Wonder in South Asia

SUNY series in Religious Studies
―――――――
Harold Coward, editor

Wonder in South Asia

Histories, Aesthetics, Ethics

Edited by
TULASI SRINIVAS

SUNY PRESS

Cover photo (from Shutterstock) of Holi, the Hindu festival of colors, Rajasthan, India, March 30, 2019.

Published by State University of New York Press, Albany

© 2023 State University of New York

All rights reserved

Printed in the United States of America

No part of this book may be used or reproduced in any manner whatsoever without written permission. No part of this book may be stored in a retrieval system or transmitted in any form or by any means including electronic, electrostatic, magnetic tape, mechanical, photocopying, recording, or otherwise without the prior permission in writing of the publisher.

For information, contact State University of New York Press, Albany, NY
www.sunypress.edu

Library of Congress Cataloging-in-Publication Data

Name: Srinivas, Tulasi, editor.
Title: Wonder in South Asia : histories, aesthetics, ethics / Edited by
   Tulasi Srinivas.
Description: Albany : State University of New York Press, [2023] | Series:
   SUNY series in Religious Studies | Includes bibliographical references and
   index.
Identifiers: ISBN 9781438495286 (hardcover : alk. paper) | ISBN 9781438495293
   (ebook) | ISBN 9781438495279 (pbk. : alk. paper)
Further information is available at the Library of Congress.

10 9 8 7 6 5 4 3 2 1

For my sister
Lakshmi Srinivas

Contents

List of Illustrations   xi

Acknowledgments   xiii

Wondering about Wonder: An Introduction   1
    Tulasi Srinivas

Section 1. Histories of Wonder

Chapter 1
Wonders Never Cease: An Ethnographic Panorama   21
    Ann Grodzins Gold

Chapter 2
Weird Tales: Ganesh, Idolatry, and the Golden Age of American Pulp Fiction   45
    William Elison

Chapter 3
Did the Masters of Disenchantment Ever Wonder? India in the Nineteenth-Century American Evangelical Imaginary   79
    Mary Hancock

Section 2. Aesthetics of Wonder

Chapter 4
Wonder: Spirit Mediumship and Devotional Music at a Mumbai Shrine of the Sidi Ancestor-Saints   105
    Jazmin Graves Eyssallenne

CHAPTER 5
Wonder as Affect on the Kuchipudi Stage 123
    Harshita Mruthinti Kamath

CHAPTER 6
In the Vicinity of Wonder: Thirunangai Devotees of
Angalamman and Narratives of Moral Astonishment 145
    Aniruddhan Vasudevan

CHAPTER 7
Wonder in the Cremation Ground: The Affective and
Transformative Dimensions of an Urban Tamil Festival 167
    Amy L. Allocco

CHAPTER 8
Economies of Wonder: The Production of Spectacle at the
Kumbh Mela 197
    Amanda Lucia

Section 3. Ethics of Wonder

CHAPTER 9
Scarcity, Abundance, and Money at Muslim Saint Shrines in
North India 223
    Quinn A. Clark

CHAPTER 10
On Wondrous Moments as the Basis for a Swaminarayan
Ethics of Sociality 245
    Hanna H. Kim

CHAPTER 11
"Guruji Rocked . . . Duniya Shocked": Wondertraps and the
Camerawork Guruship of Dera Sacha Sauda Guru
Dr. Saint Gurmeet Ram Rahim Singh Ji Insan 271
    Jacob Copeman and Koonal Duggal

CONCLUSION THE WORLDS OF WONDER 307
    Tulasi Srinivas

List of Contributors	311
Index	317

Illustrations

Figure 1.1 At the Taj Mahal in 1980, women from rural Rajasthan look out over the Yamuna River.   26

Figure 1.2 At Kuchalwara Mataji temple in 1980, the assistant priest stands before the Goddess.   30

Figure 1.3 At home in Ghatiyali in 2015, Raji Gujar (far right) and her visitors.   35

Figure 1.4 At Kuchalwara Mataji temple in 2017, ill pilgrims are camped; a shrine to Hanuman is visible behind them.   37

Figure 1.5 At the still unfinished new Kuchalwara Mataji temple in 2017; the freshly adorned image of the goddess, and, above her on the left, a pigeon's nest.   37

Figure 1.6 At the tomb of Gaji Pir, a gate densely covered with tokens of visitors' prayers and blessings; the flower-covered tomb is visible on the left.   40

Figure 2.1 H. P. Lovecraft, "Cthulhu" (1934).   63

Figure 2.2 H. P. Lovecraft, "Cthulhu" (1934).   64

Figure 7.1 A devotee who is guised or dressed as the Goddess (i.e., who has taken her *vesham*) experiences Angalaparameshwari's presence and prepares to sacrifice a chicken.   172

Figure 7.2 The ash figure (*bommai*) in an open expanse within the graveyard/cremation ground on the morning of the 2019 Mayana Kollai festival.   174

Figure 7.3	Morning *puja* for the shrouded Pavadairayan image at the head of the ash figure in the cremation ground.	175
Figure 7.4	Hindu families repaint and decorate their relatives' graves with flowers during the Mayana Kollai festival in 2019.	176
Figure 7.5	On the second day of the festival, Angalaparameshwari's elaborately decorated festival image presides over sacrificial offerings in the street in front of her temple before setting out on a multihour procession that culminates in the cremation ground late in the evening.	178
Figure 7.6	The five-faced image (*kapparai*) of the guardian Pavadairayan is revealed following the animal sacrifices in the street before Angalaparameshwari's temple.	178
Figure 7.7	As worshipers and onlookers trample and destroy the enlivened figure in the cremation ground on Mayana Kollai night, a woman scoops handfuls of the powerful ashes into a bag to bring home as *prasadam*.	180
Figure 8.1	Crowd on street at the Kumbh Mela 2019, Prayagraj.	198
Figure 8.2	Expansive camp of Bala Baldev Das Ji Maharaj, Kumbh Mela 2019.	204
Figure 8.3	Sādhu seated on swinging platform, Kumbh Mela 2013, Prayagraj.	209
Figure 11.1	Guru enters on army tank.	272
Figure 11.2	Gurmeet Ram Rahim Singh Ji Insan performing on stage with psychedelic effects projected on background screen in *Love Charger* music video.	282

Acknowledgments

As with any book, this one required the support of many friends and colleagues. First, I'd like to thank the contributors—Amy L. Allocco, Quinn A. Clark, Jacob Copeman, Koonal Duggal, William Elison, Jazmin Graves Eyssallenne, Ann Grodzins Gold, Mary Hancock, Hanna H. Kim, Harshita Mruthinti Kamath, Amanda Lucia, and Aniruddhan Vasudevan—for their hard work, their collaborative spirit, and, most importantly for an edited volume, their respect for deadlines. This work would not have seen the light of day without their enthusiasm and discipline. During the process of putting this volume together many of them became my friends and trusted colleagues.

I would also like to thank David Palmer, Andrea Marion Pinkney, Anne Mocko, Deepak Sarma, Vasudha Narayanan, and Robert P. Weller, who all supported the endeavor and appeared on panels on wonder at the American Anthropological Association and American Academy of Religion meetings amid the smoke and forest fires around San Jose, and the chaos of missed flights at Denver. They provided much needed emotional and intellectual ballast when the volume was adrift for many months.

James Peltz of SUNY Press is a thoughtful and supportive editor. He championed the book early, finding merit in the proposal and in the various essays. I am enormously fortunate in finding him and the SUNY editorial and book design team—Diane Ganeles, Gordon Marce, and Aimee Harrison—as well as the SUNY marketing team, particularly John Britch, all of whom have made this book far better than it was. Thanks also for the anonymous reviewers of the book who offered useful suggestions for making the volume more cohesive.

My colleagues at the Marlboro Institute for Liberal Arts and Interdisciplinary Studies at Emerson College, Boston, and Dean Amy Ansell at the Institute, have been a safety net of intellectual care that I can never repay. I am grateful for their continued mentoring and friendship.

This book was completed in the quiet confines of my study at the Carriage House at the Harvard Divinity School, under the auspices of a Women's Studies in Religion Fellowship. The distilled calm of the Carriage House and the friendship of my cohort of fellows—Kinitra D. Brooks, Elyan Jeanine Hill, Jordan R. Katz, Xhercis Méndez, and Rahina Muazu—the wonderful director of the WSRP, Ann Braude, and the super-efficient administrator, Tracy Wall, all contributed, in no small measure, to the smooth completion of this work. My friends at the Carriage House and the work of the legions of scholars before them who have occupied its offices remind me every day that we scholars are only as good as our interlocutors, past and present. I am grateful for the generosity of all the interlocutors who have supported the scholars in this volume and given of their time and lives to them.

And, lastly, to my family to whom I owe the biggest debt of gratitude. My mother Rukmini Srinivas, an intelligent, kind, and generous person, whose many sacrifices have shaped my life, and whose own intellectual life has informed my own. Thanks are due to my sister and colleague Lakshmi Srinivas, to whom this book is dedicated; our walks and chats (though infrequent now due to circumstance) have created the contours of my curiosities from an early age, and for that shared life, I am forever grateful.

And, finally, to my wonderful spouse Popsi Narasimhan who has taken care of innumerable small annoyances of life with great generosity and love to give me the time and space to think and write. And lastly and most importantly, to our parrot Monster, whose joyful antics make life wondrous in so many ways.

Wondering about Wonder

An Introduction

TULASI SRINIVAS

The Maze within Amazement

In 2006, I was at the Krishna Temple in Malleshwaram, a northern suburb in Bangalore[1] city in South India, one of the sites of my inquiry into ritual creativity. I was frustrated, as during the *mangalarathi* (offering of the sacred flame), I had not been able to get *darshan* (sacred sighting) of the deity, surrounded as I was by a phalanx of tall, male devotees who blocked my view. Krishna Bhattar, the chief priest of the temple, registered my frustration and annoyance. He took me aside and narrated a parable from the Hindu epic, the *Mahabharata*.

The *Mahabharata* recounts the story of a fratricidal war between two sets of royal cousins, the five Pandava brothers, and the hundred Kaurava kings. In one battle of the multiday war, one of the Pandava brothers, Arjuna, the master archer, lost faith in the meaning of the war. His wise counselor and skilled charioteer Krishna, an avatar of the Hindu god Vishnu, urged him to go to war, to kill his evil cousins, to free the kingdom of their poisonous influence, and to set the course of *dharma*, of justice.

Krishna Bhattar said that Arjuna was torn between his kinship loyalties to his cousins and his duty to purge the earth of evil. He was lost in an ethical quandary, a maze of moral problems, so much so that he laid down his bow and stopped fighting. Confused and in emotional darkness, he asked Krishna how any murder of family could be a moral act. His ethical conundrum birthed the *locus classicus* the Bhagavad Gita, the central Hindu philosophical and ethical text, structured as a conversation between himself and Krishna (Easwaran 2007).

Krishna, the god in the guise of a charioteer, argued that this battle was indeed ethical, as it was ordained by divine will. Arjuna was skeptical. To prove his divinity and clinch the argument, Krishna decided to give Arjuna the ultimate gift, to have a *darshan* of the ultimate Godhead. Krishna showed Arjuna his true form, the fount of all reality, the all-encompassing *Vishwarupa* or divine form. In the Vishwarupa Arjuna saw the multiverse, its dark skies, exploding stars and brilliant suns, the earth, all its living beings, himself included, all in glorious technicolor. As Krishna Bhatter pointedly stated to me, Arjuna saw everything *in its true colors* and was stunned, dazzled, frightened, transported and silenced all at once. He stood amazed, the ethical maze he was caught in, forgotten.

I was mystified by this parable as a response to my frustration at not being able to see the deity. Was Krishna Bhattar suggesting that I needed to be a "better" devotee like Arjuna to get a good darshan? Or that I needed an have an ethical quandary to reveal some truth about life, reality, divinity, and the universe at large? Despite, or maybe *because of* my confusion, Krishna Bhattar carried the story to its point.

Arjuna was, he said, simply wonderstruck.

Many people will recognize Krishna Bhattar's point; the transformative experience of being struck by wonder at the mysterious world and one's place in it. But the story of Arjuna's sudden access to the glorious and awe-inspiring Vishwarupa leaves us with a few questions: What exactly *was* Arjuna's wonderment? What does it *do*? How can we understand it?

The *Oxford English Dictionary* defines wonder as "the emotion excited by the perception of something novel and unexpected," and extending to an "astonishment mingled with perplexity or bewildered curiosity." Descriptions of the experience of wonder are incomplete—the sudden gasp of surprise, the childlike amazement—wonder is seen as hard to hold onto, ineffable and evanescent, merely evinced through momentary slack-jawed surprise. In an attempt to grasp this slipperiness of wonder, Phillip Fisher has recently offered us the definition of wonder, "a sudden experience of an extraordinary object that produces delight," which reveals to us the material otherness of the wonderful, and how little we actually know about it.

When we are wonderstruck, we are dazzled, lost for words, as our experience exceeds our frames of interpretation and "dissolves the ordinary meaning of things" (Schinkel 2019, 239–40). Wonder signifies that the world is "profounder, more all-embracing and mysterious than the logic of everyday reason had taught us to believe" (Pieper 1963, 102). We know that the experience of wonder breaks through the everyday, as did the Vishwarupa, allowing for a perspectival shift.

Indeed, as for Arjuna, the experience of wonder stems from this disruption, and it forces us to question our reality, perhaps even to transform it (Hepburn 1980). Wonder, as Opdal states, "is the state of mind that signals we have reached the limits of our present understanding, and that things may be different from how they look" (Opdal 2001, 332). And if modernity is a time of disenchantment, wonder enables a retrieval of enchantment and its perspectives towards a rethinking of the meaning of life itself. Not an entrenched preoccupation with the willful resuscitation of certain character traits in modern society, but rather, an acknowledgment of differential, and previously distant and invisible perspectives. Wonder enables one to you look upon oneself, as it were, from a remote corner of the universe—a flight of the imagination into the cosmos that disrupts the mundane, enabling new aesthetic, political and ethical stances.

The Genealogy of Wonder

Wonder has had a home in Western philosophies, in the quest for an ethical life, where it has been understood variously as the internal state of enlightenment, the state of bewilderment leading to Socratic inquiry, and the Kantian sublime of beauty (Bynum 1997). Pieper emphasizes the essential nature of the connection between philosophy and wonder: "Wonder is not just the starting point of philosophy in the sense of initium, of a prelude or preface. Wonder is the principium, the lasting source, the *fons et origo*, the immanent origin of philosophy" (Pieper 1963, 8, 103). In the ancient Greek idea of *thaumatazein*, which is seen as akin to wonderment, there is an echo of the Vishwarupa where wonder descends from the immortal and the cosmological to the human and mortal level (Hepburn 1980). For the Greek philosophers, wonder was seen as the internal state of enlightenment, in which truth and beauty cohabited along with a Socratic *aporia*, a disorientation of passion (Bynum 1997). In Greek myth and storytelling inciting "various forms of astonishment," a sort of constant disorientation, was of central concern (Buxton 2009). Indeed, amazement and enchantment were central to the development of the disciplines of Western religion, philosophy, arts and literature (Schinkel 2017).

Jumping forward several centuries, this focus on wonder and its enchantment developed in the fifteenth and sixteenth centuries in Europe, in tandem with the age of exploration and colonization. Responding to the enlarged geographical and mental horizons created by European exploration into distant places, wonder was found in the disconcerting effects of surprise and estrangement provoked by the burgeoning literature of global discovery, with its reports of new and wonderful lands and the beings that inhabited them. Plays and poetry, literature and cuisine, all responded to this wonderful derangement of the European senses (Schinkel 2019).

Even science and its twinned curiosities of the day, magic and alchemy, depended upon the curiosity provoked by wonder. As Dalston and Park (1998) demonstrate in their history of European naturalists from the High Middle Ages through the Enlightenment, wonder and wonders was central to envisioning themselves and the natural world. Tracing monsters, strange gems, odd horns, fossils, and plants encased in *Wunderkammern*, or cabinets of curiosity, Dalston and Park explain how wonder and wonders fortified princely power, rewove the texture of scientific experience, and shaped the sensibility of modern intellectualism.

Later, European men of science from the seventeenth to the nineteenth century inflamed wonder, fusing it forever with the unknown, the frightening, the dreadful, the awesome, and the mysterious (Dalston and Park 1998; Holmes 2010; Griffiths 2003). These early scientists and doctors understood wonder as that which clung to the mysterious, fueled curiosity, and edged the curious toward experimental knowledge. Tim Ingold has argued for a renewal of this the sense of wonder, that has been "banished from official science" (2006, 9) as it suggests new realities and new possibilities, a way of contesting the received knowledge of the limits to living, as well as a way to transform the ontological possibilities of life itself (Scott 2016, 474–75).

This idea of the excitement of discovery followed wonder in the twentieth century, where the quest to comprehend wonder was taken up tangentially by the religion scholar Rudolph Otto, in an attempt to describe encounters with the divine. *Das Heilige* (*The Idea of the Holy*), Otto's masterpiece, is a treatise on the unknowability and ineffability of wonder. In it, Otto argued that Arjuna's experience of the Vishwarupa was common to *all* human experience of divinity and that such human religious experiences of wonder and awe were the fulcrum of all religious life. He coined the neologism *the numinous*, based on the Latin word *numen* (divine power) to describe the ineffable feeling of awe, terror, and sublimity that such an interaction with the divine provoked ([1923] 1958, 15–17). For Otto, the numinous can be understood to be the experience of a mystery (*Mysterium tremendum et fascinans*) and majesty (*Majestas*) in the presence of that which is "entirely other" (*das ganz Andere*) and thus incapable of being expressed directly through human language and other media. In this physiognomic understanding, wonder included not only "the psychological process of affect, but in turn also its object, the holy," a knowable attribute of the divine mystery that is discoverable (22).

This notion of discovery invests Mary Jane Rubenstein's work on the metaphysics of wonder. In her unearthing of comparative Platonic and Aristotelian notions of wonder, she argues that they were significantly different: where Aristotle sought to dissipate wonder and move toward reason and knowledge, Plato attempted to open us to the passions, to vulnerability and joy, to a different kind of knowing (Rubenstein 2008). Yet, as Rubenstein notes, both philosophers understood wonder was provoked by difference. It is the fact that Krishna is God, a different order of being than Arjuna, who encompasses within their divine self all of creation, that provokes the wonder of the Vishwarupa.

Such alternate spaces and beings form the ground on which wonder is generated and thrives. For this reason, critical thinkers who wish to link wonder and alterity in their cultural histories or ethics begin in *otherness* (Greenblatt 1991; Arendt 1978). As Jerome Miller (1992) suggests, wonder is born in curiosity about difference. In short, the Western intellectual history of wonder recognizes it as difference that locates sublimity. Yet, oddly, until recently, despite this supposed focus on the other, wonder has been located solely in Western thought. So the provocation for our shared work in this volume arose in the question, Can wonder be located in the South Asian context?

For anthropologists and ethnohistorians like our contributors, the otherness that undergirds wonder and the curiosity it enfolds is central to our practice and theory. Margaret Mead has stated, in an oft-cited quote, "Anthropology demands the open-mindedness with which one must look and listen, record in astonishment and wonder that which one would not have been able to guess" (Mead 1977, ix). Wonder and astonishment are a part of anthropologists' interaction with "other" societies and cultures despite ethnography's dark history, twinned forever as it is with imperialism and the movement, subjugation, and exploitation of people (Pels and Salamink 2000). The recognition of an Other's potential, and right to a meaningful life, has been centrally debated in the history of the discipline, positioning it vitally to speak to otherness and the wonderment it can provoke. Our shared question developed further: Can we see a way to invite an ethnography rescued from its poisonous inheritances, through South Asian examples?

Clifford Geertz, though sensitive to ethnography's difficult history, has argued, in keeping with Mead, that ethnographers evoke wonder and relay it. See them as "merchants of astonishment" who "hawk the anomalous, peddle the strange," who with "no little success have sought to keep the world off balance; pulling out rugs, upsetting tea tables and setting off firecrackers," Geertz argues that ethnography and anthropology as whole is a disruptive discipline that elevates the disruption of wonder into a method (Geertz 2001, 64). This destabilization of worlds is what Michael Scott has written about drawing together wonder and anthropology, to suggest that if wonder is the beginning of philosophy as Greek thinkers would have it, then wonder also marks the genesis of curiosity of an encounter with the Other. It is in this sense of a method of productive disruption that the contributors to this volume have read wonder, leading to delightful essays that contemplate and probe disruptions as profitable to extend the limits of our understanding of different worlds.

The pursuit of wonder, located in many recent ethnographies, is "charged with a passionate pursuit of wonder and an earnest desire to affirm that beings and becoming(s) are wonderful" (Scott 2014, 49). The broad characterization of wonder as encompassing amazement, astonishment, awe, dread, horror, and marvel offers the center point of wonder that Arjuna experienced—an ontological destabilization (Timmer and Tomlinson 2020) rooted in multiplicity, flux, and generativity that productively engages difference.

From his deep ethnographic work among the Arosi people of Makira in the Solomon Islands, the anthropologist Scott develops different modalities of wonder that encompass such revelation of difference and alterity that attend to everyday life and engage the curiosity and bafflement that follows, forcing, to my mind, a critical and haunting engagement with ethics. This understanding of wonder—as an aesthetical concern that leads inexorably to ethics—is a call to bring us closer to an understanding of it as both index and instrument that enables an ontological destabilization of the known, the true and the real.

Here we offer an affirmative response to that call in our collection of essays by scholars, established and emergent, that invite and incite hopeful ways of thinking about difference, that engage the building of new and transformative worlds, and provoke new ethical and imaginative horizons.

The Cow in the Elevator and Ethnographies of Wonder

In 2018, I published a book titled *The Cow in the Elevator: An Anthropology of Wonder*, in which I explored creativity in ritual forms in Hindu temples in Bangalore city in South India. In the book's introduction I revealed that several ritual practitioners in the Hindu temples engaged in ritual innovation, playing with ritual forms and contexts routinely. They suggested that devotees needed *adbhuta* in their lives, which I repeatedly translated as "oddity" or "the strange." And yet, one day when I happened to translate *adbhuta* as wonder, I began to understand that the pursuit of wonder and its disorientation was the space in which ritualists wanted to dwell. It occurred to me that perhaps the traditional European understandings of wonder as an uncontrolled "act of god" were not sufficient in the South Asian context. Indeed, it became clear to me that the anthropology of wonder describes and invites a transformation, and that wonder can help us pry open the meaning of life itself (Srinivas 2018).

Through a detailed ethnography that took my interlocutors concerns seriously, I argued that these creative rituals were focused on the pursuit of wonder that, as I saw it, enabled my interlocutors to deal with the uncertainty and disorientation that neoliberal modernity brought into their lives, the waiting, the precarity, the temporal, spatial, and affective shifts. Wonder was the element of transformation individually and collectively birthing communities and new aesthetics of rituals in its wake and that these new aesthetics allowed for both a capturing and subversion of neoliberalism at the same time, enabling a joyful resistance to and acceptance of the uncertainties that neoliberal modernity brought (Srinivas 2018).

Exploring wonder as a transformative state that was pursuable, I examined how the affective experience of wonder and the ineffable quality of that which is wondrous have been indelibly braided together. I argued that wonder allowed for creative ritual in the everyday through a development of curiosity, and curiosity and creativity together birthed a compassion that built to a radical social hope in time of neoliberal precarity and uncertainty. Finally, I proposed that that wonder, and its cognates of awe, marvel, astonishment, and amazement, in its evocation of hope, was both a symptom and a mode of challenge to existing ontological assumptions about being and becoming (Srinivas 2018). But, as I finished the manuscript, I realized that rather than seeing wonder outside the Western world as reflective of the European example, wonder in non-Western societies was rarely acknowledged or understood.

For example, in South Asia, the magical experience of wonder has been a central paradigm of knowledge of the divine, found in theological treatises as wide ranging as the Bhagavad Gita or Kabir's poetry, yet the sense of dislocation that wonder provides has been seen through the lens of devotion or *bhakti*, more as a tool for the pedagogical cultivation of the devout self than an analysis of wonder itself.

Coalescing around such productive dislocations, the ontological ruptures that wonder provokes is the pivot around which this book hinges. The cultural anthropological questions that this book drew inspiration from and leads back to are: Are certain forms of wonder specific to certain cultures? Are certain peoples more primed to be sensitive to wonder than others? And these in turn lead to the other quintessential question in cultural anthropology: Is there something universal or particular about how we experience and evoke wonder?

I became curious as to how many others who studied South Asia had tripped over wonder in their own anthropological work, and had seen it as the cultivation of the devout self, or not known what to make of it and relegated it to the sidelines, uncertain of how to make space for it in their ethnographies and in their texts. My questions were simple in the beginning: Had wonder emerged in my friends' fieldwork? Had it slipped away before they could process it? As I grew bolder I asked, What does wonder look like in South Asia? Then the questions grew to become ever more encompassing: How can we begin to think of the real in relation to the braiding of the ordinary and the extraordinary in everyday life? Does the diaphanous concept of wonder play a critical role in the envisioning of the future? How does that affect people's understandings of what constitutes a good and valuable life? Can wonder transform worlds?

This collection of essays gathered together as an anthology of wonder in South Asia, presents reflections upon the history, proliferation, politics, emotional aspects, aesthetics, ethics, transformative potential, enduring appeal, meaning and the future of wonder among the religions of South Asia. It is divided into three sections: "Histories," "Aesthetics," and "Ethics." Highly respected authors and researchers, representing the varied and sometimes competing perspectives of the study of wonder in the subcontinent, provide a fascinating and instructive voyage into the social, experiential, expressive, and textual worlds of wonder, arguing that wonder is "good to think with." It is our hope that this work will broaden the discourse on wonder to use it as a helpful theorizing trope and to cultivate conversations among those who seek to interrogate or abandon modernity's fictions in search of the other-wise, the relational, the marginal, and the wonder-full in and of South Asia.

We seek together to apprehend wonder's oscillating visions through ethnographies and histories that engage wonder or the wonder adjacent. As indicated in my own struggles with linguistic translation of the idea of wonder, in the following pages wonder and language interdigitize in surprising new ways. The collective also acts as a kind of glossary of wonder in South Asia and in that sense this volume presents an anthropology all of its own (Clifford and Marcus 1986).

A secondary focus of this work is rooted in the peculiar interplay between religious philosophy and experiential wonder in South Asia. This is something that must be explored in more depth. These essays describe the many worlds of wonder in varied sites of and about South Asian life—mystical Sufi shrines, houses of Swaminarayan devotees, Rajasthani healing shrines, Tamil cremation grounds, American fantasy novels, Kuchipudi and Dhammal performances, and Dara Sacha Saudha satsangs. And, as varied as these sites are, equally varied are the evocations of wonder, its practices and meanings. Rather than a singular understanding of wonder evoked in European understandings, the multivocality of wonder in South Asia emerges in these pages.

Our invitation therefore is to illuminate and engage the plural meanings of wonder and the interversal paths between them, as we seek to disturb the singularity, universality, and totality of the Eurocentric understanding of wonder. The proposition centers around an undoing of Eurocentricism's claims and frames of knowledge and meaning, the unraveling of what Michel Ralph Trouillot has termed "North Atlantic abstract universal fictions," toward a "decolonial pluriversality" (Mignolo and Walsh 2018, 69–72).

By taking up the invitation to consider these and similar questions, we can also unveil the religiosity that undergirds Western secular theories of wonder, to provincialize the Western canon and displace the universal abstraction on which the rhetoric of Western modernity rests, to disobey the logics of colonial inheritance capitalisms. By thinking about wonder in South Asia, we open the joints of meaning, emotion, and action to consider coexistent temporalities and spatialities. The essays in the book connect and bring together histories, subjectivities, knowledges, and narratives that are in conversation with, and provide an alternative to, Western thought on wonder. The underpinning of this volume is the deep sensing by the authors that wonder enables a path to do this work of decolonization.

Additionally, we seek to interrupt the idea of wonder as purely philosophical to give it location and contours. Wonder here is the strategic creation of a bewildering yet ecstatic experience that is sought in religious publics through the introduction of the novel and the strange. Accordingly, then, we need ethnographies of wonder to get at wonder's ontology as a counterpoint to wonder's rarified existence in Western philosophical and literary texts, both to think about the mood of wonder as willed, and the pursuit of wonder as a considered and strategic act (Scott 2016). So the anthropological proposition of this work is modest, built on three pillars of inquiry: Can we eff the ineffability of wonder? Can we see the pursuit of wonder, its discourses, and practices as passionate acts that can be provoked and "stoked" to shift and transform assumptions of life and being in South Asia? And what are the ethical implications that practitioners need to consider before embracing such a creative ethos?

Lastly, in our thinking, theory and praxis are interwoven and we seek to decolonize the Western separation of theory and practice to invite us to consider the ways in which fieldwork encounters and experiences may engender wonder for the ethnographer, and assess the possibilities for capturing and representing wonder in the resulting ethnographic texts. By engaging wonder as we do in this book, we set in motion an ethnographic approach to wonder from an-other perspective, rendering an account of what generates wonder when the ontological premises at stake are those of neither the Cartesian dualism that are the understood characteristic of modernity, nor the relational nondualism commonly imputed to anthropological "others" (Scott 2016; Cicovacki 2014). If a "new world is possible," we need a new set of ideas and imaginaries to make this world possible. This volume is rooted in the idea that ethnographic texts are praxis and theory in one; deeply transformative of self and the world, and so akin to wonder itself.

South Asian Wonders

Section 1: Histories

In chapter 1, anthropologist and ethnographer extraordinaire Ann Gold considers history as biography. Drawing on field notes, diaries, interviews, and memories spanning the longue dureé of forty years in Ajmer and Bhilwara districts in the Banas River Basin of Rajasthan, her retrospective essay offers a stunning verbal panoramic sweep over vignettes from different eras in one region of North India. The earliest of these materials date from 1980 and the most recent from the second decade of the twenty-first century. Incorporating long-forgotten testimonies transpiring or originating at a single place—Kuchalwara Mataji, a healing shrine dedicated to a Hindu goddess—Gold responds to the initial provocation of wonder's architecture to consider: curiosity, creativity, compassion—as insufficient, and adds connection and communication as inherent and important to wonder stories. Telling these stories is essential to their nature, she argues, and the panorama of stories over forty years collected by one ethnographer not only reveals multiple ways that connections among people, animals and spirits are both exemplified and forged in wonderous experience, but also the singular focus and dedication that a lifetime of ethnography requires.

Chapter 2 sees William Elison trace the imagery of the elephant-headed Lord Ganesh in late nineteenth- and early twentieth-century American fiction, to reflect upon the quality or affective valence of wonder. Tracing the advent of Ganesh in literary forms such as in Rudyard Kipling's and H. P. Lovecraft's stories, as well as the Conan the Barbarian series, Elison terms these weird tales "idolatry stories" and he argues, persuasively, that they emerge from a growing American fascination with Hindu idols, and their reading as an "existential threat" to Western civilization. Interweaving Coomarasawmy's idea of the Pali term *saṁvega*, "aesthetic shock," Elison argues that these weird tales that interpolate fantasy and dread do not pose a challenge to the philosophical conditions underwriting this world's existence, rather, they open up new worlds of wonder.

In chapter 3, historian Mary Hancock shifts our temporal frame to the early nineteenth century when India or "Hindustan" acquired a vivid presence in the imaginations of many Americans. Images depicting India and Indians as "exotic and barbaric, magical and menacing, beneficial and perilous," were promulgated in fairs, expositions, and department stores, and in the cultural and geographic narratives of both Christian and secular publications. Accordingly, Hancock rewrites our understanding of wonder to include horror. Focusing on the mission in the antebellum period as the site where the most sustained connections between the US and India were forged, Hancock argues that mission practice recoiled from Hindu religious iconography and belief casting it as the "other." This Orientalist reading of wonder was in conversation with the historical and cultural analysis of wonder's persistence and mutability. Hancock makes the case for wonder acting as a fulcrum for comparative thinking about religion.

SECTION 2: AESTHETICS

In both chapters 4 and 5, performance traditions in South Asia and their evocations of wonderment are examined. In chapter 4, Jazmin Graves Eyssallenne examines the workings of wonder in the Sufi devotional tradition of Sidis (Indians of African ancestry) that centers on the veneration of African Rifai Sufi ancestral saints entombed in the Bharuch district of Gujarat. This chapter situates "play" as a technology of wonder in the Sidi Sufi tradition. Play encompasses participation in the Sidi devotional song and dance performance called *dhammal* or *goma* that invites the presence of the saints through ecstatic embodiment. Wonder in this context is identified as *wajd* encompassing reverence, excitement, and supplication that are the precursor to and prerequisite for the devotee's experience of the ineffable quality of the saints' presence via an ecstatic state of possession (*hal*). The "play" signals the confluence of Sufi, Hindu, and eastern African ideological frameworks and ritual practices in the Sidi devotional tradition, contributing to the study of wonder in different temporal, ethnic, and embodied dimensions.

In chapter 5, Harshita Mruthinti Kamath focuses granularly on the *stri-vesham*, or the donning of a woman's guise, ubiquitous to the performance and religious repertoire of Smarta Vaidiki Brahmin men of Kuchipudi village (located in the Krishna district in the South Indian state of Andhra Pradesh) to explore the aesthetics of wonder. For generations, brahmin men from the Kuchipudi village have been taking on the *stri-vesham* to enact female characters from Hindu religious narratives. Such impersonation draws on a broader repertoire of gender crossings across South Asia in which men can become women, women can become men, and gods can impersonate humans. Kamath explores how rapid transitions across male and female characters require both special costuming and manipulations in bodily movement ultimately inculcating a sense of astonishment and wonder for the spectator, as she considers both the creative and disruptive potential of wonder enacted through the body of the guised Kuchipudi dancer.

In chapter 6, Aniruddhan Vasudevan introduces us to the *Thirunangai Maruladis*, trans women performers in ritual genres in the city of Chennai, Tamil Nadu, who are deeply devoted to the worship of the goddess Angalamman, a regional deity. As the Tamil word *maruladi* suggests, this mode of devotion involves dancing the deity in states of trance. Vasudevan challenges us to think about the Thirunangais as "adjacent to wonder" through both their discourses and practices of *asandhu podhal* or astonishment that takes palpable form in the financial resources they muster for, and expend in organizing the annual rituals for the goddess. Thirunangais take pride in their ability to deliver a spectacle that turns upon the astonishment of the spectators, and see that as having moral value. Asking the productive question of whether there are ontological premises at stake in thirunangai discourses and practices of astonishment Vasudevan draws attention to a traffic in wonder that exists between thirunangai-maruladis, the goddess herself, and community at large.

Chapter 7 focuses on the spectacular urban festival of Mayana Kollai (looting of the cremation ground). Amy Allocco's beautifully detailed chapter analyzes the potential for wonder in the festival as it is performed by the community of priests, trustees, and devotees of the Angalaparameshwari (Angalamman) temple in Chennai. Allocco's reading of the festival holds open space to consider how the processes of wonder play through it. Here the prospect of wonder is assessed in light of the broader repertoire of Tamil vernacular affective categories that are identified by festival participants as essential to the festival. Perhaps most generative for the chapter's focus on "wonder" are the ritual activities that transpire in the cremation ground itself, where men from the Angalaparameshwari temple fashion an enormous figure out of cremation ashes and, in a highly charged atmosphere, the figure is quickly destroyed by those who mount and stomp on it as well as those who grab handfuls of the ash to be brought home as *prasādam*, or consecrated material. As it traces themes of ritual creativity, death, and rebirth, this chapter tests the creative potential and the limits of the category of wonder.

Chapter 8 broadens the lens on the theme of abundance that Vasudevan's and Allocco's chapters subtly introduce to relocate the interrogation of wonder to the banks of the Ganges during the Kumbh Mela festival, the largest religious gathering on earth. Amanda Lucia's study of the festival focuses on the economies of wonder, by which she means the circulatory production, distribution, and consumption practices that encapsulate a religious spectacle, proffering the affective experience of wonder. Lucia argues that there has been a marked increase in the religious exhibits designed to cultivate the affective experience of wonder at the Kumbh Melā over the past twenty years, and they have gotten larger and more extravagant, attracting many millions of spectators. The exhibits are, she states, identity-making projects for the gurus and religious organizations who host them; as also an attempt to reenchant a world that is becoming increasingly disenchanted through secular materialism. Wonder is about enchantment, and as such it draws marked contrast to the disenchantments characteristic of modernity—the tedium of the struggles of everyday life, the waiting, and the precarity. Here wonder is cyclical, as objects are discarded in the landfills of "wonder-trash" and replaced by newer and more elaborate objects of wonder.

SECTION 3: ETHICS

In chapter 9, Quinn Clark follows Lucia to consider economies of wonder, but the discussion pivots from symbolic economies of excess to the problems of hard coin in Sufi saint shrines. As he argues, Sufi shrines have acquired an idealized reputation as utopian spaces free of divisive politics, intolerance, and hierarchy, yet they are also highly politicized and economized through the distribution of cash seen as favors from the saints and God. Interlocutors see the "negative" aspects of shrine operations as a natural consequence of money being involved, whereas the "positive" aspects arise from *barakah*, or the love of God manifest as a blessing. Why is money considered corrupting in some contexts but freely and openly circulated in the ritualized context shrine-based celebrations? Based on ethnographic research in Lucknow, Clark analyzes money as both social concept and as a material object, arguing that a focus on money reflects the fundamental scarcity in which Muslims find themselves living in neoliberal India today, in opposition to what they see as its *barakah*, the infinite abundance emerging from an eternal God tilting money between hard coin and a moral or ethical object.

Chapter 10 advances the established links between wonder and the meaning of life through an exploration of how wonder flows through devotional practice of BAPS Swaminarayan followers in Gujarat, primarily through their interpretations of remembered encounters between the followers and the movement. Hanna Kim argues that follower's wondrous experiences leave an imprint that calls for interpretive strategies or ways to make sense of the affective memory though an assemblage of discourses. Kim carefully traces Swaminarayan ontologies of devotion where elements of surprise are centered and central. Following interlocutors as they reexamine moments of surprise that, by their retelling, convey a sense of something more than a memory, that builds towards "revised attitude to living," or what Kim terms an "ethics of sociality." She argues that that exposure to BAPS Swaminarayan discourses can offer the means to reify an affective experience into a playbook for ethical living with equanimity and care for others, alerting us to the experience and aftermath of an encounter with wonder and how it can guide the subject and ethnographer to productive ends, ethically and ethnographically.

Finally, in chapter 11 Jacob Copeman and Koonal Duggal build upon the idea of spectacle to explore how wonder is generated and experienced, questions that lie at the heart of the popularity of the Dera Sacha Sauda, a guru-led movement that is the focus of their analysis. Drawing on their previous work on gurus' "methodologies of presence," focusing on the Guru's spectacular entries into crowds of gathered devotees on a homemade army tank and other miraculous forms of transport, and devotees' responses to them in person and online, Copeman and Duggal argue that the Guru's strategic generation of "wonder effects" creates what Mary Jane Rubenstein has termed an appropriative stupefaction that is based on the Guru's relentless staging of new and newer marvels. Copeman and Duggal provide a provisional account of the Dera Sacha Saudha guru's experiments in wonder to argue that these spectacles are "wondertraps" (that reflect a kind of postcolonial kitsch aesthetic) that create a "devotion of attractions" for devotees. Copeman and Duggal describe the co-implication of entrapment and wonder, and how devotee labor is frequently required to set the wondertraps via which the replenishment and augmentation of the same labor supply is accomplished, which in turn enables more wondertraps to be laid. This cyclical pursuit of ever greater devotee numbers through a strategic pursuit of wonder, reflects the ethical problems that such a repeated enhancement of wonder generates.

Note

1. I have retained the colonial name of the city with which I am familiar, though the name was changed to the precolonial name of Bengaluru in 2006.

Works Cited

Arendt, Hannah. 1978. *The Life of the Mind*. San Diego: Harcourt.
Buxton, Richard. 2009. *Forms of Astonishment: Greek Myths of Metamorphosis*. Oxford: Oxford University Press.
Bynum, Caroline Walker. 1997. "Wonder." *American Historical Review* 102 (1): 1–26.
Cicovacki, Predrag. 2014. *The Analysis of Wonder: An Introduction to the Philosophy of Nicolai Hartmann*. New York: Bloomsbury.
Clifford, James, and George E. Marcus, eds. 1986. *Writing Culture: The Poetics and Politics of Ethnography*. 25th anniversary ed. Berkeley: University of California Press.
Dalston, Lorraine, and Katharine Park. 1998. *Wonder and the Order of Nature, 1150–1750*. New York: Zone.
Easwaran, Eknath, trans. 2007. *The Bhagavad Gita*. 2nd ed. Tomales, CA: Nilgiri.
Geertz, Clifford. 2001. *Available Light: Anthropological Reflections on Philosophical Topics*. Princeton, NJ: Princeton University Press.
Greenblatt, Stephen. 1991. *Marvelous Possessions: The Wonder of the New World*. Chicago: University of Chicago Press.
Hepburn, R. W. 1980. "The Inaugural Address: Wonder." *Proceedings of the Aristotelian Society*, suppl. vols., 54:1–23.
Ingold, Tim. 2006. "Rethinking the Animate, Re-animating Thought." *Ethnos* 71 (1): 9–20.
Irigaray, Luce. 2004. *Luce Irigaray: Key Writings*. New York: Continuum.
Mead, Margaret. 1977. *Sex and Temperament in Three Primitive Societies*. New York: Morrow.
Mignolo, Walter, and Catherine E. Walsh. 2018. *On Decoloniality: Concepts, Analytics, Praxis*. Durham, NC: Duke University Press.
Miller, Jerome A. 1992. *In the Throe of Wonder: Intimations of the Sacred in a Post-modern World*. Albany: State University of New York Press.

Opdal, Paul Martin. 2001. "Curiosity, Wonder and Education Seen as Perspective Development." *Studies in Philosophy and Education* 20:331–44.
Otto, Rudolph. (1923) 1958. *The Idea of the Holy: An Inquiry into the Non-rational Factor in the Idea of the Divine and Its Relation to the Rational.* 2nd ed. New York: Oxford University press.
Pels, Peter, and Oscar Salamink, eds. 2000. *Colonial Subjects: Essays on the Practical History of Anthropology.* Ann Arbor: University of Michigan Press.
Pieper, Josef. 1963. *Leisure, the Basis of Culture.* New York: Mentor Omega.
Rubenstein, Mary-Jane. 2008. *Strange Wonder: The Closure of Metaphysics and the Opening of Awe.* New York: Columbia University Press.
Schinkel, Anders. 2017. "The Educational Importance of Deep Wonder." *Journal of Philosophy of Education* 51 (2): 538–53.
———. 2019. "Wonder, Mystery, and Meaning." *Philosophical Papers* 48 (2): 293–319.
Scott, Michael W. 2016. "To Be Makiran Is to See like Mr. Parrot: The Anthropology of Wonder in Soloman Islands." *Journal of the Royal Anthropological Institute* 22 (3): 474–95.
Srinivas, Tulasi. 2018. *The Cow in the Elevator: An Anthropology of Wonder.* Durham, NC: Duke University Press.
Vasalou, Sophia. 2015. *Wonder: A Grammar.* Albany: State University of New York Press.

Section 1
Histories of Wonder

Chapter 1

Wonders Never Cease

An Ethnographic Panorama

ANN GRODZINS GOLD

> And so I claim wonder for anthropology; for its understanding of the ineffable quality of change, for the study of the existential nature of being human and enduring the vicissitudes of that, for its focusing us on the experimental and the everyday, and for its commitment to hope.
>
> —Tulasi Srinivas (2018, 214)

> This idea of the field as a break or hiatus obscures what is most crucial about the experience, its transformative power, which must be carried over somehow, across the divide between places familiar and strange.
>
> —Anand Pandian (2019, 74)

In July 2020, over a Whats App call, I told Bhojuram Gujar that I was writing an essay on wonderous and miraculous events, in Rajasthan. For forty years, Bhoju has been my dear friend, research collaborator, and frequent coauthor. I was taken aback when he responded almost angrily: "The priests put masks on all the gods. If the gods need protection, who will protect us?" Bhojuram was decidedly not critiquing divine beings but rather expressing his disregard for priests likely following government suggestions for getting across the message about the necessity to wear masks to control the spread of COVID-19. Still, his reaction gave me an apprehensive inkling: Might wonders have diminished relevance in pandemic times? News features and academic blogs tell us otherwise. Quests for manifestations of divine succor, the conviction of its possibility, are vital and pervasive.[1]

As Srinivas "claims wonder for anthropology," she suggests an expansive territory. Wonder wraps both observed phenomena and observing fieldworkers within dynamic processes where "transformative power," as evoked by Pandian, might be realized. This chapter's contribution, fully lodged in the prepandemic past, may nonetheless shed light on culturally inflected human responses to our current global crisis. In a brief retrospective essay, I offer a kind of panorama sweeping over vignettes from different eras in one region of North India that I know well.

I imagine myself gliding, as with an iPhone camera set to "pano," over a stretched-out array of subjects, contriving to create an illusory mural. I also imagine turning my lens full circle to include myself, and to think of the ethnographic project, in part, as a dialogic or mutuality of wondering. This exploration of the past may have been provoked by our wondering at Rajasthanis's perceptions of wonder, but it is Rajasthanis graciously explaining their sense of wonder to me that gives it any value readers may find. The panoramic metaphor inadequately conceals an ungainly writing struggle as I have assembled materials from notes and images, the bulk of which were mired in murky predigital times or scattered in multiple emails.

How does wonder match with concepts available in the North Indian linguistic region? Several Hindi/Rajasthani words I believed to define this volume's areas of interest did not turn up wonder or wonderment as a primary or perfect English gloss in dictionaries. Common throughout North Indian Hindi speech is *adbhut*, which I have elsewhere translated as "wonderous" (Gold 2017, 280), but which is more regularly glossed as strange or surprising. *Chamatkari* can be applied to wonder-working images or other material objects endowed with inherent agency (Flueckiger 2020). I think of it as meaning "miraculous," but once again the Hindi-English dictionary disappoints me, giving "astonishing," "splendid," and "wonderful" (but not "wondrous").

The Rajasthani/Hindi exclamation and adjective *gajab* was my best hope for a word used to mark an experience of wonder.[2] When employed as an exclamation, it most often means "Wow!" "Awesome!" or, according to several internet sites, "Fantastic!" Phrases such as *gajab kar diya* or *gajab ho gya* appear in oral performance texts, and in the past I translated these variously, with phrases such as "you have done something amazing" or "an astonishing thing happened." When I searched through relatively recent, digitized interview notes for *gajab*, however, I found that as an adjective it may signify extremes of beauty or strength, sometimes tinged with a dose of the uncanny; but it is not consistently associated with the kind of transformative power that would unify the wonderous (e.g., I heard of a powerfully *gajab* image stolen from a temple and never recovered). Perhaps all wonder has its vulnerability.

I am forced to conclude that my observations do not neatly fall within a well-defined semantic domain of wonder in my fieldwork area's languages of Rajasthani and Hindi, which troubles me. As an anthropologist trained at the University of Chicago in the brief heyday of ethnosociology (late 1970s), I only reluctantly relinquish the deep commitment to local language we were disciplined to maintain. In writing about India's cosmologies, for example, we were forbidden ever to use words that did not have comfortable equivalents, or that might violate the worldviews we were trying to grasp and transmit. The prime forbidden words for those working on Hinduism in the 1970s and 1980s were "sacred" and "supernatural," because the cosmology in question resists the binaries (sacred/profane or natural/supernatural) on which these terms rely in Abrahamic traditions. The episodes I treat here as wondrous exemplify in many ways how the cosmology of rural and provincial Rajasthan is one where the boundaries between ordinary and extraordinary are thoroughly permeable.

I draw on field notes, diaries, interviews, and memories spanning forty years of intermittent work and observations in a single region—Ajmer and Bhilwara districts located in the Banas Basin of Rajasthan, North India. The earliest of these materials date from 1980, when I was a doctoral candidate. About half my essay draws on journals and recorded, transcribed, and translated interview texts incorporating testimonies transpiring or originating at a single place, Kuchalwara Mataji, a healing shrine dedicated to a Hindu goddess. While I have not formally engaged in fieldwork since 2011, revisits to the same area extend through January of 2020, my second year as emerita. One initial inspiration when I first pondered how I might produce an assemblage of wonders for this volume was an event from the mid-1980s that I recalled vividly but imperfectly, yet acutely intuited would belong here. Bhojuram Gujar kindly obliged me by committing to writing a wonderous but frightening experience from his own life history.

Sketching wonder's horizons for this volume, Srinivas offers three central components to consider: curiosity, creativity, compassion. I have taken these as impromptu prompts for what follows, flagging one of these elements as a primary theme in each vignette or set of related vignettes. It would go without saying that, like the three "constituents of nature" (the *gunas* of Hindu cosmology), all three would be involved in each piece, but, in my interpretation, I highlight one or another that seems to predominate. And, extending the *c*-word scheme, I would add connection and communication as inherent to wonder stories. Telling these stories is essential to their nature, and connections among people, animals, and spirits are both exemplified and forged in wonderous experience.

1980 Curiosity

Curiosity and Aesthetic Thrill

My early research on pilgrimage included among its possible methods to gather memories of past journeys. Then a young and very dedicated assistant, Bhoju Ram Gujar, conducted some interviews in Ghatiyali with former pilgrims. We later translated these together. Little of this material found its way into publications, as I gave priority to my firsthand experience, but revisiting those interview texts decades later yields some gems and insights. Here is one.

Uddi Gujar, a woman in her late fifties in 1980, spoke with animation and flair about a journey she had made over a decade back in the company of a small group of pilgrims from Ghatiyali village, my fieldwork site and at that time Bhoju's home. Uddi described to Bhoju the artistic beauty of the carvings around the temple door in Puri, Orissa. Her amazement and appreciation are evident, as well as the almost startling clarity of her memories from a considerable distance in time: "At the doorway on both sides are Garudas [eagles, Vishnu's mount] and also on both sides two horse-riders. . . . The Garuda was so beautiful and lifelike its mouth seemed to speak. And those who were mounted on elephants, how did they strike you? Just as if they were alive!"[3]

Bhoju always endeavored to pursue what were in those days my central research aims. He therefore did not follow up on this picture-postcard vision of aesthetically produced wonderment. Instead, he interrupted Uddi's flow of memories to ask, rather bluntly, one of our perpetual questions: "So people go on pilgrimages (*tirthayatra*); what fruit is received from going on pilgrimage?"

This proved an awkward intrusion into Uddi's spontaneous and enthusiastic recollections of wondrous sights, and caused her to sputter out several disjointed, dismissive responses. Bhoju persisted, creatively rephrasing his question several times until he finally elicited an articulate answer by asking her what difference existed between charitable gifts given in sacred sites (*tirthasthan*) and in the village. His aim (as my employee) was to get at a mystical, invisible difference between different places of worship based on presumptions of heightened divine presence. Uddi deconstructed this quite brilliantly:

> It is all one single illusion (*ek hi maya hai*); do it in any place. Bathe in any place at all, here is water, here is stone. The thing is, to see artistic creations over there (*udhar ki rachna*). It is to see that all the world goes. If not, then do merit (*pun*) right here, *tirth* are right here only. Whether you go anywhere, the Lord (*bhagvan*) is right here, ready (*taiyar*), in this heart (*hrdya ke andar*) he is ready.

Uddi firmly dismisses any valid spiritual rationale for journeying. Sacred waters and stone icons in faraway lands are fundamentally no different from those at home. But people go to see beauty, art, and scenery, and to wonder at it. Uddi contrasts this perfectly valid reason for travel with the invalid illusion that one might find God in a pilgrimage place, when God is always present, available, in one's heart.

Curiosity and Its Opposite

In fall of 1980, Bhoju and I took more or less the same journey Uddi had taken, all the way to Orissa and back, with a busload of provincial Rajasthanis (Gold 1988, 262–98). We learned that not all pilgrims were as zealous tourists as Uddi. Bhoju tape-recorded the following exchange (which we later transcribed) between an exhausted old farmer woman from the village of Mehru, whose name I unfortunately do not have noted, and a somewhat pompous Brahmin school teacher, Krishna Chandra Dube.

This took place at the Taj Mahal. The teacher, harangued his fellow pilgrim, an uneducated woman who belonged to the same village as he did:

KCD: You have paid your money, now look at everything.

Woman [wishing to rest and walk no further]: Ah, what's to see? Nothing but stones!

KCD: Well, we have stones in our village, so then why did you come here? I read the story in a book, it is made of white marble, it was made in thus and so's memory, so why did you come here? You ought to look around you! . . . See it on a moonlit night—it sparkles! People come from other countries to see it, Ainn bai [adaptation of my name, Ann, in Rajasthan] came from another country to see it. . . . You want to rest here, but if we rest, when will we ever see? . . . Look at the scene [view of the Jamuna from the terrace outside the tomb], the Badshah found bliss seeing this scene, so we also will find bliss. . . . Look! We have paid money, we should see things.

Figure 1.1. At the Taj Mahal in 1980, women from rural Rajasthan look out over the Yamuna River. *Source*: Author photo.

K. C. Dube's argument is in keeping with Uddi Gujar's: outside one's home region one should relish artistic, storied monuments. But, to a footsore old lady, they are "nothing but stones," devoid of wonder, and not objects arousing her curiosity.

1986 Compassion and Connection: The Cobra in the Well

When invited to write a chapter on wonder, my initial thought leapt to this specific event of which my own memories, because secondhand, were quite hazy. It was a story told to me by my close friend and associate, Bhojuram Gujar. The fuzzy memory had an aura of wonder that seemed necessary for my panorama. I pestered Bhojuram to write it for me. Now a retired teacher and happy grandfather, Bhojuram is a reliable narrator, not given to exaggeration. He was not eager to relive the frightening episode, although it happened thirty-five years ago. But he wrote out his recollections for me in Hindi and sent them by email. I have translated, queried, and corrected, and I hope to have retained in the telling some clarity and awe. Bhoju titled this "An Unforgettable Event":

> This event took place in 1986 about six months after I returned from my first visit to the USA. My family—Mother, Father, elder sister—were living in Ghatiyali, my *nanihal* [mother's natal village] where my three maternal uncles and my father had lived together as a family for 55 years. In 1972 my father separated his share from the others, but everyone continued to live together.[4]
>
> For generations our family had an old and ongoing connection with Kalyan Nath's family. For any social gathering or festival we were just like one family. Kalyan Nath was known in the village as Kalla Nath. He and his wife Kanvari Devi were both tantrics. Kalla Nath had a great knowledge of magical spells and he also was able to discern both cause and cure of an illness by taking someone's pulse.[5]
>
> From time to time when our family or neighbors were troubled by any kind of ghosts, snakes, or scorpions, or if their livestock fell ill, the only person we called was Kalla Nath. He used sweeping and blowing to make them well again.[6] Even after Kalla Nath's death, about fifteen years

before this event, the connection between our families continued, as it still does, right through today. This is our good fortune.

So, at this time my middle uncle, Ratan Lalji, became mentally ill. Together with Ramdev Mali I was taking my uncle, around 2:30 in the afternoon, to Puvali ka Devji. This shrine is about three kilometers from our village.[7] There are agricultural fields on both sides of the road to Puvali; some of them belonged to Kalla Nath's family. We were about halfway there, and Ratanji, my uncle, said, "I am going to take a piss and then I'll be right back." So Ramdev Mali and I waited for him by the roadside underneath a tree.

Just then, suddenly, crying out, a flock of pigeons flew up from the well in Kalla Nath's field, and we could no longer see Ratanji. I raced to the well, and I saw Ratanji's turban floating in the water. Without a thought, not knowing what I was doing, I took off my shoes and jumped into the well with all my clothes on. I was able to grab Ratanji. Holding him with one hand, I swam with the other. As is often the case, there was a large crack in the side of the well, creating a niche where the pigeons had nested. I grabbed hold of the stone in this niche, and kept us both afloat. This well was about eighty feet deep and there were thirty feet of water in it.

As soon as Ramdev realized what had happened, he started shouting and running back to the village, which was about one kilometer distance from the well. Soon Ratan's elder brother Bhairulal and some other village people came with a rope. I was holding Ratan above water in the well for about forty minutes; as soon as they brought the rope, I tied it around him and they pulled him out of the well.

I was already very tired. While they were taking Ratan out, I wanted to rest, so I held onto the stone in the niche with both hands. And suddenly I saw that deeper within the niche where I was holding on, a huge cobra snake was coiled. As soon as I saw it, I lost my ability to speak.

When they came to get me out, and dangled the rope, I was not able to grab it properly. So then they made a kind of loop and I was able to put that around myself and they pulled me out.

Once I was out of the well, I told the others how I had seen the cobra very close to where I was holding on. My Uncle Bhairulal said immediately that it was Kalla Nath: "He saved you from drowning, and didn't bite you."[8]

We kept on going to Puvali ka Devji. There were over one-hundred pilgrims there, and everyone was talking about what happened. The shrine priest, Gopiji Char Gujar, was possessed by the deity Bhairuji. He told us right away, "Today you were saved by Kalla Nathji."

Even today, when I think about this, I wonder how I jumped into the well without even thinking! I had no guess as to the depth of the water. In my entire life, this is the most unforgettable event; sometimes, unbidden, I see the face of Kala Nathji and I see the cobra. Today neither Kalla Nathji nor my uncle Ratanji are still alive, but I continue to receive their blessings in these memories.

This story of compassion and connection, stretching across generations and caste communities, endures well beyond a single human life cycle. The power of Bhoju's experience—which he probably did not tell me until my next trip to India in 1988—always remained with me as a tale of witnessed wonder. I have walked down that road and passed that field and well countless times. I knew Ratanji, and remember him best as an old man often reclining on his front stoop right next to Bhojuram's home, where I sometimes lived for weeks or months. He would exchange superficial greetings with me every time I passed. I also know the family of Kalla Nath, whose son and nephew appear in the pages to follow. This wonderous tale exemplifies compassion: on the part of Bhojuram, whose impulse to save his uncle was stronger than self-preservation or fear; on the part of the ancestor/cobra, who didn't strike the intruders into his domain due to their families' long-established connections. Then there are the pigeons who seem to be acting as any birds will when they are startled from a roosting place. But they also serve as alarming messengers to alert Bhoju to the immediate crisis. I shall return to them in concluding.

1980–2017 Creativity: Kuchalwara Mataji

By happenstance I have a deep longitudinal account of the temple of Kuchalwara Mataji, stretching from 1980 through 2017. This place is a healing shrine, without any particular scenic attractions, unlike a number of other shrines I studied.

1980 JEEP PILGRIMAGE

About ten months into my doctoral research, which was squarely focused on pilgrimage, several of my village helpers pooled their experiences and predilections to arrive at a list of "must-see" regional shrines frequented by pilgrims from our home village of Ghatiyali. We took a four-day jeep pilgrimage, just before the advent of the monsoon season, in June 1980. Bhairu Lal Mina, Nathu Natisar Nath, and Vajendra Kumar Sharma (each from a different caste community) accompanied me. The first stop on the itinerary they had devised was Kuchalwara Mataji, located not far from the growing town of Devli. We were not able to interview the main *bhopa* or shrine-priest during our visit there. In the pre–mobile phone era, nothing was ever prearranged; one just hoped for the best.

Figure 1.2. At Kuchalwara Mataji temple in 1980, the assistant priest stands before the goddess. *Source*: Author photo.

We did record a long interview with the bhopa's helper, a Rajput named Dev Ram.

Nathu Nath was one of my traveling companions and assistants. As I seek to emphasize connections in both fieldwork and wonders, let me identify Nathu as the biological son of Kalla Nathji, although he was adopted at an early age by Kalla Nathji's brother Sundar Nath, who was childless. That several members of this Nath family came to work for me has everything to do with their old and strong bond with Bhojuram's family.

Nathu asked Dev Ram a simple question, "Why do pilgrims come?" Dev Ram's answer was effusive and emphatic: "All desires are fulfilled, sons are given, crippled limbs and polio are healed; very serious cases of *lakva* (paralysis) come. They arrive just like dead bodies, and leave well!"

I quickly interjected my own query about something just then underway that I had never seen before—women carrying stones on their heads performing a single-file circumambulation of the temple. He answered, "You labor for god with your body, and then all bodily pains are removed. It is called *begar* (labor without recompense)."[9]

In response to my question about the many strings tied on the goddess's multiple tridents (*trisul*), Dev Ram explained that they were tied *after* a successful cure. The iron tridents themselves are of course another expression of pilgrims' gratitude. I asked Dev Ram who offered them, and he responded: "Those who are sick will vow, 'O Regal Mother (Mataji Maharaj), if I get well I'll offer a *trisul* weighing such and such.'" He gave examples of different weights in kilograms. All these massed tokens are signs of wonder, familiar but nonetheless impressive.

Vajendra asked the assistant priest if he had seen "completely hopeless cases" get cured. Our interviewee replied enthusiastically that he had seen hundreds of just such cases. "Some of them arrive here completely unconscious, some stay one month, twenty days, two nights."

"What are the main ways their cures are effected?"

The priest listed a series of ritual actions common to the majority of regional healing shrines, including fanning and the administration of sacred ash along with the deity's bathwater.

Interestingly, as our 1980 interview concluded, the assistant priest proposed to us, a motley crew that included a foreign presence, "You may understand this as medicine (*davai*) or as Mataji's grace (*krpa*)." Grace could be understood as divine compassion, but the priest's suggestion, strikes me as a mode of creativity. Multiple interpretations are not only possible but welcome in the transformational world where pilgrims seek succor. There are more to come.

2003 Healing Miracles and Environments

Twenty-three years later, in the winter of 2003, I visited numerous goddess shrines in the vicinity of my earlier research site, Ghatiyali village. Shambhu Nath, whose father Gokul Nath was Kalla Nathji's brother, helped me to conduct a very long, detailed interview at the same goddess shrine, Kuchalwara Mataji (January 22, 2003).

We were fortunate to find available and willing to be interviewed a man named Durga Lal Prajapat (Kumhar) who was one of several brothers and cousin-brothers among whom the duties of daily worship services regularly rotated at Kuchalwara. These priests belonged to the Kumhar community traditionally associated with the making of clay pots, but Durga Lal himself was a retired army officer, and literate.

Durga Lal spoke ardently of the goddess's healing powers:

> Afflicted persons come here. No one comes for picnics or aimless wandering. Only the afflicted come into this Mother's shelter, seeking help with their illnesses. The big hospitals refer people here. After the doctor tells them, "we can't help you," and they are totally hopeless, then they come here and are cured, at no cost! Hindus, Muslims, all kinds of people come here and experience miracles.
>
> Persons come here with such dreadful sicknesses, you couldn't even stand to see, your eyes would fill with tears, you would feel compassion, those are the kind who come, and having come they get better.
>
> After coming here, 80 percent are totally well, and if you asked them they would tell you that they recovered because of coming here. They all say that. From every village, from every small hamlet, people come.
>
> Doctors refer patients here. Even from the hospital in Jaipur.

Throughout our interview, Durga Lal repeatedly referred to science and scientists. He seemed more on the offensive than the defensive, for neither Shambhu nor I had expressed any doubts:

People whose cures doctors have failed to effect come here. . . . These days, scientific people (*vigyanik log*) don't accept Mataji and Bhairuji, but when someone is not cured in the hospital, people refer them here, to die, to wait to die. But when they get well here, then the scientific people wonder: "How did they recover?" So they claim the cause is the pure breeze (*shudh hava*) of this place, and that this air restores health. They claim, it is not Mataji who cures, but the air. They refuse to say it is Mataji. . . .

We spoke with several of the pilgrims present at the shrine that day. One woman told us that a doctor had informed her that her lungs were "finished," and her case hopeless—thus confirming Durga Lal's statements. Her son brought her to Mataji. She declared with vehemence and directly into the recorder: "I became 75 percent well after coming here, after the doctor told me I would die! I have been here two days and I am already 75 percent completely well."

These and other compelling miracle-cure stories we recorded are replete with promise and hope. The priest was effusive and eloquent. Yet the happy tales produced cognitive dissonance for me. As I looked around the shrine, I saw affliction. Nor did the air strike me as especially pure. I had been contemplating a major fieldwork project on several healing shrines including Kuchalwara. I had been thinking I would live at those places for a few months at a time, along with the ill pilgrims and their families, to watch what went on, and to converse more deeply with sufferers. The truth is, I lost my nerve. Certainly, part of my withdrawal was based in ethical sensitivity, but I cannot claim that as the whole virtuous reason; the other part was gut-level fear.

This place disturbed me, much as does a hospital visit in the USA. I lost all desire to photograph and interview these debilitated pilgrims and their worried caretakers. The pilgrims were camped in small groups with minimal bedding and cooking utensils on an unsheltered stone terrace. Some of the sick were children; some were very aged; some were young women in disheveled dress; a few were bound with cloth or wearing awkward mittens to keep them from thrashing or scratching themselves; most appeared very weak. It was Shambhu who persisted in recording tales of wonder.

Although the priest of Kuchalwara waxed eloquent about the shrine's beneficial effects on the seriously ill, I found it hard to believe in miracles in the presence of so many suffering bodies and anxious families. Retrospectively I can analyze my desire to escape as precipitated by a discomforting sense of permeability pervaded by helplessness. Many who do social science of medicine write about the way that sick others remind us of our own fragility and inadequacy.[10]

In my journal from the 2003 visit I wrote this:

> 23 Jan at Kuchalwara I felt no religious emotion at all. Only the immense pathos of the sick, the lame and the halt. A place of illness. Amazingly as we left a small man came up to us complaining of headache. I thought perhaps he wanted money for golle [pills], but no, from somewhere a handful of bhabhut [sacred ash] appeared, and Shambhu began to rub his thumb in it, muttering what I surmised (and he later confirmed) were mantras. So then he rubbed it on the man's forehead and gave him the rest of it. This world of pain and healing, what to think of it. What am I trying to find?

As was the case with every one of my research assistants, Shambhu Nath himself was no less of a cultural source than the people he helped me to interview. In fact, as my journal reported, he could shift without any awkwardness from research assistant to priest and healer.

As we departed Kuchalwara that day, Shambhu speculated on the place's miraculous healing power in an almost poetic reverie. He pulled together Durga Lal's suggestion about the pure breezes with his own observations and imaginative notions, to offer this explanation of Kuchalwara Mataji's successful healing potency: "The birds flying, beating their wings, generate power [*shakti*], and that probably gives some special power to the breeze at Kuchalwara. There is so much power in the air there, that it increases our blood circulation, there is so much heat (garmi) in it." I wrote this down carefully.

Pigeons are attracted to shrines by grain offerings, scattered and piled by pilgrims. Reflecting now, in 2020, seventeen years after my second visit to Kuchalwara, and forty years after the first, I read Shambhu's words and speculate whether he may have sensed my cognitive alarm, visceral dismay, and spiritual/ethical disorientation—and was groping for a way to counter these. Did he lump me with the "scientific people" who required an organic explanation for something ineffable, even if contrived? In other words, to provincial Rajasthanis, no matter whether schooled or unschooled, cures at Kuchalwara Mataji were simply a deity's grace, but it required creativity to produce a different language of wonder's causality. I think it likely that Shambhu himself—a literate man, an elected village official widely trusted for his integrity—sought a way to articulate if not a "convergence" of science and religion, then at least a bridge or (better metaphor) an enveloping canopy within which we might both comfortably abide. In a way, Shambhu's creative speculation, an improvisation, counters wonder, counters at least the surprising element, rendering divine healing no stranger than hungry pigeons.[11] Pigeons nested in the well located in Kalla Nathji's field where they could also find grain; and their very natural frightened flight precipitated Bhoujram's awareness that his uncle had jumped in the well.

2005 A Cure in the Family

I had four days to spend in Rajasthan on a brief visit in the winter of 2005. I learned that my dear friend Bhoju's elderly mother, Raji, had suffered a mild stroke, or in any case something that had caused a partial paralysis. The doctor had no particular help to offer, and they had taken her to the shrine of Kuchalwara Mataji, where she spent almost two weeks. Bhoju and I stopped there on the way from Jaipur to Ghatiyali, to try to persuade her to come home. She refused.

Figure 1.3. At home in Ghatiyali in 2015, Raji Gujar (far right) and her visitors. *Source*: Author photo.

While staying at Kuchalwara, Raji had a dream in which the goddess spoke to her, chastising her for coming to the shelter of the mother to be healed, while prudently leaving her valuable silver ornaments back home for safekeeping. Gujar women of Raji's generation normally wore heavy silver ornaments night and day, year-round. In the dream, Kuchalwara Mother made Raji realize she needed to put complete trust in the goddess's power. Raji asked her son and daughter-in-law to bring her the jewelry, and they complied.

Several days later, Raji did return home, weak but nearly herself again, although her mouth remained slightly off kilter—a distortion that gradually faded over the years. Many friends came to call, to congratulate her on her recovery, and to hear from her own lips about the goddess's healing grace and wonderous power.

2017 A New Temple

I stayed with Bhoju Ram's family in Ghatiyali for eight nights in February 2017. Our days were packed with courtesy visits and meals. At last, toward the end of my stay, we felt free to take a little pleasure excursion. We decided to visit Bisalpur Dam. The water in the Banas Basin reservoir was its own kind of wonderous sight in this drought-prone region. Its existence signified the capacity to irrigate thirsty crops, and the subsequent harvest bounty of nourishment, a source of celebration, gratitude.

On the way back, we stopped to have darshan at several shrines and temples that were more or less on our route. These included Kuchalwara Mataji, which I had not visited for twelve years. I was quite unprepared to see a tall new temple rising, so different from the old shrine in architectural style.

I was almost equally unprepared to see ill persons surrounding the new temple in the same fashion as they had the old shrine in 2003. As the temple was still a construction site, and the old terrace was gone, pilgrims at this point had to camp on an unpaved area to the side, to stay safely out of the way of the crane lifting giant blocks of stone to complete the dome. That crane was itself something to be wondered at, and Bhoju's wife, Bali, was fascinated by it.

Bangles, strings, strips of cloth and other items left at shrines and temples are signs of a deity's ongoing healing blessings, sometimes left by those who seek help; often by those who have received it. These had just begun to appear around the new, still incomplete temple. I did not learn who had funded the impressive construction. I was not doing

Figure 1.4. At Kuchalwara Mataji temple in 2017, ill pilgrims are camped; a shrine to Hanuman is visible behind them. *Source*: Author photo.

Figure 1.5. At the still unfinished new Kuchalwara Mataji temple in 2017; the freshly adorned image of the goddess, and, above her on the left, a pigeon's nest. *Source*: Author photo.

fieldwork; I was visiting friends. But I know that, most often, the funds to build a new temple testify to experiences of wonder, so the building itself becomes an expression of gratitude for grace received. Pigeons were already colonizing the place.

2010 Compassion:
A Muslim Pir Heals a Hindu Merchant's Wife

My research site shifted in 2010 to the town of Jahazpur where I pursued along many trails a very broad concern with the connections between localities and identities. One of the simplest ways to talk about the qualities of place was to ask about *dekhne layakh sthan* (places worth seeing). Local sites of attraction predictably were temples and shrines. One of them was the hilltop tomb (*mazar*) of Gaji Pir.[12] Gaji's devotees often spoke very passionately of the saint's miraculous works. One such person was Nazir, a government servant and a singer of qawwali, a form of Islamic devotional song very popular in India. Wonder tales literally tumbled breathlessly from his mouth, one upon the next.

Here is just one among half a dozen he produced in a single interview in which he tells of a Hindu shopkeeper's wife who was cured of a wasting illness by Gaji, a Muslim saint. Note, however, that the words Hindu and Muslim never once appear in Nazir's narrative, nor are they the main point of this story. Rather it is a story of grace, of compassion, resulting in a healing wonder indifferent to the boundaries of identity. I would not deny that a secondary message, to me, a foreigner, and to Bhoju, a Hindu, may indeed have to do with the superiority of Gaji Pir over other sources of help and healing, but that is because of Nazir's enormous reverence for the saint whose grace, as he tells it, has permeated his entire life history. Here is Nazir's account:

> You know there is a merchant named Ram Ladda [a lineage of merchants] whose shop is near the police station, near Delhi Gate.[13]
>
> His wife was sick. She was such a beautiful woman, [to Ann] her color was just like yours [fair]. It was the month of Ramadan, and her husband and I were friends. So I went to their home to ask about her health [a courtesy visit, appropriate to the holiday; presumably he already knew she was unwell]. I went to ask about her condition.

And her husband said, "Brother, I tell you solemnly I am destroyed. I went to all the gods and now fifteen days have gone by and she hasn't even taken one grain for fifteen days, and she is like a living corpse. I went to *all* the gods."

I said to him, "You say that you have been everywhere, but there is one place you haven't been!"

He responded, "Haven't I gone to every place in Jahazpur?"

"No," I said, "in Jahazpur there is one place you haven't been!"

"Where didn't I go?"

"You didn't go to Gaji."

"Yes, friend, you're right I didn't go there."

So I said to him, "Bathe her, and don't worry about her; if she can't walk you can carry her on a cot. Don't imagine you will have to carry her all the way. Take her as far as the stairs, and then she will go up herself."

"How can that be?"

"You'll see, it is true."

So they did as I said, and brought her. When they reached the steps, she said, "Take me down," and after that she said, "Hold both of my arms and I'll walk up on my own." So with one person holding each arm she walked up. She is now completely cured!

Sometimes I myself might forget to go up the stairs, but *he* never forgets, he goes up every Thursday! And now this woman and her family are in great bliss, and they are all devotees of Gaji Baba.

This wondrous tale crosses religious boundaries and proves the compassionate potency of Gaji, a saint who bestows wellness on all who approach in need of help.

Wonder, or the Beating of Birds' Wings

In this chapter I have considered wonder as multifaceted, including curiosity about the wider world and its spectacles; creativity in finding explanatory frameworks to hold the inexplicable; compassion in the sense of grace bestowed on those in need such as a young man risking his own life to save his uncle's or a devoted husband seeking a cure for his debilitated wife. Examples ranged from purely aesthetic wonder evoked and treasured by Uddi Gujar to the effective wonder of cures for hopeless cases; from the stretching beyond death of a healer's magical power accumulated through esoteric practice to the sense that expansive, compassionate grace may fall on anyone regardless of their identity or their past.

I see wonder in the ways connections among people, spirits, deities, and nature are forged and endure, often through retellings of wonder's works. And that may be what remains at the tail end of this panorama: that wonder is fundamentally a state to be communicated or an experience of communication—one in which anthropologists, at least those with a pinch of luck and an ounce of listening skills, are privileged to participate.[14]

Figure 1.6. At the tomb of Gaji Pir, a gate densely covered with tokens of visitors' prayers and blessings; the flower-covered tomb is visible on the left. *Source*: Author photo.

Beauty and power converge in wonder, visibly manifest in artistic creations, in humans and in the natural world. I want to listen seriously to Bhojuram, Dev Ram, Durga Lal, Shambhu, Nazir, Uddi, and so many others who explained things to me. Wonder, so richly shared, is evidently a font of inspiration for storytelling, for communication. In my own anthropological questing, like Uddi Gujar, I too was motivated by curiosity about other places: "It is to see that all the world goes." But seeing isn't everything. Even the Taj Mahal can be deemed nothing but stone.

Accepting that the visible hardly holds wonder's totality renders my panorama metaphor insufficient. At shrines there are certainly visible testimonies—ribbons, bangles, strings—telling wordless stories of invisible wonder-working power, power to relieve human suffering. These are signs of compassion sought and received. But there exist also invisible wonders, or inner vision, as Bhoju describes Kalla Nath and the cobra appearing in his mind's eye.

To close, rather than futilely attempting to wrap up these fragments from my forty years of intermittent ethnographic presence into a tidy package, let us just return flightily to pigeons. Let the grains of wonder slip through our fingers for the pigeons to peck. It was pigeons who alerted Bhojuram to his uncle's plunge; and it was pigeons who offered Shambhu Nath a way to interpret the salubrious atmosphere at Kuchalwara Mataji. Call it medicine or call it grace; call it power vibrant in the heated air generated by birds beating their wings.

Acknowledgments

I am indebted to Bhojuram Gujar for writing out his unforgettable event and allowing me to incorporate it, as well as to Nathu Nath and Shambhu Nath for all the ways they contributed to my research; Kirin Narayan, Tulasi Srinivas, and Anand Vivek Taneja helped me greatly with thoughtful suggestions on earlier drafts.

Notes

1. See Roychowdhury (2020) and Srinivas (2020) for timely discussions of religious phenomena in India associated with illness, and most especially with

COVID. Arumugam (2020) addresses the ways deities may indeed sometimes be perceived as "vulnerable to the virus."

2. Sakaria and Sakaria's Rajasthani-Hindi dictionary (1977) gives as the first two glosses for *gajab* as noun, *vichitra bat* (strange matter) and *ashcharya* (a surprise); but for the adjective the first gloss is *bhayankar* (frightening).

3. Here and in all quoted passages to follow, parentheses indicate insertions that were in the original text while brackets indicate explanatory insertions made for the present chapter.

4. See Gujar and Gold (1992) for Bhojuram Gujar's connections with American scholars and their initial impact on his life; see Gold and Gujar (2002, 165–81) for the life stories of Bhoju's parents, Raji and Sukhdev Gujar.

5. For the history and roles of householder Naths see Gold (1992).

6. These are common healing techniques; sweeping is often performed with a feather fan, dipped in cow urine; blowing would include a healer muttering magical words while blowing on a patient (Gold 1992, 52).

7. For Puvali ka Devji, a Devnarayan shrine outside the village of Ghatiyali, see Gold (1988, 154–79).

8. Cobras are traditionally identified with ancestral spirits in North Indian Hindu traditions; see Gold (1988, 235–39).

9. For a discussion of begar see Gold and Gujar (2002, 151–55).

10. See for some classic discussions Rhodes (1996) and Whyte (1997).

11. See Narayan for improvised creativity as "a way to reclaim space amid repressive, disciplining cultural institutions" (2016, 29).

12. See Gold (2017, 140–45) for the shrine's origin story and for a description of the Urs of Gaji Pir as celebrated in Jahazpur.

13. For the gates of Jahazpur, see Gold (2017, 29–64).

14. See Taneja (2022) for a beautiful discussion of Maulana Azad's extensive communications with sparrows during his imprisonment—and the implications of these communications for Muslim ecological thought.

Works Cited

Arumugam, Indira. 2020. "Do the Gods Have COVID-19 Too? Protecting Idols, Cherishing Deities." Asia Research Institute blog. National University of Singapore, September 3. https://ari.nus.edu.sg/20331-44/.

Flueckiger, Joyce B. 2020. *Material Acts in Everyday Hindu Worlds*. Albany: State University of New York Press.

Gold, Ann Grodzins. 1988. *Fruitful Journeys: The Ways of Rajasthani Pilgrims*. Berkeley: University of California Press.

———. 1992. *A Carnival of Parting: The Tales of King Bharthari and King Gopi Chand as Sung and told by Madhu Natisar Nath of Ghatiyali, Rajasthan*. Berkeley: University of California Press.

———. 2017. *Shiptown: Between Rural and Urban North India*. Philadelphia: University of Pennsylvania Press.

Gold, Ann Grodzins, and Bhojuram Gujar. 2002. *In the Time of Trees and Sorrows: Nature, Power, and Memory in Rajasthan*. Durham, NC: Duke University Press.

Gujar, Bhojuram, and Ann Grodzins Gold. 1992. "From the Research Assistant's Point of View." *Anthropology and Humanism Quarterly* 17 (3):72–84.

Narayan, Kirin. 2016. *Everyday Creativity: Singing Goddesses in the Himalayan Foothills*. Chicago: University of Chicago Press.

Pandian, Anand. 2019. *A Possible Anthropology: Methods for Uneasy Times*. Durham, NC: Duke University Press.

Rhodes, Lorna Amarasingham. 1996. "Studying Biomedicine as a Cultural System." In *Handbook of Medical Anthropology: Contemporary Theory and Method*, rev. ed., ed. Carolyn F. Sargent and Thomas M. Johnson, 165–80. Westport, CT: Greenwood.

Roychowdhury, Adrija. 2020. "When Fear Leads to Faith: The Disease Gods of India." *Indian Express*, June 22. https://indianexpress.com/article/research/when-fear-leads-to-faith-the-disease-gods-of-india-6470376/.

Sakaria, Acharya Badri Prasad, and Bhupati Ram Sakaria. 1977. *Rajasthani-Hindi Shabad-Kosh*. Jaipur: Panchil.

Srinivas, Tulasi. 2018. *The Cow in the Elevator: An Anthropology of Wonder*. Durham, NC: Duke University Press.

———. 2020. "India's Goddesses of Contagion Provide Protection in the Pandemic—Just Don't Make Them Angry." *Conversation*, June 15. https://theconversation.com/indias-goddesses-of-contagion-provide-protection-in-the-pandemic-just-dont-make-them-angry-139745.

Taneja, Anand Vivek. 2022. "Sharing a Room with Sparrows: Maulana Azad and Muslim Ecological Thought." In *Cosmopolitical Ecologies Across Asia: Places of Power in Changing Environments*, ed. Riamsara Kuyakanon Knapp, Hildegard Diemberger, and David Sneath, 228–42. London: Routledge.

Whyte, Susan Reynolds. 1997. *Questioning Misfortune: The Pragmatics of Uncertainty in Eastern Uganda*. Cambridge: Cambridge University Press.

Chapter 2

Weird Tales

Ganesh, Idolatry, and the Golden Age of American Pulp Fiction

WILLIAM ELISON

> Father Ganpati, go before us
> Come back to us soon next year
> Father Ganpati, go before us
> Blessed image, go before us
>
> —Ganesh Festival chant

Introduction: Ganesh Crosses the Sea

Hinduism's gateway god, the lovable, elephant-headed Ganesh: What notion of him would have prevailed among the American public in the early twentieth century?

"Not much" is the preliminary answer. Before Independence, and the stationing there of GIs during World War II, India seemed distant indeed from the United States. Migrant communities were few and marginalized. Indian objects were curios and Indian ideas were exotic, if not esoteric. Outside of scholarly circles, the teachings of Hinduism were hardly distinguished from those of other "Eastern religions"—or, at another remove, from a generic and murky heathenism (see Altman 2017; Isaacs 1958).

When it comes specifically to Lord Ganesh, databases of historical newspapers have made it possible to draw some generalizations. News items indicate the limited contexts in which the name circulated in public media. I would demarcate one sphere of associations under the rubric of *idolatry*. Here, Ganesh *murtis* feature among other figural objects considered sacred by the world's non-Christian peoples—Laughing Buddhas from East Asia, Polynesian tikis, and the like. Most contributions by metropolitan newspapers to this idolatry discourse were not overtly hostile in tone. The prevailing approach meshes well with the "encyclopaedic tradition" as identified by Jonathan Z. Smith (1971) within the context of the academic study of religion: a collector's attitude, emboldened in this period by Americans' unprecedented access to markets (of art objects among other things) across the globe.[1] To be sure, there is a dose of fire and brimstone in the mix. In the 1920s the American Methodist Church had a noted collection of idols that were exhibited at the New York headquarters when not sent out on tours of the nation's churches.

An adjacent domain is *adventure travel*. In the dispatches of special correspondents and other visitors to colonial India, Ganesh features chiefly as an element of local color. Complementing the travelogue pieces were the serialized popular novels many newspapers used to carry, some of which took the action to India (among other romantic locales). And in voice and content alike, these fictional and nonfictional representations overlap enough to be considered together. Both kinds of narrative center on an American or British sahib or memsahib, whose perspective the reader follows; Indian arcana are decoded by white Old India Hands or, perhaps less reliably, by native informants; Indian voices are reproduced along stereotyped patterns; finally, the jungle and its animals never seem far away, and chief among those Indian animals is the elephant.

These tropes can be read critically through the analytic of orientalism. But let me hone things down to a sharper point. I think, where textual production is concerned, what really brings this body of Indian impressions together—idolatry, adventure, and orientalism alike—is the example set in late nineteenth-century Anglo-American letters by one writer: Rudyard Kipling. I will advance this point with an examination of two Kipling short stories that situates them as foundational for writers who follow.

It's in the early 1930s that Ganesh makes a new claim on the attention of the American public. Up to this point consigned to background detail, when the god's prominent features are at last brought into relief it is on a rather unlikely surface: the cheap, wood-pulp pages of *Weird Tales*, "the Unique Magazine." Across two issues in 1931, Frank Belknap Long spun the tangled tale of an extradimensional being that arrives in the form of an elephant-headed idol from the East. Two years later, Robert E. Howard published the third of his Conan the Barbarian stories. When the hero encounters the mysterious Yogah of Yag, he takes him at first for an idol and next for a demon: "Conan stared at the wide flaring ears, the curling proboscis, on either side of which stood white tusks. . . ."

Weird Tales may have been a niche publication, but it cannot be considered obscure. To be sure, its annual circulation, around fifty thousand in its heyday, was nothing special by the standards of the 1920s and 1930s, the golden age of pulp fiction. And yet: Fantasy, horror, science fiction—these genres took modern shape over the *Weird Tales* decades, and they did so in large part, and to lasting effect, within the magazine's pages. This is not to deny that much of the content was formulaic. The point is rather that within the elastic thematic of the weird, a diversity of formulas was given room and new ones emerged from the mix. *Weird Tales* in the 1930s was something like a mad scientist's laboratory, a crucible where the commonplace was amalgamated with innovative and visionary elements.

But why should it have been from this spot that the blessed Ganpati image surfaces with a higher profile? This is the question that launches my argument. Let's orient it to the theme of this volume. I propose to engage *wonder* in dialogue with a related, well-noted tendency within American speculative literature—namely, the *weird*. What was it about this historical and literary nexus that proved such inviting ground for the manifestation of the Lord of the *Ganas*? What, in short, connects wonder, the weird, and Ganesh?

In what follows I present a genealogy. From the extensive oeuvre of Rudyard Kipling (1865–1936), I select two stories. I will show how each stages the definitive encounter of the idolatry discourse: the confrontation between a rational, autonomous subject and an image that mediates the presence of a radical Other. I proceed to analyses of the *Weird Tales* stories cited above: "The Horror from the Hills," by the pulp author Frank Belknap Long (1901–94), and "The Tower of the Elephant," by the better-known Robert E. Howard (1906–36).

There is a missing link. The gap between the Victorian stories of Kipling and the Depression-era fare of the American writers is not simply chronological. If Long and Howard drew inspiration from Kipling, I argue, it was transmitted through a more proximate figure. In the present day, the reputation of *Weird Tales* is associated with one writer above all others. The customary description of Howard Phillips Lovecraft (1890–1937) as a cult author is apt in more than one sense—it was even in his lifetime. And for all his flaws as an artist and thinker, it must be conceded that Lovecraft was, and is, the acknowledged prophet of the modern American weird. Let's tighten the connection: if the weird has a mascot—a legible metonym that circulates in popular media—it is surely that therioanthropomorphic deity of Lovecraft's invention, the tentacle-faced Cthulhu.

Rudyard Kipling: Idolatry Stories

The legacy of Kipling, who won the Nobel Prize in 1907, was immense. He was well-nigh unavoidable, for better or worse, for anyone writing fiction in English about India in the late colonial period. Authors with literary aspirations contended with this centrality, and writers in popular genres did so perhaps even more, such that imaginings of locales far distant from South Asia also often bear his stamp.[2]

Lord Ganesh makes his principal appearance in Kipling's fiction in elephant form.[3] I regard "The Bridge-Builders" (1898) as a standout work, and I am hardly alone in this assessment. To secure it its place in my argument, however, the story needs to be weighed against an earlier effort, "The Mark of the Beast" (Kipling 1891c). Both texts conjure with the assumptions and conventions of a discourse about idolatry already long seated in English literature. Dramas of self-mastery, they stage an encounter between the protagonist and a spectacle that exerts an alien fascination. The image challenges the hero—and thus the reader—with a riddle: What lies behind the surface? Is it something false? Something familiar, or at least accountable? Or is there something there that is true and yet unaccountable—a thing undreamt of in our philosophy?[4]

In both these tales, the narrator pulls back the curtain, as it were, and reveals the answer behind the cultic facade. In both, the hero is an English sahib, a man of education ("a scholar and gentleman"), objectivity ("fair play"), and self-discipline ("stiff upper lip"). He is a representative of the class that built the Empire, pledged to the colonial project as its Victorian architects imagined it: the imposition of rational taxonomies of administration and science on a realm of raw material. For Kipling, this is not the "heathen darkness" of the missionary but rather a dreamlike domain; across his oeuvre, India gives the writer license to play on the reader's own repressed memories and fantasies. When he presents Indian characters—human, animal, or deity—he likes to voice them with a certain Biblical "Dost thou not know me?" cadence, a half-alien, half-intimate charge that may well trigger a reader's associations of not altogether rational experiences from private life.

"The Mark of the Beast" is a well-known horror story. Following a magazine debut in 1890, it appeared the year after in the collection *Life's Handicap*. As with many Kipling stories, it is narrated by an unnamed figure who stands in for the author himself. "I" not only contributes the tale's dominant tone—a crisp self-assurance that gets brittle as things advance—he takes an active role in the drama. Another important role is played by alcohol, which (along with religion and sex) is a force that has been known to cause even *pukka* sahibs to stray from a rational appreciation of the situation.

Fleete, a newcomer, has inherited property in India. He is befriended by the narrator and by Strickland of the colonial police, a personification of the Old India Hand. On New Year's Eve, the three celebrate at the club and get drunk, Fleete wretchedly so. On the way to put him to bed at Strickland's house, they ride past a temple where a nighttime *puja* is in session. Gatecrashing the service, Fleete "grind[s] the ashes of his cigar-butt in to the forehead of the red stone image of Hanuman." He plants himself with his back to the god. He is proud of his handiwork, the profane *tilak* on the therioanthropomorphic idol, and pronounces it the "mark of the beast."

"Then, without any warning, a Silver Man came out of a recess behind the image of the god." The Silver Man is so called because leprosy has made his body spookily pale. He is a bestial figure, "perfectly naked" and inarticulate except for noises he makes, "exactly like the mewing of an otter." He seizes Fleete and "nuzzles" his chest. A priest speaks in English: "Take your friend away. He has done with Hanuman but Hanuman has not done with him." When the trio arrive home they discover that Fleete bears a bite-mark resembling the spot of a leopard. Over the following day he horrifies his hosts with erratic behavior, snapping down undercooked meat, rolling in the dirt, and howling like a wolf. Finally, "the beast that had once been Fleete" tries to exit through a bedroom window, but Strickland and "I" tie it up with the "thongs of the punkah-rope . . . and gagged it with a shoe-horn." A doctor comes, diagnoses rabies, and goes. Strickland knows better.

Following the otter-sounds, the two sahibs stalk the Silver Man in the garden, thrash him with polo sticks, tie him up too, and put him in the dining room along with his victim. Then, repurposing more gentlemen's sporting goods—a double-barreled shotgun and a fishing line—they set about torturing him. "Strickland shaded his eyes with his hands . . . and we got to work. This part is not to be printed." In due course the captive agrees to remove the curse—it takes one touch of the hand—and is allowed to remove himself.

Fleete sleeps and is woken late the next morning. He believes it is New Year's Day, and complains only of a hangover. No trace remains of the mark. Strickland rides to the temple, "to offer redress for the pollution of the god," but the priests profess ignorance of anything untoward. Back in the dining room, Fleete, restored to himself, makes a friendly remark and "without warning" Strickland loses his composure: "It is terrible to see a strong man overtaken with hysteria. Then it struck me that we had fought for Fleete's soul with the Silver Man in that room, and had disgraced ourselves as Englishmen for ever, and I laughed and gasped and gurgled just as shamefully as Strickland, while Fleete thought that we had both gone mad." The final line is an ironic comment: "[I]t is well known to every right-minded man that the gods of the heathen are stone and brass, and any attempt to deal with them otherwise is justly condemned."

Earlier, I set up the idolatry device as a riddle: an attention-getting facade that invites a question, and the answer, the reality behind the surface. The shiny object that hooks the reader is of course the idol of Hanuman, whom the narrator describes simply as "the Monkey-god." No sooner is this front defaced by Fleete than from behind springs the Silver Man. He is an alienating figure, having literally "no face, because he was a leper of some years' standing." Let's note, however, that the sole purpose of the diagnosis is to lay the ground for some unpleasant descriptions. The Silver Man is no invalid, nor yet some ghoulish corpse-like figure. His attributes—nakedness, otter cries, leopard marks—are bestial; he is the vital embodiment of the therianthropomorphic idea.[5] (In this regard, within the visual archive of Hinduism, Hanuman is second only to Ganesh.) And yet for all his shock value, he is himself merely a symptom—a mediating element, like the idol, of the riddle's ultimate answer.

In the colonial horror story, "The Mark of the Beast," Hinduism is revealed as true, or at any rate efficacious. Therein lies the horror. Not to belabor the point, but the problem with the beast-god is not the beast part (to wit, Hindus worship animals, Hindus are themselves animals) but rather the god part. Kipling's Hanuman has power not only over subjects who recognize his mastery but also those who do not. Under the brass or stone surface, the god is real; under the skin—whether brown, white, or silver—human beings are *all*, in essence, beasts. It is in participating within the logic of the native god's power over Fleete—and by extension themselves—that Strickland and "I" "disgraced [them] selves as Englishmen forever." The rejection of sportsmanship in favor of unprintable tortures is a strictly secondary aspect of this concession; the truly unmentionable, aporetic thing is the exposure of the British gentleman and the empire he serves as ideological constructs. The tale concludes with the unmanning of Strickland and "I"—their descent into hysteria—and the sense of crisis is brought home via the contrast with the cool, clipped sahib-voice in which the narrator has delivered the rest of the story.

Hanuman and Ganesh assume speaking roles in "The Bridge-Builders," which first appeared in magazine format in 1893. This story is told in the third person, but it is centered on the character of Findlayson, an engineer in the Public Works Department, and his voice and attitudes map well onto those of the narrator of the previous piece. For three years he has directed the construction of the Kashi Bridge over the Ganges. The great enterprise nears completion, and the tale's opening stresses the scale of imperial investment: five thousand laborers; state-of-the-art industrial gear; brick, stone, iron, fire. Kipling gives Findlayson an assistant, but this junior-grade Englishman soon recedes, his place taken by a more richly realized foil. Peroo is a Lascar whose experience at sea has given him the skills and ease with authority to set him at the sahib's right hand.

Reports arrive of flooding upriver. Findlayson mobilizes all his resources to secure the works. The deluge arrives the next day, and behind his stiff upper lip the Chief Engineer, working around the clock, refusing food and rest, fears for his bridge. The day's end finds him in a boat with Peroo, who has pressed him to share some opium to see them through another rough night. The raging Ganges casts them on an islet: "An incessant lightning . . . showed all that there was to be seen . . . a grey gnarled peepul overshadowing a Hindoo shrine. . . . The holy man whose summer resting-place it was had long since abandoned it, and the weather had broken the red-daubed image of his god. The two men stumbled, heavy-limbed and heavy-eyed . . . and dropped down under the shelter of the branches." Before their dreamy gaze, animal forms emerge from the darkness and assemble around the shrine.

A garlanded bull is joined in short order by others: a parrot, a blackbuck, a tiger, a "monstrous grey Ape, who seated himself man-wise in the place of the fallen image." The first to speak is a crocodile: "The walls stand. The towers stand. They have chained my flood, and the river is not free any more. Heavenly Ones, take this yoke away . . . ! It is I, Mother Gunga, that speak." The beasts, for the most part, are the iconographic vehicles of deities of classical Hinduism, and the personalities voiced are the riders: Shiva, Kama (misleadingly spelled as "Karma"), Indra, Kali, and of course Hanuman and Ganga. They have convened around the question of the British bridge over the holy river.

Others join the circle at the shrine: Ganesh in the form of an elephant; Sitala as a sickly donkey; Bhairav ("Bhairon"), a drunken man with a staff; and, finally, Krishna, "the darling of the Gopis." Ganga's plea receives support from the other female deities. But Ganesh, supported by Hanuman, urges an Olympian view: "Let the dirt dig in the dirt if it pleases the dirt." And the latecomer, Krishna, offers an unsettling argument. The time when an old-fashioned smiting would have redeemed the gods' honor has already passed. The modern methods of the British Raj have set in motion an inexorable process of rationalization, and the material progress won by rational action will consign the gods, in their capacity as brokers of human fortune, to sure irrelevance. "The flame shall die upon the altars," Krishna warns, "till ye become little Gods again—Gods of the jungle . . . as ye were at the beginning."

The final word goes to Indra. Philosophically, he affirms the gods' ultimate impermanence. But he projects their twilight onto a cosmic time scale: "Ye know the Riddle of the Gods. When Brahm ceases to dream, the Heavens and the Hells and Earth disappear. Be content. Brahm dreams still."

The day breaks. The heads of the two witnesses clear. Findlayson dismisses the *darshan* as a fever dream. His attention is given over to a material concern: Does the bridge still stand? (It does.) The effect on Peroo, by contrast, is complex and transformative. He has indeed seen the gods, but in a dreamlike altered state. The gods are lords of a realm of dream—Hindu India—but now Peroo realizes there is an alternative dispensation, that of waking life. The Lascar is a man of practical verities. He gets things done; he wields and recognizes authority within the colonial order; he is a nascent modern. Which path will he choose?

Two things elevate this tale above much of Kipling's other work. The first is the generosity the author shows to diverse perspectives, and even subjectivities, within his diegesis and among his readerships. In the previous story, the horror of the Hindu god's curse—its undeniability—is mediated through the narrator's voice. In fact, the effect of the weird relies on this unitary standpoint. The objectivity the reader initially grants "I" is revealed as a colonial authority claim. By contrast, in "The Bridge-Builders" the narration is omniscient, if not entirely dispassionate; there is indeed an overlap with the sahib's-eye view of Findlayson, but over the course of his long, strange trip the Englishman's horizons are broadened, and the reader is made privy to the interior life of Peroo as well. What's more, the characters convened in this piece include non-human persons—gods in animal form—and these luminaries of Puranic Hinduism voice a compelling diversity of opinion among themselves.

The conclave of Hindu gods—the visitation—realizes another aspect of this work that sets it apart. Here again "The Mark of the Beast" provides a useful comparison. I propose that, where the first idolatry story unsettles the reader with a sense of the weird, the second takes mystery and curiosity a step further—into wonder.

In "The Mark of the Beast," the idolatry device has three layers: behind the Hanuman *murti* is the Silver Man, and behind the Silver Man is the power of the real Hanuman. In "The Bridge-Builders," the abandoned shrine with its broken idol is the site of a multisensory hierophany. Their senses enhanced by opium, Findlayson and Peroo not only see the Hindu gods; they hear them, even smell them. No less vividly drawn than their physical attributes are their personalities. Some are fierce: Ganga the crocodile and Durga the tiger. Some are shady: Sitala the donkey, Bhairav the drunkard. Krishna is by turns tender and passionate. And the elephant Ganesh is immense, tolerant, sympathetic.

Some characterizations are more faithful to Hindu mythology than others. (Hanuman is almost unrecognizable in Kipling's trickster conception.) And while the gods' statements are heavily allusive in style, any serious attempt to decode them with reference to Brahminical sources would contend with a twofold problem. On the one hand, Kipling is simply out of his depth where Hindu teachings are concerned. On the other, inasmuch as he was writing (as he thought) for non-Hindus, ignorance did not detract from his purpose—to intrigue his readers with suggestion.

All of which notwithstanding, two coherent themes emerge from the debate. First, the gods are exercised about colonialism. They are the land's ancient masters, and their sovereignty goes back thousands of years, although—this is a key point—they do not claim to be eternal. In the present, they find their dominion challenged by white men, upstarts whose command of technique in the material sphere encroaches on their own hold over the people's imagination. Second, it is precisely in the imagination that the Heavenly Ones stake their claim. Muddling Puranic teachings on the cosmogonic roles of Vishnu and Brahma, Kipling has the gods remind each other that they are ultimately figments in the dream of "Brahm." Their reign will endure until Brahm awakes. To this suggestively Eastern formulation of all creation as *maya*, the author holds up an alternative: modernity, whose symbol is the bridge, whose subjective state is wide awake, and whose material condition is the British Raj.

At the story's close, a sober Findlayson seems unchanged. What is at stake in diegesis is the consciousness of the Indian character. In fact, Peroo has had a sort of negative epiphany: he has seen the gods, but realizes he can dispel them if he decides to wake up. But let it be asked of this open-ended idolatry story: How does it end for the reader?

Politics and theology aside, the tale's centerpiece is surely the wondrous *darshan* of the gods. Behind the idol it turns out there are indeed elder gods in the land—and they are enchanting, charismatic, glamorous. I think the story invites reflection, even from its intended white Victorian readership. Would you ("wouldst thou") really choose the bridge over the gods? To put it another way: Does the story perhaps contain more than one bridge? Is this dreamlike fiction itself a sort of bridge? What is the reader's destination?

H. P. Lovecraft: "The Call of Cthulhu"

When it comes to Cthulhu, the bulbous-headed brainchild of Lovecraft, it is easier to show the continuities with the Ganesh-like fictions that succeed him than those that anticipate him. To my knowledge, Lovecraft never stated he was inspired by a Hindu original. Yet the family resemblance is strong.

Peter Penzoldt (1980, 67), one of the first academics to take this author seriously, writes: "The most dominant motif in Lovecraft's work is the nameless, ancestral horror lurking beneath the earth, or ready to invade us from the stars; the dethroned but still potent gods of old. Probably C. G. Jung's theories on the collective subconscious give the only explanation of such symbols as 'Great Cthulhu.'" My own explanation of Great Cthulhu will gesture to a collective unconscious of a sort, although the formulation will be anything but Jungian. Rather, in line with my analysis in the previous section, I will argue that as a pagan deity whose presence is marked in the material world by cultic artifacts—idols—Cthulhu projects horror via a gesture of ideological address. The *darshan* of Cthulhu challenges the integrity of a hegemonic subject position, that of a modern white Anglo-American male—an American sahib, you could say. This profoundly unsettling affect is the *weird*.

Let's take quick note of some influences. J. Vernon Shea (1980, 135) identifies "the three writers Lovecraft sought most to emulate—Poe, Machen, and Dunsany." In remarking this trio, I don't propose to question the centrality of Edgar Allan Poe (1809–49) to the tradition of the weird in American literature (or in others). What I offer here is confined to some observations about the cultural and geographical imagination of the 1838 work *The Narrative of Arthur Gordon Pym*. The Welshman Arthur Machen (1863–1947) and the Anglo-Irish aristocrat Lord Dunsany (1878–1957), however, are a different case. My modest intervention will be to link them in a chain with Kipling, a British contemporary.

Arthur Gordon Pym is Poe's only novel. His almost-namesake Pym stows away on a Yankee whaler, enduring generic mishaps—mutiny, shipwreck—before rescue by a British ship bound for Antarctic regions. The explorers land at the island of Tsalal, an exotic landscape devoid of the color white. The inhabitants are a lost race so dark that even their teeth are black. Their strange language, apparently sui generis, resonates uncannily with Hebrew. They turn out to be treacherous and bloodthirsty, and on his escape through subterranean passages (and on, ultimately, to the vision of an angelic figure in white) Pym encounters hieroglyphs and other portents of biblical prophecy.

The points I derive from this text are straightforward. Motifs identifiable here—southern seas as the frontier region of scientific knowledge; the association of an archeological record with primitive-seeming keepers of secrets—carry over to the "Call of Cthulhu." And, not to put too fine a point on it, the tale's racism will prove of direct relevance. *Pym* is perhaps as thoroughgoing a statement of the hatred and fear of Black people as anything to be read in nineteenth-century American letters, and, on this score, Lovecraft is indeed one of Poe's authentic twentieth-century successors.

And yet. Esoteric knowledge as challenge to rationality; atavistic populations as guardians of these dangerous truths; strange words that cloak meaning but strike affective chords: all these are characteristic of the fiction of Machen and Dunsany as well. They are also, of course, elements of Kipling's idolatry stories. In Machen, the colonial dichotomy is mapped onto Wales, with the ancestral Celtic stratum hosting magic and madness, and the Welsh language supplying strings of incantations and oaths (see Penzoldt 1980, 72–73; my own idea of the etymology of *Cthulhu* is that Lovecraft started off with *chthonic* and intended the rest to sound vaguely Welsh).

Dunsany is gentler. In *The Gods of Pegāna* (1905) and stories that followed, he spins myths around a pantheon of his own invention; where Machen cites Welsh folklore and Kipling Hinduism, Dunsany's names seem suggested by Greek mythology and bits of Orientalia. The enchanted landscape his gods tread—a step or two ahead of the human inhabitants—is a distinctly Eastern realm, well stocked with dancing girls, temples, and beggars. Immortals and mortals "thee" and "thou" each other with the sort of King James stylings that mark native speech in Kipling's India. But Dunsany's vision is pristine, uncolonized. Sequestered outside of history and known geography, his world is only opened to a modern traveler—the narrator "I"—in a few later stories, via the bridge of dream.

Lovecraft (1927) himself discusses all these writers in an erudite survey, "Supernatural Horror in Literature." The entry on Kipling is terse. The one title on which he goes into detail is "The Mark of the Beast," and, although he praises the story's power, he mentions neither the idol nor the divine agency it mediates. The idolatry theme is treated once Lovecraft reaches Dunsany, for whom his regard is unstinting. He commends two short plays, *The Gods of the Mountain* (1914) and *A Night at an Inn* (1916), whose plots both share the pivot of "The Mark of the Beast." The first play is set in Dunsany's Oriental dreamland, but the second takes place in the England of the author's day. Per Lovecraft's own summary: "*A Night at an Inn* tells of four thieves who have stolen the emerald eye of Klesh, a monstrous Hindoo god. . . . [I]n the night Klesh comes gropingly for his eye; and having obtained it and departed, calls each of the despoilers out into the darkness."

Unbelievers transgress against idols; the gods act through their idols to punish them. In so doing, they prove they exist. In his two exercises on the model, Dunsany serves up the chills with some wit—the framing invites some sympathy for the idol's point of view. No such broadmindedness diverts Lovecraft's perspective. It's time to examine "The Call of Cthulhu."

Published in the February 1928 issue of *Weird Tales*, the piece is constructed, like some detective stories (or perhaps like this essay), as a hunt through an archive. The first-person narrator guides the reader through successive items of evidence. Exhibit A is found in a box among the effects of his great uncle, late professor of Semitic languages at Brown University. Professor Angell has died in 1926 "after having been jostled by a nautical-looking negro" not far from the Providence riverfront. The box contains a "queer clay bas-relief" and a manuscript inscribed "Cthulhu Cult."

The manuscript's first half presents the case of young Wilcox, a student at the Rhode Island School of Design, who visited the professor on March 1, 1925, artwork in hand. The night before, a dream had shown him "great Cyclopean cities," their walls covered over in hieroglyphs. He inscribed the clay in a trancelike state; on properly waking, he called on Angell in hopes of decoding his own writing. Above the letters he had molded an icon. Examining this later, "I" notes: "A pulpy, tentacled head surmounted a grotesque and scaly body with rudimentary wings; but it was the *general outline* of the whole which made it most shockingly frightful." In Wilcox's mind, the form was connected with "almost unpronounceable" words from the dream: *Cthulhu fhtagn*. He reported daily on his dreams with Angell until March 23, when he entered an intense delirium lasting through April 2.

Exhibit B is the second half of Angell's manuscript, which presents recollections from the American Archaeological Society conference of 1908. A policeman, an Inspector Legrasse, had enlivened the proceedings with inquiries about an unusual object. "The statuette, idol, fetish, or whatever it was, had been captured . . . in the wooded swamps south of New Orleans during a raid on a supposed voodoo meeting." The tentacle-faced figure "was of a somewhat bloated corpulence, and squatted evilly on a rectangular block . . . covered with undecipherable characters." Of all the scholars assembled in 1908, it had stirred recognition in only one: Professor Webb of Princeton's Anthropology Department. Almost fifty years before, on an expedition to Greenland, Webb had "encountered a singular tribe or cult of degenerate Esquimaux whose religion . . . chilled him with its deliberate bloodthirstiness." He had seen the idol before which they danced and chanted, and it had been a bas-relief of a similar therioanthropomorphic deity, incised with similar hieroglyphs.

Having established that Webb's data corroborated his own, Legrasse regaled the professors with how he had acquired the artifact. Alarmed by reports of human sacrifice, Legrasse had led a force of twenty police on a trek into a "region . . . of traditionally evil repute . . . untraversed by white men." A red glare through the Spanish moss and the throb of drums had led them on to their destination. When they arrived, the sight had been such that several officers had fainted dead away. "[T]his hybrid spawn were braying, bellowing, and writhing about a monstrous ring-shaped bonfire; in the centre of which . . . stood a great granite monolith . . . on top of which . . . rested the noxious carven statuette."

Mastering their nerves, the police had charged the meeting and taken several dozen prisoners.

> Most were seamen, and a sprinkling of negroes and mulattoes . . . gave a colouring of voodooism to the heterogeneous cult. But . . . it became manifest that something far deeper and older than negro fetishism was involved. . . .
>
> They worshipped, so they said, the Great Old Ones who lived ages before there were any men. . . . This was that cult, and the prisoners said it had always existed and always would exist, hidden . . . all over the world until the time when the great priest Cthulhu, from his dark house in the mighty city of R'lyeh under the waters, should rise and bring the earth again beneath his sway.

To the mysterious chant Webb recorded in Greenland—*Ph'nglui mglw'nafh Cthulhu R'lyeh wgah'nagl fhtagn*—Legrasse, thanks to his interrogations, could add a translation: "In his house at R'lyeh dead Cthulhu lies dreaming."

Exhibit C consists of a report from the *Sydney Bulletin* and some pages from a seaman's written statement. The narrator has followed up with his own inquiries. "I was on the track of a very real, very secret, and very ancient religion whose discovery would make me an anthropologist of note." It is while taking a break (or so he thinks) at the home of a mineralogist friend that his eye is fortuitously drawn to a news clipping that lines a shelf of Australian samples. It is a report dated April 18, 1925, about a maritime mystery involving three ships.

A transpacific freighter has docked at Sydney with a disabled steam yacht in tow. On board the freighter is a Norwegian named Johansen, the second mate of a schooner swept far off course by a storm that broke out on March 1. On March 22, in an all-but-untrafficked patch of the South Pacific, it was challenged by the yacht with cannon fire. In the ensuing fight the schooner sank, but Johansen survived with eight others to board the yacht and eliminate its "evil-looking crew of Kanakas and half-castes." Then, curious about what they had been at pains to conceal, he had sailed the captured vessel to an unidentified island, where seven of his comrades were lost. With the eighth man, Braden, he had fled the scene in the yacht; at some point between a second storm on April 2 and rescue by the freighter on April 12, Braden had died. Johansen had been found, barely coherent, clutching an idol recovered from a shrine inside the ill-omened yacht.

The narrator is back on the case. To Sydney, where the idol now on display at the Australian Museum confounds all who study it. Next—reversing track—to Oslo, only to learn Johansen had recently died, expiring in the arms of two Lascars while out for a walk on the docks. His widow entrusts "I" with a manuscript in which Johansen has laid out—with a surplus of descriptive detail—his antipodean adventure of March 1925.

It bears out the narrator's direst forebodings. Accounting for global time differences, the dates of the storms bracketing Johansen's ordeal can be lined up exactly with the artist Wilcox's spell of nightmare and trance. What the sailor's statement makes clear is that, within the same window of time, the seismic activity that produced the squalls had also brought an uncharted (to that point) island from the waves: "[T]he men sight a great stone pillar sticking out of the sea, and in latitude S 47°9', longitude W 126°43' come upon a coast-line of mingled mud, ooze, and weedy Cyclopean masonry which can be nothing less than the tangible substance of earth's supreme terror—the nightmare corpse-city of R'lyeh." Behind the strange words, then, R'lyeh exists as a real geographical location. And behind the idol, a material reality—Great Cthulhu—also exists. Paraphrasing Johansen, "I" relates, inexorably, how the seamen discover a great slab they surmise is a door, how they slide it open, and how "It lumbered slobberingly into sight and gropingly squeezed Its gelatinous green immensity through the black doorway." There and then, two men die "of pure fright." The others fall to Its clutches or to slippery footing, save only Johansen and Braden, who escape to the yacht. But Braden looks back and is stricken mad, reduced to a cackling maniac.

And having now witnessed everything at one remove, the narrator fears for his own sanity. "[E]ven the skies of spring and the flowers of summer must ever afterward be poison to me. But I do not think my life will be long. . . . I know too much." His death following the completion of this text (met with, no doubt, at the hands of some nautical person of color) is signaled at its opening, where it is stated the record was "Found Among the Papers of the Late Francis Wayland Thurston, of Boston."

"The Call of Cthulhu" is an idolatry story. Comparison with Kipling will demonstrate that Lovecraft's is also a story about colonialism. To lay it out systematically: If what is at stake in "Cthulhu" is the narrator's sanity—and the integration of subjects like him within a symbolic order—then the idol wields its power as a trace (or symptom) of an alternative order, one that has been expelled (or repressed) beyond the pale of modern civilization. Cuing the reader to identify with "I," the story grounds this normative subject position in a world made intelligible and coherent by the English language—or an authoritative register thereof—and by positivist science. Yet the empire of reason has its frontiers, and the jungles of unreason are home not only to savage populations but also their gods. Elder gods, who turn out—as in "The Mark of the Beast" and "The Bridge-Builders"—to be real.

Who are the sahibs? They are well-educated white American men, and to a man they are Northeastern WASPs like Lovecraft himself. They are academics based at Brown and Princeton. Their names are almost comically Establishment: Francis Wayland Thurston, George Gammell Angell, William Channing Webb, even Henry Anthony Wilcox. Then there are witnesses who report from the field, practical men who get their hands dirty. Inspector Legrasse and Second Mate Johansen have gained officer rank, but their names mark them with second-tier ethnicities. In the whole, three-part story there is one female character: Johansen's widow, who is given no name.

Who are the natives, enthralled before the idol of their Great Old One? The Gulf Coast prisoners "all proved to be men of a very low, mixed-blooded, and mentally aberrant type." The cultists of Greenland are "degenerate Esquimaux"; the South Pacific pirates are "Kanakas and half-castes." Racism, for Lovecraft, was a matter of intellectual commitment as well as personal affect: this has been studied by critics as well as attested throughout a prolific correspondence.[6] And hybridity and creolization of the sort associated with maritime cultures seem to have been peculiarly abhorrent to the author (a native of Providence) as sites of boundary-crossing—human matter out of place. To go by the text, however, Cthulhu holds sway even over natives who appear to "know their place," which is to say, under the rational rule of colonial administration. In studying the goings-on of March 1925, Professor Angell had collected news reports from around the globe: "[I]tems from India speak guardedly of serious native unrest toward the end of March. Voodoo orgies multiply in Hayti, and African outposts report ominous mutterings. American officers in the Philippines find certain tribes bothersome about this time, and New York policemen are mobbed by hysterical Levantines on the night of March 22–23. The west of Ireland, too, is full of wild rumour and legendry." Anticolonial agitation in India, Africa, the Philippines, and US-occupied Haiti: Can the pattern behind it all be other than some worldwide, archaic cult of unreason? Lovecraft's inclusion of the Irish among the fey subject peoples may be a tip of the hat to Machen and Dunsany. As for "Levantines," the term is meant to overlap with Jews, whom he negatively identified with New York. He lived there unhappily from 1924 to 1926, and despised the city as a sinkhole of racial corruption (see Lovecraft 2000, 174, 179–81, 198).

What is the empire that is being contested? The gods of "The Bridge-Builders" assert sovereignty over India. By contrast Cthulhu and his kin, the unnamed Great Old Ones, lay claim to the entire world. Like Kipling's gods they enact their mastery by shaping the dream lives of lesser races, but they are not themselves creatures of dream, to be extinguished in waking life. Rather, the shock that concludes "The Call of Cthulhu" is that the god has been roused from his own dreaming. And the revelation of the monstrous form—unnatural yet corporeal—makes explicit what his graven likeness only suggests. The dreaming god commands the dream-bound masses; the awakened god confronts the masters of a global colonialism.

"We are proud to be definitely *reactionary* . . . ," Lovecraft (2000, 117) wrote in a letter of January 1926: "[M]y objection to Germany in the late war was that it formed a menace to our English Empire—an Empire so lamentably split in 1775–83, and so regrettably weakened by effeminate ideas of liberty. My wish was that we English reunite into one irresistible power and establish an hegemony of the globe in true Roman fashion." Anglo-American cultural hegemony is an apparent fact in "The Call of Cthulhu," and the author's wished-for political hegemony might as well be too. One thing the tale does quite effectively is to build the image of a world surveyed, classified, and managed by modern knowledge and technique. The verisimilitude is grounded in precise dates, street addresses, and names of real-life institutions. Where the panopticon's limits first become apparent is at certain blind spots of American ambition: Greenland, the far side of Canada; the Louisiana bayou, down-home heart of darkness. The story moves on to the fatal reading 47°09'S, 126°43'W, coordinates well beyond the sweep of the Pacific Fleet, over a thousand miles from Rapa Nui. The pagan monolith that surfaces there ruptures the technocratic matrix, exposing it for an illusion—possibly just another dream.[7]

Finally, where does Cthulhu come from? There may indeed be something of an Easter Island *moai* about him. But in imagining a being whose power among humans is mediated by an idol, and casting it in humanoid form with animal head, Lovecraft was surely looking to the Orient. The ancient Mediterranean world would have been one source of inspiration. Egypt actually figured as a setting in more than one of his stories; Phoenician cults, as sensationalized by Gustave Flaubert in his 1862 *Salammbô*, had appealingly sanguinary associations. But with or without these alternatives, I think a strong case can be made for India and Ganesh. There is little doubt Lovecraft was acquainted with the deity. He was a museum enthusiast, and within his New England ambit were Salem, where the Peabody Museum had counted Ganesh images from India and Java in its holdings since 1821 (Altman 2017, 6; Bean 2001, 188–89), and the Boston Museum of Fine Arts, home base of the most prominent scholar of South Asian art in the United States or anywhere else, Ananda Coomaraswamy. Of Kipling's cast of elder gods in "The Bridge-Builders," the elephant Ganesh is surely the most grand and exotic, not excluding Hanuman.

Let's wrap up with some morphological considerations. I have two. The first is Cthulhu's head, which takes the form of an octopus or squid, complete with tentacles. The resemblance of this set of appendages to an elephant's trunk—or a trunk plus a pair of tusks—or even an assemblage of trunk, tusks, and multiple arms—is well marked in his portraits of the present day. These tend to follow a comic-book style of illustration; Googling "Cthulhu" will turn up many examples. In some, the flapping wings fill in for elephant ears. In others, the combination of domed brow with curled side feelers gives the creature the look of a long-tusked mammoth.

The second concerns the body, where I want to highlight an aspect of Lovecraft's conception that gets ignored in contemporary visualizations. Cthulhu is fat. His idols show him seated on a platform. The pose described in the text, in which "fore paws . . . clasped the croucher's elevated knees," is perhaps less citational of the iconography of Ganesh than of Budai, the Chinese monk familiarly known in English as the Laughing Buddha. But when added to Cthulhu's great head and proboscislike members, a round belly contributes a Ganeshlike effect. In illustration of this, I will forego Google image search, which seems keen to assimilate even the elder gods within a generic superhero body type. I submit here two sketches taken from a letter of May 1934. The artist is none other than H. P. Lovecraft himself.

Figure 2.1. H. P. Lovecraft, "Cthulhu" (1934). *Source*: Howard P. Lovecraft Collection, Brown University Library, public domain.

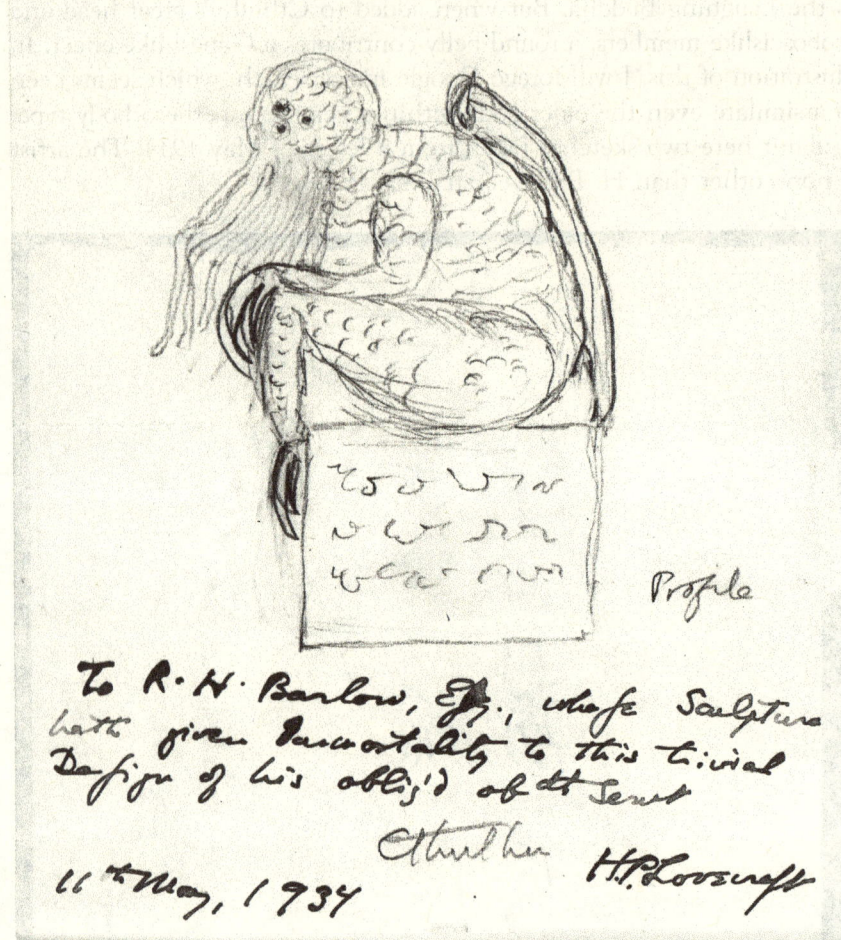

Figure 2.2. H. P. Lovecraft, "Cthulhu" (1934). *Source:* Howard P. Lovecraft Collection, Brown University Library, public domain.

This is the outline Lovecraft saw rising from the sea. A shift in the earth's crust has reimmersed him, but will he come back again next year?

Frank Belknap Long: "The Horror from the Hills"

Weird Tales ran "The Horror from the Hills" in the January and February/March issues of 1931. There is no mystery about where Long derived his titular Horror. His friend and eventual editor Robert M. Price (2010, 8; see also 208) describes his reaction to a "decorative statue" of Ganesh: "Doing a double-take, Long was much impressed with the divine effigy." The author was a friend and protégé of Lovecraft's. And indeed the correlations between his story and "The Call of Cthulhu" are such that Long's creation has been inducted into the Cthulhu Mythos, the intertextual continuity Lovecraft himself embraced in some later stories, and which the master's successors and fans continue to populate with fresh horrors. With a more-than-casual echo of "Cthulhu fhtagn," Long named his own elder god Chaugnar Faugn.

The story opens at the Manhattan Museum of Fine Arts, where the Yale- and Oxford-credentialed Algernon Harris is the recently appointed Curator of Archeology. Clark Ulman, just returned from an expedition to China, reports in on the phone. He has secured the Elephant God of Tsang. But Ulman's voice betrays strain. "You may photograph it and study it, but you've got to destroy it. You'll understand when you see what—*what I have become!*"

Deliverymen bring the green stone idol in first. "It was endowed with a trunk and great, uneven ears, and two enormous tusks protruded from the corners of its mouth. But it was not an elephant. . . . Its forelimbs were bent stiffly at the elbow, and its hands—it had human hands—rested palms upward on its lap. Its shoulders were broad and square and its breasts and enormous stomach sloped outward, cushioning the trunk." Ulman arrives, his face wrapped in a scarf. He has succeeded where other explorers failed; a single predecessor had survived the harsh plateau of Tsang to write up his ordeal. Armed with clues from this record, Ulman had won through to the cave sanctuary of the cult of Chaugnar Faugn—for so, he had learned, the god was named—and presented himself as the White Acolyte of prophecy. The head priest, one Chung Ga, had been receptive. After long ages, he agreed, the day had surely arrived for Chaugnar to seize international fame. Chung Ga would feast the White Acolyte, leave him to spend the night in the cave with the idol, and see them both off to the wider world.

But in the cave Ulman had experienced a rude awakening, assaulted by some slimy creature of the night. Shocked to find it sucking his blood, he had scrambled in the dark towards the idol, seeking refuge atop the stone throne. What had been his horror on discovering the throne was bare, vacated by the very monster he was fleeing from!

The next day the urbane Chung Ga (another Oxford graduate) had made certain things clear. Great Chaughnar was not merely a living being;

he was an "utterly cosmic god" and "beyond good and evil." He had been sustained across centuries by his Asian devotees, but he and his kind had first manifested themselves in the West, and it was to the West he was to return. It would be the American's fate to serve his master as a sort of human filling station. "[A]nd a fortnight later I reached the Bay of Bengal, accompanied by half a hundred ragged, gaunt-visaged mendicants from the temples of obscure Indian villages. . . ." The tale concludes with Ulman's unveiling: over the weeks on the seas, the feedings have not only wrecked his body but transformed his face in the god's image. He strips the scarf off his nose: "it had become a loathsome greenish trunk almost a foot in length."

Algernon meets the crisis with didactic explanations. "I've visited India, Clark, and I have a very keen respect for the hypnotic endowments of the Oriental." Ulman collapses and dies in his office. Algernon goes on talking. He persuades the coroner to attribute death to heart failure, and he attempts to persuade the Museum's president—and himself—that the prominent features could have been produced by advanced, if exotic, plastic surgery techniques.[8] But then the mutilated body of a night watchman is discovered in the gallery where he has had Chaugnar put on exhibit. The police recover a rice bowl and chopsticks from the scene: "We haven't any positive evidence that a Chinaman did it. It might have been a Jap or Hindoo or even a South Sea Islander."

In short order, two plainclothesmen appear with a Chinese interloper. Hsieh Ho throws himself at Algernon's feet, pleading:

> You are my friend. . . . I saw you in green-fire dream. In dream when big green animals came down from mountain I saw you and Gautama Siddhartha. Big green animals all wanted blood. . . .
>
> I said, "No! *Please*," I said. Then Gautama Siddhartha let fall jewel of wisdom. "Go to *museum*. Go to big museum round block, and big green animal will eat you quick. . . ."
>
> All night I have sat here. All night I said: "Eat me. Please!" But big green animal slept till American man came. Then he moved. Very quickly he moved.

If obscure, to Algernon the words ring authentic. He warns the police not to subject Hsieh Ho to "your revolting third-degree tactics," but permits them to take him as a material witness. Only then does he see something that spurs him to action. The position of the elephant trunk has shifted—the curator's own eyes attest the idol has moved in the night.

Clearly, the time has come to find a specialist. Algernon calls on Dr. Imbert, "the foremost American ethnologist." Assuring him, "The Figure is totally unfamiliar. . . . Nothing even remotely resembling it occurs in Asian . . . mythology," Imbert pays Algernon in his own coin with a scholarly monologue. Then the two seek out the reclusive Roger Little, of Queens. An expert in the paranormal and a scientific freethinker, Little is well embarked on his own self-justifying lecture when Algernon brings him up short with two words: *Chaugnar Faugn.* The response is a cry of terror.

Little explains the name had triggered a dream experience of the previous Halloween. He has taken on the persona of Caelius Rufus, a Roman official in a province of Spain. Rufus receives a report from the outpost of Pompelo. High in the Pyrenees there live a "strange dark folk," the Miri Nigri. Their twice-yearly rituals to propitiate native gods are made known to the settlers of Pompelo by the sight of hilltop bonfires, the sound of drums, and the abduction of neighbors for sacrifice. Rufus presses the authorities for a punitive expedition. A cohort is ordered to Pompelo, and Rufus rides with it into the hills at night. Overhead, to the legionaries' panic, some force of darkness blots out the stars. Then: "[A]round the swollen fires of the distant peaks we saw prancing and leaping the awful and cyclopean silhouettes of things that were neither men nor beasts, but fiendish amalgams of both—things with huge flaring ears and long waving trunks that howled and gibbered and pranced in the skyless night." Little awakes with a scream on his lips and the name *Chaugnar* in his mind:

> [F]or a moment the three men were silent. Then Algernon said: "The Chinaman had a strange dream too. He spoke of the horror on the mountains—of great things that came clumping down from the hills at nightfall." . . .
> "And you think that Hsieh Ho's dream was a prophecy?" whispered Imbert.

The phone rings. A staff member informs Algernon that the new acquisition is missing from the museum. The curator stares through the window at the glittering New York skyline. But Little steps forward and offers encouragement:

"Though Chaugnar Faugn is a very terrible menace it isn't quite as omnipotent as Ulman thought. It and its brothers are incarnate manifestations of a very ancient . . . hyperdimensional entity. . . . [I]f I am successful I can send it back to its point of origin beyond the galactic universe. . . .

"I am not," he continued, "a merely theoretical dreamer. . . . I have forged a very concrete and effective weapon to combat the cosmic malignancies. If you'll step into my laboratory I'll show you something."

The invention turns out to be an assemblage of metallic spheres that, when activated, align themselves into a "four-dimensional figure" and shoot out a powerful beam. "'I'll explain,' said Little. 'You are of course familiar with the ABCs of Einsteinian physics. . . .'" And it seems yet more explanations are in order while Chaugnar takes midtown Manhattan, accosting random New Yorkers with his nozzle and sucking them dry. After due deliberation over the hows and whys of it, however, our heroes arrive at a plan. They load the machine in Little's car (the chauffeur has the day off) and the three chase the elder god down the highway to the Jersey Shore. Cornering him on some mud flats, they point their device and flip the switch. Chaugnar Faugn dissolves in the cosmic ray, zapped back to some nether dimension.

This is *echt* pulp fiction. The story is also extremely talky. I don't know if the fiction writer's adage "Show, don't tell," was current in Long's day, but he passes up no chance here to tell. Some of the author's choices can no doubt be attributed to *Weird Tales*'s policy of paying by the word. Nevertheless, the effect on the reader of all this expository verbiage—and of the authority claim of the voice delivering it—is a factor to consider in an analysis of this piece as an idolatry story.

Chaugnar's debt to Cthulhu has been remarked. Other aspects of the world of "The Horror of the Hills" reflect assumptions underlying "The Call of Cthulhu." America's WASP elite are masters of objective knowledge about the rest of the world. Museums are an organ of this global regime of knowledge. Law enforcement defers to scholarly authority. Asian people—"Chinamen," "Hindoos," "Japs"—are much of a heathen muchness. The relation of the United States to Asia is prefigured in Rome's domination of the Mediterranean world. In fact, the entire dream sequence—the story of the Roman colonizers and the Miri Nigri—was copied directly from a letter Lovecraft sent Long that narrated a vivid dream of Halloween 1927.[9]

In "The Call of Cthulhu," the narrator collects clues until they lead him to an existential crisis. Conversely, in "The Horror from the Hills," the idolatry mystery is resolved at the story's beginning. The idol is coterminous with the material body of the god (in our dimension, anyway); the device has ample precedents in English-language fiction.[10] But in Long's story, far from a denouement, it is the premise: a New York museum has attempted to put a living god on exhibit. Again, the revelation here—such as it is—is not so shocking as to crack anyone's sanity within diegesis. Nor does the author seek to leverage this incongruity in a challenge to the reader's sense of self. What he attempts, in fact, is the opposite: this tale is about taming the absurd by explaining it. In a sense, "The Horror from the Hills" is "The Call of Cthulhu" backwards. In the therioanthropomorphic Ganesh, Long saw a chimera with which to tease self-fancied rationalists. A pot-bellied figure with an elephant's head—anomaly personified.

The story is narrated in the third person. But if Algernon is the protagonist, his didactic style is reproduced by the interlocutors whose explanations succeed his, first the ethnologist Dr. Imbert and then the visionary Roger Little. From the rationalization of Ulman's experiences as hypnotically induced . . . to the idea his disfigurement was caused by surgery . . . to Imbert's take on the religions of colonized peoples ("[M]ost of the major and minor monstrosities that figure . . . in the pantheons of barbarian races . . . are synthetic conceptions") . . . to the "transcendental mathematics" theorized by Little ("[I]f an earth-event is very disorganized and very decadent in its contours even our hypothetical distant observer would know that it has occurred very late in the course of cosmic evolution") . . . the text is dominated through its course by one lecture delivered after another in a sententious monotone.

This is—literally, within the diegesis—the voice of reason. And the educated white American men who command it are the story's normative "I." To the extent that "The Horror from the Hills" can be read as an idolatry story, this is what's at stake: the discourse of (pseudo-) scientific positivism is challenged in its global sweep by the anomalous, illogical Chaugnar. But successive waves of words poured into the breach by Ivy League types eventually mend the aporia. The world once again makes orderly sense, its every element put back in its place—and that includes its human elements. At the end, over coffee, Algernon asks: "[W]as Ulman's priest right and was Chaugnar an incarnation of the Oneness of the Brahmic mysteries, the portentous all-in-all of theosophists and occultists, or merely a product of physical evolution on a plane incomprehensible to us?" Little replies, reassuringly: "[I]t is my opinion that it is inherently, like ourselves, a circumscribed entity—the spawn of remote worlds and unholy dimensions, but a creature and not a creator, a creature obeying inexorable laws and occupying a definite niche in the cosmos."

The anomalous Oriental, the Oxford-educated Chung Ga, is exposed as a fool or liar. And the curious statement of the witness Hsieh Ho can now be revisited, too. He had gone to the museum to sacrifice himself and save the life of a real American. He is an Asian who knew his place.

Robert E. Howard: "The Tower of the Elephant"

Billed as "a strange, blood-freezing story of an idol that wept on its throne," the Conan adventure "The Tower of the Elephant" appeared in the March 1933 issue of *Weird Tales*. Robert E. Howard was an admirer and correspondent of Lovecraft's; in an early letter, he asked where he could learn more about Cthulhu, which he had taken to be a figure from some actual historical tradition. Howard lived in small-town Texas all his short life (he was a suicide at thirty). His work is far from obscure, however. His best-known creation, Conan the Barbarian, is the hero of a story cycle set in an invented period of ancient history, the "Hyborean Age." Almost all the stories were first published in *Weird Tales* in the 1930s.

Conan has subsequently gone on to fame in the movies, as well as comic books, computer games, and much additional writing outside the Howard canon. The barbarian image repurposes the American trope of the rugged frontiersman, and the Conan stories (along with other adventure writing in this vein) can be considered *Weird Tales*'s answer to that great rival pulp fiction genre, the Western. It seems likely that Howard conceived the idol of "The Tower of the Elephant" after the example of Chaugnar Faugn, who had preceded him by two years in the same magazine. But it's hard to imagine a hero less like Long's windy preppies than the rough-hewn Conan.

The stories have an omniscient narrator, but the voice closely tracks Conan's movements. The reader is thus introduced to the Hyborean world through the eyes of the barbarian, who is, as such, himself a stranger. "The Tower of the Elephant" is set in the City of Thieves, a metropolis embracing high places and low, where dark-skinned native Zamorians mingle with the rogues and adventurers of other nations. In a divey tavern a "professional kidnapper" is talking up the charms of one of his captives. "I know lords . . . who would trade the secret of the Elephant Tower for her," he crows, attracting the attention of a "tall, strongly made youth."

Conan has seen the tower, which rises behind unguarded walls enclosing a garden. What is its secret? "[A]ny fool knows that Yara the priest dwells there with the great jewel men call the Elephant's Heart, that is the secret of his magic." But why then, in this City of Thieves, has no one seen fit to steal the jewel? The kidnapper lays out the puzzle. Behind the wall is the garden, patrolled by no human guards, but patrolled nonetheless. The lower part of the tower is garrisoned by soldiers. The tower's surface is sheer. The jewel is somewhere in the upper part. But Conan refuses to concede the site's impregnability, and the speaker takes this as a personal slight. Swords are drawn. The candle goes out, and when the flame is restored the blowhard lies dead, and Conan is nowhere to be seen.

The Elephant Tower stands in a quarter known for its temples: "On all sides of him they glittered white in the starlight . . . shrines of Zamora's myriad strange gods. He did not trouble his head about them. . . . Zamora's religion, like all things of a civilized, long-settled people, was intricate and complex, and had lost most of the pristine essence in a maze of formulas and rituals." The barbarian is content to submit to the god of his own people, Crom, "a gloomy, savage god, who hated weaklings. But he gave a man courage at birth. . . ." He arrives before the tower and reflects that no one has yet made clear what it has to do with an elephant, an outlandish animal he has never seen. What he does know is that the tower's lord, Yara, is feared throughout the city for his command of dark arts. It is said he is the power behind the throne of Zamora, that he has lived for centuries and will live on as long as he possesses the Elephant's Heart.

Conan vaults over the outer wall to find an inner one. He also finds a rival who has chosen the same night to raid the tower: Taurus, Prince of Thieves. Joining forces, they clear the first two hurdles. The grounds' nonhuman guards are lions, which Taurus defeats with an exotic poison "made from the black lotus, whose blossoms wave in the lost jungles of Khitai." They bypass the tower's garrison by scaling the heights with a special rope of human hair. The Prince gains the summit only to encounter a third trial he had not prepared for: a giant spider with a deadly bite. Conan, however, rises to the challenge. He advances to a golden door and then an ivory one.

He stands on the threshold of a jeweled chamber, its air thick with incense. Facing him is a great idol on a marble couch. "[T]he image had the body of a man, naked, and green in color; but the head was one of nightmare and madness." He takes in the outlandish features and understands: this is the elephant of the tower.

> As Conan came forward, his eyes fixed on the motionless idol, the eyes of the thing opened suddenly! The Cimmerian froze in his tracks. It was no image—it was a living thing, and he was trapped in its chamber! . . .
>
> A civilized man in his position would have sought doubtful refuge in the conclusion that he was insane; it did not occur to the Cimmerian to doubt his senses. He knew he was face to face with a demon of the Elder World, and the realization robbed him of all his faculties except sight.

Petrified, he can only see. By contrast, the living idol appears to be blind. Realizing he has eluded notice, Conan unfreezes and backs towards the door. But "the sensitive trunk stretched toward him, and . . . the being spoke." It has sensed his presence but mistaken him for Yara. Tears spill from the sightless eyes and the intruder notes the marks of torture that cover the creature's body. "And suddenly all fear and repulsion went from him. . . . What this monster was, Conan could not know, but the evidences of its sufferings were so terrible and pathetic that a strange aching sadness came over the Cimmerian, he knew not why. He only felt that he was looking upon a cosmic tragedy, and he shrank with shame, as if the guilt of a whole race were laid upon him." He steps up to let the trunk pass over his features, "and its touch was as light as a girl's hand."

Now Yag-Kosha, also known as Yogah of Yag, introduces himself. "I am neither god nor demon, but flesh and blood like yourself," he begins. "[L]ong ago I came to this planet with others of my world, from the green planet Yag. . . . At last I alone was left, dreaming of old times among the ruined temples of jungle-lost Khitai. . . . Then came Yara, versed in dark knowledge handed down through the days of barbarism, since before Atlantis sank. First he sat at my feet and learned wisdom." But not satisfied with white magic, the disciple tricked the master, and forced Yogah into serving his will. "No more was I a god to kindly jungle-folk—I was slave to a devil in human form." In Conan he sees both a deliverer and an avenger. He directs the swordsman to a nearby altar and the crystal orb resting on it. Then he charges him to cut the heart out of his body and squeeze the blood over the stone. Having performed this libation, Conan is to find Yara's quarters and present the priest with the Heart of the Elephant.

Conan does as bidden. Stirred from a reverie induced by "the fumes of the yellow lotus," Yara is drawn in fascination to the gem, which has taken on a "throbbing" and then "blazing" appearance. In short order, the sorcerer shrinks to the size of the orb, it engulfs him, and Conan catches a glimpse inside of the shining green Yogah, restored to health and sight, pursuing his miniscule tormentor. The gem bursts "like a bubble" and the intruder sees the time has come to leave; he has barely exited the enchanted tower before the whole thing crashes behind him in "shining shards."

Howard's tale shows off his hero to advantage. The tower break-in unfolds as a series of trials, and these make up the narrative core. But Conan's real triumph comes after his feats of prowess, when the encounter with the radically alien Yogah presents him with a different kind of test. Mercenary and crude though the barbarian may be, he is able to master the impulse to reject the monster's looks—its weirdness—and come together with it in its pain. The test is a vindication for Howard, too, and his conception of the possibilities available to his uncouth but grounded character.

The twist "The Tower of the Elephant" puts on the idolatry story is all the more remarkable given its immediate antecedents in *Weird Tales*. Howard shares with Long the device of the idol that turns out to be a living being. He also shares the choice of a greenish Ganesh as the most chimerical possible combination. But instead of following Long's next move—to explain away the incongruous—Howard empowers his monster to state his presence in a voice of his own.

The point I stress in conclusion does not concern Yogah's testimony, which is nothing wild by the standards of the genre. (He is a life form from a distant planet, he crossed boundless space countless ages ago: this is a rehash of Lovecraftian tropes as well as Chaugnar's own origin story.) The narrative pivot is not so much that Yogah speaks but rather that

Conan is ready to listen. He has signaled himself open to the Other's address. And he has done so during the curious standoff that calls to mind the *darshan* encounter between a Hindu image and a worshipper.

Frozen, Conan effectively trades places with Yogah as the chamber's *murti*. Conversely, Yogah, cast as the perceiving subject, at first misrecognizes whom he has before him, assuming it is Yara—or possibly a different member of the class of human oppressors, the "whole race" whose "guilt" Conan feels burdened with in that moment. Here Howard's prose rings distinctly theological. Weirdness turns to wonder in Conan's eyes, and he wins through to a recognition that neither in the equation is a god or demon but both can come across difference into personhood. Crucially (so to speak), the transition is mediated for him—and made intelligible for the audience of *Weird Tales*—by the torture marks on Yogah's body. Perhaps not entirely deliberately, Howard appropriates the iconography of two traditions. He has modeled his monster's appearance on Ganesh, but the elephant in the room is really Christ.

This offbeat tale of *darshan* does not take place, of course, in India. But it would not be right to say the milieu has nothing to do with the India of Kipling and his imitators. The Hyborean Age is set on our earth but anterior to recorded history; onto an ill-defined landmass Howard maps a legible human geography. Conan's native Cimmeria and its neighbors in this world's north and west are populated by lighter-skinned people. Among the hero's Cimmerian traits—barbarous to other peoples—are his forthrightness and self-reliance; his god Crom doesn't like to be bothered. The Zamorians to the southeast are darker-skinned and inhabit teeming cities. They are fond of words, and their various deities are served by priests in elaborate temples. Farther still to the east and south are the so-called exotic lands, associated with magic and mystery. These include Khitai, where Yogah enjoyed idolatrous worship; and Vendhya (capital: Ayodhya; northwestern neighbor: Afghulistan). In this world too—to drop a cliché from Kipling—East is East.

For all that he is a cold-blooded killer, Conan moves through "The Tower of the Elephant" as a sort of innocent abroad. The intrigues of the Zamorians or the powers of lotus products are as strange to him as they are to his readership—he is a barbarian, after all. And this is the nub of the difference between him and the protagonists of the other idolatry stories. He is a white man abroad in Oriental realms, but he is no colonial master. (To be sure, several attributes cast as barbarous in diegesis—his bluntness, pragmatism, lack of spiritual imagination—are deployed to cue recognition in American readers, especially those compelled by the man-of-action ideal of the Western genre, and this is a no less ideological figuration. But it is a different ideological figuration.) Let's spell it out. Conan is unlike Kipling's sahibs, or the gentleman scholars of Lovecraft and Long, in that his subject position is not defined by a totalizing ideology that construes the globe as an object of knowledge.

An Eastern idol that interpellates rational subjects is a threatening anomaly in the modern world of 1890 (or 1920, or 1930). It's *weird*. Contrast the world of the Hyborean Age—a not merely premodern, but prehistoric realm of fantasy. Such an anomaly does not pose a challenge to the philosophical conditions underwriting this world's existence. What it does, rather, is open up possibilities. It inspires a hard-bitten barbarian to curiosity and compassion. And via the mediation of that wish-fulfillment figure, it may even have done so, in some small way, for the youthful readership of *Weird Tales* in the 1930s United States. And that is kind of wonderful.

An Afterword: Wonder

It could even be thought a special kind of wonderful. In pursuing my own research on *darshan*, I read and theorized a great deal about how the visual connection is made between the human subject and the deity in the context of Hindu ritual (see Elison 2018). But is it possible for someone from outside the tradition, who has not been conditioned to encounter god in the form of the *murti*, to experience *darshan*? Someone from Cimmeria, say, or Cross Plains, Texas, who might find the spectacle of an elephant's head on a man's body alienating at first glance?

Ancient Indian thinkers had a handle on this problem, and in one of his late essays Coomaraswamy (1943, 174) investigates the Pali term *saṁvega*, "aesthetic shock" as he dubs it, "the shock or wonder that may be felt when the perception of art becomes a serious experience." He parses the experience as twofold: on the one hand, the shock, which he likens to being struck by a whip or thunderbolt (*vajra*); on the other, an authentic transformation of the self. The Buddhist texts he is reading, of a didactic cast, evaluate the effect in terms of progress toward enlightenment. But Coomaraswamy wants to apply it to his modern American environment. "For the most part," he observes, "our 'aesthetic approach' stands between us and the content of the work of art, of which only the surface concerns us" (174n2). How inadequate, he feels, is this detached attitude in the face of Picasso's *Guernica*. Rather, consider *saṁvega*: "In the deepest experience that can be induced by a work of art our very being is shaken (*saṁvijita*) to its roots" (178).

For Coomaraswamy, the scope of art is not limited to visual forms or music; he gives the arresting example of a mathematical proof. Nor, I think, do we need to confine ourselves, as analysts of culture and religion, to conceptions of self-transformation along soteriological or mystical lines. The shocking encounter with form that resets our horizons: this could be a working definition of *saṁvega* as wonder.

Notes

1. "The encyclopaedic tradition . . . became *cabinets de curiousités*, contextless lists of strange things done by strange people in strange lands. Characteristic . . . is relatively little interest in explicit comparison. The material is NOT-LIKE-US." (Smith 1971, 78).

2. Typical is Kipling's influence on Edgar Rice Burroughs, father of Tarzan; see chapter 15 in Lupoff (1968). Examples of more direct relevance: Fraser (1905) and Casserly (1921), jungle stories featuring elephant characters named Ganesh.

3. "That great elephant-headed One" is also a character in "The Finances of the Gods," Kipling's (1891a) short retelling of an Indian fable. It offers an eerie, even weird, description of Hindu gods at large in a temple at night: "And Ganesh woke, for the money-lender heard the dry rustle of his trunk uncoiling. . . ."

4. A third story that fits this framework well is "The Incarnation of Krishna Mulvaney" (Kipling 1891b), a comic piece in which congregants in a Banaras temple are presented with a hierophany from behind an "elephant-head pillar."

5. A likely visual referent for Kipling was the Hanuman devotees (often but not always *sadhus*) who exhibit themselves with blackened faces and ash-daubed bodies after the model of silver-gray langur monkeys.

6. In addition to scholarly treatments, Lovecraft's racism has inspired Matt Ruff's 2016 novel *Lovecraft Country*, the basis of an eponymous television series that debuted on HBO in 2020.

7. One complicating factor—and perhaps the story's saving grace—is that white men can be dreamers, too. Wilcox, the sculptor, is a proper New England WASP. And when Angell queries his correspondents for reports of strange dreams, "it was from the artists and poets that the pertinent answers came."

8. For all this scenario's hokiness, let it be noted that no less a defender of the Hindu religion's honor than Narendra Modi proposed plastic surgery as an explanation for Lord Ganesh himself (see, inter alia, Express News Service 2014).

9. Lovecraft was so impressed with this dream that he wrote it up three times for different correspondents. It would be helpful to know if the "huge flaring ears and long waving trunks" that mark the gods' silhouettes was his original wording or an interpolation by Long. The Ganeshlike features are absent from the other two letters, both published in *The H. P. Lovecraft Dream Book*. Unfortunately, the book's editors could not track down the version penned to Long, and its place is marked with text taken from "The Horror from the Hills" (Joshi, Murray, and Schultz 1994, 17–29). Lovecraft did state several times that Long had changed nothing. His conceptions of the Miri Nigri also vary across the three tellings, from "strange and dark" to "little yellow [and] squint-eyed" to "Basque" (Rajala 2011, 48–53).

10. Two examples, already cited, are Dunsany 1914 and 1916.

Works Cited

Altman, Michael J. 2017. *Heathen, Hindoo, Hindu: American Representations of India, 1721–1893*. New York: Oxford University Press.

Bean, Susan S. 2001. *Yankee India: American Commercial and Cultural Encounters with India in the Age of Sail, 1784–1860*. Salem, MA: Peabody Essex Museum.

Coomaraswamy, Ananda K. 1943. "Saṁvega, Aesthetic Shock." *Harvard Journal of Asiatic Studies* 7 (3): 174–79.

Elison, William. 2018. *The Neighborhood of Gods: The Sacred and the Visible at the Margins of Mumbai*. Chicago: University of Chicago Press.

Express News Service. 2014. "PM Modi Takes Leaf from Batra Book: Mahabharat Genetics, Lord Ganesha Surgery." *Indian Express*, October, 28.

Isaacs, Harold R. 1958. *Scratches on Our Minds: American Images of China and India*. New York: John Day.

Joshi, S. T., Will Murray, and David E. Schultz, eds. 1994. *The H. P. Lovecraft Dream Book*. West Warwick, RI: Necronomicon.

Lovecraft, H. P. 1927. "Supernatural Horror in Literature." *The Recluse*, no. 1, 23–59.

———. 2000. *Lord of a Visible World: An Autobiography in Letters*. Edited by S. T. Joshi and David E. Schultz. Athens: Ohio University Press.

Lupoff, Richard A. 1968. *Edgar Rice Burroughs: Master of Adventure*. New York: Ace.

Penzoldt, Peter. 1980. "From *The Supernatural in Fiction*." In *H. P. Lovecraft: Four Decades of Criticism*, edited by S. T. Joshi. Athens: Ohio University Press.

Price, Robert M., ed. 2010. *The Tindalos Cycle*. New York: Hippocampus Press.

Rajala, J.-M. 2011. "Locked Dimensions out of Reach: The Lost Stories of H. P. Lovecraft." *Lovecraft Annual* 5:3–90.

Shea, J. Vernon. 1980. "On the Literary Influences which Shaped Lovecraft's Work." In *H. P. Lovecraft: Four Decades of Criticism*, edited by S. T. Joshi. Athens: Ohio University Press.

Smith, Jonathan Z. 1971. "Adde Parvum Parvo Magnus Acervus Erit." *History of Religions* 11 (1): 67–90.

Fiction

Most of this material can be found online. I have not given page numbers for passages excerpted from these sources, both because of the variety of online formats and because all texts quoted are relatively short.

Casserly, Gordon. 1921. *The Elephant God*. New York: Putnam.
Dunsany, Lord (Edward John Moreton Drax Plunkett). 1905. *The Gods of Pegāna*. London: Elkin Mathews.
———. 1914. *The Gods of the Mountain*. In *Five Plays*. New York: Mitchell Kennerley.
———. 1916. *A Night at an Inn: A Play in One Act*. New York: Sunwise Turn.
Flaubert, Gustave. 1862. *Salammbô*. Paris: Michel Lévy Frères.
Fraser, W. A. 1905. *The Sa'-zada Tales*. New York: Scribner.
Howard, Robert E. 1933. "The Tower of the Elephant." *Weird Tales* 21:306–22.
Kipling, Rudyard. 1891a. "The Finances of the Gods." In *Life's Handicap*. London: Macmillan.
———. 1891b. "The Incarnation of Krishna Mulvaney." In *Life's Handicap*. London: Macmillan.
———. 1891c. "The Mark of the Beast." In *Life's Handicap*. London: Macmillan.
———. 1898. "The Bridge-Builders." In *The Day's Work*. London: Macmillan.
Long, Frank Belknap. 1931. "The Horror from the Hills." *Weird Tales* 17:32–54, 245–72.
Lovecraft, H. P. 1928. "The Call of Cthulhu." *Weird Tales* 11:159–78, 287.
Poe, Edgar Allan. 1838. *The Narrative of Arthur Gordon Pym, of Nantucket*. New York: Harper.
Ruff, Matt. 2016. *Lovecraft Country*. New York: HarperCollins.

Chapter 3

Did the Masters of Disenchantment Ever Wonder?

India in the Nineteenth-Century American Evangelical Imaginary

MARY HANCOCK

Introduction

India was a vivid presence in the imaginations of many nineteenth-century Americans. Rendered usually as a Hindu space, its stock visual elements included "fakirs" reclining on beds of nails; veiled "child-brides"; bloodthirsty goddesses attended by "thuggees"; beatific "yogis" and "gurus"; swaying dancing girls; and "maharajahs" draped with opulent jewels and gold-threaded silks (Altman 2017, 30–46). Travelogues, essays, and fiction gave narrative context to these images, while works in translation, such as the *Bhagavad Gita*, offered moral and ideological alternatives to Judeo-Christian thinking. An imagined Hindustan, depicted as "exotic and barbaric, magical and menacing, beneficial and perilous," surfaced in fairs, expositions, and department stores; in Transcendentalist and Theosophical writings; in philology and ethnology; in immigrant exclusion discourse and policies; and in the cultural and geographic narratives of popular publications, such as *The Dial* and *Harper's Weekly* (Bald 2015, 26).

The historical consequences of American images of and attitudes about India have been examined productively in works dealing with the traffic in persons, images, artifacts, and texts that connected India and the

US. Scholars have explained how diverse streams of Indic thought and practice were consolidated into an "ism"—Hinduism—and categorized as a world religion; historians have uncovered the nineteenth-century roots of the diplomatic and economic ties forged in the twentieth century (see Altman 2017; Davis 2015, 2018; Edwards 2000; Foxen 2017; Iwamura 2010; Srinivasan 2011; Tweed and Prothero 1999). Recent work has also tracked the racializing project of immigrant exclusion in the US as well as the anti-racist and anti-colonialist alliances that some US citizens made with Indian activists and reformers (see Bald 2013; Bald et al. 2013; Immerwahr 2007; Slate 2012; Sohi 2014; Tyrrell 2010).

But in what forces or experiences did this preoccupation with the Indic world and the wonder that fueled it originate? And what might this tell us about the cultural and historical genealogies of wonder and its transcultural travel? Although India may have been the jewel in Britain's imperial crown, it was not a site of American military or commercial involvement in the manner of Hawai'i, Puerto Rico, Cuba, and the Philippines. Private commerce was limited and declined over the nineteenth century (Bean 2006). Despite their participation in imperial British industrial, military, and agricultural ventures in South Asia, American entrepreneurs and scientists did not advance American interests directly, nor did they make territorial claims on its behalf (Tuffnell 2014).

The most sustained connections were forged, instead, through Protestant mission activity, growing from the everyday entanglements of Christian and non-Christian ideas, persons, spaces, soundscapes, and images in mission. By 1800, American Protestants had embraced the millennialist aims of world Christianization and within fifteen years had dispatched missionaries to British India and Ceylon, as well as West Africa and the Pacific, expanding soon to East Asia, the Middle East, Latin America, and the Caribbean (Conroy-Krutz 2015). Calling upon a shared identification with evangelicalism, Congregationalists, Baptists, Presbyterians, and later Methodists established schools, churches, orphanages, and hospitals, aiming to foster self-sustaining Christian communities.[1]

As Emily Conroy-Krutz argued, Protestant missionaries were agents of Christian imperialism, who exported an orientation both American and Protestant to a world that had been opened to Western intervention through imperialism (Conroy-Krutz 2015, 11–16). Christian imperialism, moreover, was steeped in both racism and "racecraft," the latter being the quotidian practices and imaginaries that, according to Barbara Fields and Karen Fields, instantiated race as an identity, stigmatized certain racialized attributes and buttressed an institutional system that perpetuated both race as a category and racism as a pattern of discrimination (Fields and Fields 2012, 16–19; see also Wilkerson 2020). American Protestant missionaries, largely white, perceived diverse non-Christian others on a conjoined understanding of racial and religious attributes, envisioning what Conroy-Krutz called a "hierarchy of heathenism," graded according to susceptibility to Christianization (Conroy-Krutz 2015, 21–30). India's "heathens," like enslaved and formerly enslaved Africans in the US, were assigned fixed qualities linking physiognomy to intellectual capacities and dispositions, as well as spiritual malleability, with a capacity for atonement and conversion. The missionaries interpreted caste-based differences and forms of enslavement as variants of the racialized hierarchy with which they were familiar. They reproduced these sensibilities in practice by residing in segregated compounds and using linguistic and behavioral codes to create racial boundaries between themselves and their Indian neighbors, coreligionists, servants, employees, and students. At the same time, norms of spiritual egalitarianism led them to outlaw caste hierarchy in churches and schools and to experiment with housing arrangements and communal dining in an effort to weaken caste boundaries among converts.

Because those labeled "heathen" were thought susceptible to superstition and idolatry, Protestant missionaries also relied on strategies of disenchantment as a means to clear the ground for Christian conversion. They treated Hindu spaces and rituals as vestiges of superstition, using Western scientific principles to undermine local reliance on them. Indefatigable in categorizing the various stages of conversion and counting the signs of Christian progress, they adapted the rationalized techniques of double-entry accounting in quantifying these signs and their own labor. They saw themselves, in short, as spiritual entrepreneurs dedicated to the incremental task of world Christianization.

In the everyday workings of mission, however, rationalization and disenchantment were supplanted by morally ambivalent forms of wonder that were fueled as much by pity and racialized stigma, as by admiration and awe. For example, while missionaries could be transported by awe when regarding the "wondrous" engineering and design of temples and monuments, they regarded deity icons and the self-mortification of Hindu ascetics with horrific wonder. Wonder thus served as a conduit through which racially coded impressions of these distant persons and places were incorporated into religious experiences, into scholarly and philosophical projects, and into consumerism, feeding popular imaginaries while sustaining Protestant identity and religiosity. Letters, journals, and reports recounting missionaries' experiences circulated in mission print culture and were read and spoken in settings of worship, prayer, and teaching; pictures and artifacts were displayed in cabinets and handled in the course of worship and teaching. These activities and objects demonstrated the urgency of evangelization and reinforced religious identity by attracting donations and mission recruits, and engendering piety. They also mediated the spiritual and affective ties between missionaries and home churches and between US Protestants and mission field converts, neophytes, and students (Ahmed 2004; Haggis and Allen 2008).

Disseminated within mission print culture, India as "Hindoostan" traveled beyond its target audiences with unanticipated effects. And, while ascribing to normative Christianity in official reports and letters, some missionaries cultivated wonder through personal projects of collection and translation, reproducing racialized formations of Orientalist knowledge and power while also following paths of curiosity and passion. This chapter investigates how South Asia, generally, if erroneously, treated as Hindu, entered American popular imagination as a by-product of Protestant mission. I focus on the period when mission was inaugurated and sustained by the religious revivalism of the Second Great Awakening, framing this period (1790s–1850s) as a moment in the cultural and historical genealogy of wonder. The period's major sponsoring organization, the Congregationalist-led American Board of Commissioners for Foreign Mission (ABCFM), offers the principal case material. While recognizing that Protestant theology and religious practice worked in tandem with Enlightenment rationalism to domesticate the passion of wonder and to disenchant its objects, I argue that, rather than eliminating wonder from Protestantism's experiential catalogue, mission practice forced its moral revaluation and allowed it to travel along new pathways and solicit new audiences.

I first consider missionaries' entangling encounters with Hindu materiality and the wonder, morally coded as horror, that these encounters produced. I attend to missionaries' reframing of such encounters as (re)conversionary moments, opportunities to reaffirm Christian identity within the conversionary process anticipated by revivalism. The second section turns to the virtuous wonder attributed to mission print, visual, and material culture by analyzing the incorporation of mission-based narratives, images, and artifacts in rituals of worship, prayer, and pedagogy in the US and at mission stations in India, and the affective and spiritual connections between missionaries, mission subjects, and American clergy and laity that they enacted. The final section tracks wonder's resurfacing in American scholarly and popular discourses by following missionaries' efforts as translators. If their official roles, as delimited by Protestant norms and the racial project of mission, offered little scope for these endeavors, the new spaces of scholarly societies allowed them to cultivate these avocational passions and engage wider arenas of popular culture, including Transcendentalist circles. In addition to the historical and cultural analysis of wonder's persistence and its diverse moral and political valences, this chapter makes a case for wonder as a category for comparative thinking about religion.

Entangling Encounters

Protestants' commitment to South Asia's Christianization, voiced in Cotton Mather's *India Christiana* of 1721 and nurtured by the evangelical impulses of the Great Awakenings, triggered the foreign mission movement (Mather 1721). Chartered in 1810, ABCFM sent its first missionaries to join the English Baptist mission at Serampore (Bengal) in 1812; the American cohort later expanded to Burma. Shortly thereafter, it established stations in western India (Bombay, 1812), in what was then Ceylon (Jaffna, 1815), and in southern India (Madurai, 1834). ABCFM remained the major sending organization until the 1860s, at which point sixty-six of its missionaries (thirty-two men and thirty-four women) were active in South Asia.[2]

In 1833, John Lawrence, a student at Andover Theological Seminary (Massachusetts), wrote to ABCFM's secretary about his interest in mission service in India. His letter included a request to borrow an "idol" then displayed at the seminary:

> I take the liberty of making the request for . . . one of the idols of our museum during vacation. I have thought of your remarks relative to the dramatic effect of such exhibitions. . . . My conclusion is that we might as well object to . . . the phrenological busts, the anatomical skeletons, or the chemist's bell glasses, as to object to fixing an impression of the degradation of the heathen by giving some of these

palpable [emphasis original] evidences of their abominable superstitions. Will you loan me an image and inform me what one you can most conveniently spare. I will be careful of "my idol" and "Deo Volunti" will return it or another in its place by the close of vacation or the close of life . . . provided you can send me where I can find them.[3]

Although Lawrence envisioned a future dedicated to disenchantment, his reference to the seminary's museum alerts us to another dimension of mission practice, namely, its capacity to engage Americans in Indic life worlds through mission artifacts.[4] A few years after Lawrence made his request, ABCFM formalized its expectations about such collections. A published circular alluded to existing collections and requested items illustrative of conditions in mission fields, noting the benefits to science of minerals, historical coins, and artifacts. Especially sought were "idols, paintings and prints . . . illustrating the native mythology . . . [which] impressed visitors most deeply."[5] This plea implied that visual and tactile engagement with the *matter* of idolatry yielded benefit, even virtue, under Christian scrutiny. Lawrence's encounter illustrated the novel, unanticipated transactions in one object's cultural biography, from its displacement from Hindu sites of fabrication, sanctification, and worship to its re-emplacement in spaces of Christian appraisal.

Artifacts like the "idol" gave tangible form to the sometimes horrific wonder attributed to India. Drawing comparisons to pagan practices condemned in the Old Testament, missionaries emphasized that idolatry inhered in the materiality of gods: their embodiment in stone, wood, and metal forms; the tactile, olfactory, gustatory, and auditory aspects of worship; and their rootedness in the natural world. Such objects were also the targets of conversionary practices. Imagined as channels for satanic power, which missionaries like other Christians knew to be real, dangerous, and predatory, "idols" were sometimes targets of preaching and other Christian encounters, for example, by preaching in temple precincts.

At the same time, "idols" were dismissed as products of superstition, error, or imaginative excess, with scientific education prescribed as the corrective. Declaring that "true science saps the foundations of idolatry," missionaries introduced astronomy, geography, chemistry, and mathematics into school curricula.[6] To redirect the awe for idols toward natural, albeit divinely created, wonders, missionaries delivered public lectures on natural science and seized events, including eclipses and the appearance of a comet, as teaching opportunities.[7] They also tried to inculcate Western systems of astronomical time reckoning by printing and distributing Tamil-language Christian almanacs.[8] Just as missionaries felt wonder was properly directed to regularities ordained by God rather than that which transgressed the ordinary, so too they hoped that this knowledge would unseat superstition.

If mission practice was oriented to "heathen" materiality, collecting such artifacts extended the work of conversion further, while adding new chapters to objects' cultural biographies (Davis 1997). Of particular note, as illustrated in John Lawrence's correspondence, were the Christian practices of religio-moral and aesthetic appraisal and valuation of objects such as deity figures. Items in mission collections furnished knowledge of other lands and peoples, but in the contexts of sabbath school pedagogy and prayer meetings, such knowledge was meant to demonstrate both the extent of "idolatry" and the impacts of Christian evangelization.

The collection and re-emplacement of religious artifacts was fueled by the desire to both destroy these dangerous vessels of idolatry and to preserve them as objects of pious scrutiny. This affective and pragmatic duality shaped the pathways of objects' (trans)cultural biographies, which recognized their educational value as well as their dangers for Christian selves. Missionaries understood that figures like the "idol" had originated as products of ritualized techniques, in which the deity was invoked as an animating, empowering presence in its physical icon. Despite dismissing such actions as superstition, missionaries found their own traffic with such objects to be fraught transactions. In acquiring "idols," missionaries cast a disenchanting gaze on the heathen world, while also emplacing their own fragile and anxious Christian selves in a world populated by demonic forces.

Missionaries' experience of the fragility and porosity of Christian selfhood as they moved within Indic ritual space and exerted themselves in the discernment of the godly from the demonic was suggested in an 1836 letter written by William Todd. Declaring, "I fear I have polluted myself with idols," Todd recounted a "case of conscience" instigated by ABCFM's request for local artifacts.[9] Todd wrote anxiously of his fear that a "secondary species of idolatry is rising up in the churches," and questioned whether viewing such artifacts, even as curiosities, could instill virtue: "If these abominations were sentient beings they must be pleased with the unexpected attentions which they are now receiving from Christians."[10] He then described his purchase of a Ganesha figure for the ABCFM collection, and speculated that such idols, if not properly signified as the "devil's work," could pose grave moral danger to Christians. Borrowing a gesture from the Old Testament, he channeled his anger to iconoclasm, smashing the "diabolical beastly pot-gut fellow, rat and all, upon the floor."[11] Still, he concluded his entry with ironic resignation, observing that the "idols" that he so detested had already become global travelers. He anticipated that when displayed in the US, the artifacts would "probably be much more admired than they have been at Madura for many years past," adding that "heathen deities manufactured in Great Britain are sold . . . at a cheaper rate at Calcutta than those manufactured [in] this country."[12]

Todd's comments capture the tensions that suffused missionaries' encounters with the spaces and practices of Hindu religiosity (see Hancock 2021). Not only was he skeptical about Hindu ritual artifacts as triggers for Christian piety, he recognized the danger and volatility of their power to *reenchant*, and his comments alluded indirectly to the power with which "idols" were vested in the settings of their original production and display. Then, as now, deity figures were worshiped through actions known collectively as *puja*, with the propitiation of Ganesha being the first step in most sequences.[13] *Puja* invokes the deity's presence in its material icon through acts of worship; its practice is requisite both for the making of ritual objects and spaces and as a way of interacting with them in temples and in domestic spaces. Central to *puja*, which originated in medieval temple-based traditions of southern India, are substantive transactions between devotees and materialized deities that assert the simultaneity of deities' immanence and transcendence: foodstuffs and other materials are offered and redistributed as sacralized matter; devotees see and are seen by deities in an empowering visual transaction known as *darshan* (Davis 1991, 7–8). Todd, even if considering the figure an abomination, recognized the force and, for Christians, the precarity of seeing and touching such objects. Re-emplaced in the churches and mission society offices that formed nodes of Christian community in the US, Ganesha's potency might be contained while being appraised as an ethnological curiosity or displayed during monthly prayer meetings convened on behalf of missions. As Todd feared, however, he also retained capacity to entrap viewers in idolatry, reconstituting the ritual spaces of his origin as he enjoyed "unexpected attention" from new viewers.

As Lawrence's and Todd's letters suggested, objects like the Ganesha figure were both desired and feared by Christians, serving multiple functions and gaining diverse affective and moral valences as they moved between different ritual spaces. As material metonyms of heathen places, they encapsulated what Protestants defined as idolatry, both its materiality and the divine agency misattributed to that materiality. They circulated, moreover, as products of the reconversionary dynamic of mission, acquiring virtue as products of missionaries' own *encounters with* and *disavowals of* heathenism. Likening themselves to the first generations of Christians described in the New Testament's Acts of the Apostles, missionaries claimed to be reenacting the foundational moment of Christian becoming by refuting the power of the "idols" they encountered in temples and shrines.[14] When recontextualized within Christian space of churches and mission society offices, however, those same "idols" fed a nascent ethnological imagination, while encouraging audiences to form affect-laden and prayerful connections with missionaries and mission. How the morally precarious wonder of missionary encounters with idolatry was redirected to cultivation of virtue is the subject of the next section.

Wondrous Virtue

The religiosity that suffused the foreign mission movement emerged within the social ecology of Great Awakening revivalism. While consistent with the patterns of voluntarism of the early republic, the activities and concerns of evangelical bodies were distinct in their missional focus. Evangelical social ecology was anchored by local churches and educational institutions (academies, colleges, seminaries), and by myriad parachurch organizations that met for prayer, charitable works, socializing, and education. Reflecting the spiritual egalitarianism of Puritan-descended evangelical Protestantism and the specific appeals to women made by mission's advocates, both men and women were eager participants.[15]

Despite the suspicion of images and ritual formalism central to Protestantism, evangelical social ecology was structured by individual and collective rituals, deemed such by their repeatability and the transformative capacities they were understood to possess. Formal liturgical cycles included daily communal prayers, weekly Sunday services, prayer meetings, and Sabbath schools, and monthly meetings dedicated to mission-related prayer and voluntarism. Interrupting, but also sustaining, these cycles were the "seasons of revival," usually several days dedicated to prayer and exhortation, declared when church leaders detected an intensification of piety and religious affections in their congregations.[16]

In evangelical ritual milieus, wonder was cultivated, morally coded, and recirculated in the service of Christian self-making. Cyclic revivals, with their affective intensities and moments of spiritual epiphany, were crucibles for experiencing and recoding wonder and its passion. In the regularized formats that emerged for these events, fervent communal prayer, rather than "cold speculative discussions of doctrine," was central, and church leaders were advised to promote revivals with "seasons of fasting and prayer," confession of sin in churches, public sanctions and discipline of wayward members, home visitations, and "united, agonizing, persevering prayer."[17] Such prayer was meant to convince the participants of their sinful condition, and to lead them to atonement through anxiety and self-examination. Resolution came with the recognition that one was a recipient of an unearned gift of what believers called "indwelling" grace, and described as "refreshing" and "hopeful." Conversion implied a new (Christian) identity and led to moments of felt community arising from shared conversionary experiences.

Mission media yielded grist for this process, recoding wonder in morally dichotomous terms. It enabled Christians to see in words and pictures the horror of the "perishing world" of heathendom, inhabited by those whose lack of knowledge of the Christian gospel left them mired in the credulous wonder of idolatry and without possibility of redemptive wonder, with its hope of salvific grace. Mission practice was among the forms of disinterested benevolence that Protestants, especially those influenced by Congregationalism, thought that conversion compelled (Porterfield 1997, 11–20). Labor as a missionary gave hope for salvation to Christianity's others, while also affirming the possibility of missionaries' own salvation.

To foment and sustain these seasons of revival, mission narratives and artifacts were circulated and interpreted in church services and in less formal gatherings of voluntary associations, many affiliated with colleges and seminaries. Missionaries' letters and reports were read and discussed; returned missionaries were pressed for firsthand accounts of their experiences; pictures, maps, and artifacts were viewed and handled; and prayers were offered, communally and privately, for foreign and domestic mission successes. Consider Julia Ostrander's 1836 account of her conversion and her hope to realize Christian identity by helping her "sisters in India." She began with a declaration of the affective force of "missionary intelligence," explaining that it regularly "touched a chord in my heart that has vibrated through all my soul."[18] Her experience of grace was limned with piteous revulsion for heathens: "When my heart was warm with my first love [of the Savior], I thought of the heathen and they have never been forgotten by me since. Over their <u>degradation</u> and <u>want</u>, I have <u>wept</u> and <u>prayed</u>. And at the recital of their superstition and idolatry, and utter pollution, my heart has bled at every pore" (emphasis original).[19] This vivid experience compelled her calling to mission: "Yes, for my sisters in India would I toil and pray and suffer, and now for their benefit, I most cheerfully offer myself as an assistant missionary to the [A]BCFM."[20]

In these affectively charged settings, lay Protestants' curiosity about the world was aroused by geographic, cultural, and historical information organized in relation to the millennialist project of world Christianization; they acted in that world by praying, by donating cash and property, and by self-sacrifice on behalf of missions. With these gestures, the wonder that early modern writers had found in Hindoostan was recoded as horror. In that same gesture, however, the passion of wonder was invited and redirected to pity, sympathy, and imaginative identification through prayer-forged affective and spiritual connections with distant missionaries and the "heathens" they sought to convert.

Another formal liturgical innovation was the monthly concert. An 1820 account described it as a collective prayer, to be observed concurrently by congregations, for the "coming of the Kingdom and for the extension of the triumphs of the Gospel" and explained that the "first and principal object in appointing the monthly concert is to pray for [the heathen]."[21] And, such prayers were not directed simply to an undifferentiated body of heathens, but to particular, geographically identified groups. It typically began with a prayer or hymn, followed by scripture readings, and short presentations on mission field geography, supplemented by maps, charts and pictures, to illustrate mission impacts with numbers of converts, schools, and churches. Another prayer, addressing the particulars of the featured location, closed the service. In form and content, it conjoined piety and pedagogy.

Church leaders maintained that the monthly concert's efficacy rested on the inclusion of images and narratives that enabled participants to visualize the objects of their prayers and recommended it as an encouragement to revival. As one writer explained, "A *mere* prayer meeting in behalf of foreign missions cannot be well-sustained with the present small amount of precise and accurate knowledge of the heathen world, the object of the meeting is too distant, too faintly conceived to awaken an intelligent, lively, effective interest in the minds of Christians, without the imparting of precise and accurate information" (emphasis original).[22]

The monthly concert was observed, initially, on the first Monday of each month in churches in the US and Europe and in mission stations.[23] At mission stations, the monthly concert provided occasions for missionaries and local Christians to gather together for prayer and to exchange news of their work. This normative synchrony, along with the specificity of its objects, was understood as enhancing its efficacy. It was valued by diverse Protestant communities as a mechanism for linking revival at home to Christian conquest abroad, because it united, "in concert," Christians across dispersed geographic spaces affectively and spiritually. Its impacts were calculable inasmuch as it served the aims of fundraising and recruitment. Monthly donations were reported in each issue of the *Missionary Herald* with the names of individual and group donors and preferred recipients listed, along with the precise amount donated. Donations were also valued as acts of piety that emulated the sacrifices of missionaries, for example, by donating money that might otherwise have been spent on luxuries.

The ritual crucibles that anchored the social ecology of revivalism were spaces where mission narratives, artifacts, and images were conjoined with the cultivation of piety among lay Protestants in the US. And missionaries, while benefiting from the prayerful attention of home congregations, also maintained senses of felt community through rhetorics of simultaneity. Within this ritual nexus, India as object of prayer, pity, horror, and awe was affixed to another space of wonder, that of Christian self-making formed through the anxious disavowal of the "dark" and "perishing" world of humans' sinful nature and the cautious hope of god's "refreshing" presence, grace, and salvation.

Wonder Resurfacing

Interpolating mission-derived information and artifacts within Christian practices allowed those materials to circulate in expansive and unanticipated ways. Fed by missionaries' donations, ABCFM's own artifact collections grew to over three thousand objects by 1895.[24] In the late 1840s, the newly formed American Oriental Society (AOS), a philological body formed in 1842, also began soliciting "curiosities," manuscripts, and translations from ABCFM missionaries.[25] Philology's roots in Biblical studies and its place in seminary education account for the possibility of missionary participation in Orientalist projects, while also anticipating how the Christian imperialism of mission helped lay the foundation for the race science that philology sustained later in the nineteenth century (Keel 2018). Like other Orientalists, missionaries used philological evidence to buttress an encyclopedic, racialized account of world civilizational history and presumed that the languages of the colonized contained vestiges of earlier civilizational moments, recoverable through the labor of translation.[26] They also found unexpected spaces of wonder and spiritual affinity.

Many missionaries were primed for acts of collection and translation through their exposure to South Asian cultural texts and artifacts in the course of their education. In requesting a mission assignment in India, William Tracy referred to his education at Williams College and Andover Seminary, explaining, "my predilection for Hindostan [sic] may have arisen from the fact that I have been better acquainted with the mythology, manners, and customs of that country than of some others."[27] A generation later, David Scudder, who began service in Madurai in 1861, complemented his college and seminary studies by delving into the Oriental and classical collections at Boston's Athenaeum while awaiting his mission assignment. Between days spent distributing tracts and Bibles, he commenced Sanskrit study, delivered a lecture, "Philosophy of Hinduism," before the Society of Inquiry, and completed a series of articles that summarized South Asia's epics and Puranas, the Laws of Manu, Sanskrit drama, and the Vedas.[28]

Those experiences demonstrate how streams of curiosity about Indic worlds were fed not only by mission accounts, but also by secular works on scientific subjects and Orientalist scholarship. At the AOS's 1849 meeting, one of its founders, ABCFM secretary Rufus Anderson, pointed to affinities between missionaries' knowledge and Orientalist scholarship, asserting that missionaries could advance science through the comparative and historical linguistic knowledge that their translations produced, as well as through their documentation of local ways of life.[29]

Anderson's influence likely accounted for the numbers of missionaries who donated manuscripts, printed material, and artifacts to the AOS and contributed translations and commentaries to the *Journal of the American Oriental Society*. The AOS library included philological texts, studies of orthography, and translations of Indic epics and sacred texts, as well as nearly all of the publications of mission presses, from hymnals and school primers to dictionaries and scriptural translations, newspapers, calendars, and mission reports.[30] Its cabinet, too, was filled with a growing collection of ritual accouterments, ornaments, clothing, and images donated by missionaries, merchants, diplomats, and other travelers. Like ABCFM's collections, AOS collections also grew to several thousands in number and, following AOS's move to New Haven, were distributed among different repositories on Yale University's campus.

Although few missionaries gained sufficient competence to translate Sanskrit, Tamil, or Persian texts, they couched these efforts in proselytic goals, proposing that knowledge of Indic religious traditions would enable them to be more persuasive interlocutors with learned Hindus. These avocational pursuits also allowed for expressions of curiosity, even wonder, that found no outlets in the prescribed genres of missionary writing. The work of Henry Hoisington, a Ceylon-based missionary, can illustrate.

In 1834, following his education at Williams College and Auburn Seminary (Ohio), Hoisington was posted to Ceylon.[31] Deemed a man of "ardent piety," he worked as a printer and later headed the mission's theological seminary at Batticotta.[32] As required of ABCFM missionaries, he studied the regional vernacular, Tamil. He further pursued philological study of Tamil and translations of texts contained in Tamil sections of a collection on Saivite Hindu principles and practices within the larger body of works known as Agamas.[33] Like his contemporary, Robert Caldwell, Hoisington made a case for Tamil's historical primacy as an Indic language and its status as classical language of greater antiquity than Sanskrit (Hoisington 1853; Caldwell 1856).

The translations and commentaries covered the Saivite tenets and practices that Hoisington considered definitive elements of pan-Hindu systems of thought. He presented *Tattuva-Kaṭṭaḷei* (Law of the Tattuvam) as a seminal text within this group, noting that, "as help to those who would look into the mysteries of Hinduism, it is important, if not indispensable. It stands related to the whole system of that mystic philosophy somewhat as the Greek grammar does to the whole course of the Greek classics" (Hoisington 1854c, 3). His commentary on another work, the *Pantshtshara Yogam*, explained the technique for achieving experiential union with the deity (Hoisington 1851a). This technique hinged on *mantras*, formulaic utterances acquired in the course of religious instruction and deployed in ascetic disciplines and in the consecration of temples and deity figures.[34] Elsewhere, Hoisington addressed the principles of logic and reasoning by which understanding of "the three eternal entities of deity [pathi], soul [pasu], matter [pāśam]" (bracketed content original) could be reached through Saiva ritual practices (Hoisington 1851b, 138).

His translations include none of the pejorative language that usually accompanied missionary accounts, writing instead of the "wondrous powers" that Hindus' ritual utterances and actions accessed and controlled. He argued that to gain credibility as an interlocutor, the "correct knowledge of [the] living, practical system of Hinduism" was more important than linguistic competence in the vernacular (Hoisington 1851b, 151). By contrast, and of greater remark, was his presentation of the translations as comparative projects that demonstrated both the commensurability and incommensurability of Hindu and Christian concepts.

Recognition of incommensurability is evident in his treatment of the formulaic utterances of mantras, which he explained as incarnations of deities whose repetition empowered the "laws of nature" and infused divinity into material forms (Hoisington 1851a, 153–54). Mantra, treated as language that was both performative and transformative, rested on an underlying logic for which Hoisington could find no single English gloss and that he recognized as antithetical to Cartesian dualism. He explicated that logic in his discussion of the term, *tattuvam*. There, he observed that that term (from a Sanskrit word that he translated as essential nature or property) might be rendered in English variously as category, principle, organ, property, or power, but that, in a more basic sense, it "has no equivalent in our language . . . the ideas wrapped up in *tattuvam* confound the physical and the metaphysical, the real and the imaginary" (Hoisington 1854c, 5). He finessed the problem that this posed for his translation by retaining the original term, using Tamil orthography, in his translation rather than an English gloss.

Elsewhere, however, commensurability between Hindu and Christian principles was implied, though not because of Hinduism's alleged idolatry. For example, in his commentary on the *Siva-Gnâna-Pōtham*, he employed the English term "soul" to gloss a Tamil term he transliterated as *paśu*, using vocabulary that would be familiar to Protestants in their own accounts of conversion (Hoisington 1851b, 138). In presenting the "soul" as the conduit of divinity, he explained that the illumination of the "in-dwelling deity" through the agency of "grace" (glossed as *aruḷ-śakti*) brought humans to truth through union with divinity. Indeed, in his introduction to the *Siva-Gnâna-Pōtham*, he described its dogma and the forms of logical and metaphysical reasoning it prescribed as "evincing that the Hindus have some correct apprehension of the true sources of ideas, and of the way in which the human mind usually reasons when enlightened" (Hoisington 1854a, 31).

And, in counterpoint to William Todd, whose destruction of a Ganesha figure had violently refused Hindu materiality, Hoisington textually reenacted the practice of *puja* in his translation of the *Siva-Pirakâsam* (Hoisington 1854b, 125). The treatise was described as a concise commentary on the *Siva-Gnâna-Pōtham* and an authoritative source on Agamic doctrines of God, the soul, and the human organism. In his translation, Hoisington made a point to include the treatise's preamble, which asserted the benefits of worshiping Ganesha (also named Pillaiyar and Kanapathi) and invoked that deity and the other gods, saints, and gurus whose worship enabled humans to gain esoteric knowledge. This invocation read, "In order that my treatise may be useful in elucidating the three eternal entities (Deity, Soul, Matter) and for the attainment of *sāyuchchiyam*, union with god, and that it may be free from poetical blemishes . . . and that I may escape any casualty that would prevent my completing the work, I meditate on the two beautiful lotus-like feet of the elephant-face Kanapathi, who was produced by the union of Sivan and Papathi" (Hoisington 1854b, 131–32). The retention of these invocations captured the original author's treatment of the text, itself, as performative language, as a ritual enacted, while it dismissed objections of those who considered such passages ornamental or ancillary.[35] In so doing, Hoisington, in the liminal and intimate space of translation, transposed the entanglements with "idols" that so disturbed Todd to entanglements with philosophical treatises and the sacred utterances that they both explained and performed. In that space, there is a provisional resolution to what Matthew Engelke placed at the core of Protestant Christianity, its "problem of presence," the conundrum of how a transcendent deity can be made immanent (Engelke 2007).

Hoisington's translations alert us to the resurfacing of wonder in scholarly discourses. That Orientalist scholarship and Christian mission together enacted imperial power and reinforced its racialized order is irrefutable. What the works of missionary Orientalists reveal, however, are the spaces of strategic ambiguity that were also afforded.[36] Orientalist scholarship, alongside natural sciences, was understood as both available and necessary for mission preparation. But, distinct from the ways that Protestant teaching and ritual recoded the wonders of "Hindoostan" as satanically fashioned horrors, Orientalism's philological and ethnological inquiries, while asserting racialized otherness, also gave scope for curiosity, appraisal, comparison, and admiration; and it placed translators, at least provisionally, into the intimate liminality and wonder that existed in the spaces between languages. As evangelizers and teachers, missionaries dutifully catalogued the small victories that paved the way for Christian conversion by naming, claiming, and counting the signs of Christianity's advance. In the avocational tasks of translation and collection, however, some discovered new passions, made new alliances, and solicited new audiences for the wonders both of indwelling grace and of Hindu metaphysics.

Conclusion

As a broad, enabling concept, wonder has gained traction as subject of scholarly inquiry and as an attribute of and affective orientation toward such inquiry. These works encompass both genealogies of wonder and documentation of its persistent, often fugitive presence, in modernity, as it lost elite cachet and resurfaced in popular spaces of fairs, expositions, carnivals, lay scientific practices, and tabloids (Bynum 1997; Daston and Park 1998).

Lorraine Daston and Katharine Park attributed the modern recalibration of wonder less to the ascendency of science than to theological interventions and changes in class culture (Daston and Park 1998, 350–58, 360–62). They observed that, between Europe's medieval and early modern periods, "marvels," both near at hand and encountered through trade, exploration, pilgrimage, and war, were regularly and appreciatively catalogued and collected. Wonder's moral valence, however, shifted in the mid-1700s, led by Enlightenment philosophers and by Protestant and Catholic theologians and clerics. They sought to distinguish the wonder that might be directed to god's creation from that originating in the credulity of superstition, the imaginative or psychological excesses of religious enthusiasm, or even the demonic power of idolatry (see Taves 1999, 20–46). Wonder, domesticated through a new moral valuation, encompassed both the sublime and the merely vulgar, the former a matter of aesthetics and religiosity, the latter offering entertaining and sometimes horrific spectacles.

Downplayed in wonder's intellectual history are its experiential manifestations. For the American Protestants whose religiosity was forged in eighteenth- and nineteenth-century revivals, the moral distinctions of wonder were worked out both speculatively, in theology, and experimentally, in religious practice. Rather than abandoning wonder and wonders, they relocated its objects and recalibrated its passions. Indian life worlds, framed as racialized spaces of profound otherness, even monstrosity, yielded objects of wonder and invited its passion, experienced as both horror of idolatry and awe for its landscapes, art, narratives, and architecture (Cohen 1996). Spaces of wonder were also found in religious experiences where, goaded by affecting tropes of idolatry, Protestants embraced mission vocations and, through iterative ritual praxis, fashioned Christian selves.

Missionaries' experimental revaluation of wonder proceeded in an everyday milieu of entangling encounters. They moved through, saw, touched, and heard what they called "heathendom," while also struggling to maintain connections with coreligionists locally and in the US. The spatiotemporal architecture of liturgy created a context in which Protestants could live in the wondrous "refreshment" of indwelling grace and in the affective and spiritual bonds that extended across dispersed locales. And missionaries regularly invoked biblical paradigms to identify and disavow the morally depraved wonder of idolatry's materiality, its deities, shrines, and sacred landscapes. Relying on a racialized framing of Hindustan as a space of "idolatry" and "fetishism," missionaries denigrated and demeaned Hindus (as well as Muslims, Roman Catholics, Jains, and Buddhists). They were agents of intimate violence, as they imposed ways of knowing and being compatible with Protestant Christianity on Indian mission subjects. But, for some missionaries, the avocational pursuits of translation and collection offered spaces for curiosity and for the passion of wonder. Against the grain of Protestant conversionary logic, such pursuits yielded admiration and affinities, and even created an ambivalent proximity with Protestants' own struggles with the conundrum of divinity's simultaneous immanence and transcendence.

Where does wonder, even as domesticated by Protestant rationality and contaminated by the structural violence of Orientalism, bring us? Tulasi Srinivas's (2018) effort to think through an anthropology of wonder provides both provocation and inspiration. If Daston and Park's analysis reveals what Europeans made of the wonder that they attributed to India, Srinivas recodes wonder, its passions and its objects, as *products* of Hindu ritual praxis, asking what a comparative account of religiosity might look like with Hinduism at its center. She situates wonder in the ritual life of south India's Hindu temples, finding that ritual engenders wonder through its simultaneous emplacement in the world of conventional time and space, and its invocation of a beyond, an alterity that is more-than-human, organizing life in the present while orienting it toward futurity (see also Hancock 1999, 17–22).

This chapter is conceived in conversation with Srinivas's project. It reveals how the tropes of "Hindoostan" emerged and were sustained by the iterative, dialogical self-fashioning of Christian ritual and pedagogy. At the same time, I have also taken up Srinivas's invitation for a comparative anthropology of wonder by following wonder's surfacing as a cognitive and affective device for imagining alterity—something that even Protestants understood themselves as doing when they gathered for monthly concerts, for "seasons of revival," and for collective prayer.

In making these arguments, I have not lost sight of the fact that Protestants, especially those self-conscious heirs of Puritanism who led mission to India, would resist the suggestion that their actions were ritualized. Protestant religiosity was founded on skepticism about ritual formalism and about its material mediants. Yet they relied on ritualized actions and affects, such as liturgical sequences and prayer offered "in concert," for transformative ends. As conversion narratives suggest, ritualized action yielded liminal moments and created thresholds for divinity, understood as transcendent, to become immanent, even as Protestants remained attentive to the need to distinguish such moments from imaginative excess. Liminality and the wonder that it invites and cultivates offer points for comparative reflection. Rather than marking Hindu exceptionalism, paying attention to the process—the doing—of wonder is an opportunity to pry open the fugitive ritual nodes of Protestant Christianity. And, if Protestant missionaries found their way to wonder through ritual, they also found themselves unintentionally in another liminal space as they pursued avocational passions of translation. The philosophical and moral texts they grappled with provided an entry into different ontological spaces where they found both affinities and disjunctions between Christian and Hindu traditions.

In contrast with their expansive goal of world Christianization, American missionaries enjoyed only limited successes in gaining Christian converts in India. Their efforts, however, helped consolidate "Hindoostan" in the American evangelical imaginary through images and narratives in which both racist stereotypes and dialogical composites coexisted. This chapter has considered how the layered and unpredictable entanglements of mission were framed by Western discourses of wonder to which Protestants were heirs, while also inviting them to recode wonder's objects and the passion of wonder, itself, for new religio-moral projects.

Notes

1. During this period, "evangelical" denoted a millennialist-inflected commitment to missional Christianity, both its conversionary dynamic within Christian communities and the Christianization of others. Evangelicals valued personal piety, self-sacrifice for what were deemed benevolent ends, and conversionary zeal.

2. "Southern Asia," *The Missionary Herald* 56, no. 1 (1860): 7–9.

3. John Lawrence to E. Wisner, April 1, 1833, ABC 6, vol. 10, no. 32, ABCFM.

4. For example, see the account of artifacts collected by one early missionary, William Todd to Rufus Anderson, Letter, September 19, 1836, ABC 16.1.9, A467, Reel 466, no. 48, ABCFM.

5. "To the Missionaries of the American Board of Commissioners for Foreign Missions," Circular, June 27, 1838, ABC 85.3, Box 1, Folder 4, ABCFM.

6. "Minutes of Delegation Meeting at Madras, February 9, 1839," ABC 16.1.9, A467, Reel 466, no. 7, p. 8, ABCFM.

7. Reverend Daniel Poor, "Journal of a Visit to Madura," printed at Manepy, 1837, ABC 16.1.9 A467, Reel 466, no. 1, pp. 8–9; Rev. D. Poor, Journal, November, 1835, ABC 16.1.9, A467, Reel 499, no. 24, p. 4, ABCFM.

8. Reverend Daniel Poor, Journal, November, 1835; Daniel Poor to Rufus Anderson, May 3, 1836, Madura, ABC 16.1.9, A467, Reel 499, no. 34, p. 7, ABCFM.

9. William Todd to Rufus Anderson, September 15, 1836, ABC 16.1.9, A467, Reel 499, no. 33, p. 2, ABCFM.

10. Todd to Anderson, September 15, 1836, p. 2.

11. Todd to Anderson, September 15, 1836, p. 4.

12. Todd to Anderson, September 15, 1836, p. 4.

13. Unless they appear in quoted matter or in the titles of references, diacritics have not been added to transliterated terms.

14. Poor, "Journal of a Visit to Madura," p. 4.

15. As of 1830, 1634 recognized associations were listed, 608 being women-only and the remainder being either mixed gender or male-only. "Brief View of the American Board of Commissioners for Foreign Missions and its Operations," *Missionary Herald* 27, no. 1 (January 1831): 1–2; see also Porterfield (1997, 14–19).

16. See, for example, "Revival in Adams, NY," *Panoplist and Missionary Herald* 15, no. 4 (April 1819): 181, 186.

17. "Domestic Intelligence: State of Religion," *Missionary Herald* 23, no. 3 (March 1827): 89–90.

18. Julia Ostrander to Wm. Armstrong, August 15, 1836, ABC 6, vol. 8, no. 37, ABCFM.

19. Ostrander to Armstrong, August 15, 1836.

20. Ostrander to Armstrong, August 15, 1836.

21. "Concise History of the Monthly Concert of Prayer," *Christian Watchman* 1, no. 19 (April 22, 1820): 2.

22. "Miscellanies: Historical Statement Respecting the Monthly Concert for Prayer" *Missionary Herald* 35, no. 3 (March 1839): 121.

23. Its popularization in the US may even have been inspired by its observance among missionaries. An 1814 letter described a liturgical schedule that included Wednesday prayer meetings, and weekly and monthly "concerts of prayer . . . observed by all missionaries in India of every denomination." Samuel Newell to the American Board, August 2, 1814, *Panoplist and Missionary Herald* 11, no. 7 (July 1815): 208.

24. Report of the Sub-committee on Library, June 30, 1939, ABC 85.9, Box 8, museum folder, ABCFM.

25. "Miscellaneous Notices Relative to the Recent Progress of Oriental Researches," *Journal of the American Oriental Society* 1, no. 3 (1847): 319; "Proceedings of the American Oriental Society," *Journal of the American Oriental Society* 1, no. 4 (1849): xli–xliv; "Additions to the Library and Cabinet of the American Oriental Society, February 1853–July 1854," *Journal of the American Oriental Society* 4 (1854): iii–xiv.

26. Said's *Orientalism* (1978) provides a foundational critique of the Orientalist project's roots, its imbrication of power and knowledge, and its continued impacts.

27. William Tracy to the American Board Secretary, January 20, 1836, ABC 6, vol. 12, no. 57, ABCFM.

28. David Scudder, Diary, 1856–1858, ABC 56, vol. 1, pp. 38, 40, 60, ABCFM; David Scudder, "India Illustrated by Its Literature," undated clippings from *Boston Recorder*, 1860, file on David Coit Scudder, bMS 1264, Series VI, ABCFM-A.

29. "Proceedings of the American Oriental Society," *Journal of the American Oriental Society* 1, no. 4 (1849): xli. See also, Davis (1985, 7–8).

30. "Proceedings of the American Oriental Society at New York" [October 26 and 27, 1864], *Journal of the American Oriental Society* 8 (1866): lix.

31. Henry Hoisington to American Board Secretary, February 4, 1833, ABC 6, vol. 9, no. 46, ABCFM.

32. Saul Hutchings to American Board Secretary, February 9, 1833, ABC 6, vol. 9, no. 46, ABCFM.

33. Hoisington did not credit any other translator(s) in his publications, but missionaries commonly relied on local pandits for guidance.

34. "Mantras are speech acts. . . . They are also, more fundamentally, powerful divine beings or forces that exist independently of any human usage. The speech act is the signifier . . . the divine being is the signified . . . the mantra may be thought of as the sign in which the two are intimately—and not arbitrarily—united" (Davis 1991, 33).

35. The sections were "retained as worthy of notice both because they furnish a fair specimen of what is common with writers of the east, and because they contain allusions to facts and notions which ought to be known" (Hoisington 1854b, 128).

36. For a discussion of similar phenomena in the context of Portuguese empire, see Xavier and Zupanov (2015).

Works Cited

Ahmed, Sara. 2004. "Collective Feelings: Or, The Impressions Left by Others." *Theory, Culture and Society* 21 (2): 25–42.

Altman, Michael J. 2017. *Heathen, Hindoo, Hindu: American Representations of India, 1721–1893.* New York: Oxford University Press.

American Board of Commissioners for Foreign Missions Archive, 1810–1961 (ABCFM). ABC 1–91. Houghton Library, Harvard University.

American Board of Commissioners for Foreign Missions. India. 1813–1966 (ABCFM-A). bMS 1264. Harvard Divinity School Library, Harvard University.

Bald, Vivek. 2015. "American Orientalism." *Dissent* 62 (2): 23–34.

———. 2013. *Bengali Harlem and the Lost Histories of South Asian America.* Cambridge, MA: Harvard University Press.

Bald, Vivek, Miabi Chatterji, Sujani Reddy, and Manu Vimalassery, eds. 2013. *The Sun Never Sets: South Asian Migrants in an Age of U.S. Power.* New York: New York University Press.

Bean, Susan. 2006. *Yankee India: American Commercial and Cultural Encounters with India in the Age of Sail, 1784–1860.* Salem, MA: Peabody Essex Museum.

Bynum, Caroline Walker. 1997. "Wonder." *American Historical Review* 102 (1): 1–26.

Caldwell, Robert. 1856. *A Comparative Grammar of the Dravidian or South Indian Family of Languages.* London.

Cohen, Jeffrey. 1996. "Monster Culture (Seven Theses)." In *Monster Theory: Reading Culture*, ed. Jeffrey Cohen, 3–25. Minneapolis: University of Minnesota Press.

Conroy-Krutz, Emily. 2015. *Christian Imperialism: Converting the World in the Early American Republic.* Ithaca: Cornell University Press.

Daston, Lorraine, and Katharine Park. 1998. *Wonders and the Order of Nature, 1150–1750.* New York: Zone.

Davis, Richard H. 1985. *South Asia at Chicago: A History.* COSAS, new series, no. 1. Chicago: Committee on Southern Asian Studies, University of Chicago.
———. 1991. *Ritual in an Oscillating Universe: Worshiping Siva in Medieval India.* Princeton, NJ: Princeton University Press.
———. 1997. *Lives of Indian Images.* Princeton, NJ: Princeton University Press.
———. 2015. *The Bhagavad Gita: A Biography.* Princeton, NJ: Princeton University Press.
———. 2018. "Henry David Thoreau, Yogi." *Common Knowledge* 1 (24): 56–89.
Edwards, Holly. 2000. *Noble Dreams, Wicked Pleasures: Orientalism in America, 1870–1930.* Princeton, NJ: Princeton University Press.
Engelke, Matthew. 2007. *A Problem of Presence: Beyond Scripture in an African Church.* Berkeley: University of California Press.
Fields, Karen, and Barbara Fields. 2012. *Racecraft: The Soul of Inequality in American Life.* London: Verso.
Foxen, Anya. 2017. "Yogi Calisthenics: What the Non-Yoga Yogic Practice of Pramahamsa Can Tell Us about Religion." *Journal of the American Academy of Religion* 85 (2): 494–526.
Haggis, Jane, and Margaret Allen. 2008. "Imperial Emotions: Affective Communities of Mission in British Protestant Women's Missionary Publications c1880–1920." *Journal of Social History* 41 (3): 691–716.
Hancock, Mary. 1999. *Womanhood in the Making: Domestic Ritual and Public Culture in Urban South India.* Boulder, CO: Westview Press.
———. 2021. "Conversionary Christian Place-Making in 19th-Century Madurai." In *Spaces of Religion in Urban South Asia*, ed. István Keul, 39–55. London: Routledge.
Hoisington, Henry R. 1851a. "Note on the Pantshtshara-Yogam, the Formula of Five Characters." *Journal of the American Oriental Society* 2:152–54.
———. 1851b. "Syllabus of the Siva-Gnâna-Pōtham." *Journal of the American Oriental Society* 2:135, 137–51.
———. 1853. "Brief Notes on the Tamil Language." *Journal of the American Oriental Society* 3:387–97.
———. 1854a. "Siva-Gnâna-Pōtham, Instruction in the Knowledge of God: A Metaphysical and Theological Treatise." *Journal of the American Oriental Society* 4:31–102.
———. 1854b. "Siva-Pirakâsam, Light of Sivan: A Metaphysical and Theological Treatise." *Journal of the American Oriental Society* 4:125–244.
———. 1854c. "Tattuva-Kaṭṭalei, Law of the Tattuvam: A Synopsis of the Mystical Philosophy of the Hindûs." *Journal of the American Oriental Society* 4:1–30.
Immerwahr, Daniel. 2007. "Caste or Colony? Indianizing Race in the United States." *Modern Intellectual History* 4 (2):275–301.
Iwamura, Jane. 2010. *Virtual Orientalism: Asian Religions and American Popular Culture.* New York: Oxford University Press.

Keel, Terrence. 2018. *Divine Variations: How Christian Thought Became Racial Science*. Redwood City, CA: Stanford University Press.

Mather, Cotton. 1721. *India Christiana. A discourse, delivered unto the Commissioners, for the Propagation of the Gospel among the American Indians: which is accompanied with several instruments relating to the glorious design of propagating our holy religion, in the Eastern as well as the Western, Indies.: An entertainment which they that are waiting for the kingdom of God will receive as good news from a far country*. Boston. Evans Early American Imprint Collection, Text Creation Partnership. http://name.umdl.umich.edu/N01899.0001.001.

Porterfield, Amanda. 1997. *Mary Lyon and the Mount Holyoke Missionaries*. New York: Oxford University Press.

Said, Edward. 1978. *Orientalism*. New York: Vintage.

Slate, Nico. 2012. *Colored Cosmopolitanism: The Shared Struggle for Freedom in the United States and India*. Cambridge, MA: Harvard University Press.

Sohi, Seema. 2014. *Echoes of Mutiny: Race, Surveillance and Indian Anticolonialism in North America*. New York: Oxford University Press.

Srinivas, Tulasi. 2018. *The Cow in the Elevator: An Anthropology of Wonder*. Durham, NC: Duke University Press.

Srinivasan, Priya. 2011. *Sweating Saris: Indian Dance as Transnational Labour*. Philadelphia: Temple University Press.

Taves, Ann. 1999. *Fits, Trances, and Visions: Experiencing Religion and Explaining Experience from Wesley to James*. Princeton, NJ: Princeton University Press.

Tuffnell, Stephen. 2014. "Anglo-American Inter-Imperialism: U.S. Expansion and the British World, 1865–1914." *Britain and the World* 7 (2): 174–95.

Tweed, Thomas, and Stephen Prothero, eds. 1999. *Asian Religions in America: A Documentary History*. New York, Oxford University Press.

Tyrrell, Ian. 2010. *Reforming the World: The Creation of America's Moral Empire*. Princeton, NJ: Princeton University Press.

Wilkerson, Isabel. 2020. *Caste: The Origin of our Discontent*. New York, Random House.

Xavier, Angela Barreto, and Ines Zupanov. 2015. *Catholic Orientalism: Portuguese Empire, Indian Knowledge*. Delhi: Oxford University Press.

Section 2
Aesthetics of Wonder

Chapter 4

Wonder

Spirit Mediumship and Devotional Music at a
Mumbai Shrine of the Sidi Ancestor-Saints

JAZMIN GRAVES EYSSALLENNE

Introduction

This chapter examines wonder in the Sidi Sufi devotional tradition of Gujarat and Mumbai. This tradition comprises the veneration of African Rifai Sufi saints entombed in Gujarat, and other related figures, as ancestor-saints of Muslim Sidis, Indians of eastern African ancestry.[1] The three saints at the focus of this tradition are the siblings Bava Gor, Bava Habash, and Mai Misra. A network of tomb-shrines (*dargah*) and memorial shrines (*chilla*, also called *dargah*) of the Sidi ancestor-saints extends throughout Gujarat and Mumbai. These shrines are generally, though not exclusively, maintained by Sidis and visited by a multireligious body of supplicants. This chapter studies the workings of wonder at a memorial shrine of the Sidi ancestor-saints in Mumbai managed by a non-Sidi, Sunni Muslim caretaker and patronized primarily by a community of Parsi Zoroastrian devotees.[2]

The performance of devotional music and ecstatic dance called Sidi *dhammal* or *goma* catalyzes the experience of wonder among ritual participants at the shrines of the Sidi ancestor-saints.[3] Wonder in this context describes the devotee's affective experience of the charisma (*barkat*) and "miracle healing presence/assistance" (*karamat*) of the Sidi ancestor-saints (Shroff 2013, 21—22; see also Werbner and Basu 1998). This experience, characterized as *wajd*, culminates in the embodiment of that which is wondrous—the presence (*haziri*) of the saints in an ecstatic state called *hal*. In this state, the medium of the saints communicates information from beyond the devotee's ordinary scope of knowledge, a compassionate service rendered to impart healing and blessings to others.

This chapter offers a vocabulary for categorizing states of ecstasy and spirit embodiment in the Sidi Sufi tradition, with reference to pivotal studies of ritual healing and devotional music performance in other Indian Islamic contexts. The chapter draws from original ethnographic research conducted throughout the Sidi saint shrine network, and particularly at the "Parsi shrine" of the Sidi ancestor-saints in Mumbai, to detail the experience of wonder and its subsequent phases of embodiment and communication among devotees of the Sidi saints. Centering on interviews with two women, Sidi and Parsi, who serve as mediums of the saint Mai Misra at this site, the chapter illustrates the process by which the affective experience of wonder culminates in ecstatic embodiment and highlights both emic and etic perspectives on spiritual development as the pathway bridging wonder and ecstasy.[4]

As the instruments and rhythms of Sidi *dhammal* facilitate the experience of wonder, the chapter analyzes the links between *dhammal*, embodiment, and communication. The chapter traces these connections to the African diasporan heritage of Sidi *dhammal* and its sacred rhythms and instruments, positioning the *dhammal* performance, as Tulasi Srinivas's introduction notes, as a "point of convergence for . . . technologies of information and technologies of the soul and the cosmos." The chapter's analysis contributes to the study of the multivocality of the Sidi Sufi devotional tradition as a site of confluence for Sufi, Hindu, and eastern African conceptual frameworks and modes of accessing the divine (See Orsini 2014, 228; Graves 2022).

Wajd as Wonder: Defining *Haziri* and *Hal*

Embodiment, a term preferable to "possession," emerges as one of the most tangible ways by which the Sidi ancestor-saints manifest their miracle healing presence and assistance in the lives of devotees. Sidis use the terms *haziri* ("presence"), *hal* ("ecstasy"), and *sawari* ("vehicle") to describe this process.[5] Beheroze Shroff identifies this practice as spirit mediumship, whereby a Sidi ancestor-saint overtakes the voice and body of a devotee in a ritual context; participants then consult the embodied saint for blessings, prayers, and advice (Shroff 2013, 22).

It is necessary to ground this chapter's study of women's embodiment of the presence of the Sidi ancestor-saint Mai Misra in scholarship on trance and possession in Islamic ritual contexts in South Asia. Joyce Flueckiger, in her study of the spiritual healing practice of Amma, a Muslim woman and wife of a Sufi teacher (*pir*) in Hyderabad, observes the interchangeable, "inconsistent and context-specific" usage of the terms *hal* and *wajd* (Flueckiger 2006, 217). These terms denote trance states that emerge during the performance of qawwali in Amma's courtyard, and are opposed in valuation with *haziri*, which denotes possession. Flueckiger warns that, despite the observable similarities between trance and possession, "Allah and the saints do not possess, though they might be present; only *jinn* and devils possess and take over a person's body" (Flueckiger 2006, 216–17). Flueckiger thus distinguishes between trance and possession in Muslim devotional contexts, in which the former is positively valued and the latter, negatively. Likewise, Peter van der Veer distinguishes between possession or *haziri* and trance or *hal* at a Rifai Sufi shrine in Surat, Gujarat (Van der Veer 1992, 555).

The "impossibility" of possession by Muslim saints and the connotation of *hal* as trance as opposed to possession is incompatible with the conceptualization of *hal* in the Sidi Sufi tradition. Helene Basu identifies a binary valuation of possession in the context of Sidi saint shrines, where *hal* is the positively valued embodiment of a benevolent ancestor-saint and *haziri* indicates possession by a malevolent spirit; pilgrims to Sidi saint shrines often appeal to the saints for healing from the latter (Basu 2008, 249, 252). As mentioned above, terminological usage in Sidi devotional contexts complicates this binary. For example, Heena, the Sidi spirit medium of Mai Misra at the Mumbai shrine that is the focus of this chapter, uses the term *haziri* to describe embodiment of Mai Misra: "Mai Misra's presence (*haziri*) comes" (*Mai Misra ni haziri ave che*).[6] The inconsistent usage of such terms to refer to either a positively or negatively valued mode of embodiment also occurs in the context of Amma's healing practice in Hyderabad: Flueckiger observes that on one occasion, Amma conflates the terms *hal* and *haziri* and opposes *hal* with *wajd*. Ultimately, as Flueckiger states, the usage of these terms is "context-specific."

In this chapter, *haziri* signifies its literal definition of "presence," denoting the presence of a Sidi ancestor-saint that may be embodied in an experience identified as *hal*. The chapter defines *wajd* as the affective experience of wonder that sparks the embodied experience of *hal*, delineated below. The chapter develops its analysis with reference to Carla Bellamy's discussion of positively valued modes of embodiment identified in her study of *haziri* and healing at the shrine Husain Tekri in Jaora, Madhya Pradesh in central India (Bellamy 2011).

Wonder and the Embodiment of the Saints

The performance of *dhammal* during the death-anniversary (*urs*) celebrations of the Sidi ancestor-saints creates an occasion for devotees to experience the dynamic energy of the saints' presence through embodiment or through communication with the embodied saints. The following depicts such a scene from the 2018 *urs* at the Mumbai memorial shrine:

> Devotees placed satin embroidered cloths (*galef*) and woven sheets of flowers (*chaddar*) on the memorial tomb of Bava Gor and on the actual tomb of Makbul Bava, the grandfather of Yasin Bava and spirit medium of Bava Gor with whom this Parsi community's devotion to Bava Gor had begun. Men assembled in a queue, placing their hands on each other's shoulders, and sanctified the space with frankincense (*loban*). Meanwhile, women lit oil lamps (*diya*).
>
> After the recitation of prayers, *dhammal* began. Yasin Bava, the shrine's ritual authority and spirit medium of Bava Gor, collapsed on the floor in *hal* and, surrounded by men assisting him, crawled toward the *dhammal* performers. Heena stepped energetically and rhythmically in *hal*, firmly embracing a devotee. A Parsi medium of Mai Misra sat meditatively, crying nearing the life-sized, symbolic embodiment of Mai Misra installed beside the memorial tomb of Bava Gor.[7]
>
> In *hal*, the Parsi medium and Yasin Bava held audience (*baithak*) with devotees. The Parsi woman lay on the ground, her body covered in a green satin sheet. She waved her index finger to the rhythms of the *dhammal* as she received devotees' questions and salutations.[8]

This scene underscores the central role of mediums of the Sidi ancestor-saints in devotional life at this shrine. Living conduits for the charisma and healing assistance of the saints, they selflessly provide a physically taxing service that requires fortitude and endurance (Shroff 2013, 21–22). These individuals' embodiment of the saints aligns with Bellamy's analysis of *salami*, the "greeting" or blessing of a Muslim saint that allows an individual to embody the saint's presence and thereby conduct a "benevolent spirit possession-based healing practice" (Bellamy 2011, 89–91, 155).

Mediumship at the Sidi saint shrine as the embodiment of benevolent saints, akin to the concept of *salami*, aligns in key ways with Bellamy's analysis of *haziri*. Bellamy distinguishes between two aspects of *haziri*: "open" (*khuli haziri*) and "hidden" (*gum haziri*).[9] While the former denotes "a series of actions that share many characteristics with exorcism," the latter indicates "a physically painful condition of being unwell that is not observable or known to anyone other than the sufferer." Bellamy identifies *haziri* as the state of being a "*haziriwala/haziriwali*, or a person primarily characterized by presence"; thus, "*haziri* represents states of being as well as ritual action." Mediumship of the presence of the Sidi ancestor-saints likewise involves stages that, while incongruent with Bellamy's definitions of "hidden" and "open" *haziri*, parallel the respective private, experiential and public, performative aspects of these states. The private, experiential aspect of *haziri* at the Sidi saint shrine entails an affective experience of wonder, encompassing reverence, joy, awe, and supplication, as the devotee marvels at the arrival of the saints.

Crying is a relatively private, personal aspect of devotional experience that is a visible sign of the beginning stages of mediumship ability. The Parsi medium of Mai Misra explains, "I used to just cry. They also know that, 'Okay, these are the symptoms for this.' So they knew, 'Okay, this is the starting.'"[10] The young woman's crying was a "symptom" that mediumship ability was "starting." Yasin Bava, the Sunni Muslim medium of Bava Gor and caretaker of the shrine, correlates crying with the presence of the saints: "You feel like crying. [That means] you are meeting them."[11] Rumanaben, the late ritual specialist at the memorial shrine of the Sidi ancestor-saints in Ahmedabad, Gujarat, has identified this emotional state as *wajd*.[12] According to Rumanaben, one may experience *wajd* while performing devotions such as the five daily prayers. The intensity of this emotion may move the praying person to tears; likewise, women who appear to be on the verge of entering *hal* may weep as they yearn for the saints' presence and rejoice at their arrival. Whereas *wajd* defined as "a state of ecstasy, frenzy, or religious transport" is synonymous with *hal, wajd* in the Sidi devotional tradition is a precursor to the fully realized, outward display of embodiment of a saint's "presence" (*haziri*) in the ecstatic trance of *hal* (Platts 1884, 473, 1181).

Bellamy observes that the physical stress of embodiment of a saint's presence may at first render it indistinguishable from expressions of malevolent modes of embodiment until the saint speaks and clarifies the confusion (Bellamy 2011, 89). Mediums of Bava Gor and Mai Misra report that, at the beginning of development as a medium, embodying the presence of the saints involves physical or mental discomfort. Heena, a Sidi medium of Mai Misra, describes the onset of her mediumship abilities at the age of seven: "The first time it came, I was very confused and I did not understand. I could not hear the people around me. I could only hear the devotional songs and I felt very strange. I felt like something had come near me. And I cried a lot. I could not stay in control. In one second I would just forget myself."[13] Heena reports the "symptom" of crying, along with an internal state of confusion. She could only hear the devotional songs, underscoring the connection between the *dhammal* performance and the emotional transport of wonder. Heena adds later in the interview that interlocutors must ask for the name of the embodied saint while the medium is in *hal* in order to ascertain the saint's identity. This corresponds with Bellamy's observation that the saint who has bestowed their "greeting" will clarify this fact for the individual, since the experience of embodiment might appear and feel similar to the negatively valued *haziri* of that context.

The Parsi medium of Mai Misra describes a similar experience when she began to develop mediumship abilities around the age of sixteen or seventeen:

> Initially, I used to just cry, and I didn't know how to express myself or how to talk. Because it takes time. It's not something that just happens. You need to get your body used to it—the frequency. Because another energy is entering your space, your body. So, it takes time. Once that happens, then there is ease. You need to be a little advanced spiritually to be able to take that energy within you. Otherwise it just goes haywire.

The medium notes that she was unable to speak when her abilities first began. She introduces the idea of a gradual progression from the initial state of crying and confoundment to the ability to communicate the voice of the saint. This process hinges on the body's adjustment to "another energy [that] is entering your space [and] your body." Her phrasing recalls Heena's description of sensing something near her; first entering one's "space," the sensed presence graduates to embodiment. This description supports Bellamy's analysis of *haziri* as a dual-staged phenomenon involving a personally experienced state and externally expressed activity.

Bridging Wonder and Ecstatic Embodiment: Spiritual Development Viewed from within and without Sidi Sufi Ritual Contexts

In the quote above, the Parsi medium introduces a hypothesis on spiritual development as it facilitates gradual acclimation to embodying the saints' presence. She addresses the point that embodying the saints may entail pain or discomfort and can ultimately go "haywire," describing someone who used to come to the shrine ten years prior:

> She used to get [*hal*], but she used to just scream. And she used to run around the *dargah*. And then, you needed four, five people to just hold her down. So—this is my conception—if you are not even slightly spiritually inclined or you don't practice any spiritual modality, [and] your body is vibrating at that particular frequency, [then] it might reject [the *hal*]. . . . It could be also that the spirit that is entering her is a more *jalali* [hot-minded] spirit and it doesn't know how to express, it could be anything. But this is my perception of it—if you've not allowed your body to vibrate at that frequency, it could not come out in a positive way, not in a gentle way.

The medium associates pain in *hal* with lack of spiritual development, which she couches in terms of the body "vibrating at [a] particular frequency" that is not conducive to assimilating the energy of the saint. This is even more apparent in the case she cites of a new medium's embodiment of a hot-minded spirit; *jalali* saints are "easily angered, difficult to deal with and may even become harmful for those who do not respect them enough" (Basu 2000, 251). Some Sidis describe the performance of miraculous feats of physical strength associated with the *hal* of *jalali* saints, such as Bava Habash. According to popular belief, Bava Habash's tomb is far away from Bava Gor's and Mai Misra's because *jalali* saints prefer distance from others. Shroff observes that the medium of Bava Habash at the Parsi shrine is likewise too *jalali* to be touched: he keeps his distance from devotees and, rather than hold devotees' hands as the medium of Bava Gor or Mai Misra usually does, he reaches out to them with the peacock feather brush that usually sits atop Bava Gor's memorial tomb.[14] The intensity of such saints suggests that acclimating to their presence may presage pain for one who is not physically ready to assimilate that "frequency" of energy.

In addition to her mediumship role at the shrine, the Parsi medium practices alternative healing modalities and is a respected master teacher of Reiki. The discourse of Reiki energy healing work emerges in her conceptualization of the process of adjusting to the presence of the saints so as to embody and mediate it. The following excerpt from a 2017 academic study of Reiki as an "agential external authority" and "object of . . . surrender" that "allow[s] for new forms of a transformed identity" among Reiki practitioners in Britain illuminates the underlying logic drawn from this discourse as it informs the Parsi medium's understanding of *hal*:

> Reiki is a thing in the form of energy and a concept relating to a "universal energy" that is directed by practitioners. As a result of their training, Reiki practitioners direct reiki—an energy that has power as a life force—through the hands. This training, which is confirmed in the attunement or initiation ritual, can be considered a "consecration" in the sense that, through the initiation, the practitioner achieves a certain relationship with reiki that allows him/her to be aware of its presence and interact with it. (Beeler 2017, 471)

Reiki involves directing "universal life force energy" through the body, particularly the hands, into the body of another. Just as Reiki is "channeled" through the hands, the presence of the saint is likewise channeled through the medium, who sustains hand-to-hand contact with devotees during communication with them.[15] Attunement to Reiki increases the initiate's awareness of the presence of the energy and ability to interact with it. Likewise, the reflections of Heena and the Parsi medium suggest that wonder as the awareness of the saints' presence graduates to the ability to embody that presence and convey it to others through verbal communication.

This description of attuning to Reiki and directing it to others reflects the underlying logic of the Parsi medium's conceptualization of spiritual development as a process that allows for gradual acclimation to the saint's energy. A Reiki attunement is an initiation ritual by which a Reiki master teacher activates a student's ability to channel Reiki; the master will attune initiates to progressively more potent levels of Reiki energy to facilitate the student's gradual transition from beginner to master (Danell 2013, 120). The Parsi medium's guidebook for Reiki students details how Reiki attunements increase the frequency at which the mind of the practitioner is vibrating, expanding the practitioner's ability to channel Reiki in a more focused and meaningful way. The Parsi medium explains that consistently channeling Reiki advances the practitioner's spiritual development.[16] Spiritual development in the context of the energy healing modality she practices involves successive attunements to higher energy frequencies, which in turn facilitate the ability to channel more focused, potent energy. She likewise equates spiritual development with the new medium's ability to easily integrate the more intense "frequencies" of the energy of the saint and gently transmit those frequencies through the communicative interactivity of *hal*: for example, she was unable to speak in *hal* until her body adjusted. Her perspective situates spiritual development as the bridge between wonder and ecstatic embodiment.

While the Parsi medium articulates this hypothesis from her perspective as a Reiki practitioner, Sidis express the same ideas in terms that are emic to the Sidi devotional tradition. A Sidi man at the shrine of Nagarchi Pir in Jambur, Gujarat has used the term "*munki* [mute] *haziri*" to indicate a person's inability to speak while embodying a saint.[17] He along with Sidis in Ahmedabad associate this with the limitations of an uninitiated medium ("*kaccha* [unrefined; immature] *pyala*") and express that taking the cup (*pyala*) of ritual initiation from a Sidi teacher (*murshid*) to become a "*pakka* [refined; mature] *pyala*" will remedy the problem. This perspective associates ritual initiation in the Sidi Sufi tradition with refinement of spiritual abilities.

A Sidi ritual practitioner in Baroda, Gujarat explains that taking initiation from a teacher transfers spiritual power from the teacher to the initiate; aspiring initiates therefore seek a teacher with great spiritual efficacy (i.e., "the teacher's prayers are heard").[18] He counsels that initiation fortifies the initiate's spiritual abilities, advancing them from "*kaccha*" to "*pakka*," and provides spiritual protection; he likens engaging in spiritual work without initiation to handling dangerous chemicals without protective gear. The Sidi ritual practitioner's insights align with the Parsi medium's conceptions of spiritual development and advancement of mediumship ability. A Reiki master teacher attunes the student to higher frequencies of energy, amplifying the student's channeling ability and fostering the student's spiritual development. Likewise, taking ritual initiation from a Sidi teacher transfers power to the initiate and hones the initiate's spiritual abilities; for example, one who could formerly only experience the saint's presence would be able to mediate the saint's presence to others through verbal communication. The Parsi medium observes that spiritual development eases the intensity of embodiment, especially of a fiery saint; the Sidi ritual specialist likewise asserts that initiation affords protection from volatile spiritual energies.

The Parsi medium reports that when she began to show "symptoms" of mediumship, such as crying and inability to speak, she was advised to "pray more often." This prescription offered at the onset of her abilities perhaps informs the intricate connections she draws between spiritual development, mediumship, and her mastery of energy healing modalities. As an actualized medium, she channels the presence not only of Mai Misra, but at times of Makbul Bava, who is entombed in the Mumbai shrine.[19] She also channels departed souls from among the community of Parsi devotees. In her case, the gift (*bakhshish*) of mediumship was such that ritual initiation from a Sidi teacher was not necessary for the refinement of her spiritual abilities; her level of spiritual development allowed her to adjust to the saints' energies and move from marveling at their presence to mediating it for the benefit of others.

Voices of the Saints:
African Diasporan Instruments of Sidi *Dhammal/Goma*

Sidi musicians visit the Mumbai shrine once annually during the death-anniversary celebrations (*urs*) of the Sidi saints, where they perform *dhammal*.[20] Sidi *dhammal* or *goma* as a genre of devotional music and ecstatic dance participates in the tradition of Sufi ritual audition (*sama*) as it incorporates remembrance (*zikr*) of God, the Prophet, and Sufi saints to generate ecstatic states (Catlin-Jairazbhoy 2004, 184–86, 193–94).[21] Sidi *dhammal* involves the performance of devotional songs called *jikar* that articulate the praise of God, the Prophet, and Sufi saints, especially the Sidi ancestor-saints. The transition of the *dhammal* performance from an initial seated sequence to the rigorous movements and tempos of its standing sequence mirrors the way in which *wajd*, a more personal, affective experience of religious transport, culminates in the exuberant expression of embodiment of the saints' presence. Shroff describes this link between *dhammal* and the climactic states of wonder during the *urs*: "The intensified tempo of drumming and dancing invites Sidis and spirit mediums of Mai Mishra and Bava Gor among them into a state of collective spirit possession. Sidis refer to this elevated experience of high energy as *majha*, translated as collective joy or ecstasy" (Shroff 2013, 22). It is at this point that the mediums begin to communicate the blessings and counsel of the embodied saints.

The instrumentation of the Sidi *dhammal* performance orchestrates this experience of wonder and mirrors its culminating aspects of embodiment and communication. With this, Sidi *dhammal* suggests the mechanics of African *ngoma* traditions involving spirit embodiment, underscoring the significance of the genre's alternate name, *goma*, which derives from the Swahili word *ngoma*. According to Shroff, Sidis as an African diasporan community in India "reinvented the practices of ngoma from fragmented memories of Africa" (Shroff 2008, 264). This section of the chapter thus examines two of the sacred instruments of Sidi *dhammal*, including the *mugarman* drum, which has no known indigenous counterpart in South Asia, and the "Mai Misra" rattle, as they perpetuate the correspondences between instruments, rhythms, and spirits observed in continental African *ngoma* traditions (see Catlin-Jairazbhoy 2004, 189–90, 193; 2010, 129–33, 137–38, 143). This analysis highlights the Sidi *dhammal* performance as an African diasporan musical tradition that mediates the experience of wonder at Sidi Sufi saint shrines in South Asia.

In his canonical study, John Janzen identifies the *ngoma* drum as the primary instrument of *ngoma* healing and trance-possession rituals: "In the belt across the middle of the continent, from Kongo to Swahili . . . *ngoma* refers primarily to the elongated wooden drum with a single membrane attached at one end with pegs. . . . In societies where trance-possession and therapeutic cults are present, *ngoma* more than any other drum is used in this therapeutic setting, to the accompaniment of shakers and singing" (Janzen 1992, 70). Likewise, the Sidi *goma* performance features the sacred *mugarman* drum and the "Mai Misra" rattle, which accompany the recitation of devotional songs (*jikar*). Amy Catlin-Jairazbhoy compares the *mugarman* to a Zimbabwean *ngoma* drum, noting, "Similar types of pegged drumheads and footed drums are widespread on the east coast of Africa, while they are otherwise unknown in India."[22] She cites Abdulaziz Lodhi's etymology of the term *mugarman* as an "abbreviation of the [Bantu/Swahili] phrase '*ngoma ya magulu mane*' (four-legged drum). In several places, '*magulman*' is not only the name of the drum but also the dances danced with it and the songs sung with it." The term *mugarman* therefore describes a four-legged *ngoma* (drum), and in some sites among Sidis carries the same semantic range as *ngoma* ("song" and "dance") does in continental African contexts, rendering *mugarman* synonymous in such instances with the usage of the term *ngoma*. What the *ngoma* drum is to the *ngoma* healing and trance-possession rituals of eastern, central, and southern Africa, the *mugarman* is to the Sidi *dhammal/goma* tradition of South Asia.

Sacred instruments of African origin played in honor of African Sufi saints memorialize the African heritage of the Sidi devotional tradition and its custodians not only in India, but in Pakistan as well. Detailing the Pakistani Shidi community's *urs* observances in Karachi, Basu observes that the *mugarman* "is treated as one of the most sacred objects of the cult . . . [and] orchestrates the interplay of rhythms created by other drums" during the *goma* performance (Basu 2000, 260). These rhythms correspond to seven sister saints, among whom Pakistani Shidis name Mai Misra as well as a figure called Mai Goma: "Seven rhythms, each of which is associated with one female saint, are played on different types of drums. Collectively, these rhythms—which establish a relationship with the female saint Mai Goma—are referred to as *goma*, i.e., by the word that also denotes the dances and is suggestive of the Swahili meaning of *ngoma*, dance" (Basu 2000, 259–60). Basu discerns that the names of the Sidi saints serve as "tags for memorial clusters"—Mai Misra and Bava Habash, for example, point to Arabic names for Egypt and Ethiopia respectively, from whose markets enslaved Africans entered other polities in the northwestern Indian Ocean world (Basu 2000, 260). Likewise, the name of the saint Mai Goma recollects the *ngoma* traditions of eastern, central, and southern Africa, which the Sidi *dhammal/goma* performance memorializes in South Asia.

The Karachi *urs* associates each of the seven rhythms of the *goma* performance with one of seven ancestor-saints. A precedent for this direct correlation between rhythm and spirit exists in Tanzanian *ngoma* traditions. "In Tanzania, . . . waganga [healers] and music experts also point to the association of spirits in ngoma and distinctive rhythms. . . . For Botoli Laie, a mganga [healer] from Kilwa in Tanzania, specific instruments play distinctive rhythms appropriate to each spirit" (Janzen 1992, 126). Additionally, "the drumming is considered to be the voice or influence of the ancestral shades or other spirits" (Janzen 1992, 1). Thus, a particular rhythm can be understood to be the cadence of the voice of the unique spirit with which it is associated. For example, the healer Botoli Laie works with Ngoma Mbungi, a type of *ngoma* therapeutic cult that features five ngoma drums. These drums "represent five up-country *masheitani* [spirits] . . . each of which is roused and manipulated by its own drum" (Janzen 1992, 25). This suggests a bidirectionality of the *ngoma* drum, which rouses and manipulates the spirit associated with it and articulates that spirit's voice or influence.

The Gujarati lyrics of one Sidi devotional song gesture toward this intercommunicative dynamic: "The *damama* beats, the *musindo* beats, the 'Mai Misra' beats. Tell us, Mother, tell us will you come playing or not?" (*Damamu vage, musindo vage, vage Mai Misra. Bolo Mari bolo ramva avsho ke nahi?*). The narrator of this verse asks whether Mai Misra will make her presence known in response to the rhythms of *dhammal*, produced by percussion instruments such as the coconut-shell rattle that bears her name. Among the Tanzanian healer's paraphernalia are "gourd shakers" which here find a counterpart in the "Mai Misra" rattle (Janzen 1992, 24). The gynomorphic appearance of the rattle, its component parts, and its method of assembly evoke Mai Misra's water-pot (*kalas/ghat*), a symbolic embodiment of the saint that shares in the materiality of the ritual installation of a jar-form of a Hindu goddess (*ghatasthapana*) (see Graves 2022). The protocol for assembling the rattle suggests that its preparation, like that of the *kalas*, is a symbolic process of embodiment. The rattle is wrapped in a "ritually sanctioned cloth" of the same kind that is used to cover the *kalas*.[23] The rattle's adornment with this cloth signifies its function as a material medium not only of Mai Misra's voice, but of her charisma. For example, Sidis playing the "Mai Misra" may pass its cloth skirt over the head of an infant, a gesture that denotes the transference of Mai Misra's blessings to the child through the instrument (see Catlin-Jairazbhoy 2010, 137–38). The rattle's appearance, assembly and usage indicate its sacredness as a percussion instrument directly associated with Mai Misra.

Furthermore, the storage of the "Mai Misra" rattle emphasizes its role as a musical medium of the saint's voice and charisma. As a sacred instrument, the rattle must be placed inside of a shrine, including a household shrine, or hung above the ground in a special red or green bag (*jholi*) made specifically for holding *dhammal* instruments. The rattle or the bag holding it must never be placed on the floor: a fallen "Mai Misra" augurs the death of one of her companions (*sahelis*)—that is, a Sidi woman. Similarly, mishaps with other *dhammal* instruments portend the death of a *dhammali* (*dhammal* player)—a Sidi man. These omens underscore the notion that *dhammal* instruments communicate messages from the saints.

Housed ceremonially inside of shrines, decorated with ritually sanctioned cloth, and even venerated with incense, the sacred instruments of Sidi *dhammal/goma* mediate the spiritual energy of the ancestor-saints.[24] This section's brief study of connections between musical instruments, rhythms, and spirits in continental African *ngoma* traditions underscores the role of the instruments of Sidi *dhammal* in, like spirit mediums, embodying the charisma and conveying the voices of the Sidi ancestor-saints. The instruments of the *dhammal* performance orchestrate devotees' experience of wonder, an ecstatic state that culminates in the verbal conveyance of information and physical conveyance of healing energy from saints, through their mediums, to supplicants.

Conclusion

This chapter explores the workings of wonder, identified as *wajd*, in the Sidi devotional tradition. The music performance called Sidi *dhammal* or *goma* facilitates the affective experience of wonder at the immaterial presence of the Sidi ancestor-saints. This state culminates in the ecstatic trance of *hal*, connoting the embodiment of the presence (*haziri*) of the saints. The instrumentation and dynamics of the *dhammal* performance influence the experience of ecstasy in ritual contexts and set the stage for the embodied saints' communication of blessings and counsel to devotees.

The Sidi *dhammal* performance and the vocabulary of mediumship at the Sidi saint shrine evidence the multivocality of the Sidi devotional tradition.[25] The term multivocality in this context suggests that a single element may convey multiple meanings simultaneously. As discussed above, the terms *haziri* and *hal* are multivocal both within the Sidi tradition and in other Indian Islamic contexts of healing and devotional practice. The *dhammal* performance itself is multivocal, suggesting at one level a genre of Sufi devotional music based on the practice of remembrance, and on another level expressing the logic of continental African *ngoma* traditions, as its alternate name *goma* suggests. In this way, Sidi *dhammal* evidences the African diasporan heritage of this Indian Sufi devotional tradition, its saints, and the Sidi community of devotees.

Notes

1. For more on the Sidi devotional tradition and its saints, see Basu (1998, 2003). See also Jeychandran (2020), Catlin-Jairazbhoy and Alpers (2004), and Graves (2019). For more on the history of the African diaspora in India, see Robbins and McLeod (2006) and Pankhurst (2003). For more on the Sidis of Mumbai, see Shroff (2007).

2. For more on the history and devotional life of this shrine, see Shroff (2004, 2008, 2013). See also Graves Eyssallenne (2022).

3. For more on Sidi *dhammal*, see Catlin-Jairazbhoy (2004, 2010, 2012).

4. Interviews conducted by the author in Mumbai in March and April 2019.

5. See Erndl (2006, 164) for use of the term *sawari* in the context of possession by the Hindu goddess Durga.

6. Interviewed by Beheroze Shroff in her 2005 film *Voices of the Sidis: Ancestral Links*.

7. For a description Mai Misra's *ghat*, see Shroff (2013, 22). For Mai Misra's *ghat/kalas* rituals, see Graves (2019, 2022).

8. From participant-observation in Mumbai in April 2018.

9. Bellamy (2011, 26). Unless otherwise noted, quotations in this paragraph are drawn from this page.

10. From an interview conducted by the author on March 29, 2019. Unless otherwise noted, all quotations from the Parsi medium are drawn from this interview.

11. From an interview conducted by the author in Mumbai on October 30, 2019.

12. Communication in Ahmedabad in December 2018.

13. From an interview conducted in Hindi on April 2, 2019, in Mumbai. Unless otherwise noted, all quotations from Heena are drawn from this interview and have been translated by the author.

14. From personal communication on July 8, 2020.

15. The terminology of "channeling" Reiki is used in the Parsi medium's Reiki guidebook. For the use of this terminology with regard to spirit mediumship, see also Spencer (2001, 343–60).

16. From the Parsi medium's Reiki manual and personal communication on December 14, 2020.

17. Communication in Jambur on April 7, 2019.

18. Communication in Baroda on December 12, 2018.

19. From meetings with Beheroze Shroff and Parsi mediums of Mai Misra on August 11–16, 2017.

20. The subheading for this section is inspired by Shroff's *Voices of the Sidis* documentaries.

21. For a discussion of trance and *qawwali*, see Flueckiger (2006, 211–21).

22. The information in this paragraph is drawn from Catlin-Jairazbhoy (2010, 129).

23. Phrase in quotes from Catlin-Jairazbhoy (2010, 130).

24. For a description of this regarding the *mugarman* see Catlin-Jairazbhoy (2010, 129–30).

25. See Orsini (2014, 228) for definition and application of the term "multivocality." See also Graves (2022) for the application of this term in the context of the Sidi devotional tradition.

Works Cited

Basu, Helene. 1998. "Hierarchy and Emotion: Love, Joy and Sorrow in a Cult of Black Saints in Gujarat, India." In *Embodying Charisma: Modernity, Locality, and Performance of Emotion in Sufi Cults*, edited by Pnina Werbner and Helene Basu, 87–101. London: Routledge.

———. 2000. "Theatre of Memory: Ritual Kinship Performances of the African Diaspora in Pakistan." In *Culture, Creation, and Procreation: Concepts of Kinship in South Asian Practice*, edited by Monika Bock and Aparna Rao, 243–70. New York: Berghahn.

———. 2008. "A Gendered Indian Ocean Site: Mai Mishra, African Spirit Possession and Sidi Women in Gujarat." In *Journeys and Dwellings: Indian Ocean Themes in South Asia*, edited by Helene Basu, 227–55. Hyderabad: Orient Longman.

Beeler, Dori. 2017. "Reiki as Surrender: Evidence of an External Authority." *Journal of Contemporary Religion* 32 (3): 465–78.

Bellamy, Carla. 2011. *The Powerful Ephemeral: Everyday Healing in an Ambiguously Islamic Place*. Berkeley: University of California Press.

Catlin-Jairazbhoy, Amy. 2004. "A Sidi CD? Globalisation of Music and the Sacred." In *Sidis and Scholars: Essays on African Indians*, edited by Amy Catlin-Jairazbhoy and Edward Alpers, 178–211. Noida: Rainbow.

———. 2010. "Sidi Music in Western India: Remembering an African Heritage." In *Remembered Rhythms: Essays on Diaspora and the Music of India*, edited by Shubha Chaudhuri and Anthony Seeger, 125–58. London: Seagull.

———. 2012. "Sacred Pleasure, Pain and Transformation in African Indian Sidi Sufi Ritual and Performance." *Performing Islam* 1 (1): 73–100.

Danell, Jenny-Ann Brodin. 2013. "On the Boundaries of Medicine and Spirituality: Professionalization and Self-Regulation of Reiki in Sweden." *International Journal for the Study of New Religions* 4 (1): 113–38.

Erndl, Kathleen. 2006. "Possession by Durga: The Mother Who Possesses." In *The Life of Hinduism*, edited by John Stratton Hawley and Vasudha Narayanan, 158–70. Berkeley: University of California Press.

Flueckiger, Joyce Burkhalter. 2006. *In Amma's Healing Room: Gender and Vernacular Islam in South India*. Bloomington: Indian University Press.

Graves, Jazmin. 2019. "Filling the Pot: The Remembrance of African Sufi Ancestor-Saints and the Reclamation of African Historical Heritage in Ahmedabad, Gujarat." *Journal of Africana Religions*, 7 (1): 94–104.

———. 2022. "A Tree Enrooted: African Sufi Saints as "Lineage Deities" of a Muslim Community of East African Ancestry in Western India (Gujarat and Mumbai)." In *Routledge Handbook on Islam in Asia*, edited by Chiara Formichi, 335–50. London: Routledge.

Graves Eyssallenne, Jazmin. 2022. "Mumbai, Where Indian Ocean Diasporas and Cosmopolitanisms Meet." *JSTOR Daily*. https://daily.jstor.org/mumbai-indian-ocean-diasporas-cosmpolitanisms-meet/.

Janzen, John. 1992. *Ngoma: Discourses of Healing in Central and Southern Africa*. Berkley: University of California Press.

Jeychandran, Neelima. 2020. "Charismatic Afterlives of African Saints and Martyrs: Sidi Sacred Geography and Spiritual Practices in Gujarat." In *Afro-South Asia in the Global African Diaspora: African Diasporan Communities across South Asia*, edited by Omar H. Ali et al., 77–91. Greensboro: University of North Carolina at Greensboro Ethiopian and East African Studies Project.

Orsini, Francesca. 2014. "'Krishna Is the Truth of Man': Mir 'Abdul Wahid Bilgrami's *Haqā'iq-i Hindī* (Indian Truths) and the Circulation of *Dhrupad* and *Bishnupad*." In *Culture and Circulation*, edited by Allison Busch and Thomas De Bruijn, 222–46. Leiden: Brill.

Pankhurst, Richard. 2003. "The Ethiopian Diaspora to India: The Role of Habshis and Sidis from Medieval Times to the End of the Eighteenth Century." In *The African Diaspora in the Indian Ocean*, edited by Shihan de Silva Jayasuriya and Richard Pankhurst, 189–222. Trenton: Africa World Press.

Platts, John T. 1884. *A Dictionary of Urdu, Classical Hindi, and English*. London: W. H. Allen.

Robbins, Kenneth X., and John McLeod, eds. 2006. *African Elites in India: Habshi Amarat*. Ahmedabad: Mapin.

Shroff, Beheroze. 2004. "Sidis and Parsis: A Filmmaker's Notes." In *Sidis and Scholars: Essays on African Indians*, edited by Amy Catlin-Jairazbhoy and Edward Alpers, 159–77. Trenton, NJ: Red Sea Press.

———. 2005. *Voices of the Sidis: Two Documentaries*. Irvine, CA: B. F. Shroff. DVD.

———. 2007. "Sidis in Mumbai: Negotiating Identities between Mumbai and Gujarat." *African and Asian Studies* 6:305–19.

———. 2008. "Spiritual Journeys: Parsis and Sidi Saints." In *Journeys and Dwellings: Indian Ocean Themes in South Asia*, edited by Helene Basu, 256–75. Hyderabad: Orient Longman.

———. 2013. "Goma is Going On: Sidis of Gujarat." *African Arts* 46 (1): 18–25.

Spencer, Wayne. 2001. "To Absent Friends: Classical Spiritualist Mediumship and New Age Channeling Compared and Contrasted." *Journal of Contemporary Religion* 16 (3): 343–60.

Van Der Veer, Peter. 1992. "Playing or Praying: A Sufi Saint's Day in Surat." *Journal of Asian Studies* 51 (3): 545–64.

Werbner, Pnina, and Helene Basu, eds. 1998. *Embodying Charisma: Modernity, Locality and the Performance of Emotion in Sufi Cults*. London: Routledge.

Chapter 5

Wonder as Affect on the Kuchipudi Stage

HARSHITA MRUTHINTI KAMATH

As the lights rise on a darkened stage, the clanging sound of a bell resounds against the backdrop of the melodious notes of a flute. From the far corner of stage right, two dancers dressed in cerulean blue costumes enter onstage, their steady walk matching the beats of the *mridangam*, the South Indian double-barrel drum. The dancers gracefully move toward upstage center while holding a white curtain stretched wide between them. Glimpses of red silk pleats and black cloth peak from underneath the white curtain, which is held in midair to shield a third dancer from view. The voice of a male vocalist, who is seated with the orchestra to the side of stage right, is amplified over the symphony of instruments as he begins to sing a Sanskrit hymn (*stotra*) in praise of the Hindu deity Shiva and his consort Parvati.

Reaching the center of the stage, the two dancers position themselves in front of a golden wooden archway, flanked by a silvery trident. The third dancer, still hidden from view, sits down on a bench covered with animal skin and stretches out their left foot, the visible portion of the dancer's leg draped with pleats of red silk. The other two dancers remain in place, holding the curtain between them and striking their feet flat on the floor in synch with the music. When the vocalist finishes the final line of the hymn, the two dancers walk rhythmically toward stage left, carrying the curtain with them. As they exit, the third dancer, seated on the bench in the center of the stage, comes into view. This dancer holds the corner of a sheer black veil in their raised right hand.

The other edge of the veil is vertically pinned down the middle of the dancer's body, thus preventing the audience from seeing their right side. The left side of the dancer, however, is clearly visible: the stitched silk costume in auspicious red tones, white and orange flowers adorning the crown of the head, and golden bangles dangling from an outstretched left hand. A female vocalist begins to sing:

> champeya gaurardha sharirakayai
> champeya gaurardha sharirakayai
>
> Her body shines like a golden flower.
> Her body shines like a golden flower.[1]

With the second repetition of the line, the dancer slowly rises and gracefully moves forward, alternating from right to left foot to move toward center stage. Adorned with glistening gold ornaments, the dancer's movements are sinuous and slow, prompting the audience to connect the words—*champeya gaurardha sharirakayai* (her body shines like a golden flower)—with the embodied form of the dancer onstage. The vocalist then sings the next line of the song:

> karpura gaurardha sharirakaya
> karpura gaurardha sharirakaya
>
> His body shines like white camphor.
> His body shines like white camphor.

With these words, the dancer deftly transfers the corner of the black veil from right hand to left, and now the dancer's righthand side appears in view, with the left hidden behind the veil. A velvet tiger-print cloth covers the dancer's chest, which is adorned with long golden chains. An ornamental armband, decorated with the hood of a snake, sits on the dancer's upper right arm, and rows of bells are wrapped around their wrist. Three horizontal white lines are painted across the dancer's forehead and a topknot of brown matted hair adorns the crown of their head. With this shift of the veil from left to right hands, the goddess transforms into Shiva:

> dhammillakayai cha jatadharaya
> dhammillakayai cha jatadharaya

Her hair is studded with ornaments, his is matted.
Her hair is studded with ornaments, his is matted.

With these next two lines, the dancer nimbly moves the black veil back and forth, revealing the left-hand side of the goddess and the right-hand side of Shiva in quick succession. As the stanza comes to an end, the vocalist sings:

namah shivayai cha namah shivaya
namah shivayai cha namah shivaya

I bow to the goddess, I bow to Shiva.
I bow to the goddess, I bow to Shiva.

Then, shifting the veil from left hand to right, the dancer turns clockwise in a circle, and the goddess comes back to face the audience, her eyes darting alluringly in a sideways glance. As the two lines repeat again, Shiva appears once more, his facial expressions emoting a serious tone.

For the remainder of the piece, the dancer alternates across both sides of their body, sometimes displaying the graceful movements of the goddess and sometimes displaying the vigorous steps of Shiva. The shifts from goddess to Shiva and back are often exaggerated, alternating from coy glances to fierce looks intending to demarcate a clear shift in gender. The black veil nimbly transferred from right to left aids the gender transformation, with costume seamlessly supporting bodily movement. Bare chested male attendants, who enter onstage after the first verse of the song, dance alongside the center dancer, and their energetic jumps serve as a contrast to the goddess's graceful steps when she appears from behind the veil. The item ends as the attendants gather in a circle in the center of the stage, the main dancer once again hidden from view. As a group, they exit the darkened stage.

This item serves as the climactic scene of the Kuchipudi dance drama *Ardhanareeswara* choreographed by Chennai-based guru Vempati Chinna Satyam (1929–2012) in the 1990s and performed in the United States under Chinna Satyam's direction in 1998. The main dancer described here is Vempati Ravi Shankar (1969–2018), Chinna Satyam's youngest child and second son, who played the role of Shiva in the start of the drama and the role of Ardhanarishvara in the second part of the drama. *Ardhanareeswara* is a collection of Puranic stories featuring Shiva, beginning with the story of how Shiva bears the burden of the river Ganga, personified as a goddess. Upset at her husband's attention to Ganga, the goddess Parvati angrily leaves Shiva's heavenly abode. Shiva appeases Parvati by agreeing to merge with her form, resulting in the climactic scene of the dance drama with the appearance of Ardhanarishvara, whose name literally translates as "the god who is half woman."

Trained in Chinna Satyam's style of Kuchipudi, I have always marveled at Ravi Shankar's ability to enact the character of Ardhanarishvara in the final scene of the *Ardhanareeswara* dance drama. In fact, every time I have watched Ravi Shankar perform Ardhanarishvara, particularly his nimble manipulation of the veil from one side of his body to another, his expertly cast glances of the goddess, and his sharp gestures as Shiva, I am washed over with wonder. In these moments, I am reminded of wonder as a break from the everyday through "its extraordinariness, suddenness, and seemingly divine-like rupturing of the mundane" (Srinivas 2018, 6). Wonder is grounded in the creativity of the embodied gesture, particularly the nimble shift of the veil from one hand to the other.

In this chapter, I trace the affective experience of wonder in watching Ravi Shankar's enactment of Ardhanarishvara in the Kuchipudi dance drama *Ardhanareeswara*. I turn to the work of Sara Ahmed ([2004] 2014) to frame wonder as an affective emotion grounded in past histories of contact between bodies and objects, particularly between brahmin bodies and Sanskritized Indian dance. I read wonder as an affective emotion that sticks to Ravi Shankar's brahmin body and generates a caste-based aesthetic of beauty for me, a brahmin audience member. In reading wonder through the lens of affect theory, I explore what T. M. Krishna (2018) refers to as the "ugliness of beauty," or the casteist practices that undergird the production of aesthetics on the Kuchipudi stage. I also interrogate the utility of Indian aesthetic theory for reading wonder in Kuchipudi and Indian dance, more broadly.

Although I first watched the dance drama live when it was performed in the United States in 1998, I draw on the publicly available VHS recording of *Ardhanareeswara* (Chinna Satyam 1998) distributed by the Sri Venkateswara Temple in Pittsburgh to ground my performance analysis in this chapter. I also draw on my ethnographic fieldwork with Kuchipudi dancers based in the eponymous village of Kuchipudi, Andhra Pradesh, and in Hyderabad, Telangana, and Chennai, Tamil Nadu (Kamath 2019). In particular, my conversations and interactions with Vempati Ravi Shankar in Chennai and his sister Chavali Balatripurasundari in Hyderabad undergird my experience of watching *Ardhanareeswara*.[2] My training in Kuchipudi dance with Atlanta-based dancer, Sasikala Penumarthi, a disciple of Chinna Satyam's, as well as with dance teachers in India, including Ravi Shankar and Balatripurasundari, inform my analysis of wonder in Ravi Shankar's enactment of the role of Ardhanarishvara.

Ravi Shankar as Ardhanarishvara

I first met Vempati Ravi Shankar in October 2009 in Vijayawada, Andhra Pradesh, when I attended a performance of his dance drama *Navadurga* (Nine Goddesses). At the time, I had just started fieldwork in Hyderabad and was taking weekly classes with Ravi Shankar's sister Chavali Balatripurasundari (whom I refer to as Baliakka) to keep up my dance practice. Baliakka was performing as one of the goddesses in her brother's dance drama and invited me to attend the performance. I had heard about Ravi Shankar's legendary dance skills and was excited to watch his choreography. A few weeks after the dance drama, Ravi Shankar's kidney suddenly failed after a successful transplant a number of years earlier. His sisters were distraught at the news of their younger brother's health; at the time, Ravi Shankar's career was on the rise, and he was becoming known in Kuchipudi dance circles as an experienced dancer and choreographer. By the time I met Ravi Shankar again in spring 2010, his life revolved around his dialysis schedule, and many of my interviews were punctuated by the sounds of dialysis machines and the chatter of staff at the Chennai hospital where he received dialysis three times a week. During my fieldwork, I had the opportunity to watch Ravi Shankar teach the role of Ardhanarishvara to a younger male dancer visiting from the United States, and I also learned items from Ravi Shankar's choreography. Ravi Shankar never recovered from this kidney failure and passed away in February 2018 due to complications from a kidney transplant. My experiences interacting with Ravi Shankar were limited to this final decade of his life, in which his health overshadowed his ability to engage fully with dance. However, his extensive collection of video and VCD recordings and his willingness to speak to me about his background, choreography, and dance techniques inform my understanding of his performance of Ardhanarishvara.

A few years before Ravi Shankar was born, his father, Vempati Chinna Satyam, opened the Kuchipudi Art Academy (KAA) in Chennai in 1963, a dance school that would soon revolutionize the Kuchipudi curriculum and train hundreds of dancers over the course of Chinna Satyam's lifetime. A brahmin from the Kuchipudi village who moved to Chennai early in his career, Chinna Satyam abandoned the custom of only teaching the village's brahmin men and began to teach men and women across castes in his urban dance school. However, Chinna Satyam had little interest in teaching his five children to dance. In particular, he discouraged his three daughters from dancing, citing that it was not custom to teach women from the village's brahmin families to dance.[3] Despite his father's disinclination to formally initiate him in dance, Ravi Shankar began learning from Bala Kondala Rao, a lead female dancer at the KAA who took an interest in her guru's son. Ravi Shankar described to me that these lessons with Kondala Rao were done in secret after everyone else in the dance institute was asleep. He began learning around the age of eight and soon mastered the basic steps (*adavus*), combination of steps (*jatis*), and dance items of his father's repertoire. Soon, Kondala Rao felt the time was right to show Ravi Shankar's dance to his father; Ravi Shankar narrates:

> On the day of Vijaya Dashami [a Hindu festival], she made me wear silk clothes, and put me in the front row. My father saw me and said, "Why did he come? Make him go aside." She responded, "Give him a chance to dance also. Please watch him." So, I started dancing with everybody, and he finally saw me. He didn't say anything but afterwards he told my mother, "It's okay. He's doing well." That was it. After that he never used to bother how I was dancing.[4]

With his father's tacit consent, Ravi Shankar soon began taking part in the KAA's various dance dramas, which usually involved a cast of thirty to forty dancers. Ravi Shankar first performed smaller roles and made his way up to performing the lead roles of his father's dance dramas. During the height of his career, Ravi Shankar was frequently cast as Shiva in his father's dance dramas, including *Srinivasa Kalyanam* (Marriage of Srinivasa), *Haravilasam* (Play of Shiva), and *Ardhanareeswara*. Among these three, Ravi Shankar described his favorite portrayal of Shiva to be in *Ardhanareeswara*. In the dance drama, Ravi Shankar began the opening scenes by portraying the character of Shiva and then rapidly changed costumes at the end of the drama to portray the dual-gendered character of Ardhanarishvara. Ravi Shankar said that he first performed the character of Ardhanarishvara in a solo item performance staged at the Sri Venkateswara Temple in Pittsburgh in 1994. Then, in 1997, his father engaged scriptwriter S. V. Bhujangaraya Sarma, who composed the script for the dance drama *Ardhanareeswara*, which was performed the following year on the KAA's tour in the United States. The choreography, according to Ravi Shankar, was a collaborative effort between father and son:

> When doing the composing, so many changes came about. My father researched how to show Shiva from one side and how to show Parvati from one side, and which angle to turn to show the depth of the face. I used to practice every day. My father taught me the basic framework of the movement, but that's it. He didn't tell me anything else. He would tell me, "Whatever is natural for Shiva, do it like that. Whatever is natural for a woman, do it like that."[5]

Initially, Ravi Shankar struggled with the movements, particularly when portraying the gender distinction between Shiva and the goddess. While he felt comfortable portraying Shiva, he described that he struggled with enacting the goddess; initially, he felt the movements were too rigid and then, after a period of time, he thought they were too expressive of the goddess's femininity. It was only after several practice sessions that Ravi Shankar felt comfortable with the transition between Shiva and the goddess, particularly when doing the character of Ardhanarishvara in *vesham* (costume). He described:

> There's the line in the item, "*Ambodhara shyamala kuntalayai*," which means that the Goddess's braid is so long, it's very black and thick. When moving the right leg, I used to point it. When moving the left leg, I used to move my hip in this way. This way, that way. This way, that way. It used to be lots of fun, that walk. At first, I used to feel that it was a bit difficult. But after wearing the *vesham* and dancing, I was able to do it with ease and a happy feeling would come about. I told you that although my father only taught me the basic movements, I thought about how to enact the character, how to walk, how to move. When looking as Shiva, I looked like

this. When looking as the goddess, I used to look like this. I created all of these myself.[6]

When donning the costume, which was specially designed for this role, Ravi Shankar never enlisted the help of a makeup artist, which is common for most India-based Kuchipudi dancers. Instead, he insisted on doing his own makeup; he described this process to me:

> Everything must add up: your face, the proper proportion of each part of your body, they all add to the beauty of the presentation. [*signaling with hands*] Your forehead has to be this much, your nose has to be this much, your lip size has to be this much, your chin must be proportionate. . . . Your nose must be sharp. The makeup for your eyes shouldn't be too big, but it shouldn't be too small. Everything should add up. If you wear makeup, it should be mind-blowing. In the *Ardhanareeswaram* photos, I did my own makeup.[7]

Ravi Shankar's enactment of Ardhanarishvara marked the height of his career; although other KAA dancers eventually learned to perform the character, no one could match his skill enacting two characters—Shiva and the goddess—in a single piece. Speaking to me more than two decades after his 1998 performances as Ardhanarishvara and Shiva, Ravi Shankar expressed satisfaction that no other dancer was able to enact the character in the way he could. "No one did the character after me. Nobody is daring to do that character," he said simply.[8]

Although other dancers have, in fact, tried to perform Ardhanarishvara over the years, at the time, I found myself agreeing with Ravi Shankar's frank assessment: he is, at least according to me, the most successful dancer to portray Ardhanarishvara. In fact, when I watch Ravi Shankar enact the character of Ardhanarishvara in the final scene of the *Ardhanareeswara* dance drama, I am still washed over with wonder. But where is this feeling of wonder generated? How does my embodied experience as a brahmin woman and dancer shape my experience of wonder? Why do I read Ravi Shankar's wondrous performance as aesthetically beautiful? In the next section, I attempt to engage these questions of wonder by turning to affect theory to reframe my approach to wonder in Kuchipudi. I contend that affect, rather than Sanskrit aesthetic theory, is a more useful frame for untangling the relationship between wonder and caste on the Kuchipudi stage.

Wonder as Affect

In *The Cultural Politics of Emotion* ([2004] 2014), Sara Ahmed turns to affect to frame the feelings of pain, disgust, shame, and love. She asserts that feeling is neither simply an internal emotion residing within the body nor is it an external state generated outside the body that impresses itself within (10). Rather, Ahmed proposes that emotions are economic; they circulate, or *slide*, between bodies, objects, and signs (44). This movement across bodies generates *affect*, or the intensities or resonances that move from body to body (Seigworth and Gregg 2010, 1). For Ahmed, affect is historically grounded; she analyzes how emotions such as fear and disgust are grounded upon histories of racism and imperialism by turning to examples such as when Charles Darwin feels disgust when his food is touched by a "naked savage" ([2004] 2014, 62, 82).[9] Ahmed underscores that "these histories have already impressed upon the surface of the bodies at the same time as they create new impressions. So while emotions may be experienced as 'inside out' or 'outside in,' they actually work to generate the distinction between inside and outside" (194). Emotions, for Ahmed, are performative: in reading the other as being "disgusting," for example, "the subject is filled up with disgust, as a sign of the truth of the reading" (194). In other words, the affective experience of disgust enables us to experience an external object as disgusting within our bodies.

The concepts of repetition and stickiness are also important for understanding the affective economies Ahmed analyzes. In the case of disgust, for example, Ahmed (94) notes that the speech act—"That's disgusting!"—must be repeated to have affect, in line with Judith Butler's ([1993] 2011) analysis of the performativity of speech. However, repetition must be coupled with *stickiness*, a term that Ahmed employs to understand how an affect such as disgust or fear clings to certain bodies and objects as opposed to others (91). When analyzing disgust, for example, Ahmed notes the discursively constructed nature of stickiness: "To name something as disgusting is to transfer the stickiness of the word 'disgust' to an object, which henceforth becomes generated as the very thing that is spoken" (94).

Ahmed's notion of stickiness is taken up by Jasbir Puar (2007) when analyzing hate crimes committed against Sikh turbaned men in post-9/11 America. For Puar, "the turban is thus a 'sticky' signifier, operating as a fetish object of fear, and the ontological becoming of the turbaned Sikh is intrinsically tied into the temporal logic of preempting his futurity, a deferred death, a becoming that is sutured through its failure, its decay" (187). More recently, Shailaja Paik (2022) employs Ahmed's notion of stickiness to discuss how the concept of *ashlil* (vulgar) sticks to Dalit bodies particularly in the context of Tamasha performance. Linking stickiness with caste, Paik writes: "Although Ambedkar did not himself use the word *ashlil*, he did capture the essence of the ashlil sticking to the Untouchable when he referred to a 'protective discoulouration' that cannot be peeled off and that prevents the realization of an authentic selfhood. Untouchables could not escape their ascribed status due to the caste order" (3).

Indebted to the work of Puar (2007) and Paik (2022), here, I employ Ahmed's theorizations on affect—including its histories of contact, sliding movement across bodies and objects, and the stickiness of signs—to read wonder on the Kuchipudi stage. Returning to the opening vignette, dancer Ravi Shankar is hidden behind a white curtain and slowly enters onstage, accompanied by two supporting dancers. When he reveals his identity as both the goddess and Shiva through the first lines of the item, a breakthrough into wonder materializes through the transference of the veil. By shifting the veil from his right hand to left, Ravi Shankar as the goddess becomes Ravi Shankar as Shiva, a sideways movement that is repeated throughout the item. As an audience member, I watch transfixed, eagerly anticipating the next shift of the veil, which entails the next transformation from goddess to Shiva and back. When watching Ravi Shankar as Ardhanarishvara, wonder washes over me.

Indeed, my own dance training frames this feeling of wonder. While I struggled (and continue to struggle) to fashion a gesture or emote an expression in my dance classrooms, Ravi Shankar exhibits an ease in performing Ardhanarishvara, one I witnessed firsthand when he taught a student to perform the role in Hyderabad during my fieldwork. This feeling of wonder, I have always assumed, must extend not only to me, but to all others watching Ravi Shankar. For example, I regularly show clips from the Ardhanarishvara item to my undergraduate students and find myself eagerly listening for the audible gasp in the classroom after the repetition of the first line—*champeya gaurardha sharirakayai*—when Ravi Shankar, as the goddess, shifts the veil and transforms into Shiva. I feel a sense of satisfaction when I hear the gasp, knowing that the students likely feel some sense of wonder just as I do when watching Ravi Shankar as Ardhanarishvara.

Where is this feeling of wonder generated? Reading wonder through the lens of affect, I argue that wonder is both produced by the embodied movements of the dancer and generated inside me, the viewer. The fact that Ravi Shankar can easily shift from the goddess to Shiva with the flip of the veil generates wonder in me, the cisgender brahmin female dancer. As I watch the male body dancing the goddess, I marvel at the skill of a man donning the *stri-vesham* (a woman's guise) better than I ever can. My years of dancing and failing in dance impress the feeling of wonder on my body. My ethnographic experience of dancing in India and being told that I am not womanly enough in my dance further this impression of wonder (Kamath 2019, 26). Wonder is thus generated "outside in" (from Ravi Shankar's dancing body) and "inside out" (from my own gendered, dancing body).

However, it is no accident that Ravi Shankar, and not another dancer, invokes wonder in me, a brahmin viewer. Ravi Shankar as Ardhanarishvara generates an affective response of wonder in me because of my past histories of contact. As a brahmin woman educated in a brahmin-dominated art form, the genealogy of which I will return to later in this chapter, I hold in my body years of knowledge that can discern the perfect execution of Chinna Satyam's brahmin choreography. In other words, as a brahmin dancer, *I am trained to view the brahmin body as wondrous*. Very few dancers are capable of enacting Chinna Satyam's choreography with precision; Ravi Shankar is one. This sense of wonder is augmented with the manipulation of the veil, which enables the rapid gender transformations throughout the item; wonder slides from inorganic matter (veil) to organic matter (Ravi Shankar's body), to paraphrase Puar (2007, 187). Ravi Shankar's brahmin body and the veil he holds are "sticky" signifiers that operate as aesthetic, fetishized objects of wonder.

To help further contextualize wonder, it is helpful to turn to the work of Carnatic musician and activist T. M. Krishna (2018). The presumption that art is beautiful, according to Krishna, is always already rendered through a gendered and casteist lens, a process he characterizes as the "ugliness of beauty." When describing his first entry into the realm of Indian classical music, Krishna states:

> I started learning music when I was six years old. . . . Like they put a lot of young brahmin boys and girls in [music] class, I was also put in [music] class. And I started learning at

six. From that moment, the moment that someone presumes you have talent and enters you into that domain of art, there are multiple things that come to be understood. First, that you're doing something beautiful. It's presumed. It's presumed the moment that I sing *sa, pa, sa* that something beautiful is happening. That beauty is presumed by the teacher, by the student, by the environment. (2018)

Drawing on Krishna's observations, we can see that various factors—performer, teacher, art, viewer, and space—undergird the production of beauty. Beauty is manufactured by certain bodies located in particular spaces and situated in particular histories. In other words, beauty is a cultural production, rather than an aesthetic ideal that is always already there, waiting for the educated connoisseur to relish it, as Indian aesthetic theory assumes.

Wonder as *Rasa*

Thus far, I have employed affect theory to read my experience of wonder when watching Ravi Shankar perform the character of Ardhanarishvara. However, when discussing aesthetics in neoclassical Indian dance forms, including Kuchipudi, dancers usually invoke Sanskrit aesthetic theory, particularly the concept of *rasa*, or aesthetic taste. Sanskrit aesthetic theory has a technical term attached to wonder: *adbhuta*. According to Bharata's *Natyashastra*, the Sanskrit foundational text on dramaturgy composed in the early centuries CE, *adbhuta* is one of eight *rasas*, or aesthetic tastes, that can develop in the context of a dramatic or literary work. In the *Natyashastra*, *adbhuta* arises in the audience member due to external factors, known as *vibhavas*, such as seeing a wondrous person (a divine being) or visiting a wondrous place (a beautiful garden or palace).[10] These external determinants, coupled with internal emotive states, comingle to produce the aesthetic flavor of *adbhuta* in the connoisseur watching the performance.

Indeed, Ravi Shankar's performance of Ardhanarishvara seems to be an example of *adbhuta* as articulated in Indian aesthetic theory. In my earliest work on Kuchipudi (Kamath 2012b), I turned to *rasa* theory to analyze the aesthetic experience of watching a male dancer don the guise, or *vesham*, of another character. However, the invocation of *rasa* theory to frame Indian dance practice must be interrogated, including my own prior research, due to the Sanskritization of Indian dance over the course of the twentieth century. Framing neoclassical dance forms such as Bharatanatyam and Kuchipudi as grounded in Sanskrit aesthetic theory, particularly the *Natyashastra*, is an explicit attempt to elevate these dance forms within the boundaries of "classical." Drawing on M. N. Srinivas's (1956) analysis of Sanskritization, Uttara Asha Coorlawala (2004) describes how the process of Sanskritization can be mapped on to Indian dance, with a focus on the South Indian dance form of Bharatanatyam. Coorlawala writes:

> In dance, sanskritization has become a legitimizing process by which dance forms designated as "ritual," "folk," or simply insignificant, attain social and politico-artistic status which brings the redesignation, "classical." Whereas in 1958 it was agreed [in the All-India Dance Seminar] that there were four classical dance forms in India, the number has more than doubled as "classical" dance forms are continuously being recovered from oblivion in different parts of India. In the 1970s, almost every dance form claiming antiquity and sophistication, noted references within the canonized *Nāṭyaśāstra* and texts in regional languages, and demonstrated how postures, movement units and narrative techniques were organized according to this text. (53–54)

As Coorlawala notes, the appeal to Sanskrit texts, particularly the *Natyashastra*, undergirded the classicization of Bharatanatyam and other regional dance forms in the postcolonial period. Other scholars writing on the history of Bharatanatyam have noted the privileging of Sanskrit texts and deities to transform the dance from a hereditary courtesan form to a privileged-caste, middle-class dance tradition over the course of the twentieth century (Srinivasan 1985; Allen 1997; Soneji 2010).[11]

In the case of Kuchipudi, the turn to the *Natyashastra* to legitimize its classical status is clear. Rumya Putcha (2013) outlines the contestations over Kuchipudi's classical status in the 1958 All-India Dance Seminar in Delhi and the subsequent 1959 "Seminar on Kuchipudi Dance" hosted by the Andhra Pradesh Sangeeta Nataka Akademi (APSNA). In the preface to the souvenir booklet distributed in the 1959 dance seminar, it is clearly stated:

> There was a feeling in Andhra that Kuchipudi dance style was not considered to be classical during the discussion in the Dance Seminar held in Delhi in March 1958 and so it was omitted from the list of classical dances. This caused great dissatisfaction in Andhra Pradesh. Eminent scholars who can speak with authority on the subject expressed strong sentiments of disapproval. . . . As a result of the discussion at the Seminar, it was authoritatively demonstrated that Kuchipudi style of dance is an ancient and classical one and that it follows Bharata's Natya Sastra and commentaries thereon. (Andhra Pradesh Sangeeta Nataka Akademi, as cited in Putcha 2013, 102)

Here, the designation of Kuchipudi as "ancient and classical" relies entirely on turning to the authority of the *Natyashastra* and its commentaries. This discursive move became practice in Kuchipudi dance classrooms where aspects from the *Natyashastra* and the later Sanskrit text, Nandikeshvara's *Abhinayadarpana* (c. tenth to thirteenth centuries CE), were explicitly incorporated into dance movements, particularly in Chinna Satyam's KAA. Earlier generations of dancers from the village practiced bodily exercises, such as *dandemulu*, *gunjilu*, and *baskilu*, which are Telugu technical terms for types of push-ups and squats (Jonnalagadda 1996, 58). Dancers also learned movements from Sanskrit manuals such as the single-hand gestures (*samyutahastamudras*) and double-hand gestures (*asamyutahastamudras*) of the *Abhinayadarpana* (Jonnalagadda 1996, 60). However, urban dancers from the mid-twentieth century onwards explicitly framed movements through Sanskrit terminology, with the vernacular vocabulary of various kinds of squats, push-ups, and backbends mostly forgotten.

The Kuchipudi curriculum soon coalesced around these Sanskrit terms and techniques in a manner similar to Rukmini Devi Arundale's Bharatanatyam dance institute, the Kalakshetra, established in Chennai in 1936 (Coorlawala 2004, 54).[12] After establishing the KAA in Chennai in 1963, Chinna Satyam crafted a strict dance curriculum that turned to the *Natyashastra* and the *Abhinayadarpana* for framing facial expressions, hand gestures, foot movements, and bodily postures, in a manner similar to the nearby Kalakshetra. Through the course of the latter half of the twentieth century, Chinna Satyam's KAA pedagogy became *the* curriculum for Kuchipudi dance. Although there are minor modifications in movement and order, I have danced the same basic steps (*adavus*), combination of steps (*jatis*), and dance items in Chennai, Hyderabad, Vishakapatnam, Atlanta, and the Kuchipudi village in my three decades of training in Chinna Satyam's style. I have also learned the same set of Sanskrit technical terms for framing my bodily gestures, spanning from the twenty-four single-hand gestures (*samyutahastamudras*) to the six foot-gestures (*padabhedas*). Telugu bodily techniques, such *dandemulu* and *baskilu*, were referred to by my interlocutors from the Kuchipudi village as practices of the past, namely, exercises they used to do (or their teachers used to do) before Chinna Satyam came along. By drawing on Sanskrit texts on dramaturgy and aesthetics, beginning with Bharata's *Natyashastra*, Chinna Satyam Sanskritized Kuchipudi, thus enabling it to adopt the sobriquet as "classical" Indian dance.

Adding to this overt Sanskritization of Kuchipudi dance are the bodies that populate the streets of Kuchipudi village, the halls of KAA, and the transnational Kuchipudi stage. As I have discussed elsewhere (Kamath 2019), Kuchipudi arises from the eponymous village in the Krishna district of Andhra Pradesh and is historically grounded in a community of fifteen or so hereditary Vaidiki brahmin families from the village who were and continue to be associated with dance in some capacity. Citing restrictions on women's appearance in public spaces, the brahmin men of the village's hereditary families historically served as the sole proprietors of Kuchipudi dance and would take on guises—both male and female—to enact stories from Hindu religious narratives. Donning the *stri-vesham*, or woman's guise, was a unique aspect of Kuchipudi dance, one that propelled it onto the national stage in the years following India's independence and the creation of Andhra Pradesh state.[13] Although there were many other flourishing dance forms, including the performances of Kalavantulu (courtesan) dancers from the nearby East and West Godavari districts, Kuchipudi, with its cadre of brahmin male dancers, became *the* "classical" dance form of Telugu-speaking South India (Soneji 2004, 2012; Putcha 2015, 2022; Thakore 2021b, 2022). Through his urban-based dance institute and his cosmopolitan, Sanskritized form of Kuchipudi, Chinna Satyam (himself a brahmin from the Kuchipudi village) enabled the rise of women dancers from brahmin backgrounds and other dominant castes. Although once women began to dance, village brahmin men were no longer needed for donning the *stri-vesham* in Chinna Satyam's dance dramas, he did employ village brahmins for a host of other male characters, such as sages, demi-gods, and demons.[14]

Through Chinna Satyam's institute, Kuchipudi as "classical" dance became reliant on a Sanskritized repertoire and a cast of brahmin and other *savarna* (privileged-caste) performers, especially urban brahmin women and village brahmin men.

Alongside these histories of Kuchipudi as a dance form grounded in a brahmin community of dancers and Sanskritized to adapt to the twentieth-century urban dance revival, space also plays an important role in framing Kuchipudi as "classical." Chinna Satyam's style of Kuchipudi was first targeted toward the *sabha*, or proscenium theater of Chennai, which itself is grounded in brahminical taste (Rudisill 2007, 93; see also Soneji 2012, 25). Chinna Satyam's choreography was intended for these brahmin audiences in the Chennai *sabha*, and he framed his style of Kuchipudi to appeal to the city's taste-makers in the same model as the Kalakshetra's brand of Bharatanatyam. When Chinna Satyam began touring in the United States in the 1990s, although his location may have shifted, his audiences remained the same; he was still appealing to Indian privileged-caste audiences in the diaspora *sabha*s who immigrated to the United States in the years following the Immigration and Nationality Act of 1965 (Putcha 2022, 8). In migrating from India to the United States, Tam Brams (the colloquial term for Tamil brahmins) and Telugu brahmins carried their tastes with them, and Chinna Satyam crafted his transnational tours in light of these brahminical aesthetics infused in the spaces where he performed.

In his well-known essay "Is There an Indian Way of Thinking?," A. K. Ramanujan (1989, 54) asserts that Indian culture is characterized by context-specific behaviors and rules. According to Ramanujan, there are important context-free exceptions, including the context-free aesthetic ideal of *rasa*, which is generalizable to everyone. In Ramanujan's context-free model, *rasa* can stick to all bodies, generate an emotive response in all viewers, and apply to all spaces. However, in reality, such a universalizing aesthetics is never truly possible. Not all bodies are deemed worthy of creating *rasa* and not all performances are designated as art, a point made evident in T. M. Krishna's (2018) observations on beauty in Indian classical music.

In this chapter, I have chosen to read wonder through the lens of affect theory in order to highlight the brahminical histories of contact undergirding the production of aesthetics in Indian dance: *rasa* is intended to invoke aesthetic relish in the educated connoisseur who, in the context of the twentieth-century revival of Indian dance, is situated within a brahminical frame. Even those dancers who may not identify as *savarna* or brahmin are judged through this brahminical lens. Clear examples are the casteist reviews of hereditary dancer Nrithya Pillai by *savarna* dance critic Leela Venkatraman in the online journal Narthaki.com (Prakash 2023).[15] Venkatraman's reviews, which were published in 2019 and 2023 and subsequently edited, illustrate how hereditary dancers like Pillai must discipline their bodies and performances to appeal to the brahminical tastes of the urban Chennai *sabha* or risk public criticism. Venkatraman's reviews lay bare the structures of brahminical supremacy undergirding the formation of Indian dance (FCHS Collective 2021).

Extending the analysis of aesthetics to wonder, we can see that the very notion of what is wondrous, or *adbhuta* in Sanskrit, sticks to the brahmin body, particularly if that brahmin body enacts a Sanskritized dance form in the context of the brahmin-oriented *sabha*. Just as saying "That's disgusting!" (Ahmed [2004] 2014, 94) sticks to certain bodies and objects, the speech act "Wonderful!" adheres to brahmin and *savarna* dancers and choreographies of Indian dance in brahminical spaces. Certainly, affective responses of wonder are possible beyond the brahmin dancer and brahmin viewer; however, the Indian dance world is conditioned to uphold and praise brahminical dance as worthy of generating *rasa*, while critiquing non-brahmin dancers, including those who belong to hereditary dance communities, as unworthy of such approbation. What is wondrous in Indian dance is a brahminical enterprise, and it is only by recognizing the casteist structures of wonder—or the "ugliness of beauty" (Krishna 2018)—that we can begin to reframe aesthetics in Indian dance. Reorienting ourselves to alternative aesthetic possibilities beyond *rasa* can open up new spaces for wonder beyond the brahmin body in *vesham* (Ahmed 2006).[16]

Conclusion

In the penultimate chapter of *The Cultural Politics of Emotion*, Ahmed proposes an alternative reading of wonder as affect. She writes: "Wonder, as an affective relation to the world, is about seeing the world that one faces and is faced with 'as if' for the first time . . . wonder allows us to see the surfaces of the world *as made*, and as such wonder opens up rather than suspends historicity" (Ahmed [2004] 2014, 179; emphasis in original). She continues by arguing that "wonder is about learning to see the world as something that does not have to be, and as something that came to be, over time, and with work" (180). Ahmed's reading of wonder as a possibility of encountering the world *as if* for the first time and also as "something that does not have to be" expands the scope of wonder beyond past histories of contact. What happens if wonder is dislodged from the brahmin body and the brahmin *sabha* and sticks to new bodies in new spaces? What would such a wondrous world look like?

To answer this question, I will turn to Yashoda Thakore, a dancer from the hereditary Kalavantulu families who is also trained in Kuchipudi dance. When reflecting on the gendered aesthetics of her dance practice, Thakore (2021a, 5) notes how her Kuchipudi training taught her to open her shoulders, maintain a straight spine, and cast sideways glances. When performing the Kalavantulu repertoire, by contrast, Thakore had to retrain her looks and posture to embody a different kind of feminine aesthetics. I observed this distinction when Thakore recently performed at Emory University on February 25, 2023. Prior to performing the *padam Rayabaram ampinada* ("Did he send a message?"), Thakore framed the piece for the audience:

> This *padam* that I will be performing for you next is done in a seated position. This is a challenge for you and me because I am not moving around. I will sit here and look straight in front of me. I see this whole act of sitting down and doing the *padam* and looking at the person just opposite you as a power of strength, as a symbol of the dancer's strength and power. In the neo-classical dance of Kuchipudi that I perform, always the hero or friend are on the side—we turn to the side and perform. But [in the Kalavantulu repertoire], she or he is right in front, and the dancer questions them. She doesn't have to use the rest of the body to keep the attention of the audience. (2023)

Departing from the neoclassical movement vocabulary of Kuchipudi, Thakore shifts the aesthetic frame for the audience, training us to expect her straightforward looks and seated posture. Watching Thakore dancing the *padam Rayabaram ampinada* generated a new kind of wonder in the audience, one that moved beyond the brahminical strictures of *rasa*.[17] In Telugu, this form of wonder is most clearly encapsulated by *vichitramu*, a capacious term that highlights the beauty of the extraordinary, the rare, the exceptional.

I will conclude by turning to the various translations of the term "wonder" that Tulasi Srinivas (2018, 59) employed in her field notes from her ethnographic work in Malleshwaram, Bengaluru. When reading the various translations in her field notes, her father, renowned anthropologist M. N. Srinivas, marked the translations with question marks and even an emoticon smiley face, alluding to the ineffability of capturing wonder in words. An affective reading, like Srinivas's translations, prompts a search for new meanings for wonder—"as 'oddity,' 'strangeness,' 'alien,' 'astonishment,' and in one case as 'divine'" (Srinivas 2018, 59)—or simply vernacular *vichitramu* in the everyday.

Notes

Thanks to Sailaja Krishnamurti, Joyce Burkhalter Flueckiger, and Petra Shenk for their feedback on this chapter.

1. These lines are from the *Ardhanarinateshvara stotra* attributed to eighth-century philosopher Adi Shankara. For the complete Sanskrit *stotra* and English translation, see Goldberg (2002, 104–5).

2. Kamath (2019) features my fieldwork with Kuchipudi dance communities, including an extensive discussion of Chavali Balatripurasundari in chapter 5. I interviewed Vempati Ravi Shankar on several occasions in spring 2010 and continued to interact with him in the years leading up to his death. A selection of my interviews with him are featured in a short article published for the journal *Nartanam* (Kamath 2012a).

3. Despite this restriction, his third daughter, Chavali Balatripurasundari, went on to have a successful career as a dance teacher and now runs her own dance institute in Hyderabad. See Kamath (2019, ch. 5) for a discussion of Balatripurasundari and other brahmin women from hereditary village families.

4. Interview with Vempati Ravi Shankar, May 26, 2010. This contrasts with how Chinna Satyam responded to his daughter Baliakka's attempts to dance. See Kamath (2019, 148).

5. Interview with Vempati Ravi Shankar, April 8, 2010.

6. Interview with Vempati Ravi Shankar, April 8, 2010.

7. Interview with Vempati Ravi Shankar, April 8, 2010.

8. Interview with Vempati Ravi Shankar, April 8, 2010.

9. Turning to the example used in psychological literature of a child who sees a bear and runs away, Ahmed argues that the affect of fear is reliant upon

past histories of contact: "When we encounter the bear, we already have an impression of the risks of encounter, as an impression that is felt on the surface of the skin. . . . This contact is shaped by past histories of contact, unavailable in the present, which allow the bear to be apprehended as fearsome" ([2004] 2014, 7). See also Puar (2007, 188).

10. See *Natyashastra*, chapter 6, translated by Ghosh (1951).

11. As Davesh Soneji notes, "The search for antiquity of Bharatanatyam in Sanskrit texts in the twentieth century disassociated the dance from its social roots in highly localized non-brahmin communities, and universalized its aesthetics and history. It also enabled a nationalized 'pan-Indian' reading of aesthetic history, with the *Natyasastra* read as 'the common root' of all regional performance traditions" (2010, xxv).

12. Soneji notes that the *Abhinayadarpana*, which was translated by Ananda Kentish Coomaraswamy (1917) and Manmohan Ghosh (1944), became the textbook for dance theory at Rukmini Devi's Kalakshetra (2010, xxvii, xlivn19). See also Matthew Harp Allen's (1997) discussion of Rukmini Devi Arundale's Kalakshetra.

13. As an example, we can turn to the popularity of impersonator Vedantam Satyanarayana Sarma discussed in Kamath (2019), chapter 1.

14. For example, Vedantam Rattayya Sarma, a senior performer from the Kuchipudi village, played leading sage roles in Chinna Satyam's productions of *Haravilasam* and *Ramayanam* in the 1990s.

15. See also Nrithya Pillai's articles on caste and Bharatanatyam (2022a, 2022b).

16. Here, I refer to Sara Ahmed's notion of disorientation as discussed in her book *Queer Phenomenology* (2006). See also FCHS Collective (2021) for a discussion of disorientation and reorientation in relation to Hindu studies.

17. Related to this reframed aesthetics, Marathi literary critic Sharankumar Limbale calls for a new aesthetic when reading Dalit literature: "Rejecting traditional aesthetics, [Dalit] writers insist on the need for a new and distinct aesthetic for their literature—an aesthetic that is life-affirming and realistic" (2004, 19).

Works Cited

Ahmed, Sara. (2004) 2014. *The Cultural Politics of Emotion*. Edinburgh: Edinburgh University Press.

———. 2006. *Queer Phenomenology: Orientations, Objects, Others*. Durham, NC: Duke University Press.

Allen, Matthew Harp. 1997. "Rewriting the Script for South Indian Dance." *TDR* 41 (3): 63–100.

Butler, Judith. (1993) 2011. *Bodies That Matter: On the Discursive Limits of "Sex."* London: Routledge.

Chinna Satyam, Vempati, chor. and dir. 1998. *Ardhanareeswara.* Pittsburgh: Sri Venkateswara Temple. VHS.

Coorlawala, Uttara Asha. 2004. "The Sanskritized Body." *Dance Research Journal* 36 (2): 50–63.

FCHS Collective. 2021. "Feminist Critical Hindu Studies in Formation." *Religion Compass* 15 (5): e12392. https://doi.org/10.1111/rec3.12392.

Ghosh, Manmohan. 1951. *The Nāṭyaśāstra Ascribed to Bharata Muni.* Vol. 1. Calcutta: Asiatic Society of Bengal.

Goldberg, Ellen. 2002. *The Lord Who Is Half Woman: Ardhanārīśvara in Indian and Feminist Perspective.* Albany: State University of New York Press.

Jonnalagadda, Anuradha. 1996. "Traditions and Innovations in Kuchipudi Dance." PhD diss., University of Hyderabad.

Kamath, Harshita Mruthinti. 2012a. "A Legacy to Follow: Vempati Ravi Shankar." *Nartanam* 12 (3): 92–96.

———. 2012b. "Aesthetics, Performativity, and Performative *Māyā*: Imagining Gender in the Textual and Performance Traditions of Telugu South India." PhD diss., Emory University.

———. 2019. *Impersonations: The Artifice of Brahmin Masculinity in South Indian Dance.* Oakland: University of California Press.

Krishna, T. M. 2018. "Beauty and Its Ugliness—the Politics of Aesthetics." Public talk at Kalady University, Kerala. Biju Mohan (YouTube channel), December 18. https://www.youtube.com/watch?v=j3EakaBCtD4.

Limbale, Sharankumar. 2004. *Towards an Aesthetic of Dalit Literature: History, Controversies and Considerations.* Trans. by Alok Mukherjee. New Delhi: Orient Longman.

Paik, Shailaja. 2022. *The Vulgarity of Caste: Dalits, Sexuality, and Humanity in Modern India.* Stanford, CA: Stanford University Press.

Pillai, Nrithya. 2022a. "Cycles of Cultural Violence within Performance and Scholarship of Bharatanatyam." *News Minute*, June 21. https://www.thenewsminute.com/article/cycles-cultural-violence-within-performance-and-scholarship-bharatanatyam-165159.

———. 2022b. "Re-casteing the Narrative of Bharatanatyam." *Economic and Political Weekly*, February 26. https://www.epw.in/engage/article/re-casteing-narrative-bharatanatyam.

Prakash, Brahma. 2023. "To Truly Democratize Indian Art and Culture, the 'Classical' Must Be Declared Dead." *Scroll.in*, March 19. https://scroll.in/article/1045681/opinion-to-truly-democratise-indian-art-and-culture-the-classical-must-be-done-away-with.

Puar, Jasbir. 2007. *Terrorist Assemblages: Homonationalism in Queer Times.* Durham, NC: Duke University Press.

Putcha, Rumya. 2013. "Between History and Historiography: The Origins of Classical Kuchipudi Dance." *Dance Research Journal* 45 (3): 91–110.

———. 2015. "Dancing in Place: Mythopoetics and the Production of History in Kuchipudi." *Yearbook for Traditional Music* 47:1–26.

———. 2022. *The Dancer's Voice: Performance and Womanhood in Transnational India*. Durham, NC: Duke University Press.

Ramanujan, A. K. 1989. "Is There an Indian Way of Thinking? An Informal Essay." *Contributions to Indian Sociology* 23 (1): 41–58.

Rudisill, Kristen. 2007. "Brahmin Humor: Chennai's Sabha Theater and the Creation of Middle-Class Indian Taste from the 1950s to the Present." PhD diss., University of Texas at Austin.

Seigworth, Gregory J., and Melissa Gregg. 2010. "An Inventory of Shimmers." In *The Affect Theory Reader*, edited by Melissa Gregg and Gregory J. Seigworth, 1–25. Durham, NC: Duke University Press.

Soneji, Davesh. 2004. "Performing Satyabhāmā: Text, Context, Memory and Mimesis in Telugu-Speaking South India." PhD diss., McGill University.

———. 2010. *Bharatanatyam: A Reader*. New Delhi: Oxford University Press.

———. 2012. *Unfinished Gestures: Devadāsīs, Memory, and Modernity in South India*. Chicago: University of Chicago Press.

Srinivas, M. N. 1956. "A Note on Sanskritization and Westernization." *Far Eastern Quarterly* 15 (4): 481–96.

Srinivas, Tulasi. 2018. *The Cow in the Elevator: An Anthropology of Wonder*. Durham, NC: Duke University Press.

Srinivasan, Amrit. 1985. "Reform and Revival: The Devadasi and Her Dance." *Economic and Political Weekly* 20 (44): 1869–76.

Thakore, Yashoda. 2021a. "Complicating Caste: Blood, Body and Practice." Unpublished manuscript.

———. 2021b. *Her Story of Dance* (podcast). Episodes 1–6. https://www.sunoindia.in/her-story-of-dance/.

———. 2022. "Dancing caste, rethinking heredity: A Kuchipudi artist reflects on her multiple lineages." *Scroll.in*, April 10. https://scroll.in/article/1021494/dancing-caste-rethinking-heredity-a-kuchipudi-artist-reflects-on-her-multiple-lineages.

Chapter 6

In the Vicinity of Wonder

Thirunangai Devotees of Angalamman and Narratives of Moral Astonishment

ANIRUDDHAN VASUDEVAN

Introduction

In this essay, I focus on the place of wonder in the ritual and social lives of *thirunangai-maruladis* in Chennai in southern India.[1] Thirunangai-maruladis are Tamil transgender women[2] who are deeply devoted to the worship of the goddess, especially Angalamman, a regional deity worshipped by people across castes.[3] As the Tamil word "maruladi" suggests, this mode of devotion involves dancing (*aadi/aadudhal*) the deity in states of trance (*marul*). Thirunangais who express an intense attachment to Angalamman place her at the center of their ideas of selfhood, gender identity, and ethics.

In the first section of this essay, I show the "wonder discourses" and "wonder practices" (Scott 2016) that are in operation in thirunangais' devotion to Angalamman, especially with respect to the fanfare with which annual rituals for the goddess are conducted. I focus on the importance that thirunangais attach to the experience of *asandhu podhal*, which I translate as astonishment.

Drawing on Tulasi Srinivas's (2018) work on the conspicuous place money occupies in the modern ritual "economy of wonder" in Hindu temple worship in southern India, in the second section I show that thirunangais' emphasis on astonishment takes the most palpable form in the financial resources they muster for, and expend in, organizing the annual rituals for goddess Angalamman, especially the *Mayana Kollai* ("pillage in the cremation grounds") ritual (Meyer 1986; Craddock 2012; Allocco, this volume). Thirunangais' talk about festival expenses indexes their concern for moral reputation within the communities in which they dwell.

In the third section, I detail the various ethical relationships that thirunangai-maruladis are part of: their natal families, neighbors, friends, local merchants, and others. We encounter some conflicting accounts of thirunangai moral personhood: as a mode of renunciation of familial attachments and normative social roles; as involving a rearticulation of normative kinship and obligation; as a site of proliferating attachments and multiple demands for care; and more. An interest in wonder, I suggest, is an interest in moments of clarity about thirunangai social personhood.

Finally, I examine the ontological premises that are at stake in thirunangai discourses and practices of astonishment. I draw attention to a traffic in wonder that exists between thirunangai-maruladis, other devotees of Angalamman, and the goddess herself. And I suggest that this mutuality of wonder, especially as it manifests in thirunangais' desire to see astonishment in those who witness their commitment to the goddess, serves to throw into relief and bring to momentary crisis some conflicting ontologies of gender (including those held by thirunangais themselves) that are in circulation within the Tamil world today.

Thirunangai-maruladis are constantly theorizing on their identity, social location, moral frameworks, and ethical practices. In deliberately highlighting a form of wonder as a valued ethical affect, thirunangais hint at a metapragmatics of wonder in operation, which I hope to detail here without overburdening it with my own theoretical and analytical interventions.[4] However, I have drawn on some frameworks from the anthropology of wonder, kinship, religion gender, and sexuality to illuminate the force of the ethicality that thirunangai-maruladis articulate and embody.

To Astonish and to Be Astonished

One striking aspect of my initial meetings with thirunangai-maruladis in north Chennai was that nearly all thirunangais were keen on showing me photo albums of the festivals they had conducted for Angalamman in their own little shrines or in the neighborhood temples for the goddess. These albums contained photos of the Mayana Kollai and Aadi (July–August) rituals they had conducted in the recent past, but, in some cases, the earliest albums went back a few decades. In showing me these photos, the thirunangai-maruladis were particularly keen that I noted the pomp and splendor with which they had organized these festivals over the years, and they spoke about the money, time, and labor it took to organize them. All my thirunangai interlocutors referenced a kind of astonishment, *asandhu podhal*—an astonishment they claimed others experienced when they witnessed the energy and resources thirunangais expended on these festivals. It was an astonishment they hoped to elicit from others and one they said they witnessed in me when I browsed through their photo albums. They were, indeed, right about the astonishment I felt at the degree of their commitment to Angalamman worship. In this essay, I do not offer a critical history of astonishment or wonder as aesthetic categories. I take as my starting point thirunangais' concern with the experience of *asandhu podhal*, and I seek to understand why it matters to them. Let me begin with some examples of this talk of astonishment.

Looking at how engrossed I was in the festival photo album she had placed on my lap, Ragini Amma, a thirunangai elder in her late sixties, said: "Even you are astonished [*asandhu poyitteenga*], aren't you? You are only looking at the photos, and even you are astonished. Then imagine the people who witnessed it directly, how astonished they must have been [*evlo asandhu poyiruppaanga*]? I do this every year for her [the goddess]. It will be forty-five years next year. To the best of my abilities, I make sure nothing is spared for her. That is my duty. You go and ask anyone in this area. They will tell you, 'No one does masaana kollai [Mayana Kollai] like Ragini Amma does, no one conducts Aadi month festivities like Ragini Amma does.' That's the reputation I have here. She is responsible for that. She alone is."

Mala is in her early fifties, and she is a well-known thirunangai-maruladi in north Chennai. Among the thirunangais in the area, she is particularly known for the incredible grace with which she moves when she enters a state of trance and embodies the goddess. Responding to a question from me about what Angalamman meant to her, she said: "If I tell you all that she [the goddess] has done for me in my life, you will be astonished [*asandhu poyiduveenga*]. . . . Truly. Even I, when I think of some of the things that have happened in my life . . . a problem will crop up, and just when I wonder 'how am I going to face this?' it will get resolved on its own. I won't have to do anything. She will take care of it. . . . She does so much for me. So I do a lot for her. You ask anyone here. Everyone in this area comes to our temple. They know how elaborately [*vimarisaiya*] I do everything for Amman."

Noticing how impressed I was with her photo albums of the festivals, she remarked, "When I see these photos, even I cannot believe [*namba mudiyala*] I managed to do all this! Even I am astonished [*malaippa irukkum*] sometimes." Quickly turning to the subject of expenses, she said, "How do you think I raise that amount? By printing donation receipts and flyers and asking for contributions? I do that for sure. But I'd get something like ten thousand rupees from that. Where does the rest of it come from? It is the money I earn from sex work."

Before I focus on the moral economy indexed by these remarks—reputation within the community, reciprocity with the goddess, value placed on personal hardship and commitment, and so on, I wish to draw attention to the emphasis on forms of astonishment that this kind of "ethical talk" generates (Venkatesan 2014). Personal responsibility and obligation, gratitude for divine grace, and a regard for how others view thirunangais' commitment to the goddess—all these aspects of devotional practice are not simply signaled as valued forms of recognition, but are framed in the charged language of *asandhu podhal* or astonishment. A set of ethical relationships are framed here using the affective register of astonishment. Insofar as these instances of ethical discourse (and the other examples I will offer in this essay) highlight thirunangai-maruladis' own concern with astonishment as an appropriate response to certain actions and relationships, I consider them to be part of what Michael W. Scott (2016) has called "wonder discourses." They fulfill the two criteria that Scott sets for "wonder discourses": (1) they evidence "a heightened interest in or mood of wonder in a given context"; and (2) they are part of a discursive practice of "cultivating wonder," as I seek to show below (475). Whether or not my thirunangai interlocutors succeed in evoking a sense of astonishment in others through their embodied commitment to Angalamman, they make certain criteria for ethical evaluation intersubjectively relevant through such ethical talk.[5] And the capacity to both experience and evoke wonder appears to be important to this ethical discourse and practice.

Money and the Economy of Astonishment

Thirunangai-maruladis place great value in conducting the annual festivals for the goddess with much fanfare, with no expenses spared. They see that gesture as necessary for their own reciprocal relationship with the goddess as well as for a recognition from others of their commitment to the goddess. To this end, thirunangais emphasize the expenses involved in the two main annual festivals for Angalamman: the Mayana Kollai in late February/early March and the festivities in the month of Aadi (July–August). Each of these festivals can cost up to 2 Lakh Rupees (US$2,700, approx.), which is a huge amount of money for my interlocutors, who make their living through ritual labor, sex work, alms-seeking/begging, and part-time employment in community-based organizations for transgender rights and health advocacy.

In order to highlight the ways in which financial resources and transactions work in the context of thirunangai performance of Angalamman rituals, I would like first to draw on an ethnographic work on wonder and ritual economy in contemporary southern India that provides both a productive contrast and some theoretical directions.

In her work on the emergent and experimental ritual practices of the urban Hindu middle class and the temples and public rituals they attend, Tulasi Srinivas (2018) "explore[s] money as part of the everyday calculus of ritual life through its usage as adornment for the deity to create *an economy of wonder* that interweaves with and illuminates the monetary economy" (103). In Srinivas's analysis of the use of money as part of an "aesthetic of adornment" in the temples of Bangalore city, the sensory experience of money as adornment for the deity undercuts a practical approach to money: "Aesthetic experimentation with currency that appeals to our visual senses changes the way we see. These experiments consciously oppose the practical use of money, to focus on seeing the brilliance and lustrous shine of coinage and gold, and to look at the visual splendor of plastic credit cards and paper money" (103). Money here enters ritual transaction not as a medium of exchange. Instead, it comes to "reside in" in the ritual as an object of dazzling aesthetic appeal produced by its sheer materiality: its color, sheen, and texture. It thus slips "from the realm of transaction to the realm of wonder" (104). The instability of middle-class affect toward money, engendered by the proximity of plenitude and precarity in neoliberal economy, manifests as a moral muddle: gratitude and greed, happiness and insecurity (that the inflow of money should last), consumerism and calculation, a tendency to value money alongside a moral unease about one's attachment to money, and so on. Srinivas reads the Bangalore priest's focus on money—coins, currency, cards—as adornment for the temple deity as a ritual technique to creatively transmute such unstable and ambivalent attitudes toward money into moments of wonder. It is money's sheer material forms, and less its transactional power, that anchor this "economy of wonder."

Important to the purposes of my analysis is Srinivas's reading of this ritualization of money as bringing together the aesthetic and moral dimensions of money. The priest who is staging this ritual adornment apprehends money in its "excessive and spectacular forms" as well as for its inescapable moral affordances that are signaled not only by the dangers of greed and attachment but also by the undeniable presence of inequality and poverty in the city. In presenting the visual splendor of money as ritual adornment, he offers a glimpse into a potential approach to money that resists "accepted regimes of value, thrift, sacrifice, and saving" (106). It is reframed from its current moral domain to signal a potential one, of plenitude for all.

In the devotional context I seek to describe, money is not ritual adornment. Its primary value here is an eminently transactional one. The aspects of money that evoke astonishment here are its capacity to enter a set of local economic relations and, through these exchanges, add pomp and splendor to the ritual and the festivities. Just as in Srinivas's ethnographic context, markers of material well-being have a privileged place in the ritual enactments of my thirunangai interlocutors too. But the key difference is that, while in Srinivas's Bangalore temples money is foregrounded in all its resplendent materiality, in the rituals that my thirunangai interlocutors seek to perform, money first functions as a medium of exchange before it comes to take wondrous forms at the scene of the ritual.

As mentioned above, conducting one of the annual festivals for Angalamman can cost up to 2 lakh rupees (a conservative estimate). Thirunangai-maruladis manage to raise the amount by gathering together their earnings from ritual work, earnings from sex work, income from other kinds of work (alms-seeking/begging, community organizational work, etc.), donations from neighbors and friends, neighborhood chit fund schemes, and loans (with or without interest).[6] In thirunangais' devotion to Angalamman, while money is not explicitly aestheticized as seen in the ritual context that Srinivas documents in the temples of Bangalore, money does, in fact, play a demonstrative role. For instance, the not inconsiderable amounts spent on renting loudspeakers, printing flex banners and leaflets, erecting the thatched pandal awning to cover the entire street, and so on, are deemed by the thirunangais themselves as expenses extraneous to the ritual. But they are, nevertheless, important.

As Radhika, a young thirunangai-maruladi, put it, "If we have decided to do the festival, we should do it properly, without cutting corners." Eveline Meyer (1986), in her magisterial work on the Angalamman cult in Tamil Nadu, has highlighted the link between financial resources and the proper conduct of rituals as well as the question of the status of the family or caste group that is organizing a festival: "Aṅkāḷamman temples are, on the whole, temples which were originally established by a clan or family of a particular caste and it would be this group (the descendants of the founder) that would feel responsible for the maintenance of the temple and the proper celebration of their *kula teyvam*'s festivals. As long as the community associated with the temple is prosperous and not fraught with dissension, the temple is likely to flourish" (1986, 156). Meyer highlights the importance of the community in Angalamman worship, but it is a caste-based community, which relates to the deity in the temple as its *kula deivam* or clan deity. Thirunangai devotees of Angalamman do not relate to the goddess as a clan deity. Even in cases where they maintain ties with their natal families (which may sustain caste affiliations and identity), the thirunangai-maruladis I work with do not assert caste identity. In fact, they largely eschew caste identification and affiliation and instead articulate their attachment to Angalamman through a gender ontology that gives the goddess a causal role in the formation of thirunangai identity (Vasudevan 2020). I examine certain aspects of this human-divine gender ontology in the final section of this essay.[7]

Meyer also discusses the extraneous aspects of ritual expenditures as markers of prestige: "For reasons of prestige, things which are 'modern' or which enjoy popularity often take precedence over older customs. Thus, for instance, more money will be spent on the electrification of the goddess' chariot or on sound equipment" (1986, 155). This partly aligns with my thirunangai interlocutors' acknowledgment that some expenses are not toward the core aspects of the ritual. Nevertheless, such expenses are not only markers of prestige. They demonstrate thirunangais' commitment to conducting the goddess's festival elaborately (*vimarisaiya*) and sincerely (*siratthaiya*). These expenses also weave in the labor and livelihood of a number of local merchants and vendors. Money first enters a set of relations of exchange as a medium of transaction before taking various sensorial forms in and around the ritual site. Those transactions and the relations they mediate are central to thirunangai-maruladi discourses and practices of wonder.

Proliferating Attachments—Kinship and Care

The transactions of which we get a glimpse in thirunangais' efforts toward conducting Angalamman festivals place them squarely within relationships mediated by neighborhood and class. These relationships overflow the bounds of transgender identity. Community here includes cis-gendered, heterosexual persons and family units that constitute the majority in the neighborhoods in which my thirunangai-maruladi interlocutors live. Thirunangais share the worship of Angalamman (and other deities) with others who live around them. In the neighborhoods of north Chennai, my thirunangai interlocutors live amid heterosexual family units that belong to various castes, primarily Vanniyar, Nayakkar, Reddy, Naidu, Chetty, Mudaliyar, and Dalit castes. Intimacies and enduring relationships with neighbors are vital features of thirunangai lives in this setting. This complicates some dominant readings of hijra and other transfeminine lifeworlds in India as primarily constituted through ritually structured and hierarchical forms of kinship among similarly identified persons (Reddy 2005; Nanda 1999). I also suggest that the way thirunangais perform and evaluate these relationships offers a productive counterpoint to readings that emphasize the renunciation aspect of transfeminine selfhood (Reddy 2005).

One afternoon in January 2016, a month or so before the annual Mayana Kollai ritual, I was walking with Mala through a vegetable and flower market in the Old Washermanpet area of north Chennai, when a flower vendor called out to her. "Malamma, come! How are you? When are you going to place orders for flowers? The festival's round the corner, isn't it?" Mala returned his greetings and told him she would call later, once she had a clear sense of the kinds of flowers she would need for that year's festival. As we walked away, the flower vendor said, "Call me. We can get it all done just like last year." Later that day, Mala spoke to her thirunangai daughter Shanthi to find out why she had not finalized things with the flower vendor yet. It turned out that Shanthi had a different vendor in mind, someone who might offer a better price. Mala was upset about this. She said, "You cannot just suddenly change these things. We have been buying from him for so many years now. He is expecting an order from us. What will happen to his livelihood [*pozhappu*] if we don't buy from him? Go talk to him." She then remarked to me, "If I suddenly break it off with him like this, how can I even go to the market after that?" She made a similar argument for erecting the pandal awning to cover the entire street. Here, however, in addition to caring about keeping up her support of a local business, she also took into consideration her relationship with her neighbors in the street: "We cannot leave out some houses. They will feel we are neglecting them. The pandal should extend to the end of the street."

This vignette illustrates the durable nature of the relationships that thirunangai-maruladis have cultivated within their neighborhoods. It hinges on mutual expectations, questions of livelihood, and concerns about social face, all of which are periodically addressed through transactions undertaken periodically for the goddess's festival.

I also got to witness the care that thirunangai-maruladis took to sustain these relationships beyond the lifetime of an individual devotee. Kameela Amma had been an influential maruladi in the Old Washermanpet area of north Chennai. After her sudden death, all her thirunangai disciples/daughters had found kinship with other gurus/mothers.[8] But her absence left a gap in the kinds of transactions I have been describing. A group of priests and drummers, whom Kameela Amma used to hire for her elaborate festivals for Angalamman, had now lost an important source of income. One day, one of the poosaris from this group, Ganesan, came to see Lakshmi Nani, a thirunangai elder and maruladi. She took him to see a few thirunangais in the area, recommending Ganesan and his team's festival services to them, and highlighting the long years of connection he had had with Kameela Amma and how her death had created a major gap in his support network. What we see here are relationships of mutual dependence conducted through an ethic of responsibility and solidarity that extend through a shared commitment to the goddess.

The third example I have to offer illustrates the kinds of intimacies thirunangais form with their non-thirunangai neighbors. Lakshmi Nani does not have her own temple for Angalamman. She spends her time in a neighborhood temple that belongs to a large family of several heterosexual family units. Thirunangais use the word *duniyadar* ("people of the world"/"the worldly ones") to refer to people who come within regimes of heterosexual marital and familial economy.[9] As a neighbor and fellow vegetable vendor in the local market, Lakshmi Nani has built years of intimacy with all members of this family, especially the three sisters whose spouses, children, and grandchildren constitute this large family. One day, Nani reached out to other thirunangais for help with borrowing some money for a festival at this temple. It turned out that she had used all her savings to help one of the sisters, Vijaya, with repaying a personal loan. So now she was left without money to contribute toward the annual Mayana Kollai ritual. Here we see Nani's commitment both to her duniyadar neighbor Vijaya as well as to goddess Angalamman, and both commitments are expressed through the idiom of money.

These instances bring to the fore some ethical relationships that thirunangai-maruladis engage in, relationships that are not subsumed by an identitarian logic of community or an instrumental rationality. But what has this got to do with wonder or astonishment? If the people who are part of the thirunangai network of relations are aware of, and rely on, their enduring relationships with thirunangais in the locality, why would they be astonished by the commitment that thirunangais show toward the goddess and the resources they expend in her worship?

The immediate community—the neighbors and friends with whom and in whose presence and company thirunangais engage in Angalamman worship—is periodically astounded not by thirunangai devotion per se, but by the extent of thirunangais' capacity for giving. The way thirunangais look at it, this astonishment is grounded in the neighbors' realization of their own limitations as duniyadars, as "people of this world," as people enmeshed in social as well as species reproduction. This is where thirunangai-maruladis invoke a selfhood and social location that resembles that of the renouncer that Gayatri Reddy (2005) has discussed among hijras in Hyderabad. For instance, Mala offered the following rationale for the intensity of thirunangai attachment toward Angalamman even though the goddess is not exclusively a thirunangai deity: "There are lots of rules and restrictions for men and women. For duniyadars. But not for us. Angalamma prefers thirunangais, she makes us thirunangais because then we won't have family, children, and all that. We can give our full attention [*muzhu kavanam*] to her. We are different from men and women." In a sentiment that echoes functionalist readings of nonnormative gender roles (cf. Turner 1969; Roscoe 1996), Mala suggests that being a thirunangai is to be extracted from heteronormative reproductive economy in order to be assigned to ritual-spiritual labor.[10]

The idea that the world of duniyadars, however proximate and intimate, can still be astonished by the degree of thirunangai commitment to the goddess was also echoed by one of Mala's neighbors, a woman in her sixties: "People like us have husbands and children and grandchildren and all that. We have to think about weddings and valaikappu [ceremony performed for pregnant women] and this and that. So we do what we can [for the festival] . . . But they [thirunangais] don't have all that. So they do it elaborately. They can do it in such a way that the entire Vannarapettai is astonished [*asandhu pora alavukku*]." Note that the woman's theory of thirunangais' freedom from familial attachments still makes room for wonder at how they conduct the festivals. Both Mala and her non-thirunangai neighbor traffic in a heuristic distinction between the householder and the renouncer. However, they do not frame this renunciation as an agentive one. Mala believes that the goddess actively makes some people thirunangais, and the neighbor subscribes to a widely held misconception that thirunangais are congenitally incapable of engaging in procreative sex (Padmabharathi 2013; Ramakrishnan 2016). In this case, both the thirunangai and the cis-gendered neighbor attribute this gender/sex difference to divine grace. As the neighbor put it to me, "They are divine creations [*deiva piravigal*]." There is an irony here. While the neighbor sees thirunangais as people without familial attachments and obligations, the photo albums of thirunangais' festivals for the Angalamman suggest something else. They resemble the photo albums that people make of weddings and other lifecycle rituals among close kin; they suggest that thirunangais have made kinship with the goddess.

The figure of the thirunangai as a person freed from familial attachments and the social reproduction of the heterosexual family falls apart on closer examination. For instance, Mala herself divides her time between her private dwelling and her natal home in the next neighborhood. The temple where she performs rituals and conducts festivals for Amman is located next door to her parental home where she grew up as a child. When, as a "young boy" [*china payyan*], she started channeling Angalamman at a family ceremony, her family's expectations of her underwent an important shift. Within this lifeworld of ecstatic devotion and trance embodiment, a frequent "arrival" of the goddess on a young male person signals the possibility that the person would grow up to be an androgynous person. So, a recognition that Angalamman had "chosen" Mala to be her medium facilitated her family's acceptance of the shift in her gender self-presentation and her subsequent espousal of thirunangai identity. Mala now, therefore, attends to multiple kinship ties: her natal family; her place in thirunangai kinship as a mother, daughter, and more; and her mentoring of younger thirunangai-maruladis who seek to learn the ritual protocols of Angalamman worship. All these relationships involve various forms of care, including financial support. So, far from a severing of familial ties, what we see is a proliferation of attachments. Hers is not an exceptional case. Many thirunangais (especially those who are devoted to the goddess, but not only) have reestablished functional relationships with their natal families, often after a period of separation and estrangement. Karuna, a thirunangai performer in her thirties, spent all her savings on her niece's (sister's daughter) wedding. "Now I am her *chitti* [mother's younger sister]. If I had stayed a boy, I'd have been the girl's *mama* [maternal uncle] now. As a mama, I would have taken the lead in arranging things for the wedding. But I can do it now too. They need my help." Not only did the family acknowledge their need for her assistance with the wedding; they even printed the wedding invitation in Karuna's name, a clear mark of respect for her.

What we see with Mala's and Karuna's relationships with their natal families brings to mind the "kinship trouble" that Lucinda Ramberg (2014) discusses in the context of Yellamma devadasis in Karnataka. The jogatis, in being given over to the temple in marriage to the deity by their families, undergo a shift in their social personhood. They come to occupy the place of sons for their natal families, in the sense that the role of the son is linked to the responsibility to ensure the material well-being of the family, which they now fulfill. In the thirunangai instances I described above, there appears to be a kind of restoration of normative familial kinship expectations and roles, whereby the thirunangai member stays or returns to care for the family. Reddy's (2005, 173–74) documentation of hijras' attenuated ties with natal families and the value placed on "the renunciation of natal kinship" does not seem to be the uncontested case in Chennai. It is possible that transgender rights activism and visibility have shifted familial and social acceptance, giving rise to renewed affections and regimes of care. What I wish to highlight is that both the kind of "kinship trouble" that Ramberg analyzes and the kind of creative reformulation of kinship I am beginning to document in my work seem to hinge upon the provision of material care. My thirunangai interlocutors have, indeed, engaged in a form of renunciation. But it is not a renunciation of natal familial attachments per se. Instead, it is a renunciation of one's relationship to the family as a caste institution. When thirunangais return (or stay on) to provide care for their parents and siblings, they do so as people who have forged other important attachments and hold other obligations: to their thirunangai kin, to friends and intimate others, and to the goddess. My ongoing work contributes to this complex discussion of renunciation as a proliferation of sites of care.[11]

All this talk of astonishment, the explicit attention paid to thirunangai-maruladis' commitment to Angalamman worship, and the marshalling of available theories of thirunangai personhood as well as experiences of neighborly intimacy—all point to a moral economy in operation. Exchanges among people and between people and deities take forms that are semiotically recognizable within a meaningful set of relationships; they are imbued with value as well as patterns of evaluation and judgment, and they serve to hold those relationships together beyond considerations of individual self-interest and economic rationality. This aligns with a longstanding concern in the social sciences with norms and practices of exchange and their inseparability from questions of values, moral personhood, and relationships.[12] However, what is truly interesting about the ethnographic context I have tried to describe is that an interest in others' sense of astonishment serves as an affective node for thirunangais to reveal their investment in this moral economy. Wonder is not just anchored in religious ritual, it is drawn into the metalanguage of conversational talk, and it worlds an apparent paradox: thirunangai-maruladis' emphasis on others' astonishment at their commitment to the goddess seems to be an attempt at setting themselves apart as exceptional devotees of Angalamman, but at the same time it also argues for their place within a world of shared devotion and social intimacy.[13] Talk of *asandhu podhal*, of astonishment, then, serves as an ethical affordance for thirunangai-maruladis to both hint at and actually world a moral economy into being. The practice of wonder seems to be a way to cut through the mire of contradictory notions of identity and personhood to get at an ethic of being and relationality.

The "wonder discourse" we find instantiated in the ethical talk about astonishment appears to hinge on a valorization of thirunangai capacity for giving. One topic around which this value is asserted is money, especially the money spent in organizing the annual festivals for goddess Angalamman. Why should festival expenses serve as a kind of exemplary site at which this moral capacity is seen to be demonstrated? When thirunangais are clearly giving to others in so many ways—to their natal families, to neighbors and friends, to their thirunangai kin, and to local merchants—why valorize "giving to the goddess" (*avalukku seyyanum*) as the gesture that exemplifies thirunangai capacity for giving?

Ontological Premises, Social Capacities, and the Work of Wonder

I turn to Ragini Amma, a thirunangai-maruladi elder, who has her own temple for the goddess in Royapuram and who has been conducting annual rituals for the goddess for over forty years now. I asked her why thirunangais insisted on mounting the festivals with such fanfare and expense. In her response, she made a broad distinction between two kinds of moral community: one is the immediate community among which thirunangais live and perform their devotion to Angalamman and the other is what she referred to as the "general society" or "common society" (*podhu samoogam*), which is, potentially, boundless and encompasses the rest of the world, but often refers to the broader Tamil world of public opinion and normative morality. She suggested that people from both these categories marveled at thirunangais' capacity for giving (especially in the context of Amman rituals), but in slightly different ways and for slightly different reasons.

According to her, in the course of their everyday intimacies and "fights and arguments" (*sandai saccharavu*), the *duniyadars* among whom thirunangais live can forget that thirunangais are different from them, that being a thirunangai is a particularly felicitous mode to worship the goddess (*ammanukku ugandhavargal*). So, "when they see how sincerely we do the rituals, how well we do the festivals, they understand." As for the "general society" and its dominant views about thirunangais, Ragini Amma had this to say: "All year round, they see us as beggars and sex workers. But when they see us during the festival, they are astonished (*asandhu poyidaranga*). They think, 'How diligently [*siratthaiya*] they serve the goddess! They are, indeed, divine beings [*deiva piravi*].' It makes them think [*sindhikka vaikkudhu*]."

Ragini Amma appears to suggest that the wondrous enactment of the Amman festivals brings a moment of challenge and clarity to certain ontological premises others might hold about transfeminine identity and embodiment. In her view, the neighbors seem to forget that thirunangais have a special relationship with the goddess, while the world out there comes to see thirunangais only as sex workers and beggars. They both have a very human idea of what being a thirunangai is, one occluded by neighborly intimacy and the other informed by ideas of social pathology. She suggests that the spectacle of the festivals, the expense of resources and energy it indexes, and the thirunangai commitment to Amman that it signifies all pose a moment of stunning challenge to those ideas and open a space for the recognition of thirunangais' special relationship with Angalamman. Her explanation, nay theorization, suggests the possibility that an experience of astonishment offers a challenge to certain ontological premises others bring to their relationship with thirunangais.

In the theoretical framework he proposes for a comparative ethnographic approach to the anthropology of wonder, Michael W. Scott (2016) foregrounds ontology as a key site of wonder's operation. He has argued that wonder, through its instantiation in the "wonder discourses" and "wonder practices" of a people, comes to be "an index and a mode of challenge to existing ontological premises" (Scott 2016, 476).[14] In the thirunangai context, Ragini Amma's views support Scott's argument that discourses and practices of wonder might involve questions of ontology. We might see her as foregrounding a nondualist ontology in which there is a mutual, constitutive imbrication of the goddess and thirunangai embodiment. She seems to offer this claim in response to what she sees as others' refusal or forgetting to accord thirunangais their divine ontology. It is important for me to point out that this nondualist, human-divine ontology of gender that Ragini Amma and several other thirunangai-maruladis project is not shared by all thirunangais and even those who subscribe to it do not foreground it at all times. Transgender activism for rights, for instance, is broadly premised on a secular gender identity grounded in self-identification and self-expression (Kothari 2020; Semmalar 2020). In the Tamil context, the discourse of transgender rights is inflected by the Dravidian discourse of self-respect and gender autonomy (Nataraj 2019). Further, Ambedkarite critiques from within the trans community, which challenge both the Hindu-casteist underpinnings of the LGBTQ rights discourse in India and the elitism of liberal identity politics, eschew religious gender ontologies.[15] Therefore, it is important not to generalize thirunangai-maruladi assertions of divine causality of transfeminine identity as the singular claim of all thirunangais in the Tamil region. Far from it. However, for those thirunangais who are devoted to the goddess and whose lifeworlds are situated amid others who share such devotional forms, cultural practices, and class locations, a belief in Angalamman's constitutive role in thirunangai gender identity and expression appears to be central.

Ragini Amma offered me a narrative that brings together goddess Angalamman and the figure of the Thirunangai in a dramatic account of generosity, reciprocity, and mutual transformation:

> When Angalamma is taken over by brammahatti dosham [after rescuing Sivan from the clutches of the severed head of Bramma] and she wandered around, she came across a hut that was in the shade of a date palm tree. A thirunangai was living there. She had built that hut, and she was living there under the date palm tree. It was the month of Maasi [mid-February to mid-March], and Amma was under a curse from Kalaivani [Saraswati] for stomping on her husband Bramman's head. So she had become a possessed woman. Her eyes were bulged out, her teeth had grown longer, she wore a garland of entrails. She was wandering all over the place, from village to village, looking for something to eat. She comes to Thazhanoor, she comes to Poongaavanam, she comes to Koovathur. Then finally she came to [Mel]Malayanur. She sees the thirunangai's hut under the date palm tree. . . .
>
> Angalamma went to that hut. She went there as an ordinary woman. The thirunangai said to her, "You can stay in my house." But that thirunangai was unwell, so Amma healed her by finding the right herbs and making a medicine for her. Then when the month of Maasi came the next year, Amma again took her horrific form because of the curse. She needed the entrails of an animal to wear as a garland. Where would she go to find one? Looking at this, the thirunangai tore open her own stomach and offered her intestines to Amma. And she said, "Amma, when you sit down here as saami, you should not sit down in your form, you should show yourself in my form. This place should become green and lush [*pacchai pasel*]. We should hear the chatter of parrots. Peacocks should dance, cuckoos should sing, and my people should thrive here." She took this promise [*satya vaakku*] from Amma. That is why Angalamma looks like a thirunangai in the temple. She is a thirunangai.[16]

Angalamman here appears as a tired and wandering woman who finds refuge in the home of a thirunangai. The thirunangai takes her in, feeds her, and restores her to health. When the goddess in her *ugra* or fierce form needs sacrifice, the thirunangai offers her own innards, asking in return that the goddess should take the form of a thirunangai.

And Angalamman obliges. Here we have a narrative in which it is not the goddess who creates thirunangai identity, it is the thirunangai who turns the goddess into a thirunangai by the force of her generosity and sacrifice. This is only one of the many instances where the thirunangai capacity for generosity and the imperative to give to another at the risk of undoing oneself finds expression.

My point here is not to essentialize sacrifice as a thirunangai trait, but only to show that certain thirunangai-maruladi narratives highlight that capacity as an ethical quality. It is possible to see such narratives as part of a larger network of moral stances made by communities within a society. For example, Eveline Meyer (1986) documents two stories in which we see upper castes and wealthy landowners refuse to offer help either to the goddess or to her devotees in need. In one story, a *zamindar*, a wealthy landlord, refuses to offer the goddess some land even after she asks him directly and later through her priest several times. The only way Angalamman is able to secure land for a temple is by appearing in front of the landlord in the most terrifying appearance and threatening him with downfall for his lack of generosity: "Isvari went to the zamindar's house with her trident, sat on his chest and said, choking him with his hand, 'If you don't donate any land, I will open your stomach, take out your intestines and wear them as garlands" (253). Meyer records another story where the person who refuses to come to the aid of a devotee and even insults the goddess is a wealthy brahmin man (253–54).[17] The actions of these two men from upper castes and landowning classes is comparable to that of the ruthless farmer in the Yellamma story Lucinda Ramberg offers us: "The landlord saw her eating from his fields and became angry. Her ran into the fields swinging his scythe and shouting. Shouting and shouting, swinging his arms and that scythe" (2014, 39–40). These figures occupy the same paradigmatic location in the narrative—as those who fail to help the goddess even when asked.

In contrast to this, in Ragini Amma's narrative and in the Yellamma-Mathangi story recorded by Lucinda Ramberg, a thirunangai and a Dalit woman, respectively, emerge as people who are ready to put their own lives at risk in order to protect the goddess. These narratives' assertion of the capacity of the most marginalized to act in the most selfless ways need not be seen as essentialist moves. Instead, by placing these narratives alongside each other, we can see that the plot offers some interesting paradigmatic positions for different local groups to occupy.

As part of these discursive emplacements, we see the selflessness of the most oppressed within these worlds highlighted against the meanness of the wealthy and the powerful.

Conclusion

The narrative Ragini Amma offers is not an authoritative account that all thirunangai-maruladis hold as an explanation for their special connection to Angalamman. For many of the thirunangai-maruladis with whom I conducted my fieldwork, their sense of connection to Angalamman is anchored in other modalities of faith: an intuitive affection for the goddess; a vacillation between a religious and a secular sense of self; the importance of their first encounter with the goddess, which was a moment of trance embodiment in a ritual context; and so on. What we see here are multiple secular and religious ontologies of gender and multiple, often conflicting, perceptions of thirunangais' social personhood and the nature of their social attachments. But what allows me to see these plural accounts of identity, moral personhood, and ethical relationality is an attention to thirunangai-maruladis' insistence on the world's astonishment at their commitment to the goddess. This wonder, this commitment, and this valorization of thirunangai capacity to give are all wondrously despiritualized and framed in terms of money, expense, festivities, pomp, and splendor. But what Ragini Amma's myth tells us is that even the goddess is wonderstruck by thirunangai generosity. In fact, she is revived and revivified by thirunangai sacrifice. In exchange for that stunning act of sacrifice on the part of the thirunangai, Angalamman turns herself into a thirunangai. In this poetics of identity, what links thirunangais to Angalamman is not merely devotion but a fundamental mutuality of being.

Read through Ragini Amma's theorization, thirunangais' insistence on astonishment (*asandhupodhal*) as a valued emotional response to the splendor of ritual appears like an openness—both a faith in the possibility of, and a willingness to work toward, moments that powerfully call into question certain everyday assumptions. Especially assumptions about the social and moral personhood of thirunangais. Assumptions that directly impact their material lives and relationships. Assumptions about who thirunangais are, what relationships matter to them, how they go about attending to those relationships, whether being a thirunangai is a place outside normative sites of attachment, love, and obligation, or whether it is, in fact, a site where ethical relationships and commitments explode and proliferate. In a field of such proliferation of commitments, "the determination of what is excess and what is necessity is riven with questions" (Srinivas 2018, 120). Srinivas here refers to the "excess" and "necessity" of ritual enactments. That question certainly applies to thirunangai practices of ritual, but it also applies, obliquely, to the relationships they sustain. How much to give, to whom, when, in exchange for what, and so on, are questions that my thirunangai interlocutors suggest should not be calculated too neatly. There is an ethic of excess here; an ethic that, in its fulfillment, generates astonishment. This ethic of excess is also an ethic of exhaustion, for the Tamil expression *asandhupodhal* could also be related to *ayarndhupodhal*, to be exhausted by something. To err on the side of excessive giving is also to court exhaustion; and to exhaust oneself in giving to the goddess is also to prepare oneself for replenishment and renewal.

Notes

The research for this paper was made possible by a Junior Research Fellowship (2016–17) from the American Institute of Indian Studies and funding through a Link-Cotsen Postdoctoral Fellowship (2020–23) at the Society of Fellows, Princeton University. The ethnographic material for this essay comes from research conducted in Chennai with thirty-five thirunangai-maruladis and several other thirunangais who were themselves not maruladis but many of whom were devotees of the goddess.

1. *Thirunangai* is the widely recognized, accepted, and respectful Tamil label that refers to transgender women in and from the Tamil region. It combines the honorific *Thiru* and the word *nangai*, meaning woman, to foreground a gender identity that is broadly secular in its juridical aspirations and is inflected by Dravidian political ideology of the self-respect and self-assertion of marginalized communities. See Nataraj (2019).

2. I use "transgender" not as an unproblematic gloss for "thirunangai" or to suggest commensurability of identities and embodiments, but merely to facilitate some provisional cross-context understanding. Here I take cue from my thirunangai interlocutors who themselves use "transgender" and "TG" as identity labels alongside "thirunangai" when addressing anglophone contexts and audiences. See the most recent glossary of terms produced by the LGBTQAI community in Chennai (http://orinam.net/content/wp-content/uploads/2022/01/Glossary_LGBTIQA_Jan2022.pdf).

3. Angalamman is among the many Amman mother goddesses worshipped across the region. For a detailed account of the similarities and variations in the representations, narratives, worship, and rituals of the goddess across Tamil Nadu, see Meyer (1986). For an ethnographic discussion of Angalamman rituals, see Nabokov (2000), Craddock (2012), and Allocco (this volume).

4. I use "metapragmatics" here in the sense in which Webb Keane (2008) does when he refers to "metalanguages of action" that involve "reflexive characterizations (explicit but more often implicit) of the kind of event now taking place, and the kinds of participants entering into it" (33).

5. For analyses of ethical talk and intersubjective alignment of ethical stances, see Lempert (2013), Prasad (2004), and Venkatesan (2014).

6. A popular savings and loan scheme that operates both in large professional networks investment and in smaller community arrangements. It is the latter I refer to here. For an account how chit fund schemes operate within communities of urban poor, see Roberts (2016, 99–101).

7. In a separate work in progress, I argue that thirunangais steer clear of both the *kula deivam* (clan deity) and *ishta deivam* (personal deity) formulations in devotional Hinduism and instead place a divinely ordained transfeminine identity as anchoring both personal and collective attachment to the goddess.

8. In organizing their kinship, thirunangais invoke both the monastic/pedagogic terminology of *guru* (teacher) and *chela* (disciple) and also an improvised matrilineal one of *amma-ponnu* (mother-daughter).

9. Thirunangais draw this vocabulary from their links to Hijra lifeworlds primarily in Mumbai and Delhi. For a discussion of *duniyadar* and *duniyadari* and the householder/renouncer distinction, see Reddy (2005).

10. Turner (1969) extends Arnold van Gennep's concept of liminality to a discussion of "liminal personality," "liminal entities," and "threshold people" as figures in whom liminality as a temporary condition has taken a more permanent form. The "structure" relates to these liminal figures as people who are exempted from some cherished norms but whose outsider status is nevertheless "hedged around with prescriptions, prohibitions, and conditions" (109).

11. For a recent and important reinterpretation of kinship, violence, and asceticism in hijra lifeworlds, see Saria (2021).

12. See Keane (2008), Mauss (1967 [1928]), Venkatesan (2016), Zelizer (1997) as select examples of analyses of moral economies in operation and transformation.

13. See Keane (2019) for an argument about the place of everyday ethics, forms of social interaction, and semiotic affordances in both instantiating and transforming moral economies. Also see Keane (2008) on "moral meta-language."

14. Through an analysis of "wonder discourses" among the Arosi of Solomon Islands, Scott (2016) shows that the inhabitants of island of Makira are able to challenge their own ontological premises: the earlier solidity of a "socio-cosmic order" whose entities are independently arising, matrilineally structured, and

discontinuously grouped gives way to "intimations of something amazingly at odds" with this ancestral ontology, a sense of the entire island as possessing an ontological unity (476). Scott locates this "scalar shift" (483) in the ontological premise of the Makirans within a discussion of colonialism, Christianity, and the ethnopolitics of the postcolonial nation-state.

15. See Semmalar (2017) and Asif (2021). Also see Living Smile Vidya (2014).

16. Neither the *sthala puraanam* (history/hagiography of a holy site) of the Melmalayanur temple, nor the range of myths collated by Eveline Meyer (1986) make mention of this mythology that Ragini Amma has to offer. It was, however, corroborated by some of the other thirunangai-maruladis.

17. In another narrative detailing Angalamman's meanderings in the Tamil country, the goddess approaches a toddy-tapper for some nourishment for her children. But the toddy-tapper refuses, saying the harvest has been poor on account of drought and he has no toddy to give away. In yet another story, fishermen express their willingness to help the goddess but ask in exchange that they should be blessed with plentiful catch. See Meyer (1986, 28–30).

Works Cited

Asif, Afrah. 2021. "A Phase of 'Fight, Fight, Fight.'" *DeCenter Mag*, Spring. https://www.decentermag.com/interviews-grace-banu.

Craddock, Elaine. 2012. "The Half Male, Half Female Servants of the Goddess Ankalaparamecuvari." *Nidan: Indian Journal for the Study of Hinduism* 24 (1): 117–35.

Keane, Webb. 2008. "Market, Materiality, and Moral Metalanguage." *Anthropological Theory* 8 (1): 27–42.

———. 2019. "How Everyday Ethics Becomes a Moral Economy, and Vice Versa." *Economics* 13 (1). http://dx.doi.org/10.5018/economics-ejournal.ja.2019-46.

Kothari, Jayna. 2020. "Trans Equality in India: Affirmation of the Right to Self-determination of Gender." *NUJS Law Review* 13 (3): 1–13.

Lempert, Michael. 2013. "No Ordinary Ethics." *Anthropological Theory* 13 (4): 370–393.

Living Smile Vidya. 2014. *I Am Vidya: A Transgender Woman's Journey*. New Delhi: Rupa Publications.

Meyer, Eveline. 1986. *Ankalaparamecuvari: A Goddess of Tamil Nadu, Her Myths and Cult*. Stuttgart: Steiner Verlag.

Nabokov, Isabelle. 2000. *Religion against the Self: An Ethnography of Tamil Rituals*. Oxford: Oxford University Press.

Nanda, Serena. 1999. *Neither Man nor Woman: The Hijras of India*. Second Edition. Belmont, CA: Wadsworth Publishing Company.

Nataraj, Shakthi. 2019. "Trans-formations: Projects of Resignification in Tamil Nadu's Transgender Rights Movement." PhD diss., University of California, Berkeley.

Padmabharathi, K. 2013. *Thirunangaiyar: Samooga Varaiviyal* [Thirunangais: An Ethnographic Study]. Chennai: Tamizhini Publications.

Prasad, Leela. 2004. "Conversational Narrative and the Moral Self: Stories of Negotiated Properties from South India." *Journal of Religious Ethics* 32 (1): 153–74.

Ramakrishnan, V. 2016. *Adithala Makkalin Panpaattu* Puridhalgal [Subaltern Cultural Understandings]. Chennai: Paalam Publications.

Ramberg, Lucinda. 2014. *Given to the Goddess: South Indian Devadasis and the Sexuality of Religion*. Durham, NC: Duke University Press.

Reddy, Gayatri. 2005. *With Respect to Sex: Negotiating Hijra Identity in South India*. Chicago: Chicago University Press.

Roberts, Nathaniel. 2016. *To Be Cared For: The Power of Conversion and Foreignness of Belonging in an Indian Slum*. Oakland: University of California Press.

Roscoe, Will. 1996. "Priests of the Goddess: Gender Transgression in Ancient Religion." *History of Religions* 35 (3): 195–230.

Saria, Vaibhav. 2021. *Hijras, Lovers, Brothers: Surviving Sex and Poverty in Rural India*. New York: Fordham University Press.

Scott, Michael W. 2016. "To Be Makiran Is to See like Mr Parrot: The anthropology of Wonder in Solomon Islands." *Journal of the Royal Anthropological Institute* 22 (3): 474–95.

Semmalar, Gee Imaan. 2017. "Why Trans Movements in India Must Be Anti-caste." *Feminism in India*, December 28. https://feminisminindia.com/2017/12/28/trans-movements-india-caste/.

———. 2020. "Re-cast(e)ing Navtej Singh v. Union of India." *NUJS Law Review* 13 (3): 1–24.

Srinivas, Tulasi. 2018. *The Cow in the Elevator: An Anthropology of Wonder*. Durham, NC: Duke University Press.

Turner, Victor. 1969. *The Ritual Process: Structure and Anti-structure*. Ithaca, NY: Cornell University Press.

Vasudevan, Aniruddhan. 2020. "Between the Goddess and the World: Religion and Ethics among Thirunangai Transwomen in Chennai, India." PhD diss., University of Texas at Austin.

Venkatesan, Sowmhya. 2014. "Talk and Practice: Ethics and an Individual in Contemporary South India." *Cambridge Journal of Anthropology* 32 (2): 26–41.

Zelizer, Viviana. 1997. *The Social Meaning of Money*. Princeton, NJ: Princeton University Press.

Chapter 7

Wonder in the Cremation Ground

The Affective and Transformative Dimensions of an Urban Tamil Festival

Amy L. Allocco

A portal opens in the canopy shading the street, allowing a cascade of multicolored flower petals to shower the Goddess's gorgeous, many-armed processional image. Devotees throw cucumbers, coins, flowers, and boiled chickpeas into the air and, as these offerings rain down on us, some spectators bend to scoop them up from the ground, running the risk of being trampled by the surging crowd. Live chickens are swung around in front of possessed women dressed as Angalaparameshwari—a police officer standing near me was whacked in the face with one!—and several women who are dancing the Goddess bite their heads off and drink the warm blood from their necks, their eyes closed in evident bliss. The entire street is packed, body to body—so, too, the street's balconies and rooftops are crowded with onlookers. Drums ring out, worshipers with eyes fixed on the Goddess chant "Om Shakti," possessed women scream and lurch, colored lights twinkle, baskets full of food offerings are distributed: what a spectacle. . . . Five goats are cut (oh, the blood!) and the priests dance by with the goats' headless bodies draped around their necks and shoulders, blood coursing down their bare torsos, droplets flying everywhere. The five-headed image of Pavadairayan is now visible—whether deliberately revealed or unveiled from energetic dancing, I don't know—and is spattered with blood. One priest carries a winnowing basket filled with the goats' innards aloft, and the god-dancers jump and lunge at these delicacies as the procession starts out on its excruciatingly slow journey to the cremation ground. It will take perhaps six hours or more for it to reach the graveyard, where the Goddess's processional image will have darshan of the enormous figure that was fashioned out of cremation ashes after midnight last night—we will meet her there.

—March 6, 2019

This excerpt from my fieldnotes on the 2019 Mayana Kollai festival (Mayāna Koḷḷai tiruviḻā; Looting of the Graveyard/Cremation Ground festival) at a temple dedicated to the Hindu goddess Angalaparameshwari (Aṅkāḷaparamēsvari) in Chennai, Tamil Nadu reveals the intensity of this spectacular scene.[1] Spectacle, particularly as it may encode or enact transformation, can engender wonder in an audience, as Tulasi Srinivas has demonstrated (2018, 207). In my analysis of the Mayana Kollai festival I follow Srinivas's proposal that wonder is a generative force that operates in a "landscape of possibility" (57) and highlight two key types of wonder. First, wonder exerts an affective force that reshapes relations between the Goddess and her devotees. The narratives of festival participants suggest that they experience a certain kind of possibility-expanding wonder as their relationships with the Goddess are redefined and reframed in this intense and intimate set of performances. Their wonder exists within a repertoire of affective possibilities, including the fear and shock that devotees and temple leaders discursively mark when they reflect on their sense of being overwhelmed at seeing the Goddess in her heightened, frenzied form, given that she is experienced as gentler and more accessible throughout the year. Second, there is the sense of wonder that I, the ethnographer, have experienced each time I participate in the multiday Mayana Kollai festival with the community at this modest Angalaparameshwari temple. The force of this wonder collapses binaries and raises questions about our scholarly frameworks for understanding the extra/ordinary, ultimately compelling us to reconsider and expand several interpretive categories. In focusing our attention on the festival as a site of transformation, my analysis highlights the fluidity of spatial and gender norms in this sequence of rituals and emphasizes the striking ways that categories of purity and pollution are renegotiated and the boundaries between the living and the dead and myth and everyday life may be dissolved or suspended. These fluidities and renegotiations are inextricably linked to the wonder that the spectacle of the festival engenders, and they propel devotees and the anthropologist alike into a space of almost limitless possibility.

During the festival events of Mayana Kollai, which take place over two days and two nights, the goddess Angalaparameshwari herself manifests in a range of forms, evoking multiple reactions from her devotees and attracting diverse interpretations. This non-brahminic goddess, who is now cast as a local manifestation of Parvati and identified as exclusively vegetarian outside of this festival context, is worshiped in her temple throughout the year by people from a broad range of castes. On the Mayana Kollai day she explodes into the streets in a heightened, resplendent form and, accompanied by Pavadairayan (Pāvāṭairāyan̲), her blood-eating guardian deity, and frenzied human hosts, travels to the cremation ground to participate in *darshan* and destruction before her devotees gently rock and sooth her with lullabies that night. Eveline Meyer, whose comprehensive 1986 study of Angalaparameshwari remains the only detailed treatment of the festival to date, underscores the goddess's inherent complexity and multiplicity, observing that devotees perceive her as "a complex whole, made up of fluid images" (iv). In addition to this fluidity, there is a great deal of creativity on display in the Mayana Kollai festival context as the Goddess assumes her fullest form in order to revive and temporarily regenerate all who fall under her jurisdiction. Whereas the festival's ritual process might at first seem like a dramatic and self-conscious rupture of the ordinary world, in the estimation of the temple priests, trustees, worshipers, ritual musicians, and others with whom I have discussed Mayana Kollai since I first witnessed its performance in 2007, it is very much embedded in the everyday. Indeed, my interlocutors are clear that participating in the festival helps them to know the Goddess more fully, more abundantly, and more expansively, and that their everyday interactions with her are profoundly shaped and enriched by this intimate, deeper knowing. Srinivas argues that rituals, although threaded through ordinary life, nevertheless have the capacity to "allow practitioners to enter another extraordinary state, characterized by an internal, often magical logic" that transforms them and their everyday worlds (2018, 12). The festival's transformative potential lies at the heart of Mayana Kollai, which, I argue, should be understood as a remarkable and spectacular (even potentially wonder-full) cluster of ritual performances situated in the flow of everyday life rather than a radical departure from it.

The Festival Process: Preparations, Decorations, Vows, and Processions

The Mayana Kollai festival takes place at the new moon of the Tamil month of Masi (February–March), immediately following Maha Shivaratri (the Great Night of Shiva).[2] The festival sequence is inaugurated on the full moon day two weeks prior, when a ritual vessel is established in Angalaparameshwari's temple and members of the hereditary priestly line tie ritual wristlets (*kappu*; see Allocco 2009, 398–401). This priestly family belongs to the inland fisherman caste (i.e., the Sembadavar or Meenavar caste) for whom Angalaparameshwari is the lineage deity (*kuladeivam*) and on whom the traditional right to serve as her priests was conferred.[3] Several additional preparatory rituals punctuate the waning moon period leading up to the new moon, including the sprouting of assorted tender shoots in a pot installed next to the goddess's image inside the temple, which strongly signals the festival's themes of regeneration, enlivening, and fertility.[4] Following these preparatory practices, the festival itself unfolds across multiple ritual events on the darkest night of the month, during the new moon (*amavasai*), which is dedicated to worshiping Angalaparameshwari in her sanctum and features the construction of a *padivilakku*, a temporary ritual vessel within which a distinctive oil lamp (*vilakku*) is set.

The roads flanking Angalaparameshwari's temple are lavishly decorated for the festival: crisscrossing strands of colored lights flash and twinkle and huge light displays depicting the Goddess, Ganesha, and other deities stretch skyward. Beneath the decorative canopy that stretches over the temple a marching band clad in tasseled velvet uniforms plays, trading off periodically with an energetic ensemble of Kerala-style *chenda* drummers. *Thappattai* drummers wait for their turn to perform and a *tavil-nadaswaram* pair, who will accompany the procession later that evening, drink tea nearby. Whenever there is a break in the live performances, devotional songs blare from enormous speakers stacked at the ends of the bunted pavilion.

Where the atmosphere in the street is carnivalesque, a more focused devotional mood prevails inside the temple. A steady stream of worshipers flows through the Goddess's sanctum, which is festooned with flower garlands and swags of crisp rupee bills. The priests handle the near-continuous *puja*: they receive food, fruit, and flower offerings from devotees who then impale lemons on the Goddess's trident as they exit the small temple, clutching their *prasadam*. Meanwhile, drummers from the troupe of ritual musicians (*pambai-udukkaikkarar*) who have been hired to preside over the festival proceedings sculpt the distinctively styled *padivilakku*, a flower-decorated ritual display into which an oil lamp (*vilakku*) is set. Over the course of several hours, they use clay to craft both a decorative base for the lamp—through whose flame the Goddess must communicate her satisfaction with the festival arrangements and give permission (*uttaravu*) for them to proceed—and an anthropomorphic image of Angalaparameshwari seated on a lion. Her feline vehicle is intended to be fearsome with his protruding *kumkum*-smeared tongue, garlic-clove fangs, and bulging egg eyes. This flower-wreathed ritual assemblage is kept concealed behind a curtain throughout this process and is revealed only after life is transferred to it from Angalaparameshwari's central image and it is definitively identified with the Goddess.

As the evening wears on, the street in front of the temple begins to fill with worshipers, spectators, and votaries. Women petition Angalaparameshwari for bodily healing and pregnancies with offerings of small dough figures and silver milk cups, while others present the saris and other accoutrements that they will wear when they guise or dress as the Goddess (i.e., take her *vesham*).[5] Eventually, the procession coalesces and—led by the temple's priestly family—sets out for the nearby temple of Goddess Mundakkanni (Muṇṭakakkaṇṇi Amman; see Allocco 2009, 12–17; 2018) for the "gathering the Ganges" (*Gangai tiraṭṭu*) rite. Although no water is actually recovered from the well at Mundakkanni Amman, an enormously popular local goddess who is understood as the "big-sister" to many of her counterparts in the surrounding neighborhoods, the Ganga-collecting rite opens up flows of power between the two sites.[6] As one woman explained to me, even symbolically carrying a pot of water from one powerful location to another along with *pambai* and *udukkai* drumming will "make the dead feel happy and attract them to that place." Drawing both the dead and the Goddess into communion with the living, then, is one of the chief goals of the Mayana Kollai festival.

Dozens of women who have vowed to take up the Goddess's *vesham* don gem-studded foil crowns, peacock feathers, and strings of multicolored cloth scraps (see fig. 7.1) that recall the curse to wear rags and feathers that the Goddess bears in the story of Shiva's sin of brahminicide (*brahmahatti dosham*), which is one of the key myths associated with this festival.[7] In that story Shiva and the Goddess both suffer after he angrily excises Brahma's fifth head when Parvati mistakes Brahma for her simi-

Figure 7.1. A devotee who is guised or dressed as the goddess (i.e., who has taken her *vesham*) experiences Angalaparameshwari's presence and prepares to sacrifice a chicken. Note her rag dress and the characteristic skull-like ash pot held by the man behind her. *Source*: Author photo.

larly five-headed husband. The Mayana Kollai festival commemorates the elimination of Shiva's curse, accomplished when Brahma's skull, which has been attached to Shiva's palm since his murderous act, descends to devour the food that has been scattered in the cremation ground and the Goddess takes on a huge, fearsome form and smashes it. Children, too, wear headbands strung with cloth scraps tied around their heads in conjunction with vows for their protection, especially from pox and other illnesses. One mother, for example, tells me that both she and her son keep this practice in gratitude for the Goddess enabling his safe delivery despite the fact that his umbilical cord was wrapped around his neck "like a garland" in utero. The ritual musicians insert skewers, spears, and piercings (*alagu*) of various sizes into the cheeks and tongues of male and female votaries, and other devotees prepare to carry blazing, unglazed firepots. Once the ritual musicians start to play their drums and sing, several vow-keepers and worshipers exhibit the presence of Angalaparameshwari and other goddesses, and they are given time and space to dance and offer divination (*kuri solluthal*) before the procession sets out toward Angalaparameshwari's temple.

The spectacular return procession takes several hours and includes multiple types of drumming, energetic dancing, and the sacrifice of chickens for those who embody the Goddess. Once we reach Angalaparameshwari's temple, platters of offerings are laid out before her and a gigantic banana leaf is mounded with vegetarian foods particular to this festival. The ritual musicians sing directly to the *padivilakku*, heaping praise on and describing the Goddess while those who are embodying her engage in further prophecy-saying (*arul-vakku*). It is well after midnight when the hereditary priests retrieve a shrouded ritual object from their home behind the temple (as seen in fig. 7.3). Often called the *kapparai*, this item is identified as Pavadairayan, the Goddess's son and guardian (see fig. 7.6).[8] Because his gaze is believed to be lethal when he is hungry, his five-faced image will remain concealed until the following afternoon, when it will feed on the blood of the sacrificial goats in the street in front of the temple.

Ritual Creativity in the Cremation Ground

With the cloaked image of Pavadairayan in hand, a few male temple leaders set off for the cremation/burial ground with shovels and other supplies loaded aboard a wooden cart graced with Angalaparameshwari's processional image. We walk the two kilometers to our destination and arrive there shortly before 2 a.m. Our group heads directly to an open expanse within the compound, past the cremation sheds and the areas filled with close-set graves. There, an enormous mound of ash that the site's attendants have been saving from the electric crematorium awaits us. The sari that covers the pile is weighted down by a sack of human bones, which they will use to adorn the massive, supine figure (*uruvam*) that they will create from the ashes. Significantly, Meyer notes that the majority of castes who worship Angalaparameshwari bury their kin, meaning that this figure is effectively produced from the ashes of dead who belong to other communities (1986, 104). While some of the men immediately begin fashioning the ash effigy (*bommai*) with its head stretching southward toward the King of Death's realm (Yama Lokam), others collect skulls and bones from the surrounding cemetery to be used in their final decoration work (*alankaram*). Although no gravesites were disturbed during the festivals I attended, the use of bones as embellishments is frequently described as the remaining vestige of what was once the actual robbing of graves during Mayana Kollai, whose name may also translate as "pillage" or "plunder" in the cremation ground.[9]

By dawn the figure is complete (as seen in fig. 7.2). Dusted with *kumkum* and turmeric powders, it is draped with a long garland of lemons.[10] Lemon eyes now punctuate the effigy's face, and its limbs are adorned with bones. Who the figure represents is a subject of some debate: this temple community's *bommai* is sometimes identified as the Goddess's guardian, Pavadairayan, but I have also been told that it is the demon/king Vallalakandan/Vallalarajan, his wife, or even the Goddess herself.[11] Even as the volunteers who have spent the night sculpting the ash heap into a figure that is now twenty-five feet long and perhaps four feet high nap on the hard earth, the cemetery around us is springing to life. Families of those buried here arrive with brooms, flowers, paint cans, and brushes in order to spruce up their relatives' graves while members of Angalaparameshwari's temple community congregate around the ash figure.

Figure 7.2. The ash figure (*bommai*) in an open expanse within the graveyard/cremation ground on the morning of the 2019 Mayana Kollai festival, the one-hundredth anniversary of its performance at this Chennai Angalaparameshwari temple. *Source*: Author photo.

Some parents and children carry out vows in thanksgiving for progeny and to protect against illness, including dressing the kids as the guardian deity Madurai Veeran, complete with traditional outfits, mustaches, and floral hair decorations. The temple priests arrange lush flower garlands on the Goddess's processional image, the still-hidden five-headed image of Pavadairayan, and the ash figure and then lay out a spread of raw vegetables and cooked foods. These offerings tie in with the festival's themes of abundance, nourishment, renewal, and regeneration, which are extended later in the day as foodstuffs are thrown and scattered to reflect elements of its animating myths. Cellphone communication with the priest at the Angalaparameshwari temple ensures that the morning bathing ritual underway there coincides precisely with the *puja* for Pavadairayan (as pictured in fig. 7.3) and the ash figure in the cremation ground, effectively collapsing temporal and spatial distinctions between the two ritual arenas and drawing the Goddess and her guardian into powerful communion with the living and the dead. Finally, once the worshipers have prostrated before the effigy's skull-decorated feet, the

Figure 7.3. Morning *puja* for the shrouded Pavadairayan image at the head of the ash figure in the cremation ground. Children dressed as Madurai Veeran are visible in the background. *Source*: Author photo.

group sets off for the temple. They carry the shrouded Pavadairayan with them, leaving the *bommai* alone for the time being.

My practice at this point is to stay back to observe how the hundreds of families, whose relatives are buried or have been cremated here, mark the Mayana Kollai festival. Living kin clear weeds from, repaint, and decorate graves and offer clothing and the departed's favorite food items (see fig. 7.4). Later that day I meet a dear friend at her family's burial plot and watch as she carries heavy buckets of water to wash the single concrete slab atop her five relatives' graves before sprinkling it with colored powders and roses. She then arranges the special foods and drinks she has purchased from nearby shops: she pairs sweet, milky tea with a pack of biscuits for her recently deceased niece, scoops out biryani for her in-laws, and carefully mixes brandy and water in a flimsy plastic cup to accompany Chicken 65 and samosas for her husband. The family lights camphor and, wiping their eyes frequently, prays for their dead. As one of them explained, "On Mayana Kollai day the spirits of the

Figure 7.4. Hindu families repaint and decorate their relatives' graves with flowers during the Mayana Kollai festival in 2019. Many of them leave food and clothing offerings at their gravesites on the new moon day in the Tamil month of Masi. *Source*: Author photo.

dead roam unrestricted, because Angali releases them of their misdeeds and sets them free to eat the foods spread in the cremation ground and satisfy their hunger." After watching attentively to see that the food they have left out for a crow, emissary to the dead, is consumed, they return home to lay out additional offerings before the niche in the center of their home where they light their ritual lamp (*nadu veedu*).

Creative and beautiful flower decorations draw my eye as I walk among the graves: these range from thick flower garlands, to rows of marigold blossoms arranged in alternating colors along tomb ledges, to a display of bright-hued gerbera daisies on a diaphanous fabric canopy created by a professional florist. The cremation area is similarly busy, as the living kin of those who were burned there pay their respects and arrange banana leaves of homecooked foods to nourish their dead. To these they add slices of bread and biscuits favored by children and store-bought fried snacks enjoyed by many men, as well as sweets and bananas. Families thoughtfully complement each of these heaped leaves with the departed person's beverage of choice: a squat paper cup of tea, a water bottle, local liquor, or a tall bottle of beer. This intimate time, when kin networks concentrate on feeding and honoring their dead, contrasts sharply with the intense public activities that recommence at the Goddess's temple that afternoon and that climax in the graveyard that night.

Angalaparameshwari's festival intensifies when her elaborately decorated processional image appears in the street before her temple later that day (see fig. 7.5). She is multi-armed and magnificent, armed with weapons and ritual accessories. Massive flower garlands and blossoms of every shade surround her and jewelry glitters at her wrists, necks, ears, and waist. A golden garland of skulls rests against her gem-encrusted breastplate and small bands of skulls adorn her ankles as well as her primary arms, which hold a shining trident-spear aloft. The enormous crowd parts to accommodate the frenzied dancing of women who are embodying the Goddess (as shown in fig. 7.1). Their eyes fixed on her towering, stunning image, one after another these goddesses in human form sink their teeth into chickens' necks and drink their blood. Other devotees have brought savory chickpeas, dumplings, and other homemade delicacies, which they distribute among onlookers and toss into the air, much as the Goddess once strew food in the cremation ground on this precise new moon day to entice Brahma's skull to leave Shiva's hand to feed (Meyer 1986, 36–37).

Figure 7.5. On the second day of the festival Angalaparameshwari's elaborately decorated festival image presides over sacrificial offerings in the street in front of her temple before setting out on a multihour procession that culminates in the cremation ground late in the evening. There she displays her rage and madness as she participates in visual exchange with and the destruction of the massive ash effigy fashioned the previous night. *Source*: Author photo.

Figure 7.6. The five-faced image (*kapparai*) of the guardian Pavadairayan is revealed following the animal sacrifices in the street before Angalaparameshwari's temple. Sated from his feasting, his gaze is no longer regarded as dangerous. *Source*: Author photo.

The seething crowd grows tense when the five goats that have been reserved for the Goddess are sacrificed at the end of the street.[12] Men from the temple's priestly lineage push through the maze of bodies with the now-headless goats draped over their shoulders, blood streaming down their bare torsos, and the priest from a nearby Draupadi temple holds a dripping winnowing fan piled with goat viscera high above our heads. Another member of the priestly family careens and spins through the street carrying the previously cloaked image of Pavadairayan, whose five blood-streaked faces are now visible (see fig. 7.6). Satiated from his feasting, his gaze is no longer dangerous. Those who are dancing the Goddess grow agitated as the goats and the basket of entrails draws close to them and they lunge forward hungrily. Eventually the cart carrying the Goddess lurches into motion and begins to inch its way toward the graveyard. The crowd of worshipers accompanying the procession swells as it moves through the neighborhood, whose streets quickly become littered with scattered flowers, chickpeas, and other ritual detritus. Faces pressed against metal grates and gates, upper-caste and upper-class spectators view the raucous procession from the safe distance of their balconies and other vantage points along the way, consuming and participating voyeuristically in the wonder that the spectacle generates. Because her festival image is forced to halt again and again to accommodate the many residents who wish to worship and present offerings to the Goddess, it takes more than five hours for the procession to cover the less than two kilometers to reach the entrance to the cremation ground.

Inside, the scene is festive. The usually deserted burial/burning ground has been transformed into a fairground pulsating with sound and light. Every space seems filled with people: spectators line the branching roads that lead to different sections of the graveyard and cremation ground and onlookers perch on walls, stand atop mausoleums, and sit in the branches of large trees strung with colored lights. Devotional and popular music alternately blasts from speakers and vendors selling cotton candy, *pani puri*, and ice cream hawk their treats. Children clamber aboard amusement park rides, women browse at carts offering bangles, and flower-sellers enjoy a brisk trade.

The crowd's anticipation builds further in the additional hour it takes for the Goddess's procession to reach the open field where the enormous ash-soil image lays on its back, dreadlocks splayed around its head (see fig. 7.2). There the Mayana Kollai festival hurtles toward its culminating moments as Angalaparameshwari's elaborately decorated processional image finally meets the supine image, whom the priests infuse with life by thrusting the winnowing fan full of dripping goat organs deep into its abdomen. The five-headed Pavadairayan oversees this ritual enlivening, his now-visible faces spattered with the blood of the goats on which he has been feeding all afternoon (as seen in fig. 7.6). In a highly charged atmosphere intensified by widespread possession and the frenetic energy of male youth, the figure is quickly destroyed by those who mount and stomp on it as well as those who grab fistfuls of the vivified body to carry home (as pictured in fig. 7.7).[13] The ash-soil mixture is now regarded as highly valued *prasadam* and believed to have protective and healing properties for those who come into contact with or ingest it.

By this time, it is 10 p.m. and most worshipers immediately disperse. A few, however, escort Angalaparameshwari back to her temple, where small clusters of women take turns rocking the Goddess's festival image in a swing and singing soothing lullabies to her throughout the night. These ministrations continue the next day up until the final, evening *puja* in front of the *padivilakku*, when the dead who were invited to earth are urged to return to feast again next year. As one participant put it, on this day we "loot the graveyard in order to bring the dead

Figure 7.7. As worshipers and onlookers trample and destroy the enlivened figure in the cremation ground on Mayana Kollai night, a woman scoops handfuls of the powerful ashes into a bag to bring home as *prasadam*. *Source*: Author photo.

back to life." Then, after a community feast that includes the sacrificed goats' meat is served that night, the festival formally concludes when participants' wristlets are removed and all the *puja* materials except for the ritual lamp are deposited in the ocean just beyond the cremation ground. Drawing attention to what he perceives as the uniqueness of his temple's Mayana Kollai celebration, one of the priests emphatically declared, "*No* other temples and *no* other festivals call the dead. We do this because Angali is a Kali who goes to the cremation ground. The dead are invited, honored, and dismissed."

The Festival's Subtle Landscapes

Although this complex and vibrant Hindu festival is performed with great fanfare in some Chennai neighborhoods and elsewhere in Tamil Nadu's northern districts, it has largely escaped scholarly notice.[14] The key exception is Meyer's *Aṅkāḷaparamēcuvari: A Goddess of Tamilnadu, Her Myths and Cult* (1986), which is based on a survey of more than sixty Angalaparameshwari temples in the South Indian state, relying primarily on interviews with priests to elucidate the Goddess's ritual and mythic expressions. Her study situates this festival, which she calls the ritual "trade-mark" of Angalaparameshwari (iii), in relation to its animating myths, particularly the story of Shiva's brahminicide (36–38, 176–83). Shiva cut off Brahma's fifth head after Parvati confused Brahma with her five-headed spouse, so Brahma cursed Shiva to wander the cremation ground begging for food, with his skull (*kapalam*) stuck to Shiva's palm, poised to eat everything he collected. Famished and seeking relief, Shiva came to the cremation ground at Mel Malaiyanur (Mēl Malaiyanūr), which Meyer calls the "oldest and most famous" among this Goddess's temples (103) and "the origin and center of the Aṅkāḷamman cult in Tamilnadu" (97). Here Parvati threw food offerings into the air, enticing the *kapalam* to descend from Shiva's hand to eat the morsels on the ground, and Parvati assumed the huge, "frightful" form (*aghora rupam*) of Kali/Angalaparameshwari and smashed the skull, thus expunging Shiva's curse. These events earned Mel Malaiyanur its renown both for its Mayana Kollai celebration and as a site where black magic, curses, and other afflictions can be resolved throughout the year for devotees, who carry home healing soil from the anthill wherein the Goddess undertook penance (see Allocco 2009, 36–37; Nabokov 2000, 76–78).[15]

While there are numerous versions of this story and the other two myths associated with Angalaparameshwari—one wherein she slices open the pregnant belly of the demon/king's wife and destroys them both, and the other being Daksha's sacrifice—they are seldom retold in festival celebrations I have attended or mentioned in my interviews/conversations about it. The myths are, however, discursively invoked and performatively signaled by priests, ritual musicians, and devotees alike, and several of the festival's ritual elements are either explicitly or implicitly related to these narratives. They are also consistently referenced in vernacular sources related to the Goddess and Mayana Kollai, including the Tamil-language profile of the temple that the priests have proudly framed and hung on an interior wall (Centilkumār 2011).[16] The most obvious connection between these narratives and festival events is the mythical basis for food being thrown aloft in the streets and cremation ground during Mayana Kollai. The characteristic sacred ash pot associated with Angalaparameshwari (visible in the man's hand in fig. 7.1), which features in her iconography and is used on an everyday basis at her temples, is frequently linked with Brahma's skull, and vow-keepers extend this association to the fire pots that they carry in Mayana Kollai processions. Many of them also cast the colorful rag dresses that they wear during the festival—which one ritual drummer described as "the pride of Angalaparameshwari"—in relation to the curse to wear ugly, tattered clothes that the Goddess endured due to Shiva's brahminicide.

Startlingly little has been written about Pavadairayan, the Goddess's son and guard, especially considering his central role in the festival.[17] Meyer calls him the "most interesting" among the attendant deities and notes that he displays an "effeminate, yet heroic nature" when he gains favor as the son who offers his innards to his mother when she expresses her hunger (1986, 81–83).[18] While my interlocutors agreed that he is the guardian deity (*kaaval deivam*) for Angalaparameshwari and serves as her support (*thunai*) and even chaperone in some mythic confrontations, they had little more to add about his significance to the festival. The invitation leaflet that the temple distributes annually notes only that Pavadairayan takes form in the cremation ground (*rudra bhumi*) on the night that the ash figure is constructed there. When I attempted to elicit stories about him, one priest relayed that in a display of his unwavering devotion, Pavadairayan once presented his own tonsils and intestines to the Goddess on a petticoat (*pavadai*). Myth, festival performance, and everyday practices are clearly interwoven in this context, much as the boundaries between the living and the dead are at least temporarily dissolved via the ritual processes that move back and forth between the Goddess's temple and the cremation ground, a place where "even death can be conquered" (Zotter 2016, 45). As we shall see, these suspensions and dissolutions operate alongside the fluidities and renegotiations of particular Hindu norms and categories, leading us deeper into a landscape of possibility, where devotees' relations with the Goddess may be transformed.

Wonder in a Landscape of Possibility

Where some elements of the Mayana Kollai festival (e.g., *puja*, processions, and vow-taking) will read as entirely familiar to observers of Hindu ritual practices, other components (e.g., an ash figure decorated with bones and skulls, grave-decoration, and worship in the burning/burial ground) are certain to raise questions, provoke confusion, and even, perhaps, inspire wonder. These latter reactions owe much to the fact that scholarly work on mainstream Hinduism almost without exception represents the cremation ground as polluting, liminal, and dangerous.[19] Such depictions rely more on orthodox and brahminic formulations that link death with impurity, the disruption of normal, ordered life, and the temporary suspension of social and ritual participation. For these and other reasons, elite discourses characterize the cremation ground as an unsuitable and even hazardous place for women to go, even at the time of their own loved ones' last rites. These discourses have produced an almost exclusive focus on cremation, despite the fact that burial is practiced by many middle- and low-caste Hindus in Tamil Nadu. By extension, Hindu burial practices are rarely discussed in the academic literature and worship in the cemetery is almost entirely overlooked.[20] Dominant frameworks also present blood/animal sacrifice as impure and threatening and code ritual contexts where nonvegetarian offerings are made as inferior to those limited to "purer" vegetarian ones. Even possession, which figures among everyday practices for navigating the world in vernacular Hinduism, is often rendered as marginal and inviting risk.

Given this backdrop, the juxtaposition of women who are experiencing the Goddess's presence biting off the heads of chickens and goats being sacrificed in the streets of a traditionally brahmin enclave, in the shadow of Chennai's grand, thoroughly vegetarian Kapaleeswarar Temple, is noteworthy. In light of inherited scholarly purity and pollution categories, it also seems decidedly unusual to contemplate women preparing food in the precincts of the cremation ground and living kin spreading out food there so that they may partake in a meal with their dead. Nevertheless, cooking, offering, and eating food in the graveyard is precisely what hundreds of families do on Mayana Kollai here. One local woman, for example, explained, "We are Goundars, a high-class *jati*; traditionally we farm paddy. Every year I cook *pongal* and savory chickpeas at the cremation ground and then throw them when Angalamman's procession comes. We do this for the dead persons of all generations in our family."

Srinivas's anthropology of wonder extends to our own wonder as ethnographers encountering different worlds (2018, 33). She proposes that we as anthropologists can also experience an "eruption into perception of another order" made possible through wonder because fieldwork itself is "an object of wonder . . . [that is] vivid, occluded, and complex" (223n36). Alf Hiltebeitel's discussion of "the mood of wonder" (*adbhutarasa*) in the *Mahabharata* and *Harivamsa* operates in the same register: he suggests that wonder does *work* in these texts, principally in terms of "churning up thought" (2022, 247). My experiences documenting the complex, layered Mayana Kollai festival certainly churned up a great deal of thought and even inspired a sense of wonder, as I came to recognize the remarkable fluidities evident in its ritual performances. This experience of anthropological wonder raises the possibility that we as scholars ought to reconsider our own articulations of the ordinary and extraordinary vis-à-vis our fieldwork contexts and in ethnographic writing, particularly because perceptions of wonder may not be identical (or even translatable) across cultures and languages (see Leavitt 1996). In terms of Mayana Kollai, most striking are the ways that the categories of purity and pollution are renegotiated and the boundaries between the living and the dead as well as myth and everyday life are temporarily dissolved or suspended in the festival sequence. Following my interlocutors' articulations and examples, I was able to see beyond discourses that represent the cremation ground as polluted and inaccessible, an entirely inappropriate place for worship and, especially, for women to enter. Female participants' seemingly effortless embrace of this space and unselfconscious reflections about their graveyard *pujas* prompted me to recognize the constructed nature of the purity/pollution paradigm at this level of vernacular practice.

The cemetery hardly seems frightening and polluted if we consider the instance of Rani, who told me that on any day of the year when she is particularly missing her sister-in-law, she goes there to lie down on her grave to talk with and feel close to her. This intimacy is certainly evident in the unscripted moments that punctuate the vibrant worship of Mayana Kollai, when kin groups may pause their decoration and beautification practices to crouch near or sit on their relatives' graves and chat, snack, or reminisce. I came to know that many Hindu families visit their relatives' gravesites on death anniversaries and birthdays and that they relish the opportunity to serve—and share in—a meal there with their loved ones (see Allocco 2020). Likewise, the materiality of death, evident in the commingled cremation ashes that are used to fashion the *bommai*, are identified as esteemed *prasadam* rather than a defiling substance.

Much as the gender norms surrounding temple and cremation ground reveal themselves to be fluid in the context of this festival, so, too, spatial norms and attendant categorizations of "pure" or "polluted" are called into question by the Mayana Kollai procession itself. One of the central functions of festival processions is to demarcate the boundaries (*ellai*) of a deity's jurisdiction and performatively mark the deity's sphere of control. As is the case during Angalaparameshwari's journey on Mayana Kollai day, the delineation of insides and outsides is underscored when priests scatter handfuls of cooked rice mixed with blood as offerings intended to keep malevolent spirits at bay, beyond the border of the Goddess's territory. Angalaparameshwari's festival procession not only clearly includes the burning/burial ground within her precinct, but it also establishes flows of power between this site and her temple that spill over into and redefine the everyday devotional imaginary of her worshipers.

Additional fluidities are operative in this festival context, and they work together to open up possibilities for transformation both of participants' experience of the Goddess and our scholarly frameworks. For example, worshipers who visit this site on Mayana Kollai day do not rush to bathe afterwards, as they would to ameliorate pollution following an interment or a cremation. Instead, they regard the food, ash, and other items that they return home with as *prasadam*, blessed substances. Women, some of whom do not visit the cremation/burial ground on other occasions in the year, not only make up the preponderance of worshipers during this festival but also assume ritual leadership and authoritative roles there.

Writing about feminism and wonder, Sara Ahmed notes that emotions can "take us to a different relation to the world in which we live" (2015, 178). Drawing on Descartes, she describes wonder as "a departure from ordinary experience" that "works to transform the ordinary . . . into the extraordinary" (179). Here the festival's rich ritual, sensory, and aesthetic landscapes, characterized by periods of intensity alongside moments of intimacy, encode the capacity for affective engagement as well as emotional transformation. This capacity is in line with Ahmed's portrayal of wonder as an affective relation to the world that "expands our field of vision and touch," catalyzed "when we are moved by that which we face" (179). Likewise, Srinivas describes wonder as shifting our discourses and practices, firing our imaginations, and inspiring us to consider "a broad horizon of possibility" (2018, 6, 56; see also Scott 2014).

In a series of conversations spanning more than a decade, Chamundiswari, a ritual leader at another nearby goddess temple, made it clear that her participation in the "special time" of this festival changed her orientation to the Goddess and her temple during ordinary time. Chamundiswari's account of Mayana Kollai stretching her awareness of the Goddess's characteristics suggests that at least some devotees experience the festival's transformative potential whereby the ordinary becomes briefly extraordinary in ways that then redefine the post-festival everyday. Chamundiswari described the cremation ground as being "like a temple" on Mayana Kollai day and said that visiting it to remember her dead kin who are buried there makes her "feel like crying." Her comments highlight the range of emotional responses the festival provokes in its participants and underscore the ways in which its affectively heightened dimensions can restructure and transform devotees' ongoing devotional relationships with the Goddess. Chamundiswari explained that participating in the festival year after year has helped her to become acquainted with Angalaparameshwari's many forms and moods, which she variously described (in a mix of Tamil and English) as awe-inspiring, frenzied, formidable, and excessive, and to know her more deeply. In her words, "Once we know the goddess in this new way, our daily worship of her changes. Even when I just think of her, I <u>feel</u>."

Although Chamundiswari does not verbally mark "wonder" (*viyappu*) in her description, Chamundiswari expresses the sense of an expanded relational field with the Goddess and suggests that she is moved (sometimes to tears) and transformed by the new ways of knowing Angalaparameshwari that Mayana Kollai makes possible. While there may be limits to discursive modes of apprehension and expression, Chamundiswari's descriptions indicate that wonder is part of an oscillating array or cluster of affects at work in this context. By virtue of her participation in the festival, Chamundiswari's relationship to her ordinary devotional world, populated as it is by a range of local goddesses, is reoriented, expanded, and made extraordinary. These shifts open up new landscapes of possibility that are not confined to the festival but rather inform and even profoundly reshape the everyday.

Other participants confirm that Mayana Kollai elicits a range of emotions and draws them into fundamentally different relationships with the Goddess that restructure their regular, non-festival devotional worlds, shifts that I read as being catalyzed by a certain kind of wonder. The goddess who is experienced as accessible, protective, and beneficent throughout the year is transformed in the festival context: as she dances to the cremation ground to participate in removing Shiva's curse and the charged visual exchange at the moment of the destruction of the ash figure, she displays rage (*agrosam*) and madness (*baittiyam*). Most prominent in the repertoire of affects that festival participants say they experience in response to these displays are horror (*bayangaram*), shock (*adhirchi*), and fear (*bayam*), but these extend and enlarge their apprehension of Angalaparameshwari's essential nature rather than displacing her everyday characteristics. At the moment when the Goddess, who is embodied by her human hosts and simultaneously manifest in her towering processional image, assumes her *aghora rupam*—the fearsome form that is understood by many as her true self, though only temporarily revealed—devotees must confront and assimilate this image into her complex range of attributes. As one woman put it, "Angalaparameshwari comes dancing into the cremation ground in a terrifying manner and bites the bones and the human remains there; this frightens us." Another worshiper's comment signals not only the capacity for transformation inherent in Mayana Kollai, that is, the opportunity to participate in the possibilities of the world in new or expanded ways that it presents, but also the potential for festival realizations to become embedded in everyday relations. She observed, "After you know the Goddess in this way, that awareness does just not go away. It does not disappear. You think about her and yourself differently once you go from the temple to the burial ground and come back."

In these words, this long-time devotee of Angalaparameshwari captures how the Mayana Kollai processional journey is an affectively transformational one. This alternately intense and intimate set of performances has the capacity not only to reorient worshipers' understandings of and relationships with this goddess, but also to reframe their connections to the wider devotional landscape and the world. Nevertheless, while it is clearly remarkable, spectacular, and even wonder-filled for participants, the festival remains firmly situated in the flow of everyday life. In this context we can observe striking fluidities of spatial and gender norms alongside renegotiations of purity and pollution paradigms and the dissolution of the boundaries between the living and the dead and myth and life. As worshippers take in its spectacle and partake in its dynamism, Mayana Kollai opens up for them a wondrous space of possibility where the ordinary and the extraordinary coalesce.

Notes

I am grateful to the American Institute of Indian Studies, the National Endowment for the Humanities, Fulbright-Nehru, and Elon University for generously supporting my fieldwork on Mayana Kollai in 2019, 2016, and 2007. Elon colleagues Geoffrey Claussen, Tim Peeples, and Gabie Smith made it possible for me to take a mid-semester research trip to participate in this Angalaparameshwari temple's one-hundredth anniversary celebration of Mayana Kollai in 2019. Deep appreciation is also owed to G. Pandiaraj and Vaishnavi Ramanathan for research assistance, to the temple's hereditary priests and trustees for warmly welcoming me into festival performances, and to the many devotees and ritual musicians who have patiently discussed the festival and its broader context with me. I am indebted to Eva Ambos, Emilia Bachrach, Jenn Ortegren, and Brian Pennington for their feedback as I developed this chapter and to Anya Fredsell and James Ponniah for being enthusiastic conversation partners about all things Mayana Kollai.

    1. The *Tamil Lexicon* defines *mayānakkoḷḷai* as the "ceremony among Cempaṭavas [fisherman caste] of bringing offerings to the burning ground, heaping them and allowing them to be looted and carried off by the people, celebrated in memory of Kāḷi's destruction of Takṣa's sacrifice" ([1924–36] 1982, 3074). Although the story of Daksha's sacrifice occasionally surfaces in connection with the festival, in my experience it does so far more rarely than the myths of Shiva's sin of brahminicide and the Goddess scooping the fetus from the wife of the demon/king Vallalakandan/Vallalarajan (Vallālakaṇṭan/Vallālarājaṉ; see Arumugam 2020; Hiltebeitel 1988, 1991; Meyer 1986). In the interest of

readability, I have rendered Tamil terms phonetically and included diacritics only for a few key terms and deity names at their first usage. For example, although this goddess's Tamil name is Aṅkāḷaparamēcuvari, I use Angalaparameshwari throughout. Colloquially, she is also called Angali and Angalamman, as we see in the previous chapter of this volume. All names used herein are pseudonyms and English words used in conversations otherwise conducted in Tamil are indicated by underlining.

2. Mayana Kollai is the most important festival at this particular Angalaparameshwari temple, but not all temples dedicated to her celebrate it. Much like many local goddess temples in Chennai, other Angalaparameshwari temples host annual festivals in the Tamil month of Adi (Āṭi; see Allocco 2009).

3. They also refer to themselves as Parvadaraja Sembadavar to signal their descent from the mythical king Parvadarajan and some use Nāṭṭār as a title. On the Sembadavars and their link to this goddess, see Meyer (1986, 53–54, 98–104) and Thurston with Rangachari (1909, 6:350–59). Some participants suggested that only Angalaparameshwari temples where Sembadavars preside are entitled to celebrate Mayana Kollai; I am aware, however, of temples whose priests are from other castes who host this festival annually.

4. Nine specific seeds (*navadhanyam*) are sprouted in various Tamil ritual contexts and suggest fertility, whether new growth or regrowth (including of the dead). Ritually planting *mulaippari*, the tender seedlings, is an element in many Tamil weddings, symbolizing both the "planting" of the bride into the groom's family and the expectation that from this union new life will sprout. This planting is also performed after some cremations, when mourners create furrows in a small patch of soil and "plant" seeds so that the soul/body may sprout anew. Agriculturalists offer pots of vibrant green shoots at annual goddess celebrations as well as at the Adi Perukku festival, which coincides with the traditional time for farmers to sow paddy (see Allocco 2009, 361–62). Earthen pots of *mulaippari* are also cultivated at home by some families in the context of rituals to invite their dead home to be installed as desired family deities, or *puvadaikkari* (see Allocco 2021).

5. While in this temple community it is women who take the Goddess's *vesham*, men from other temples frequently dress as the Goddess in this and other festival contexts. David Dean Shulman interprets what he calls "ritual transvestism" in this context as an expression of self-sacrifice to the goddess, wherein the devotee who dresses as a woman symbolically presents his power, his seed, and perhaps even his very life to her (1980, 298–99; see also Meyer 1986, 111). On *vesham* in another South Indian goddess tradition see Flueckiger (2013).

6. Because the dead are believed to lurk in watery places and to be accessible and retrievable through water sources such as wells, *puvadaikkari pujas* to propitiate deceased relatives are frequently performed at this temple's well. Some version of the *Gangai tirattu* rite consistently features in the dozens of *puvadai-*

kkari pujas to invite the dead back into the family home that I have recorded: typically, a string is sunk into the water source so the dead may travel along this conduit and take up residence in the pot to which the string is attached (see Allocco 2021; Nabokov 2000, 203n13). That pot is then installed in the family's home shrine, thus relocating the dead from outside to inside the house and permanently installing them as household deities (*veedu-deivam*). The Mayana Kollai festival stands alongside *puvadaikkari pujas* in the broader repertoire of ongoing engagements with the dead in Tamil Nadu that I consider in my book project, *Living with the Dead in Hindu South India*.

7. On this myth see, for example, Hiltebeitel (1988, 1991), Meyer (1986, 36–38, 176–84), Nabokov (2000, 89–90), and Visuvalingam (1989).

8. Although this festival's participants identified the *kapparai* as Pavadairayan, Eveline Meyer's report that it represents Brahma makes a great deal of sense (1986, 160–67, 210–11; see also Shulman 2006; Thurston with Rangachari 1909, 6:356). Pūṅkuṉṟaṉ and Rōculeṭ (1999, 78–80) link the *kapparai* with Daksha in the context of another Tamil Mayana Kollai festival. The *Tamil Lexicon* defines *kapparai* as the "bowl of a beggar or medicant" ([1924–36] 1982, 720), which fits with the mythic sequence where Brahma's decapitated skull becomes stuck to Shiva's hand and eats all of the cursed god's food. While Meyer describes small pots with offerings fastened below the side-by-side red faces, each with a black moustache and crown (1986, 111; see fig. 6), and this precise description surfaced in one of my interviews, a pot was only fixed to the *kapparai* in some of the years that I attended this festival.

9. Accounts of actual grave robbing in past Mayana Kollai festivals surfaced in more than a dozen of my interviews with devotees, priests, and ritual drummers. Several interlocutors reported that families who experience a death in the days preceding the festival delay burying their dead out of fear that their bodies might be exhumed and put to ritual use during Mayana Kollai. On this motif see also Sriram (2015), Thurston ([1906] 1989, 222–25), and Thurston with Rangachari (1909, 6:357–59).

10. In light of Tulasi Srinivas's (2018) emphasis on ritual creativity, it is worth noting that Mayana Kollai *alankaram* has shifted dramatically in recent years in ways that may well evoke a sense of wonder (see also Ramanathan 2019 on iconographic transformation and *alankaram*). For example, while this Angalaparameshwari temple has so far favored turmeric and vermilion to decorate its ash figure, other temples whose Mayana Kollai festivals I observed have shifted to trendy jewel-toned powders. Light displays are ever more elaborate, and mechanized and other decorations are now commonplace. A new emphasis on professional-style costuming, in lieu of more modest rag dresses, is evident among the Goddess's devotees. Some ritual drummers have stepped into this market and now sell fancy crowns and extra arms and heads via Facebook for

those dressing as the Goddess. Meenakshi Madan's (2020) stunning photo essay documents this elaborate costuming.

11. One year there was intense disagreement about who the figure should represent and, at the last moment, the ash breasts that had been added to the figure were scraped away, thereby transforming it from female to male. On another occasion a few bystanders identified the image as *kodumbavi pen*, which means "the worst woman," a heinous sinner who is used as a public scapegoat and destroyed, especially to bring rain (see Clark-Decès 2007, esp. ch. 2). On variations in the figure's identity in different festival contexts see also Hiltebeitel (1991, 434) and Meyer (1986, 76).

12. Outside of this festival, this Angalaparameshwari receives only vegetarian offerings.

13. Scholar M. D. Muthukumaraswamy has suggested that the destruction of these figures during Mayana Kollai (see Meyer 1986, 112) should be interpreted in dialogue with demolition of similar earthen Duryodhana images (see Hiltebeitel 1991) in the context of *Mahabharata* dramas called *therukoothu* (*terukkūttu*). He believes this performance tradition might serve as a "touchstone" for Mayana Kollai rituals (personal conversation, February 27, 2019; see also Muthukumaraswamy 2016). This is plausible since there is overlap across the genres of *therukoothu*, the songs of the ritual drummers who officiate at this festival (*udukkai pattu*), and the bow song (*vil pattu*; see Valk and Lourdusamy 2007), which has recently been (re-?)introduced at one Chennai temple's Mayana Kollai festival. The Mayana Kollai participants pictured in Thurston ([1906] 1989, 220–21) and Thurston with Rangachari (1909, 6:356–57) appear to be costumed much like *therukoothu* actors; one carries a winnowing fan and has intestines spewing from their mouth. In an unpublished chapter, Alf Hiltebeitel (n.d.) also makes note of the parallels between the effigies as sacrificial victims in the Draupadi and Angalamman cults: both "lie on their backs as if dying or dead."

14. Edgar Thurston, superintendent of the Madras Museum from 1885 to 1908, provides fascinating but brief accounts of the annual "looting the burning-ground" festival at Malaiyanur and elsewhere ([1906] 1989: 200–225; Thurston with Rangachari 1909, 6:356–59), while Michael Moffat includes just a mention (1979, 164). Where it has been treated in recent scholarship, the Mayana Kollai festival has primarily been considered in light of the ritual roles that transgender persons (*thirunangais*) play in its performance in some places (Craddock 2012; Vasudevan, this volume; Vasudevan 2020, ch. 5; for a journalistic source, see Barry 2016). Although transgender persons neither officiate nor participate in this temple's Mayana Kollai festival, several elements in Elaine Craddock's brief description of the 2012 festival performance in Mel Malaiyanur align with my experiences in Chennai, and her discussion confirms the links to the myths of Shiva's brahminicide and the demon king Vallalakandan and

his wife as well as the variation in whom the earthen image represents (2012, 127–32). Writing about sacrificial beauty, Hiltebeitel (n.d.) considers the cult of Angalaparameshwari within the phenomenon of Tamil *kuladeivam* religion. In his discussion of the "pillaging of the crematorium" festival, Hiltebeitel engages the aesthetic of the macabre (which he argues can be "rasically beautiful") in relation to what he calls the "most beautiful moment" of one Mayana Kollai festival he witnessed, where—in the name of their lineage deity, Pavadairayan—members of the sponsoring weaver community unfurled shimmering sari after shimmering sari over Angalaparameshwari's twenty-foot-long earth-ash effigy. Finally, within a larger study of Hindu shrines built on public (*poramboke*) land, Pushkal Shivam (2016) documents one inaugural Mayana Kollai festival near Chennai.

15. In addition to being performed in a grand fashion in certain places in North Chennai, the Mayana Kollai festival is famously celebrated at the Angalaparameshwari temple in Chennai's historic Triplicane neighborhood, which is understood as a "branch" of the Mel Malaiyanur temple, established with soil transferred from the anthill that graces Malaiyanur's inner sanctum (Cailapati 2019).

16. For other examples, see *Aruḷmiku Aṅkāḷamman̲ Tirukkōyil Tiruttal Varalāṟu* (n.d.), Cantiracēkar (n.d.), Pandian (2020), and Pūṅkun̲ran̲ and Rōculeṭ (1999).

17. Outside of Meyer's (1986) discussion of him, I have identified only a handful of passing references to Pavadairayan (e.g., Amirthalingam 2008; Masilamani-Meyer 2004; Srinivasan 2012; Valk and Lourdusamy 2007; Venkatachalapathy 2004).

18. Shulman (1980, 299) and Hiltebeitel (1988, 307, 304n28) both reference Meyer's work in their brief treatments of Pavadairayan self-sacrifice (more accurately, self-disembowelment) and "transvestism," which is how they characterize his wearing of a girl's lower garment (*pavadai*). In Shulman's account, Pavadairayan ("King of the Long Skirt") inadvertently wounds the goddess who is dwelling in an anthill and, to atone for this violence, offers his entrails to her as food. Pleased, Angalaparameshwari orders him to serve as her attendant henceforth, granting him eternal life.

19. See Craddock (2020) for references to the cremation ground in Tamil sources and Shaiva *bhakti* literature. James Ponniah (2011) and Christof Zotter (2016) discuss other religious practices associated with this space.

20. But see Lubomír Ondračka (2020) on Hindu burial and David Mosse's discussion of Tamil Catholic offerings and worship in the cemetery, especially in the context of the All Souls festival (2012, 76–77, 121–22, 247). In my experience participating in Kallarai Day (Cemetery Day) with Catholics in Chennai, this observance involves not only individual families offering prayers, decorating, and lighting candles at their burial plots, but also congregational worship in the form of a Mass celebrated in the graveyard.

References

Ahmed, Sara. 2015. *The Cultural Politics of Emotion.* London: Routledge.
Allocco, Amy L. 2009. "Snakes, Goddesses, and Anthills: Modern Challenges and Women's Ritual Responses in Contemporary South India." PhD diss., Emory University.
———. 2018. "Flower Showers for the Goddess: Borrowing, Modification, and Ritual Innovation in Tamil Nadu." In *Ritual Innovation: Strategic Interventions in South Asian Religion*, edited by Brian K. Pennington and Amy L. Allocco, 129–48. Albany: State University of New York Press.
———. 2020. "Vernacular Practice, Gendered Tensions, and Interpretive Ambivalence in Hindu Death, Deification, and Domestication Narratives." *Journal of Hindu Studies* 13 (2): 144–71.
———. 2021. "Bringing the Dead Home: Hindu Invitation Rituals in Tamil South India." *Journal of the American Academy of Religion* 89 (1): 103–42.
Amirthalingam, M. 2008. "Role of Sacred Natural Sites in the Conservation of Tropical Dry Evergreen Forests of the Tamil Nadu Coast." *Indian Journal of Environmental Education* 8: 22–25.
Aruḷmiku Aṅkāḷamman Tirukkōyil Tiruttal Varalāṟu. n.d. Dindivanam: Gayatri Offset Printers.
Arumugam, Indira. 2020. "Migrant Deities: Dislocations, Divine Agency, and Mediated Manifestations." *American Behavioral Scientist* 64 (10): 1458–70.
Barry, Ellen. 2016. "Mortal to Divine and Back: India's Transgender Goddesses." *New York Times*, July 24. https://www.nytimes.com/2016/07/25/world/asia/india-transgender.html.
Cailapati. 2019. "Ciṉṉamalaiyaṉūril Mārc 4-m Tēti Mayāṉakkoḷai Mācip Poruviḷā!" *Vikaṭan*, March 2.
Cantiracēkar, R., comp. n.d. *Mēl Malaiyaṉūr Srī Aṅkāḷamman Stala Varalāṟum Vaḷipāṭṭu Muṟaikaḷum.* Shivakashi: Balaji Notebooks.
Centilkumār, Es. Ār. 2011. "Kuḷantaikkaḷaik Kattaruḷum Kāval Teyvam." *Tiṉakaraṉ*, September 31.
Clark-Decès, Isabelle. 2007. *The Encounter Never Ends: A Return to the Field of Tamil Rituals.* Albany: State University of New York Press.
Craddock, Elaine. 2012. "The Half Male, Half Female Servants of the Goddess Aṅkāḷaparamēcuvari." *Nidān: International Journal for the Study of Hinduism* 24: 117–35.
———. 2020. "Kālī Dances into the Cremation Grounds of the Tamil Land." In *Regional Communities of Devotion in South Asia: Insiders, Outsiders, and Interlopers*, edited by Gil Ben-Herut, Jon Keune, and Anne E. Monius, 31–53. London: Routledge.
Flueckiger, Joyce Burkhalter. 2013. *When the World Becomes Female: Guises of a South Indian Goddess.* Bloomington: Indiana University Press.

Hiltebeitel, Alf. 1988. *The Cult of Draupadī*. Vol. 1, *Mythologies: From Gingee to Kurukṣetra*. Chicago: University of Chicago Press.

———. 1991. *The Cult of Draupadī*. Vol. 2, *On Hindu Ritual and the Goddess*. Chicago: University of Chicago Press.

———. 2022. *World of Wonders: The Work of Adbhutarasa in the Mahābhārata and the Harivaṃśa*. New York: Oxford University Press.

———. n.d. "Warts and All: Sacrificial Beauty in the Draupadī Cult and the Aṅkālamman̠ Festival at Veḷḷekaun̠tan̠ Pāḷaiyam Explored as Examples of Lineage Deity (*Kulateyvam*) Worship." Unpublished manuscript.

Leavitt, John. 1996. "Meaning and Feeling in the Anthropology of Emotions." *American Ethnologist* 23 (3): 514–39.

Madan, Meenakshi. 2020. "Colours of Trance-MayanaKollai." April 23. https://www.behance.net/gallery/95898191/Colours-of-TranceMayanakollai.

Masilamani-Meyer, Eveline. 2004. *Guardians of Tamil Nadu: Folk Deities, Folk Religion, Hindu Themes*. Halle: Verlag der Franckeschen Stiftungen.

Meyer, Eveline. 1986. *Aṅkāḷaparamēcuvari: A Goddess of Tamilnadu, Her Myths and Cult*. Stuttgart: Steiner Verlag Wiesbaden.

Moffatt, Michael. 1979. *An Untouchable Community in South India: Structure and Consensus*. Princeton, NJ: Princeton University Press.

Mosse, David. 2012. *The Saint in the Banyan Tree: Christianity and Caste Society in India*. Berkeley: University of California Press.

Muthukumaraswamy, M.D. 2016. "When Graveyards Throb with Life and Women Power." *Times of India*, March 17. https://timesofindia.indiatimes.com/entertainment/events/chennai/When-graveyards-throb-with-life-and-women-power/articleshow/51447808.cms.

Nabokov, Isabelle. 2000. *Religion against the Self: An Ethnography of Tamil Rituals*. New York: Oxford University Press.

Ondračka, Lubomír. 2020. "Burial (Hinduism)." In *Hinduism and Tribal Religions*, edited by Pankaj Jain, Rita Sherma, and Madhu Khanna, 308–12. Encyclopedia of Indian Religions. Dordrecht: Springer. https://www.academia.edu/43210104/Burial_Hinduism.

Pandian, A. T. S. 2020. "Mayāna̠ Koḷḷai En̠rāl En̠na? Or Cir̠appu Kan̠n̠ōṭṭam . . . !" Accessed March 30, 2020. https://www.patrikai.com/what-is-mayana-kollai-a-special-overview/?fbclid=IwAR3g-k1Cw-axzsqwUH8sDZIIEgLUozRbquRzuSv32Dx9C7_LxXCrTNP54JU.

Ponniah, James. 2011. *The Dynamics of Folk Religion in Society: Pericentralisation as Deconstruction of Sanskritisation*. New Delhi: Serials Publications.

Pūṅkun̠ran̠, Ti., and Jē. Rōculeṭ. 1999. *Aṅkāḷaparamēcuvari Varalāru̠m Vaḻipāṭum*. Ponnamaravathi: Thirumanappu.

Ramanathan, Vaishnavi. 2019. "New Iconographies: Gods in the Age of Kali." In *The Contemporary Hindu Temple: Fragments for a History*, edited by Annapurna Garimella, Shriya Sridharan, and A. Srivastham, 98–113. Mumbai: Marg Foundation.

Scott, Michael W. 2014. "To Be a Wonder: Anthropology, Cosmology, and Alterity." In *Framing Cosmologies: The Anthropology of Worlds*, edited by Allen Abramson and Martin Holbraad, 31–54. Manchester: University of Manchester Press.

Shivam, Pushkal. 2016. "Sacred Occupancies, Space, Practices: The Politics of 'Public Land.'" MA thesis, Indian Institute of Technology, Madras.

Shulman, David Dean. 1980. *Tamil Temple Myths: Sacrifice and Divine Marriage in the South Indian Śaiva Tradition*. Princeton, NJ: Princeton University Press.

———. 2006. "Toward a New Theory of Masks." In *Masked Ritual Performance in South India: Dance, Healing and Possession*, edited by David Shulman and Deborah Thiagarajan, 39–58. Ann Arbor: Centers for South and Southeast Asian Studies, University of Michigan.

Srinivas, Tulasi. 2018. *The Cow in the Elevator: An Anthropology of Wonder*. Durham, NC: Duke University Press.

Srinivasan, Perundevi. 2012. "The Ascetic Goddess Who Is Half Woman: Female Authority in the Discourses of Māriyamman̲'s *Tapas*." *Nidān: International Journal for the Study of Hinduism* 24 (1): 66–83.

Sriram, V. 2015. "The Night of the Dead." *The Hindu*, February 20. https://www.thehindu.com/features/metroplus/the-night-of-the-dead/article6916283.ece.

Tamil Lexicon. (1924–36) 1982. 6 vols. and supplement. Madras: University of Madras.

Thurston, Edgar. [1906] 1989. *Ethnographic Notes on Southern India*. New Delhi: Asian Educational Services.

Thurston, Edgar, with K. Rangachari. 1909. *Castes and Tribes of Southern India*: Vol. 6. Madras: Government Press.

Valk, Ülo, and S. Lourdusamy. 2007. "Village Deities of Tamil Nadu in Myths and Legends: The Narrated Experience." *Asian Folklore Studies* 66 (1/2): 179–99.

Vasudevan, Aniruddhan. 2020. "Between the Goddess and the World: Religion and Ethics among Thirunangai Transwomen in Chennai, India." PhD diss., University of Texas at Austin.

Venkatachalapathy, A. R. 2004. "Triumph of Tobacco: The Tamil Experience." In *South-Indian Horizons: Felicitation Volume for François Gros on the Occasion of his 70th Birthday*, edited by Jean-Luc Chevillard and Eva Wilden, 635–41. Pondichéry: Institut français de Pondichéry; Paris: École francaise d'Extrême-Orient.

Visuvalingam, Elizabeth-Chalier. 1989. "Bhairava's Royal Brahminicide: The Problem of the Mahābrāhmaṇa." In *Criminal Gods and Demon Devotees: Essays on the Guardians of Popular Hinduism*, edited by Alf Hiltebeitel, 157–229. Albany: State University of New York Press.

Zotter, Christof. 2016. "The Cremation Ground and the Denial of Ritual. The Case of the Aghorīs and Their Forerunner." In *The Ambivalence of Denial: Danger and Appeal of Rituals*, edited by Ute Hüsken and Udo Simon, 43–79. Wiesbaden: Harrasowitz Verlag.

Chapter 8

Economies of Wonder
The Production of Spectacle at the Kumbh Mela

AMANDA LUCIA

Wonder, or the willingness to "let something [unexpected] happen to you" (Srinivas 2018, 214) is the inherent promise of the Kumbh Mela. Over the course of eight weeks, approximately 150 million pilgrims converge and camp on the dried river bed at Sangam, the confluence of the Yamuna, Ganga, and mythical Saraswati rivers, in the city of Prayagraj (Allahabad). In season, the entire area is underwater, but between mid-January and early March (bookended by the Hindu holidays of Paush Purnima and Maha Shivratri) the riverbed becomes home to *sādhus* (ascetics), *kalpavāsis* (pilgrims who stay the entire duration of the mela), and other short-term pilgrims from across India and around the globe. The Kumbh Mela began as a gathering of the *akhāṛas* (sectarian groups of Hindu ascetics), who used the gathering as a meeting place to connect, conduct business, exchange information, and socialize—all with the primary purpose of taking an auspicious holy bath (*śahi snān*) at Sangam, a ritual believed to remove all sins.

And, indeed, the Kumbh Mela is rich in the production of wonder. Its sheer magnanimous size (see fig. 8.1), the astonishing diversity of the pilgrims, the extraordinary extremities of ascetic practice, the expanse and expense of renowned guru camps, the carnivalesque atmosphere, not to mention the holy bath—wandering the fair becomes a multilayered sensorial extravaganza. The overwhelm of sights, sounds, and experiences intermingle with titillating anticipation and potentially dangerous unpredictability (the potential to get lost or trampled at the mela has always been a reality and inheres in its historical lore and captivating allure). In fact, it is this open-ended possibility, unpredictability, and, most vitally, the radical interruption silencing the mundane that produces its potentiality for wonder. Building on Tulasi Srinivas's recent work theorizing wonder, I concur that these increasingly wondrous and spectacular religious productions are an attempt to reenchant a world increasingly disenchanted through secular materialism. Wonder is about enchantment, and as such it draws marked contrast to the disenchantment characteristic of modernity—the tedium of the struggles of everyday life, the waiting, and the precarity. As Srinivas writes, "Tedium, after all, is the enemy of wonder" (Srinivas 2018, 148). But while wonder can be a tool for resistance to neoliberal modernity, as Srinivas argues, I question whether the intentional production of wonder also follows the same consumptive logics of that which it resists.

To say this is to acknowledge that that which was once wondrous, repeated again and again, no longer evokes the same effect. In the economy of wonder, there is an ever-expanding threshold that must be constantly surpassed, in order to successfully interrupt the mundane and catalyze its

Figure 8.1. Crowd on street at the Kumbh Mela 2019, Prayagraj. *Source*: Author photo.

affective response. In other words, the production of wonder involves a constant demand for scaling-up and expansion; it simultaneously interrupts and yet, accelerates the neoliberal logics of late-capitalist modernity. Like the latest technology, there is always a newer more impressive mode of wonder, that which attempts to rupture, and once captured is no longer wondrous.[1] The demand for newer, more elaborate, and larger objects of wonder correlates to exponential increases in scale. The Kumbh Mela, at its current trajectory of exponential expansion, exemplifies this trajectory. This chapter considers the consequences—religious, political, and environmental—that such expansive economies of wonder create.

Creating Wonder: Akhāṛas

The Kumbh Mela began as an auspicious bathing day frequented largely by itinerant populations of ascetics and a smaller contingent of lay pilgrims. Devout Hindus regard the twelve-year cycle of Kumbh Melas, the six-year half-*melās* (Ardh Kumbh Mela), and the annual practice of the Magh Mela at Allahabad (Prayagraj) to be an ancient ritual practice.[2] There are references to it in the Purāṇas and in Tulsidas's *Ramcharitmanas*, wherein he writes, "In Magh, after the harvest, when the sun enters Capricorn, everybody goes to the lord of all pilgrimage places (Prayag). Gods, demigods, divinities and men gather and bathe in the Triveni with great reverence" (Tulsidas, Ramcharitmanas, Balkand 43; cited in Maclean 2008, epigraph). While it is likely that there was a bathing festival of some importance at Prayagraj since antiquity, historian Kama Maclean argues that it was only in the mid–eighteenth century that the Kumbh Mela at Prayagraj was formalized and ordinary pilgrims began to attend in large numbers (Maclean 2008, 12). At that time, the historical record of the mela at Prayagraj was also elaborated by British colonial administrators who projected their fears of religious fanaticism and epidemic diseases, as well as their desires to control the Indian population (particularly the population of militarized Hindu ascetics) onto the mass gathering.

British accounts routinely marveled at the spectacle of the gathered naked *sādhus*, the performers of ascetic penances, and the masses of traveling pilgrims. Colonial officials and Christian missionaries alike tended to view the gathering through an exoticized Orientalist gaze, describing the event as simultaneously abhorrent, dangerous, and wondrous. Depictions of the wonder of the Kumbh Mela abounded, but they are inseparable from the construction of the fair as an event requiring governmental policing and population control. For example, as early as 1918, the *Advocate* writes, "Anglicised Indians, globe-trotting foreigners, missionary propagandists—the human butterflies were found flitting from scene to scene eagerly taking snapshots. . . . [P]rompt and adequate punishment should be meted out to those who take photographs of the bathing pilgrims at Tribeni [Triveni]."[3] Perhaps the authors were concerned that such photographs transmitted wonder even beyond the geographical boundaries of the Kumbh, and thus expanded its influence. For example, a collection of circulated colonial-era photographs from 1930 includes a photo with the caption, "A sadhu hanging upside down over a charcoal fire at the Kumbh Mela, Allahabad."[4]

As is well known, there is a lengthy colonial history of the exoticized and Orientalist display of ascetical prowess, which aimed to stimulate the affective experience of wonder among audiences. Yogis sometimes performed ascetical feats for British officers, as in the unidentified yogi who was buried alive (*bhumipat samādhi*) in presentation to Sir Harold Wilberforce-Bell while he toured Mandi in Himachal Pradhesh in 1937.[5] On international circuits, yogis and religious virtuosi also displayed their ascetical feats in circuses, and on vaudeville and speaker-circuit stages (Deslippe 2018). During the colonial era, India and its wonders were also displayed to wild acclaim and astonishment at world's fairs and expositions in England (Taylor 2018, 48–63) and in the United States (Howard 2021, 79–135). As historian Richard Altick explains, exhibitions of human progress at the world's fairs during the Victorian Era ministered to "the desire to be amused or instructed, the indulgence of curiosity and the sheer sense of wonder, sometimes a rudimentary aesthetic sensibility" (Altick 1978, 1). The relation between Orientalist fascination, religious exoticism, and the provocations of the affect of wonder among audiences are historically intertwined and often mutually constituted. Wonder is the catalyst that captivated European, and later American, fascinations with Indian yogic and ascetical worlds and possibilities, which were—often are—activated in Orientalist and exoticist modes (Lucia 2020).

However, as an analytical category, wonder itself should not be overdetermined by these ideological frames. In today's Kumbh Mela, the economy of wonder exists to catalyze affective, emotional, and devotional reactions among pilgrims, and that economy includes, but also extends beyond, the historical legacy of wonder as one of the generative forces behind Orientalism. In the Kumbh Melas of the present, while media journalists endeavor to capture the wondrous spectacle of the yogic ascetic for international (and often exoticist) display, ideally, the spectacle is subordinated to the devotional experience of wonder generated in the performance of the ritual. For example, in 2001, photographers entered the water first before the *akhāṛas* in their efforts to get frontal images of the bathing *sādhus*.[6] That transgression became a highly publicized faux pas, and since then, the Kumbh Mela administration has built reserved bleachers and high-tower stations for photographers and journalists, thereby heavily restricting media access. In 2013, photographers were restricted behind barricades to ensure that the *akhāṛas* were the first to enter into the holy waters, but still some of the most aesthetically striking *sādhus* emerged from the river surrounded by three to five photographers. While some appeared annoyed at what could easily be perceived as harassment, others posed for cameras and held press conferences.

While such media attention has accelerated since 2001, the intent to display ascetic prowess inheres in the gathering of Hindu[7] ascetics at the Kumbh Mela. Historian D. P. Dubey argues that the primary impulse behind the Kumbh Mela is the holy bath, but it is also important for ascetics to attend in order to display their ascetical accomplishments. He writes that once religious aspirants have mastered the twelve components (the senses, intellect, and bodily functions) it is, in fact, incumbent upon them to attend the *melā*. They attend not only as a prerequisite for *mokṣa* (release from rebirth), but to exhibit their spiritual prowess, "demonstrating to others by their own example the efficacy of this practice" (D. P. Dubey 2001, 18; my emphasis). In this sense, a fundamental purpose of the fair is the dialogue between the public display of ascetic prowess and the evocation of wonder for observing audiences. Thus, the commonplace practice of ascetical display aimed to generate wonder should not be understood only through the lenses of self-exoticization, Orientalism, or commodification, but rather as a fulfilment of an indigenous religious injunction—a distinctive darshan intended to prove ascetical accomplishments while simultaneously catalyzing wonder, reverence, and devotion among pilgrims.

Following this injunction, many *sādhus* from the *akhāṛas* engage in public demonstrations of extreme ascetic practices. Select *nāgā bābās* (naked Shaivite *sādhus*) demonstrate their rejection of sexuality and their nonattachment to the physical body in public displays of radical bodily mortification. Ascetics who have raised one arm above their head or stood on one leg until the unused appendage wholly atrophies exhibit the results of their prolonged self-discipline. There are also renunciates who lie on beds of nails and thorns and others who endure the extreme cold of an early dawn holy bath or the extreme heat of meditation in the midst of multiple fires as in the ancient Vedic tradition. Though many Hindu ascetics identify with particular *sampradāyas* (sects), many have personalized, individuated, eclectic amalgamations of spiritual prowess and proclivity.

In the *akhāṛa* camps, *sādhus* exhibited their ascetic skills intentionally for the viewing public. For example, in the Juna Akhāṛa camp, the largest of the *akhāṛas*, tents housing the renunciates spread outward from a central thoroughfare upon which pilgrims promenaded. In the cool evening hours, pilgrims—both the curious and devout—walked through this central thoroughfare wherein the *nāgā bābās* clustered in small groups around a series of fire pits lined sequentially on either side of the lane. Some conversed with each other and ignored the promenading laity. Others engaged the public by sitting in displayed meditation or squatting on their haunches ready composed with a peacock feather fan and sacred ash (*vibhūtī*) to give blessings and *ṭīkās* (forehead markings applied at the third eye *cakra*). On busy nights, some of the most popular *nāgā bābās* drew large crowds and lines of lay pilgrims to seek their blessings and give donations. At Mahānirvāni Akhāṛa, Devpuri and Shivanandapuri explained that one *sādhu* must always sit at each fire pit during peak laity traffic times, to give blessings and collect donations from the public. At their fire pit, it was usually Premananda, one of the most junior acolytes, who was elected to sit on display for the public in the evenings. He wore only sacred ash smeared over his body, dozens of *rudrākṣa* necklaces, a hat comprised of curled strands of *rudrākṣa* seeds, and marigold garlands (*mālās*). At many *akhāṛa* fire pits, it was often the most physically striking, indeed—wondrous—*nāgā bābās* who were selected to give public blessings.

In addition to the daily display of extreme ascetical practices, the *akhāṛa* processionals to Sangam on auspicious bathing days produce an extraordinary display of pomp and circumstance, creating a highly orchestrated and hierarchical ritual as the *akhāṛas* arrive on horseback and on foot in their scheduled order of appearance. On the most auspicious bathing days, the processionals lay claim to the Sangam, and they also denote hierarchies within the ascetic community—both visually and temporally. The processional is a time honored South Asian religious tradition, and one that has become increasingly prevalent in the Hindu sphere alongside the rise in nationalism. Observant scholars have noted that as the power of Hindu nationalism has increased, so too has the intensity and scale of the processional and circumambulatory displays—particularly on festival occasions (Fuller 2001; Jacobsen 2020). Analyzing temple processionals in Bangalore, Srinivas argues that processions are "mobile sites of worlding, a generative space of wonder" (Srinivas 2018, 94). At the Kumbh Mela, these processionals are also improvised spaces wherein the *akhāras* map and create their worlds very practically, by asserting their position in the hierarchies of their own stratified religious field. The *akhāras* bathe first, at the most auspicious times, and in a hierarchical order, as is regulated by the *melā* authorities. Afterwards, non-*akhāra*-affiliated religious leaders arrive at the Sangam in opulent style, carried forward sitting on thrones affixed to the rooftops of white TATA jeeps and lorry trucks decorated with chains of marigolds and with royal umbrellas towering high above. As they pass by, they are observed and discussed by the crowds of lay pilgrims, who crane their necks and raise young children to their shoulders to have *darshan* of the promenade of religious virtuosi.

Creating Wonder: Gurus

The Kumbh Mela not only exhibits the ascetic discipline of the *sādhus* in the *akhāras*, but also the religious capital of the richly clad, heavily marketed, and polished personas of modern celebrity gurus. Jacob Copeman and Aya Ikegame use the term hyper-gurus to describe those "Indian godmen" who function as CEOs of business empires, "engage in high-profile development works," and "achieve hegemony in public discourse and representation" (Copeman and Ikegame 2012, 5). Celebrity gurus such as Ashutosh Maharaj, Devkinandan, Asaram Bapu, Sri Sri Ravi Shankar, Chinmaya Bapu, Ramanandacharya, Chidanand Saraswati, Pilot Baba, and Swami Nithyananda boasted exceptionally elaborate camps replete with loudspeakers, chandeliers, gift shops, fans, fountains, and gigantic carpeted pavilions (see fig. 8.2).[8] Interestingly, with some exceptions, most of these gurus direct their spiritual messages and their proselytizing aims at domestic audiences of Indian middle classes. For example, of these, the only gurus with a significant international presence are Sri Sri Ravi Shankar, whose Art of Living Foundation is globally renowned, Swami Nithyananda, who has become globally famous both through criminal allegations and self-promotion, Chidanand Saraswati, who has created Parmarth Niketan as an international yoga center, and Pilot Baba, who has cultivated a considerable community of devotees in Japan and in Russia, Belarus, and the Baltic States. The remaining gurus attract Indian audiences almost exclusively, evidenced by the fact that they speak and produce materials predominantly in Hindi (and some in southern Indian languages). Many are made famous through their popular *bhajan* performances and their religious discourses distributed through YouTube and on religious television channels like Aastha and Sanskar TV.[9] At the Kumbh Mela, celebrity gurus reproduce these media practices and connect with pilgrims through similarly styled popular educational and entertainment programming. They host guided meditations during cool mornings, devotional music (*bhajans*) and devotional plays (*līlās*) to pass the afternoon heat, and religious discourses and cultural programs to enliven festive evenings.

In 2013, Balak Lokeshwara Das was among the many hyper-gurus who displayed their influence and prowess by offering elaborate *homas*

Figure 8.2. Expansive camp of Bala Baldev Das Ji Maharaj, Kumbh Mela 2019.
Source: Author photo.

that were immense in scale—with 108 or even 1,008 participants forming the ritual simultaneously at separate *homa* pits. In another camp, hundreds of families molded 108 clay balls into miniature Shiva *lingams* and adorned each with red vermillion and rice grains, preparing them for offering in one of the largest *homas* at the *melā*. As they steadily worked, devotional music played loudly over the speakers and a sixty-foot-tall statue of Shiva—replete with a Ganga fountain spouting from his dreadlocks—watched over their efforts. In 2019, Ashutosh Maharaj (the guru who is famous for being cryogenically preserved by his devotees since his *samādhi* in 2014) and his organization Divya Jyoti Jagrati Sanstan (DJJS) boasted a massive camp with a towering fountain gracing the entrance. That same year Chinmayanand Bapu and his organization Vishva Kalyan Mission Trust-Haridwar also had a huge camp wherein the guru led discourses and *bhajans* most afternoons and evenings for thousands of pilgrims seated under the shade of their tented canopy. Some guru camps spread the length of entire city blocks and formed two- and three-story structures with ornate pavilions in the interior spaces. Each of these guru camps provided interactive religious entertainment and ritual opportunities—all the while asserting the grandiose importance of the guru. The immense scale and luxury of the camp is an exhibit of the guru's authority in itself; the experience of wonder translates into proselytizing power.

The guru camps at the Kumbh Mela also serve practical purposes. Prior to the government-supported tent accommodations, it was the gurus alone who provided food and lodging to those affiliated with their group, and even still they often set aside a portion of both aside for traveling pilgrims arriving at the camp without reservation. The *akhāṛas* provide the same service, as do some famous temples. For example, in 2019, the Annapurna temple of Varanasi—the Kashi Annapurna Annakshetra Trust—hosted a camp close to the Sangam from which they distributed tens of thousands of free meals each day. Traditionally, gurus would offer basic ashram-style shared accommodations and a modest meal plan (*thalis* [plates] consisting of dal, rice, and a vegetable) for minimal costs (usually anywhere from 300 to 2,000 Rs. per night (US$4–$27). But, in recent *melās*, there have been notable increases in more luxurious accommodations targeting Indian upper and middle classes and foreign travelers.

In 2013, Parmarth Niketan was one of the most luxurious guru camps situated on the opposite bank of Sangam, a peaceful reprieve far away from the busy epicenter of the bustling temporary city. But, in 2019, the opposite bank had expanded into miles of multiple formal sectors with some luxury camps charging US$500 or more (over 37,0000 Rs.) per night (Denton 2019). In 2019, from Sector Twelve, I was able to reach Parmarth Niketan only by moped or auto-rickshaw, and when I arrived I found an expansive celebration of yoga (Yog Kumbh) cosponsored by the celebrity gurus Baba Ramdev, Sri Sri Ravi Shankar, and Chidanand Saraswati. There the gurus and their associates offered continuous postural yoga programming and boasted a bookstore sponsored by the Indian Yoga Association, the Yoga Institute, the Art of Living Foundation, and the Indian government tourism office: Incredible India. As occurs at Parmarth Niketan in Rishikesh, each evening Chidanand Saraswati and Sadhvi Bhagawati Saraswati offered *ārati* (a ritual offering of flame to the divine) at sunset, accompanied by crowds numbering in the hundreds. In 2013, I had also attended Parmarth Niketan's evening Ganga *ārati* wherein Prem Baba (the now infamous Brazilian guru)[10] was a special guest and devotees performed a whimsical play celebrating eco-consciousness.

Gurus offer programming in order to spark the public's curiosity and cultivate recognition of their religious authority. They do so through evening *āratis* like the one at Paramarth Niketan, and also through museum exhibit-style educational presentations, massive *satsaṅgs*, *kīrtan* (devotional music), plays, yoga instruction, and public lectures. Some gurus extend even further and perform ascetic feats for audiences alongside opportunities for the public to receive their darshan, blessings, and counsel. For example, in 2001 and 2013, Yogimata Keiko Aikawa (a Japanese female ascetic who is spiritual companion to Pilot Baba) was buried underground without food or water (*bhumipat samādhi*) in the area in front of Pilot Baba's camp; in each case, three days later she was extracted with ritual celebration and emerged apparently unscathed.[11]

Even nonpresent and posthumous gurus have active camps at the Kumbh Mela; for example, the Sri Sri Anandamayi Sangha, the Neem Karoli Baba Ashram, and the Sri Sathya Sai Seva Organization each host camps dedicated to their posthumous gurus. In both 2013 and 2019, large processions of chanting Hare Krishnas accompanied by a two-team bullock cart pulled a life-sized wax statue of their posthumous guru, A. C. Bhaktivedanta Swami Prabhupada, through the streets. In 2013, proselytizing devotees distributed devotional literature in front of Swami Nithyananda's camp, while pilgrims were welcomed to view and worship a life-sized wax statue of the guru in his absence. In the religious economy of the Kumbh Mela, it is incumbent on the guru to be represented—both in life and in death.

Creating Wonder: Pilgrims

The mass gathering of Hindu religious virtuosi at the Kumbh Mela creates highly unusual spaces for dialogue between adepts and laity. The majority of the laity whom I interviewed within various guru camps and *sādhu* tents said that they attended the *melā* first to bathe (*snān karne*), then to learn (*sīkhne*) and to be in the presence of the divine (*darshan lene*), and more generally to wander for amusement (*gūmne*).[12] The religious adepts of the Kumbh Mela display their spiritual prowess in performative gestures that remind the laity of the extremities of Hindu devotion and of important otherworldly aims of existence.

But the spectacle arises from the extraordinarily diverse crowd, and not only from the wondrous ascetical acts of the *sādhus*. The Kumbh Mela draws participants from all across India, creating an unlikely nexus of the urban and rural. Affluent urban nuclear families intersperse among entire rural villages who cling together tightly, starkly aware of their geographic, linguistic, caste dislocation. Crowds are often thick, the regional diversity of India on vibrant display as women in Gujarati-styled tied saris bustle close those in Bengali-style tied saris, posh loafers walk alongside weathered bare feet adorned with heavy tribal anklets (*payals*), and ochre-robed Dandi swamis walk next to *māhāmantra*-singing Hare Krishnas. In the streets, amid the diversity of pilgrims, there are elephants and camels, children performing circus acts, fortune tellers, *mālā* makers, protective amulet peddlers, and mobile trucks broadcasting the latest Ayurvedic and yogic techniques. Camps open up to the streets and hawkers invite pilgrims in for a respite in the shade, a free meal in the form of *prasād* (blessed food), *līlā* performances, *kīrtan*, and religious discourses. Shopping stalls also beckon pilgrims to a wide assortment of wares for purchase: religious objects (*mālās*, *murtis*, *yantras*, calendars, and pamphlets), trinkets (toys, fancy *bindīs*, and purses), and camping necessities (cookery, clothes, and blankets). Traversing the streets of the *melā*, the sights and sounds shift as one camp abuts another. Their presence informs their distinctive and multisensory geographical footprint, crafting sounds and sights specific to the Brahmakumaris, or the Vishwa Hindu Parishad, or the Shankaracharyas, or the Bharat Scouts and Guides (BGS).

The wonder of the Kumbh Mela is expressed as potentiality and possibility, the uproarious interruption of the fantastical into the mundanities of daily living. The diverse cacophony of the streets provides countless opportunities for such interruptions—moments when the unexpected and awe-inspiring intentionally interjects into the status quo of daily existence. Wonder erupts in mundane interactions generated by the unique collected assemblage of humanity in all of its variance. In their relatively uncommon abutment in the public spaces of sociality in the *melā*, wealthy urbanites and tribal villagers alike encounter each other with an air of mutual curiosity and amazement. All the while, mahouts and camel keepers wield their animals through these dense crowds, and they too draw curious attention from pilgrims and excited cries from children. Such eruptions are relatively commonplace, as in my walk home in 2013, when I randomly passed a *nāgā sādhu* standing atop of an elephant, resplendent as he brandished a long, curved sword and shouted to the assembled crowd below.

Ascetic display also interlaces with the carnivalesque as some ascetics perform ascetic "tricks," such as lying on a bead of thorns or suspending heavy objects from their flaccid genitalia. In both 2013 and 2019, one *sādhu* sat suspended on a swinging platform above a fire pit. His seat was made of nails, pointed upwards and attached to the entire contraption was a long, heavy chain. On most days the chair sat empty, but on occasion, the fire was stoked and he sat on the throne of nails in meditation while pilgrims were encouraged to pull the heavy chain in order to swing him back and forth over the flames (see fig. 8.3).

The secular carnivalesque has also expanded in recent years. Cobra charmers, fortune tellers, astrologers, palm readers, and magicians set up stations on roadsides and attract curious pilgrims to wondrous astonished amusement. Many of these performers belong to agrarian nomadic tribes of performers and musicians who travel to the Kumbh Mela from Rajasthan.[13] Traditional acrobat troupes also come to the Kumbh Mela and their skilled children perform tightrope balancing acts high above the heads of assembled crowds. There are also carnival-style games for prizes, Ferris wheels, and even the famed Well of Death.[14] These popular curiosities blend with the more religious aspects of the *melā*, combining to create a fair that both global and Indian media outlets routinely and repeatedly describe as "the greatest show on earth" (Mishra 2007; see also Wood 2013; DeHart 2013; Yorke 2001; Kermani 2013).

Figure 8.3. Sādhu seated on swinging platform, Kumbh Mela 2013, Prayagraj. *Source*: Author photo.

Expansive Economies and Wonder Trash

As the Kumbh Mela has grown in size and scale, there are many parties who view the *melā* as a unique opportunity to spread their ideology and to access broad audiences of the Indian populace. And the Kumbh Mela at Prayagraj *has* grown considerably over the past fifty years. The official estimate for the number of pilgrims at the 1977 Kumbh Mela was 10 million. By 1989, the official figure was estimated at 15 million bathers at Sangam (Tully 2001, 11). In 2001, the estimated figure was 60 million (*Britannica* 2021), and by 2013 that figure had doubled to 120 million (Boghani 2013). In 2013, according to *India Today* (drawing on Indian government statistics), "the Kumbh has its own administration: A district collector, a senior police superintendent, a chief medical officer, a chief engineer, electricians, restaurateurs, boatmen, and garbage collectors. It has 156 km. of steel-plated roads, 18 pontoon bridges, 980 km. of electricity wires, 550 km. of water pipelines, and a budget of Rs.1,200 crore [approx. US$222 million]. It is a fully functional metropolis conjured out of nothing, only to be dismantled 55 days later" (Pradhan 2013). Mani Prasad Mishra, the Mela Adhikari (District Magistrate) of the Kumbh explained that "in terms of density of population, this is the largest city in the world. . . . The only catch is that this city doesn't really exist. It is El Dorado, Camelot, Shambala, or Dvaraka" (Pradhan 2013). At the end of the festival, it is all dismantled, the metal plumbing and toilet facilities ripped up, the lampposts and electricity disassembled, and the tents stored.

In 2019, the Ardh Kumbh exceeded all of these figures with an estimate of 150 million pilgrims bathing at Sangam. The Indian government also tripled the 2013 budget for the Kumbh, swelling the cost to an astounding US$600 million (Denton 2019). The Kumbh Mela in 2019 was only an Ardh Kumbh and thereby, usually half the size of the magnanimous Maha Kumbh Melas that occur at the Sangam at Prayagraj every twelve years (2001, 2013, 2025, and so on). But, in 2019, the government expanded the Ardh Kumbh into a massive-scale government-sponsored production celebrating the strength and diversity of Hindu religiosity. The management of the Kumbh Mela fell to twenty-eight government departments and six central government ministries; fifteen state government departments implemented 261 projects. These managerial collaborations resulted in a twenty-sector megacity sprawling over 32,000 hectares, including 250 kilometers of roads and twenty-two pontoon bridges (PTI 2019). In addition to transportation infrastructure, the city also included hospitals, police stations, emergency stations, water towers, electricity, sewage piping, and fresh water. In these exponential increases, the notion of an economy of wonder that characterizes the Kumbh Mela extends beyond a metaphorical idea of an economy of religious actors engaged in the production of wonder and becomes a literal production of an economy of both geographical scale and capital.

Doubling the geographic footprint of the *melā* had significant consequences for engagement within it. In 2019, the Ardh Kumbh Mela was spread over forty-five kilometers, more than double the size of the Maha Kumbh Mela of 2013, which covered a mere fifteen to twenty kilometers. During the Maha Kumbh Mela in 2013, travel by car was an unnecessary luxury. In contrast, in 2019 there was considerable auto traffic, scooters, and pilgrims queued for rikshaws at busy intersections. Many *kalpavāsis* were given temporary camping parcels in a sector on the outskirts of the *melā* and walked ninety minutes each way to access the Sangam, where the *akhāṛas* were camped.

In 2019, the Ardh Kumbh Mela fell just before the elections, and Prime Minister Narendra Modi was keenly aware that it provided an important means to demonstrate the successes of his administration. To pilgrims, it was readily apparent that the government was deeply involved at every level of the facilitation of the *melā*. Some *sādhus* and pilgrims even took to calling it "the government Kumbh." There was often a mild cynicism in the air as they spoke of the upcoming election and the importance of the Kumbh Mela for Modi's reelection campaign. The Kumbh not only had to be safe for hundreds of millions of pilgrims (no catastrophic bridge collapses), but it also had to be a grand extravaganza, a successful display of governmental organization, extraordinary feats of engineering, and an exemplar of ecological consciousness. Not only that, but there was an urgency to produce wonder—on a never-seen-before scale.

In the months leading up to the *melā*, Modi championed the event in advertising and spiritual tourism campaigns and, as mentioned, renamed it a Kumbh Mela in its publicity campaign (PTI 2019). At the airport in Delhi, massive posters and video screens depicted Modi inviting travelers to the Kumbh Mela. The slogan *Chalo Kumbh Chale* ("Let's go to the Kumbh") echoed on commercials, billboards, and in a popular devotional song[15] throughout the subcontinent. All governmental correspondence in Uttar Pradesh (UP) bore the logo of the Kumbh Mela on its letterhead and across the state all cinema halls also displayed its logo immediately after the national anthem was played. Billboards advertising the Kumbh Mela blanketed not only government buildings, but also the countryside, both urban and rural. Trains, too, did their part: 1,600 coaches of 800 special trains traveling to and from Prayagraj were wrapped in vinyl depicting the Kumbh Mela logo alongside images of *nāgā bābās* at *śahi snān* and performing *ārati* (IANS 2018).

Once at the Kumbh Mela, it was also readily apparent that the Kumbh Mela was being frequented by many high-ranking government officials. Notably, Yogi Adityanath (Chief Minister, Uttar Pradesh) traveled to the Kumbh Mela and even had an encampment office with the Nath yogis; Prime Minister Narendra Modi himself bathed at Sangam on February 24, 2019 (ET Online 2019). Billboards and placards of Adityanath and Modi adorned many intersections in the *melā*, highlighting the active state-sponsorship of the event, and, by extension, a unified Hindu political agenda. Multiple high-level organizing meetings brought together influential gurus and religious leaders for political discussions. At the Vishwa Hindu Parishad (VHP) camp, there were 320 luxury tents sprawled over fourteen acres and a model of the Ram Mandir to be built at Ayodhya (Sen 2019).

Government officials have long used the Kumbh Mela as an important site for crafting and cultivating public opinion. The British were keenly aware of this and used the *melā* as a site to, in Maclean's phrasing, enact the business of "disseminating good will," and in large effect their campaign was successful. They not only sterilized, organized, and managed the event, but in 1808 the Company waived pilgrim taxes for native soldiers "with the express aim of strengthening their attachment and loyalty to the British government" (Maclean 2008, 61). In many cases (though not all), British East India Company support for the Kumbh Mela seemed to produce the desired effects. For example, Maclean notes that the *Asiatic Journal* quoted the pilgrims as saying, "Dhunyu tera raj, tera raj joog jog ruhe! Kysa chyn ka koombh kuvaya!" (May your rule be blessed! May your reign extend for ages to come! You have produced a magnificent kumbh!)[16]

Since independence, the Indian government has recognized similarly that the production of a wondrous and magnificent Kumbh can have positive effects on pilgrims' opinions of the government. For example, in BBC reporter Mark Tully's travelogue account of the 1977 Kumbh Mela, he writes that the VHP "was present in strength at the Mela" and used its platform there to advocate for the destruction of the Babri Masjid at Ayodhya and for what is known today as *ghar wapsi* (*vāpsī*) or the (re)conversion of Muslims and Christians to Hinduism (Tully 2001, 28). Nearly fifty years later, in 2019, religious leaders, politicians, and political parties used the Kumbh Mela similarly as an important platform from which to mobilize support the campaign to construct a Ram temple at Ayodhya.

But it seems that every time the Kumbh Mela threatens to be co-opted by political forces there is also protectionist backlash. While tensions between the political and the religious often hover in the background, in 2019, the Akhil Bharatiya Akhāṛa Parishad (ABAP), the apex body of Hindu *sādhus* governing all thirteen *akhāṛas*, fostered a considerable rift within the Sangh Parivar when it refused to attend (and encouraged *sādhus* to boycott) the VHP-organized two-day Dharma Sansad (religious Parliament) at the Kumbh Mela. The Dharma Sansad was scheduled to discuss the building of the Ram temple at Ayodhya and Sabarimala. In response to the *sādhus'* rejection of the meeting, Yogi Adityanath made an unscheduled visit to the Kumbh to meet with RSS chief Mohan Bhagwat and VHP officers in an attempt to resolve the issue.[17] Lanes were closed and crowds lined the streets as Yogi Adityanath's sizeable motorcade sped through the *melā*, kicking up clouds of dust as the people cheered.

But, despite Yogi Adityanath's efforts, ABAP refused to attend and the VHP held its Dharma Sandad in their absence. In so doing, the *akhāṛas* asserted their will, power, and independence and resisted what they saw as the governmental takeover of the Kumbh during an election year. Swami Martand Puri, a Mahamandaleshwar (a high-ranking position) in the Māhānirvāni Akhāṛa, expressed frustration over the fact that the government had renamed the Ardh Kumbh as a Kumbh Mela at all. He explained, "Kumbhs and Ardh-Kumbhs are calculated in accordance with the positions of celestial bodies. They can't be changed by a government order or for the sake of helping BJP in the election. They should have questioned this change. This is a political jamboree organised to send the message of the RSS and not that of the Kumbh" (Jha 2019). In his view, ABAP's refusal was a rejection of the Sangh Parivar's "growing interference in the world of sādhus" (Jha 2019). When Yogi Adityanath's own tent at the Nath camp burned down on February 5, 2019, many saw it as a divine intervention and reprimand, to prove that the Kumbh cannot be controlled by politicians (ABP News 2019).

It is a delicate balance for the Sangh Parivar to exert its influence over the Kumbh Mela without overshadowing its central religious and ritual focus. Some influence could produce big gains for the Sangh Parivar in an election year, but too much can breed cynicism and schism—backfiring and erasing potential political strides. In 2019, it seems that the BJP-backed government overreached in its desire to produce wonder at the Kumbh (Khanal 2019). The popular presumption that the government had usurped the *akhāṛas* and the *melā*'s primary ritual aims produced tension and condemnation from key religious leaders. The renaming of the Ardh Kumbh to the Kumbh Mela created cynicism among the pilgrims and seeded unrest among the *sādhus*. And, lastly, the concluding point to which I will now turn, the enormous and wildly spectacular geographical scale of the Kumbh Mela, which was designed to produce wonder in its magnanimity, had extraordinary negative environmental impacts and subsequently diminished favorable public opinion of the event, despite all precautions to the contrary.

Prime Minister Modi was adamant that the Kumbh Mela should exemplify the pinnacle success of his campaign for an environmentally conscious and clean India (Swacch Bharat).[18] In order to avoid the conventional dramatic increase in pollution levels that occurs with a massive Kumbh Mela, the Indian government closed tanneries upriver in the cities of Kanpur and Unnao between December 15, 2018, and March 15, 2019, and released extra water from Tehri dam upstream in Uttarakand. To minimize public defecation, government authorities laid sewer lines throughout the *melā* and built 122,000 toilets (another source quoted this figure at 275,000 toilets and 20,000 urinals) (Sharma 2018). Armies consisting of one lakh (100,000) Swacchagrahis (cleaning-staff) were deployed to monitor and clean the streets and Sangam area, while 16,000 trash receptacles were installed and serviced by government trucks (Sharma 2018; *Times of India* 2019).

Environmentalism has been a major platform for Modi, and his is the latest Indian government attempt to clean the Ganga. In 2014, he launched the Namami Gange (Salutations to Ganga) program to clean the Ganga and its tributaries—a massive project with a budget allocation of more than 200 billion Rs. (US$2.8 billion) to be spent by the end of 2019. Thus, there was much at stake for him (and the UP government) to make bathing at Sangam in 2019 a positive experience for pilgrims and—particularly—one in which there was minimal illness as a result of bathing in polluted waters.[19] And, in fact, it was largely a success—the waters at Sangam were remarkably clean during the Kumbh Mela, and pilgrims delighted at the unusually clean streets and clear rivers. But river experts and environmental activists condemned the "band-aid solutions" with Manoj Mishra, a Convenor of the Yamuna Jiye Abhiyan (Living Yamuna Campaign) decrying the release of 6,000–7,000 cusec (cubic foot per second) of water into the Ganga from the Tehri dam (when normal flow in the river does not exceed 1,000 cusec) as "an election period chimera at best" (Sarkar 2020). Aside from this mirage of clean water, in April 2019 after the close of the Kumbh Mela, the National Green Tribunal (NGT) declared that Prayagraj was on the verge of an epidemic that it claimed must be dealt with "on an emergency basis." Furthermore, 2,000 tons of unsegregated solid waste was dumped at Prayagraj's only solid waste treatment plant at Baswar village, which the administration knew had been nonfunctioning since September 2018 (Kaur 2019; Kanaujia 2019). According to DownToEarth environmental advocates, the mass of untreated waste threatened to fall directly into the Yamuna River (also known as Jumna), which meets with the Ganges at Sangam (Kaur 2019).

Conclusion

Whether among the *akhāṛas*, celebrity gurus, pilgrims, or the governmental politicizing and scaling-up of the *melā*—there is a fine line between that which is interpreted as a spontaneous eruption of wonder and a manufactured production of synthesized wonder. Historian Kama Maclean laments the pernicious impact that the voyeuristic Western media has had on the *melā*, yet she admits that "pilgrimages such as the Kumbh have always been about being seen, especially for the mela's traditional elites—rajas and akharas—who were seeking to communicate their wealth, power, and influence. The narcissistic and ostentatious display of certain akharas on their shahi snans [holy bath days], and the importance that they place on the processions, makes this clear. But this is about being seen *in context*" (Maclean 2008, 52). At its genesis the Kumbh is designed to be spectacular; its aim is to cultivate curiosity and wonder. And, as Srinivas argues, there is an inherent creativity and optimism in the large-scale production of wonder. She writes, "Wonder undoes older ontological assumptions of dystopic visions and creates new joy-filled ways of being that enable localites, to see further, to enjoy more, to experiment repeatedly, to improvise and create. . . . Wonder suggests the hope and possibility of an alternate reality, a better future more conducive to joy and care. It celebrates a dexterous opportunism" (Srinivas 2018, 212–13). Certainly, the economy of wonder of the Kumbh Mela produces joy and cultivates affective experiences of awe and splendor.

But in order to sustain the experience, the creative spectacle produced at the Kumbh Mela must conform to an expansive economy of wonder. In order to continually cultivate wonder, it must be bigger and better, and then bigger and better still. This self-conscious drive to produce wonder through spectacular scale threatens the event—not only in its distraction from its intents and purposes, but also in its public perception as an event that has become overly commercial, political, and environmentally devastating. There is a delicate balance between the affective experience of wondrous astonishment, the chimera of over-the-top extravagance, and the desperate environmental consequences of the production of spectacle. At its current rate of exponential expanse—this delicate balance will be difficult to maintain. But so long as pilgrims have faith in the rewards of the *śahi snān* that supersedes all other concerns, it is likely that the Kumbh Mela will continue to be perceived to be wondrous no matter its commodification or politicization—so long as the rivers at Sangam flow clean.

Notes

1. See Srinivas for the notion of "rupture-capture" as endemic to the creative ritual process (2018, 6).

2. The Kumbh Mela (celebrated every twelve years), Ardh Kumbh Mela (celebrated at the halfway point every six years), and the annual Magh Mela all occur at Sangam at Prayagraj. In intervening years, on every third year, the Kumbh Mela changes location and is celebrated at the pilgrimage sites of Nasik, Haridwar, and Ujjain. This article focuses exclusively on the Kumbh Melas held at Prayagraj.

3. "Selections from Indian-Owned Newspapers of the United Provinces," *Advocate*, March 17, 1918; cited in Maclean (2008, 40).

4. Photo 66/2 (57), Photographers B. S. Dhaman; Director of Public Information, Delhi; D. Baljee; Mela Ram & Sons; R. B. Holmes and others unknown. British Library, photo 66/1-2.

5. "Visit of their Excellencies the Viceroy and the Marchioness of Linlithgow to Mandi, Oct.1937." "The Yogi who performed feats before their Excellencies," photo 1/5(26), Wilberforce-Bell Collection, British Library.

6. This account is widely known and also documented photographically in Maclean (2008, 49).

7. The Kumbh Mela can be characterized as an intrafaith Hindu festival, meaning that Hindus of all allegiances attend. In previous years, some non-Udāsin Sikhs attended, as did the Dalai Lama. But in 2013 the Dalai Lama was scheduled to attend, but cancelled when groups of Hindus protested his visit (see *IBTimes* 2013).

8. Some of these celebrity gurus also hold honorary titles of Mahamandaleshwaras in the various akhāras (i.e., Pilot Baba in Juna Akhāra and Nithyananda in Māhānirvāni Akhāra), but they have established independent camps.

9. Devotional television is a growing business in India, through which many gurus purchase time slots and transmit their messages directly to Indian

middle-class audiences. For example, Baba Ramdev, whose appearance at the Kumbh Mela in 2019 was made famous by his admonitions to *sādhus* against smoking (Malaviya 2020) has a controlling stake in and operates ten different Hindu devotional channels (J. Dubey 2019).

10. In 2018, many Prem Baba devotees defected due to accusations of sexual abuse against the guru (see, "Prem Baba" 2018).

11. This *samādhi* event is depicted in the famous documentary film, *Shortcut to Nirvana* (see Benazzo and Day 2004).

12. I attended the Kumbh Mela for four weeks in 2013, and for two and a half weeks in 2019. During this fieldwork, I was housed at the Society of Pilgrimage Studies camp inside the Kumbh Mela. During my fieldwork, I interviewed approximately twenty religious adepts and ten laity and took dozens of audio files of lectures, gatherings, rituals, and conversations. The majority of my fieldwork consisted of participant-observation, experiencing the festival along with and in dialogue with attendees. In 2013, I also spent considerable time with *nāgā bābās* in the Māhānirvāni Akhāṛa camp and joined their procession during Vasant Panchami Snān on February 15, 2013. Independently, I also attended the Magh Mela in 1997.

13. For more on the Kabeliya, see Treza (2015).

14. The Well of Death is an amusement wherein cars and mopeds circle a large barreled basin using centrifugal force to propel them high above the ground (see Kumar 2019).

15. P. P. Dubey 2019.

16. "The Great Mela at Hurdwar," *Asiatic Journal and Monthly Register*, n.s., 9 (November 1832): 121; cited in Maclean (2008, 61).

17. For more on this, see Jha (2019).

18. Swacch Bharat website: https://swachhbharatmission.gov.in/sbmcms/index.htm.

19. In 2013, scientists from the Harvard School of Public Health reported a 5 percent incidence of diarrheal diseases over a 23-day period and a surge in bloody-diarrhea just two days after the bathing day on January 29—both a result of bathing in the heavily polluted waters at Sangam (Sridhar, Gautret, and Brouqui 2014).

Works Cited

ABP News. 2019. "Fire Breaks Out at Yogi Adityanath's Tent in Kumbh Mela." 2019. ABP News (YouTube channel), February 5. https://www.youtube.com/watch?v=gCwAN2X0mX8.

Altick, Richard. 1978. *The Shows of London*. Cambridge, MA: Belknap Press of Harvard University Press.

Benazzo, Maurizio, and Nick Day. 2004. *Shortcut to Nirvana: Kumbh Mela*. Mela Films. DVD.
Boghani, Priyanka. 2013. "Maha Kumbh Mela Saw Record 120 Million Devotees." *The World*, March 11. https://www.pri.org/stories/2013-03-11/maha-kumbh-mela-saw-record-120-million-devotees-photos.
Britannica. 2021 (updated). S.v. "Kumbh Mela." https://www.britannica.com/topic/Kumbh-Mela.
Copeman, Jacob, and Aya Ikegame, eds. 2012. *The Guru in South Asia: New Interdisciplinary Perspectives*. Oxford: Routledge.
DeHart, Jonathan. 2013. "Kumbh Mela: Consuming the Greatest Show on Earth." *The Diplomat*, March 7.
Denton, Bryan. 2019. "At the World's Largest Religious Gathering, Nirvana and 'Glamping.'" *New York Times*, February 25. https://www.nytimes.com/2019/02/25/world/asia/india-kumbh-mela.html?auth=login-google.
Deslippe, Philip. 2018. "The Swami Circuit: Mapping the Terrain of Early American Yoga." *Journal of Yoga Studies* 1:5–44.
Dubey, D. P. 2001. *Kumbh Melā: Pilgrimage to the Greatest Cosmic Fair*. Allahabad: Society of Pilgrimage Studies.
Dubey, Jyotindra. 2019. "Owned by Corporates, Run by Babas—the Economics Behind India's Devotional Television." *The Wire*, April 14. https://thewire.in/media/owned-by-corporates-run-by-babas-the-economics-behind-indias-devotional-television.
Dubey, Prem Prakash. 2019. "Chalo Kumbh Chale." Ambey Bahkti (YouTube channel), January 13. https://youtu.be/QrPyLmz-wxo.
ET Online. 2019. "PM Modi Takes Holy Dip at Kumbh Mela." *Economic Times*, February 24. https://economictimes.indiatimes.com/news/politics-and-nation/watch-pm-modi-takes-holy-dip-at-kumbh-mela/videoshow/68138262.cms.
Fuller, C. J. 2001. "The 'Vinayaka Chaturthi' Festival and Hindutva in Tamil Nadu." *Economic and Political Weekly*, May 12–18, 1607–9, 1611–16.
Howard, Thomas Albert. 2021. *The Faiths of Others: A History of Interreligious Dialogue*. New Haven, CT: Yale University Press.
IANS. 2018. "Mela-Themed Images, Slogans to Adorn 1,600 Kumbh Special Rail Coaches." *Hindustan Times*, November 27. https://www.hindustantimes.com/art-and-culture/mela-themed-images-slogans-to-adorn-1-600-kumbh-special-rail-coaches/story-lRULtENp07WXMSV6QeRBbP.html.
IBTimes. 2013. "Maha Kumbh Mela 2013: Dalai Lama Visit Cancelled after Security Fears." February 3. http://www.ibtimes.co.uk/articles/430914/20130203/maha-kumbh-mela-dalai-lama-tibet-vhp.htm.
Jacobsen, Knut Axel. 2020. "Hinduization of Space and the Case of Ayodhyā." Conference paper, American Academy of Religion Virtual Annual Meeting, November.

Jha, Dhirendra K. 2019. "RSS and the Akhāṛas." *Fountainink*, March 8. https://fountainink.in/reportage/rss-and-the-akhāṛas.

Kanaujia, Vertika. 2019. "60,000 Tonnes of Waste: The Kumbh Mela Effect." *Health Issues India*, May 21. https://www.healthissuesindia.com/2019/05/21/kumbh-mela-waste/.

Kaur, Banjot. 2019. "Faith to Filth: Thanks to Kumbh, Prayagraj Sinks in Solid Waste." *DownToEarth*, May 20. https://www.downtoearth.org.in/news/pollution/faith-to-filth-thanks-to-kumbh-prayagraj-sinks-in-solid-waste-64579.

Kermani, Faris, dir. 2013. *Kumbh Mela: The Greatest Show on Earth*. Crescent Films.

Khanal, V. 2019. "Kumbh Mela 2019 More a Grand Platform for Politics than Religion; Parties Pitch Camps to Spread Ideology among Pilgrims, Tourists." *Firstpost*, January 24. https://www.firstpost.com/politics/kumbh-mela-2019-more-a-grand-platform-for-politics-than-religion-parties-pitch-camps-to-spread-ideology-among-pilgrims-tourists-5954781.html.

Kumar, Akshat. 2019. "Exclusively, Well of Death at Kumbh Mela Carnival 2019." A Kumar Lifestyle (YouTube channel), January 28. https://youtu.be/AF3GBGwjrSQ.

Lucia, Amanda. 2020. *White Utopias: The Religious Exoticism of Transformational Festivals*. Oakland: University of California Press.

Maclean, Kama. 2008. *Pilgrimage and Power: The Kumbh Mela in Allahabad, 1865–1954*. New York: Oxford University Press.

Malaviya, Smriti. 2020. "On Ramdev's cue, Naga sādhus pledge to give up clay pipes." *Hindustan Times*, April 13. https://www.hindustantimes.com/india-news/naga-sādhus-pledge-to-give-up-clay-pipes/story-eeHimsVJ6oTqoDMHmy4srM.html.

Mishra, J. S. 2007. *Mahakumbh: The Greatest Show on Earth*. New Delhi: Har Anand.

Pradhan, Kunal. 2013. "Mahakumbh's Engineering Miracle Contrasts with Tragic Allahabad Stampede." *India Today*, February 15.

"Prem Baba, guru espiritual faz posicionamento sobre a acusação de assédio sexual." 2018. YouTube video, August 30. https://youtu.be/Lb8npgeSQtQ.

PTI. 2019. "Kumbh Mela: Because the World Is Here." *New Indian Express*, January 14. https://www.newindianexpress.com/lifestyle/travel/2019/jan/14/kumbh-mela-because-the-world-is-here-1925066.html.

Sarkar, Soumya. 2020. "Clean Kumbh, Dirty Ganga: River's Transformation during Mela Was 'Event Management,' Not Sustainable Solution." *Firstpost*. https://www.firstpost.com/long-reads/clean-kumbh-dirty-ganga-rivers-transformation-during-mela-was-event-management-not-sustainable-solution-6251441.html.

Sen, Priyadarshini. 2019. "Ayodhya, Ghar Wapsi, Gau Raksha: How BJP, RSS and Affiliates Used Kumbh Mela to Push Hindutva." *The Print*, March

4. https://theprint.in/politics/ayodhya-ghar-wapsi-gau-raksha-how-bjp-rss-affiliates-used-kumbh-mela-to-push-hindutva/200887/.

Sharma, Vishwajit. 2018. "Let's Get Ready for a Clean and Healthy Ardh Kumbh Mela 2019." *Tour My India*, December 21. https://www.tourmyindia.com/blog/pledge-for-clean-and-healthy-kumbh-mela/.

Sridhar, S., P. Gautret, and P. Brouqui. 2014. "A Comprehensive Review of the Kumbh Mela: Identifying Risks for Spread of Infectious Diseases." *Clinical Microbiology and Infection* 21 (2): 128–33.

Srinivas, Tulasi. 2018. *The Cow in the Elevator: An Anthropology of Wonder.* Durham, NC: Duke University Press.

Taylor, Miles. 2018. *Empress: Queen Victoria and India.* New Haven, CT: Yale University Press.

Times of India. 2019. "Ardh Kumbh Mela 2019 to Be Eco-Friendly This Time; More Highlights." January 24. https://timesofindia.indiatimes.com/travel/destinations/ardh-kumbh-mela-2019-to-be-eco-friendly-this-time-more-highlights/as67525205.cms.

Treza, Raphael, dir. 2015. *Cobra Gypsies.* Raphael Treza (YouTube channel), February 28. https://youtu.be/aNUYGRn3W9Q?list=PLCeA8iExp5arCXmj4My_k9aqP81ZBK56l.

Tully, Mark. 2001. *The Kumbh Mela.* Varanasi: Indica.

Wood, Michael. 2013. "Memories of the Kumbh Mela: The Greatest Show on Earth." *BBC*, February 1. http://wwwnews.live.bbc.co.uk/religion/0/21235888.

Yorke, Michael, dir. 2001. *Kumbh Mela: The Greatest Show on Earth.* Rex Mundi Production.

Section 3
Ethics of Wonder

Chapter 9

Scarcity, Abundance, and Money at Muslim Saint Shrines in North India

QUINN A. CLARK

Introduction

Every Thursday evening at the shrines of Muslim saints in North India, money falls onto the open laps of Sufi *pirs* (living saints).[1] The *pirs* rarely reach out for it, and they never ask for it. Instead, it finds them, as if traveling under its own power, never coercively sought after, always passively received. When *qawwals* (performers of *qawwali* devotional music) play at the shrine, people drop money in front of them or in the lap of the singer but rarely before letting the *pir* touch the money or waving the cash in the direction of the tomb of the interred saint.[2] Occasionally, when someone reaches a state of *hal* (euphoric ecstasy brought about by the overwhelming power of the interred saint, a state that overrides the rational faculties), they may flamboyantly shower the performers with money so that cash rains down over them as the droning, hypnotic *qawwali* music loudly plays. This is referred to as *vel*, which historically was a means of compensating the *qawwals* for their time and labor, and the flashy enthusiasm was meant to encourage others to do the same (Nayyar 1988, 8). Today, *khadims* (shrine caretakers) often arrange compensation privately, and *vel* serves a ritually symbolic function, which is clear to anyone present: At a time in North India when Muslims are increasingly economically left behind, socially marginalized, politically threatened to be stripped of citizenship rights, and, in cruel irony, held responsible for these hardships and also those of the nation as a whole as the purported descendants of medieval Muslim "invaders" who are accused of having plundered an otherwise flourishing land, why would any rational person literally throw away money unless she or he were not out of one's senses, fully dependent on the love of God, and truly free of want?

Ethereal and unseen forces dazzle. The tremendous power of the Divine commands marvel and attention. The miraculous insight of sages inspires awe. But while all of our attention is focused on the altar, so to speak, another wondrous object goes unnoticed in plain sight like a purloined letter, but no less powerful, awe-inspiring, or theologically significant than deities, ritual objects, and miracles. At one and the same time, money is quotidian in the sense that it is everywhere—though more available for some than others—and money is also far more than an ordinary, inert object. It exerts a force so powerful that it can warp the soul and compromise individuals' eligibility for salvation. It entices the *nafs al-ammarah* (the unruly animal soul). It is responsible for the toppling of hubristic empires. And because of the tremendous power that it is said to exert on individuals, keeping it contained, controlled, and moderated carries the potential to preserve the religious purity of the Islamic community, or any other religious community for that matter. For Muslims in Lucknow, if one can identify where, when, and upon whom money has exerted its influence, one is able to peek beyond the veil of revelation (*kashf al-mahjob*) to discern true Sufism from its corrupt impostors.[3]

Against the backdrop of rising communalism in India, the shrines of Muslim saints have acquired a reputation for being apolitical, all-inclusive, and anti-elite.[4] This depiction of shrines sits awkwardly next to another set of images.[5] Fierce intra-Islamic rivalries are hashed out over the Quranic acceptability of shrine veneration, and these tensions have even manifested as terrorist attacks, especially in Pakistan.[6] The inheritance of the ownership of sacred real estate generally aligns with upper-caste descent, and today Sufis are divided among themselves over the question of whether a "true" Sufi must be a Sayyid, who are said to be descendants of the Prophet and also represent the apex position of the Muslim caste system. The sacred assets included in estates are often managed by Waqf Boards, which are subsidiary bodies of the Indian government. These Waqf Boards manage just under US$16 billion worth of assets (although some reports claim as much as $39 billion) (Prime Minister's High Level Committee 2006; Badkar 2012), and Sufi *pir*-politician alliances have come under immense scrutiny due to allegations of corruption.

When I asked my interviewees in Lucknow about these kinds of tensions—the demonization of so-called "Wahhabi" rivals by an all-inclusive community; the Sayyid caste identities of anti-elite Sufis; the political entanglements of an apolitical space—their explanations were consistent and confident: that is just what happens when money gets involved. The idea that money accounted for the "negative" aspects of Sufi shrine operations became a consistent theme over the course of my fieldwork. Why would money, and not *Shaitan* (devil, demon) or the *nafs* or theological "decay" or any other credible explanation, play this role today? What does this say about the wider social and religious significance of Sufism and shrines? And what are the conceptual underpinnings of money's ability to produce such theologically consequential effects on Sufi Islam? This chapter argues that, today, the social concept of money can play the crucial role of demarcating the boundary between "true" Sufism and its corrupt, inauthentic imposters because money, as it is experienced by many Muslims in Lucknow, is associated with eminent scarcity emblematic of the social conditions effected by the neoliberal commercial economy—ever depreciating, always fleeting, unfaithful even when present—and it is semiotically counterposed by *barakah*, the love of God manifest as a panacean blessing forever emitted by the bodies of Sufi *auliya* (sing. *wali*; "companions of God," saints) interred in shrine-tombs.

Whose Inclusivity? Which Tolerance? What Makes Sufi Shrines So "Good"

The association of Sufism and Muslim saint shrines with "good" Islam cannot be understood outside of the context of Western academic priorities and the politics of ethno-religious communalism in India.[7] Because Sufis are said to model forms of Islamic piety that are consistent and compatible with modern democratic tolerance, they have sometimes been seen as peaceful and as syncretic. Accordingly, scholarship on South Asian Sufism and Muslim saint shrines has often focused on the theme of boundary-breaking: multifaith visitation as breaking down communal borders; South Asian expressions of Sufi piety as challenges to Islamic orthodoxy;[8] poetry and *qawwali* as precommodified, free-form artistic expression; or renunciation as a way of snubbing elite culture. Although some Sufis have historically courted controversy, rebelled against religious authority, or rebuffed the solicitations of political elites, their reputation as counternormative rule-breakers has been overstated in the modern period, and scholarship's attention to it is more reflective of contemporary concerns with freedom, identity, agency, liminality, heterogeneity, and related concerns oriented around a general circumspection toward boundary-building and the preservation of ideological or communal purity.

Many of my interviewees often held similarly rosy views of Sufism and Muslim saint shrines, albeit for very different reasons that had little to do with those transgressing social strictures that stifle individuality or communal self-expression. *Barakah* can be accessed by the touch of a living *pir*, the internal cultivation of piety, or dutiful prayer. Because the *auliya* are considered to be "near" the Divine, some schools of Islamic thought contend that their bodies radiate this powerful, healing love of God. Their tombs, then, ultimately end up serving as never-ending reservoirs of this panacea, oases of eminent dependability amid the unforgiving, unpredictable landscape of India's neoliberal political economy. While scholars have often assessed the social significance of Sufi saint shrines in terms of communalism and religio-ethnic identity, shrines often appeal to demographically diverse cross sections of Indian society because of this panacean power, which can satisfy any need, including those either unmet by or unavailable in India's commercial economy. For many of my interviewees, shrines were not apolitical because multifaith visitation represents an abstract gesture of pluralism unsullied by nationalist politics but rather because the infinite abundance of *barakah* meets everyone's need, which make them less dependent on extortionate politicians, bureaucrats, or patrons. Shrines were not all-inclusive because modern Sufism is compatible with democratic secularism but because truly generous *auliya* provide to all. Shrines were not anti-elite because the social heterogeneity observed there is a form of resistance to discourses of the dominant but because the healing power of *barakah* produces a social leveling effect that makes competition or bigotry obsolete once everyone's needs are met. Whenever it appeared as is if politics, intra-Islamic strife, or Muslim caste privilege were involved, interviewees reliably circumscribed the realm of "true" Sufism as that which excluded the corrosive, corrupting influence of money because the infinite abundance of *barakah* neutralizes its corrupting effects.

The elision of *waqf* corruption, intra-Islamic sectarian rivalries, Sayyid Sufis, and, above all, money from studies of Sufi shrines is perhaps not without good reason: many Indian Muslims are not likely to consider those things a part of Sufism at all, or at least not in its ideal form. But what makes the concept of money so useful here is not just a matter of what it means but how it makes meaning, how the concept is used in everyday life. Many of my interviewees often referred to it in the process of making distinctions between true Sufism and that which is viewed as a corruption, thus erecting a boundary between authentic and inauthentic religiosity. Methodologically, this presents the anthropologist with a classic ethnographic conundrum but also an analytic opportunity: a sympathetic ethnographic account that includes that which interviewees explicitly insist should be excluded but the fact that they continue to volunteer *this particular explanation* itself warranting explanation. The manner in which many of my interviewees circumscribed the domain of "true" Sufism, I suggest in this chapter, reflected important dimensions of the immediate context in which many found themselves living. As the conditions of that immediate context change—sometimes day to day, sometimes moment to moment—so too does the boundary between true Sufism and its other, a line constantly drawn and redrawn. Because "neoliberal economy" is not itself a stable, ahistorical category either, redrawing the line that separates pure Sufism from a world corrupted by money also redefines the latter when the domain of God's eternal love is contrasted with that of the tumultuous, instable conditions of the Indian economy. The process of continually drawing and maintaining the boundary between authentic Sufism and its other is generative of new worlds and always creatively reshapes the realm of true Sufism but also that of the neoliberal commercial economy.

How to Make Sense of Money in the Anthropology of Religion

Tulasi Srinivas's *The Cow in the Elevator: An Anthropology of Wonder* shows how wonder, "sublime yet everyday," enables "the *process* of making, crafting, and manufacturing worlds, possibilities, and dispositions, in its embryonic and collaborative stages" (2018, 5–6; emphasis in original). For Srinivas, a consideration of the transformative power of wonder turns anthropologists' focus toward fracture and creativity and away from the stability and fixity of the structure of the world described by Victor Turner. If the antistructure of ritual space is characterized by liminality and ephemerality, "for Turner, the stasis of structure is normative and eternal," as Srinivas aptly puts it (2018, 5). Srinivas shifts attention away from fixity by arguing that "practices of wonder align with moments of ritual creativity of improvisation that occur sporadically but then sediment and become instituted as part and parcel of the ritual" (Srinivas 2018, 4). Building on Srinivas's work and pushing against Turner's conflation of ordinary, nonritual life with stability, this chapter asks what happens to ritual for those whose ordinary lives are marked by states of protracted precarity and instability, when money in everyday life becomes associated with ephemerality and the ritual manifestation of God's eternal love becomes associated with stability, and what kinds of worlds are created by wonder's transformative ability to remake money as its opposite in a ritual context: something you do not need. Srinivas notices that the wonder evoked by aesthetic displays of garlanded cash found in Hindu temples in Bangalore produces a paradox wherein one gives up money to an already-wealthy deity because "[the excess of money] not only invites devotees to marvel at the unimaginable radiant wealth of God but also offers them hope to be similarly prosperous themselves" (Srinivas 2018, 106; and also 120). While it is not aestheticized in the same way, the transmission of money at shrines is similarly a visual spectacle, which becomes especially clear in the extravagance of *vel*. But the wonder inspired by the spectacle of *vel* also draws out a key difference. The wondrous display of cash raining down fixates onlookers' gaze not because they aspire to be like the man throwing away money because he has so much that it is devalued. Rather he is overcome by the love of the God to the extent that he no longer desires or depends on money, no matter how little of it he may possess.

In many ways, the anthropology of money had been framed around functionalist analyses of money's effects on social formations and modes of sociality, debates that stem from the "great transformation" thesis put forward by Karl Polyani, who argued that "money freed people from corporate statuses but left them with nothing but money itself with which to evaluate and judge the social and natural worlds around them" (Maurer 2006, 19–20). Over time, a separate trend in scholarship redirected focus away from the material effects of money on social life and toward the social effects of money as a material object. In other words, money was not seen only as a force in the world that influences sociality but also as a material object that mediates social relations and possesses its own historically specific, context-dependent semiotic ideology.[9] This is not to say that the meaning of money in a given historical or social context is reducible to a projection of human concerns onto objects. Instead, it plays a role in a broader constellation of signifiers, and the signification of that constellation is made "real" through the presence of concrete, material objects. Consider Timothy Mitchell's concept of the "state effect." Mitchell argues that, because the state is

> an object of analysis that appears both as material force and as ideological construct, [and a theory of state-formation] must begin with the assumption that we must take seriously the elusiveness of the boundary between state and society, not as a problem of conceptual precision but as a clue to the nature of the phenomenon . . . [w]e must take such distinctions [between state and society] not as the boundary between two discrete entities but as a line drawn internally, within a network of institutional mechanisms through which a social and political order is maintained. (Mitchell 1999, 76–77)

This boundary is maintained by the presence of concrete objects, such as barbed wire fencing around government facilities or continuous, habitual references to "the law," that render the state hyperreal because "the phenomenon we name 'the state' arises from techniques that enable mundane material practices to take on the appearance of an abstract, nonmaterial form" (Mitchell 1999, 77). For Mitchell, state-formation is better thought of as the production of a state effect, that is, the state and civil society as things made intelligible only because of a somewhat arbitrary boundary that ostensibly distinguishes one from the other.

This chapter analyses "true Sufism" in a way similar to Mitchell's analysis of the state. The material object of money and the attribution of Sufi shrines' negative aspects to it establishes the boundary—a "Sufi effect," so to speak—that keeps the unpredictable conditions of the commercial economy at bay from the unwaveringly pure Sufi markets of the religious economy.[10] This is the specific sense referred to above in which continuously reestablishing and diligently maintaining this boundary becomes a creative, generative process insofar as constantly redrawing the line between religious and commercial economies correlates with the character of constantly reimagined new worlds. Money functions as a meaning-making medium when used to make pragmatic differentiations in day-to-day life between that which arises from forces structured by the scarcity that defines commercial economic activity and that which arises from the abundance of the Sufi markets of India's religious economy. In the ritual setting described at the beginning of this chapter, money becomes an object of wonder when it is miraculously transmutes into its opposite. Like a *camera obscura* image, the ritual transmutation of money inverts the ritual world so that money plays by different—fairer, my interlocutors insisted—rules.

The Real Ones and Big Money

A bookstore clerk named Sajjid[11] and I were chatting one day in the neighborhood Chowk, the old city of Lucknow where I had been living. I asked if he had any books about the *auliya*, and he handed me a book about twenty-two *auliya* of Delhi. "Bis! Twenty *auliya!*" he proudly declared. He dragged his finger across the title and read aloud, "Bais . . . Twenty-*two auliya!*" I mentioned that on my way to this bookstore, I had passed many small shrines along the road with sheets overlaid—he interrupted me:

> Those are wrong, those are improper [*galat*]. Totally useless [*bekar*]. Don't pay attention to those. All this shrine stuff. It's wrong. Totally useless. I'll tell you what, it's really about money. Underneath, that's what those people want: money and nothing else. Those tombs along the roadside, they're nobodies. But then people think, "Oh, I can make a little money. Trick people." So they put a sheet over it. Put up some flowers. Then, people leave money and sweets. They pocket the money, and they eat the sweets. All the shrines and these offerings. It's all nonsense.

I told him that I had heard others voice similar concerns, especially about money. And what about Shahmina Shah, an especially prominent shrine in the neighborhood, I asked. He became somber. "No, that's different. Shahmina Shah is different. He's a *wali*," he explained. "The *auliya*, these are the real ones. All of those others, those are fake, just interested in money. But the *auliya*, these are the real ones. They're from for a long time back. Very old. So that's different. Nowadays, people are shallow. But the *auliya* themselves are real. Like those twenty in Delhi." His posture softened but his face hardened:

Lucknow used to be great. But now, it has gone down. Eighty percent of the people are from outside. But only 20 percent, this 20 percent are the real Lucknowis. But that's all. Twenty. These are the real ones. The *tahzib* [culture]. The language. It's all going down now nowadays. Those outsiders, they've just come here for money. From rural areas [*dehat se*]. From Bihar. Even from Agra. From outside [*bahar se*]. They're not like us. You see, in every place, people speak their own language, their own manner of speech. That's how you know they're outsiders. In Lucknow, we say *"ham"* for "me," but they say *"main"* for "me." But even that has gone down nowadays in Lucknow. If you want to learn about these, you have to find the real ones. Don't mess with all of those roadside shrines. It's all about money nowadays.

After I left Sajjid, I hurried further down the alleyway to get some of Lucknow's world-famous *kulcha-nihari* and write down the details of the conversation. While circumspect positions regarding shrine veneration, such as theological concerns regarding the attribution of the metaphysical powers of God to that which is not God (e.g., humans), might be associated with Islamic modernism, that does not appear to be Sajjid's real issue.[12] For Sajjid, money enabled him to differentiate between "the real ones" and those inauthentic ones who only cared about themselves. His view of Sufi shrines did not neatly align with doctrinal or communal lines. Instead, concerns over theology, transregional flows of migrant labor, ethnolinguistic heritage, and sincerity came together to form a constellation of signifiers overhanging Sufi shrines: shrines, connected to the *auliya* of Islam, connected to the twenty *auliya* of Delhi as the "real ones," connected to the 20 percent of "real ones" in Lucknow, connected to distinguishing real Lucknowis by their speech from outsiders, connected to "outsider" migrant laborers. The imagined space of Lucknow is indispensable context. Although Lucknow continues to industrialize and acts an important international hub of, to name at least one example, aerospace manufacturing, it is still culturally characterized in terms of nostalgia for an imagined bygone Nawabi era during which Urdu was pure, old Lucknow (or Chowk) was central, and the city's people were respected as refined and sophisticated. As the city continues to urbanize and diversify and as wealth inequality continues to grow for Lucknow's Muslim population, which is concentrated in Chowk and adjacent neighborhoods, a straight but gradually descending line is imagined from 1856 with the Annexation of Lucknow by the British Raj until Chowk's present. This is most succinctly observed in the *chikan* markets. *Chikan* is a style of handstitched embroidery made famous in Lucknow. Today, the textile market is flooded with cheaply made, inexpensive *chikan* that is loom-woven, which is considered *nakli* (fake, reproduced). The presence of "fake" *chikan* is not just a nuisance for discerning commodity consumers but viewed as emblematic of a much broader loss of cultural purity effected by the influx of "fake" Lucknowis attempting to capitalize on the city's historic heritage. Sajjid's point is straightforward: small, roadside tombs are graves of ordinary people that have been fashioned as shrines merely for the purpose of making money. But the significance of his point is not reducible to theological modernism. Instead, he delicately linked concerns regarding the decaying authenticity of the culture of a city that he loves, transregional migrant labor flows, the untoward production of fake goods, the duplicitous nature of people, and the authenticity of "the real ones."

It is in this context that Sajjid's motif of "the real ones" became such a central theme. Purity, and the corruption of that purity by the self-interested pursuit of money, becomes spatialized by the city itself. The real ones are characterized by authenticity, depth of lineage, and a love for others and Lucknow. Sajjid counterposed inauthenticity and the real ones: the actual *auliya* as figures who are not motivated by monetary gain, unlike migrant workers who have to come to Lucknow *from outside* in hopes of earning money. But the significance of Sajjid's reaction to roadside shrines is not just what he was saying but also what he was doing. Instead of merely explicating a fully formed thought system, Sajjid stitched together thoughts not unlike Freud's dreamer might, creating associational bridges between feelings and thoughts (Freud 1913). For example, he mistakenly remembered the title of the book as "Twenty" instead of "Twenty-Two," but nevertheless the word "twenty" remained in his consciousness and functioned as an associational bridge between the "twenty real ones" (i.e., the *auliya* of Delhi) and the "20 percent" of real Lucknowis who remain in Chowk today. The actual title of the book is, of course, immaterial. What matters is that he creatively formed a picture of Sufism within modern society but did so in such a way to make fine-grained distinctions, a central one being the differentiation between the real ones and those outsiders who only care about money.

Just as I was concluding my notes and finishing my meal, a man sat at my table, introduced himself as Faisal, politely commented on the *kulcha*, and praised the restaurant and its traditional cuisine. "It's real Lucknow," he said.[13] He asked me about myself, and I told him that I was in Lucknow to study shrines. Again, I mentioned the small, roadside shrines, noting that most books only focus on big ones. He raised his eyebrows and gave a wry smile. "Big," he said. "Big *money*," he said, in English, and then repeated for emphasis, "*Big* money." He said that the people working at shrines don't care about religion, just money. "Just go see all of the houses and cars they have. All tax-free, too. Huge donations." I asked him to be specific about which shrines were especially corrupt. All of them, he said. "This is the case with all religions. Hindus, Christians, Jews, everyone. There's a political connection, too," he told me. "The politicians come to the shrine, and they give all kinds of money to the managers. Then in return, the managers tell the people how to vote. They influence the people." I told him that I found many people who frequent shrines to be full of earnest, sincere love for the saints. He said that, yes, there were real ones, and I thought of Sajjid's "real ones." "There used to be real ones who didn't care about money. Every time money gets involved in spirituality, this spiritual level [*ruhani satah*] goes down." He paused and reflected, and then he told me that he was coming back from working in Saudi Arabia. "If you can believe it, there were no traditions associated with the grave of the Prophet. Visitors were not permitted to kiss even the pillars of the roof covering the tomb. You're not allowed to pray to the Prophet or ask him for anything. The Saudis said that if you want something, you need to ask God. The Saudis, they have so much money, big money, but they don't have to take donations at shrines." When it felt as though we had run out of conversational steam, he leaned back in his chair and said in precisely the same manner as before, "Well, anyway, big money. *Big*."

Faisal enunciated an idea that I had heard repeatedly during my fieldwork all over North India: that *pirs* and politicians enjoyed a codependent relationship in which *pirs* secure votes for politicians by exerting influence over trusting admirers in exchange for financial compensation. It was often explained to me that politicians and *pirs* rely on each other to satisfy their greed, but because the structure of the commercial economy is such that there is necessarily never enough to go around—that it is simply a brute reality that not everyone can have what they need—they are able to achieve mutual gain by ensuring that the deprivation falls on the "have nots." Faisal contrasted this presumed *pir*-politician duplicity with two specific signifiers. First, he contrasted this current-day *pir*-politician alliance with the *auliya* as the real ones from *before* the influence of money made "the spiritual level go down."[14] Second, he stressed the difference between India and Saudi Arabia, where the veneration of the Prophet is not, Sajjid suggested, associated with superfluous rituals. By circumscribing the arena of "the real ones," both Sajjid and Faisal spatialize this zone (albeit differently; the spatialization of purity changes as the Islamic core shifts from the Lucknow to Saudi Arabia) and also chronologize it. In earlier periods, *auliya* were more present, worshipers more authentic, and money less of an all-consuming concern. This chronologization, or what Ewing has described as "splitting time," is consistent with a broader Islamic chronotope in which the Islamic *ummah* is more susceptible to losing its way the further away it gets from Revelation (Bakhtin 2004). That may be a Shi'i Imam who carries the message of Revelation going hidden or it may be the days of the Prophet ever receding as time marches on. For many Muslims, then, Mecca is both spatially and temporarily closer to the time of the true "real ones": the *Ahl-e-Bayt* (Lit., "People of the House").[15]

The function that Saudi Arabia played in the semiotic chain formed by Faisal goes beyond the area's place in the history of Islam. As in Sajjid's case, while it may initially appear as if he is voicing modernist views that consider shrine-based rituals to be historical additions to a sealed Sunnah tradition when he appears to commend Saudi prohibitions against kissing the Prophet's tomb or supplicating him—and he very well may have those views—he was doing more than simply rehearsing a theological position. Faisal is part of a growing trend of South Asian Muslims who travel to Gulf States to perform migrant labor, and so his view of Saudi-prescribed manners of tomb veneration is also formed in the context of labor migration. Because the Saudis are already independently wealthy, Faisal may have been suggesting, they are not under the same kind of socioeconomic pressures that would drive someone to exploit and defraud. This is of particular importance because the wealth of Saudi Arabia is imagined to free them from the kinds of wants, anxieties, and desperation that compel individuals to cheat, shortchange, and coerce each other. For those who do not possess this kind of wealth or who seek goods and services unavailable in the commercial economy, such as the miraculous healing of terminal illness or the forgiveness of sins of deceased family members, this is precisely what the *barakah* of the Sufi markets of India's religious economy offers: infinite abundance that consequently renders coercion, compromise, or competition obsolete. But the Saudis were imagined to have such a degree of effectively unending wealth that they could recreate those conditions in the Saudi commercial economy.

The *Dargah* as a Doorway between Two Worlds

Faisal admired the Saudis' wealth because it makes them less exposed to coercion, and this illustrates the degree to which, symbolically at least, money is not uniformly bad as much as money is ambivalent because one must rely on it despite its eminently unreliability (e.g., changing its value every moment with near-constant fluctuations in foreign exchange markets). In this way, money becomes an object of both desire and resentment. The love of God as *barakah* is eternally perfect and normatively assessed as such. Money, on the other hand, is useful but fleeting. At the moment one attains it, it can begin to depreciate. It is never stable and can abandon you without notice, as it did for many during the 2016 demonetization of the Indian economy. Unlike the *barakah* of God, dependence on which brings its own satisfaction, money must be depended on, but as a *bevafah* (unfaithful) companion.[16] Money can betray, but God reliably provides for the faithful. As pieces of sacred real estate that simultaneously represent both eternally replenishing wellsprings of God's healing love but also state-managed objects of immense financial wealth that are competed over by sectarian rivals, government bureaucrats, real estate mafias, and Muslim caste groups, one can imagine the *dargah* (lit., "doorway" or "threshold") as sitting at the intersection of two realms operating in the here and now of Muslim life in India: a commercial economy defined by scarcity that is ruled by the laws of supply and demand administered by politicians; characterized by competition; and epitomized by money, and, on the other hand, a religious economy defined by abundance that is ruled by the laws of God administered by the saint (*wali*: friend of god, or governor; often with epithet "Shah": king); characterized by communal harmony; and epitomized by love (Urdu: *mohabbat*).

When seen through this model, the *wali* is "split" diachronically (belonging to an earlier, purer time period) but also synchronically between these two realms (the Sufi *qutb* as the ruler of a shadow government operating parallel to worldly governments; see Ewing 1983, 254). As such, "worldly" politics and statecraft are placed on the other side of the boundary, separating them from places like Dewa Sharif, a particularly prominent *dargah* located north of Lucknow where Haji Waris was laid to rest and continues to answer prayers. Without the presence of Haji Waris and his *dargah*, I was told, there would be no commerce in the town of Dewa and considerably fewer jobs, making it just another roadside town. Despite a population of under sixteen thousand people, little industry to speak of, founded by the saint himself, and located outside of Lucknow but too far for easy commuting, Dewa Sharif still manages to attract millions of travelers every year to the shrine and the town's annual animal trading fair. It is the star attraction of the Uttar Pradesh Department of Tourism's "Sufi Circuit." Despite its rural setting, the shrine attracts considerably more visitors and notoriety than its urban counterparts in Lucknow. A steady flow of visitors, tourists, and grandstanding politicians provides business to hotels, shops, and restaurants of all socioeconomic levels. Surely, the blessings of Haji Waris Sahib—or as visitors refer to him, "Sarkar"—pervade the entire town. When I asked a visitor from Benares named Gufran about the immense popularity of the *dargah*, he described Haji Waris as a *jamali* saint.[17] While *jalali* (strong, harsh) saints specialize in dangerous blessings, such as exorcisms, that could harm the supplicant, Sarkar Sahib was so beloved because this *jamali* (beautiful; here, soft) saint was reliable and generous regardless of religion, class, or caste. He told me that there was a *jalali* saint nearby in Dewa but few people were willing or able to endure the intense, painful treatments, which often are not intended for ordinary ailments. This did not make the saint bad or mean, of course, but Haji Waris enjoyed such broad-based popularity because his blessings were given "softly." Gufran attributed the peaceful atmosphere of the area to the love of the saints and contrasted both modes of transmitting *barakah*—*jamali* and *jalali*—"inside" Dewa from the "outside" world. He told me that everyone loves Sarkar Ji, referring to the saint, because he provides to all, no matter what, and this is why people seek calming retreat at these *dargah* compounds: to gain reprieve from the corruption, division, and politicizing *outside* of it. While *sarkar* (the government) divided and deprived, he explained, Sarkar Ji provided and accepted all.

This idea that there are two "sarkars" is important because it reflects a vision of parallel realms operating conterminously in the lives of Muslims and other shrine-goers. Here, the Indian government and its politicians are seen as distinct from the saint-rulers—regulators of the religious economy but not necessarily of an entirely different type insofar as they both are tasked with providing for ordinary people, even if "worldly" regimes do so unevenly. This was even spelled out at a different *dargah* complex in Barielly. I met a man there who used to work in the Gulf States but now was a schoolteacher and volunteered at the shrine in the mornings. He said that he felt sorry for those people who did not allow themselves to visit shrines for misguided theological reasons. He said that this *dargah* complex was unique because it is so clean and they do not accept money. I asked why they don't accept money or put out donation boxes, as other shrines do. "Who needs money," he asked rhetorically, "when all of the power is with the *auliya*? We come before them, and we ask for things, for food or for help, just as you would ask a king for help. Even the kings come and ask them for things. Why? Because they are the true kings: the kings of the unseen world ['*Alam-e-ghaib*]." In practice, this unseen world is contrasted with the neoliberal commercial economy, and it is precisely because of the barrier dividing them that the former remains perfect and uncorrupted. Analytically, however, the two fit together as oppositions. In this way, the *barakah*-rich Sufi markets accessed at shrines act as "spaces of resistance to this corrosion of neoliberalism, while allowing for a pragmatic capturing of what might work in the moment. . . . This radical social hope is key to anti-alienation, to a sense of feeling and being 'at home' in the modern world" (Srinivas 2018, 8–9). But if money is so closely associated with corruption, and if it demarcates the boundary keeping one realm at bay from another, and if the "kings of the unseen world" have no need for money, then one must ask, Why is there so much money involved in shrine-based rituals, and why does its presence not detract from the religious wonder of the ritual by inviting suspicions of scandal or controversy?

Scarcity and Abundance: The Transmission of Money at Shrines

Thursday evenings are the night of *mehfil-e-sama* (lit., "gathering of audition"; Qawwali performance) when *qawwali* music is played near shrines, especially those associated with the Chishtiyya. Amid the colorful, aromatic, and festive atmosphere, the transmission of money—passed silently but in no way hidden from plain sight—from the visitors or devotees to a *qawwal*, *pir*, or interred saint is a ubiquitous ritual at Sufi saint shrines in South Asia. More often than the aforementioned *vel* process of showering performers with cash, listeners and devotees approach the *qawwals* directly and drop money either in the lap of the singers or in front of the performers. When approaching the singers, visitors are careful to never turn their backs to the tomb, and they often swirl the money in the air in the direction of the tomb before giving it to the *qawwals*. When the *pir* is seated near the *qawwals*, one may instead hand the money directly to the *pir*, who will touch it and then pass it to the performers. If one chooses to donate the money to the *pir*, he rarely touches it with his hands. Instead, he sits with open arms, and one drops the money into his lap. Alternatively, visitors and devotees can choose to donate money to the interred saint as an act of self-sacrificial devotion. One may place the money on top of the tomb, and, oftentimes, not before whispering a prayer of blessing over the money. Alternatively, one may give it to the *pir*, who touches it and then returns it to the individual so that they can then place the money on the tomb themselves to receive the blessing afforded by this act of generosity.

The various modes of exchanging money are fairly systematic and patterned by the dynamics of *barakah*. The *barakah* that imbues the bodies of the *auliya* interred within a tomb radiates outward as an ethereal, invisible force. It is due to this ethereal quality that one can merely wave cash in the direction of the tomb to bless it. Nevertheless, it does often have a tactile quality, and this why visitors touch the tomb of *wali* either with their hands or eyelids to receive the blessing power of *barakah*. This is also why one can transmit money to a *qawwal* by way of the blessing touch of a *pir*. By virtue of being the spiritual inheritor of the *wali's khilafa* (leadership role of a Sufi order or suborder), a *pir* can transmit the *barakah* onto the money, thereby ritually blessing it before passing it to the *qawwals* or onto the tomb. It is important that the *pir* rarely touches the money himself when he is the recipient but instead passively allows it to find him, which is reflected by the fact that, without reaching out for it, it lands on his lap without his own intervention. Finally, visitors may simply deposit cash into metal or wooden boxes that remain locked and overseen by a volunteer. These donations, in particular, are referred to as *nazar*, or "gift," as they are understood as a kind of charitable contribution for the upkeep and maintenance of the shrine complex.

Given all of that has been argued so far about the morally ambivalent status of money, and in light of the scandals and controversies regarding graft and corruption, the highly visible and normative presence of money at shrines strikes one as odd. Today, the financial reporting of donations is often carried out in an unsupervised manner only by the *pir* and his or her own family, and one often hears murmurs of suspicions that they skim the top off of donations. The volunteers overseeing the locked donation boxes do not escape scrutiny either, as it is whispered that volunteers are selected by the *pir* in exchange for some kind of favor, and in return, it is implied that the volunteer may help themselves to a percentage of the collected *nazar*. Aside from *mehfil-e-sama* or other shrine-centered ritual contexts, a *pir* may also prescribe a *tauviz* (amulet) for particular ailments. While the administration of *tauviz* is often attended by a monetary gift to compensate the *pir* for his or her time and efforts, some question just how freely given these cash donations really are. These apprehensions about the flow of money in and out of shrines exceed low-level graft or improper accounting. The staggering wealth managed by Waqf Boards has led to suspicions of the "maladministration," and these boards have been at the center of numerous high-profile scandals usually involving the illegal sale of sacred property to real estate mafias or fraudulent acquisition by the Indian government (Prime Minister's High Level Committee 2006, 217–35).

How, then, does one explain the apparent contradiction between the fact that, in the ritual context described above, money is blessed, and, outside of that ritual context, money's involvement in shrines signifies an inauthentic or degraded form of Sufism? The ritual symbolism of the circulation of money is produced by the combination of polarities, "aspects of social differentiation and even opposition between the components of society which ideally it is supposed symbolize as a harmonious whole" (Turner 1967, 24). The combination of scarcity and abundance inverts money's mode of transmission, which can be observed by onlookers. *Barakah* is invisible but is characterized by its infinitude and, thus, reliability as an extension of the eternal constancy of God. Outside of this ritual context, money is a concrete, tangible object that, for many, is characterized by its scarcity. When money (a concrete object associated with scarcity) is combined with *barakah* (an invisible, ethereal force of love associated with abundance), money is transmuted and its mode of transmission is inverted, because it is no longer driven by coercion or self-interest. Instead, it is freely given—and passively received, which exonerates *pirs* of the kind of scrutiny that might otherwise be "corrosive of the aspirational . . . [and] creates limits to the conditions of wonder"

(Srinivas 2018, 107)—like showering *qawwals* with cash as a spontaneous act of literally throwing money away, something signifying a complete lack of self-interest due to perfect satisfaction from the love of God. This is why "exchange" does not adequately describe money's movements in this context. Here, the transmission of money becomes a wondrous spectacle when it acts as a vehicle of *barakah* and individuals "made money part of the 'perfect world' of ritual interaction, thereby creating new space for it to reside in and simultaneously, they slipped money from the realm of transaction to the realm of wonder" (Srinivas 2018, 103–4). When money is included in Sufi ritual repertoires, it becomes transmuted from something that arouses feelings of ambivalence or resentment into something that brings joy by providing refuge and reprieve whenever it comes into contact with the love of God. The nature of money's ritual transmutation still bears a relationship to its "natural" state outside of ritual contexts, just as a photographic inversion represents a *camera obscura* image of what it both is and is not.

Conclusion

What could be more disruptive, counternormative, and fracturing to the logic of neoliberal capitalism than actually throwing money away? In a Turnerian sense, this act directly reflects its opposite: Muslim precarity in North India. But while Turner suggests that the ritual combination of opposites creates a "harmonious whole," the combination of money's unpredictability with the reliability of God's love paradoxically fractures the norms of neoliberal capitalism in the same motion that it ensures stability for the participant. It is not simply that the *barakah*-rich Sufi markets of India's religious economy are an escape from the "real world." They are in the real world. The vow prayers and blessings address real needs, such as those of a mother hoping to ensure her son passes exams, newlyweds struggling to conceive a child, grieving families praying for the existential comfort of the recently departed, or a woman just hoping for a peaceful place to pray (Pearson 1996). The infinite abundance of God's blessing love can always be relied on, and God never betrays the faithful. This stands in stark contrast to the *bevafah* tumult of the commercial economy, but it is not reducible to escapism. Perhaps because the ethereal nature of *barakah* is panacean, it can remain immutably adaptive. And, in this way, the dynamics of the religious economy mirror but invert those of the commercial economy, because it is filling in gaps left by neoliberal society—satisfying unmet market demand, so to speak—by becoming present in those interstices where the capitalist conditions of North India have created absences, hollowed out people's lives. In this way, "through the pursuit of wonder—in which wonder is a rhetorical and aspirational catalyst to create rituals that not only rupture and resist but also embrace and extend modernity's enduring and seductive paradigm—ritual practitioners explore, interrogate, and slyly resist the dominant model of a Western-derived neoliberal modernity to which they are subject, and that these discourses and practices are potentially transformative of contemporary modernity, capturing, yet also rupturing, both past and future conditions" (Srinivas 2018, 9–10). The meaning of money shifts historically and also from ethnographic moment to moment. But because the semiotic ideology of money is ever-shifting, it is also producing meaning whenever it is used to differentiate between this and that. This is why the shifts of meaning themselves must be accounted for, analyzed, and interpreted, instead disavowing them from the anthropology of religion, even if—or maybe especially if—our interlocutors do.

Notes

This chapter draws on chapter 1 of the author's own unpublished dissertation. This includes fieldwork data, analysis of that data, and, in some cases, verbatim phrases. See "Who Are the Real Kings? Scarcity and Coercion, Indian Politics, and Money," in Clark (2021, 35–77).

1. "Saint" is an imperfect gloss. *Pir* is a general term that refers to Sufi or saintly figures in South Asian Islam. Other terms denote specific roles, such as *sajjadah nashin* or *gaddi nashin*, which refers to the leader of a particular Sufi tradition, or terms that denote vows of poverty, such as *faqir*.

2. The English terms "shrine" or "tomb" do not do full justice to these sites. They can be variously referred to in Urdu as *mazar* (lit., place of visitation), *dargah* (lit., doorway, threshold), or *qabar* (tomb, or grave).

3. Historically, Sufi literature has taken up the concept of *kashf* with particular verve. Al-Hujwiri's *Kashf al-Mahjob*, in particular, dedicates considerable attention to differentiating true Sufis from impostors (al-Hujwīrī 2014).

4. Fait Muedini's (2015) important study analyses the global politics of this characterization.

5. Each of these four themes (i.e., politics, Waqf, "Wahhabis" and theological disputes, and caste) are taken up in the author's dissertation (Clark 2021).

6. There are relatively few cases of shrine bombings in India, but the most notable attack, which occurred in 2006 at Ajmer Sharif, was carried out by right-wing Hindu terrorists.

7. Katherine Ewing and Rosemary Corbett's recent edited volume is an important contribution to our understanding of the politicization of Sufism in South Asia today (see Ewing and Corbett 2020).

8. Nile Green provides an excellent demonstration of the way that the insistence of Indian secular nationalist discourse regarding Sufism's uniquely Indic qualities obscures Indian Sufism's historical connections with the broader Islamic world but also why the disavowal of these connections to the Middle East is itself consistent with the secular nationalist discourse (Green 2012).

9. For more on the concept of semiotic ideology, see Keane (2018).

10. The "religious economy" model was popularized by the work of Nile Green. Green uses the concept in historical analysis. In my study, I attempt to adapt the model for ethnographic analysis (see Green 2013).

11. All names of interviewees and interlocutors are pseudonyms. Sajjid and I spoke in Urdu.

12. Brannon Ingram's work offer the best direct treatment of a Deobandi conception of *tasawwuf*, which is understood as the cultivation of inner piety. Shrine veneration and the metaphysical status of the *auliya* has been a matter of contention among Deobandi thinkers, but this is not to say—as both scholars and theological rivals have suggested—that they roundly reject Sufism or *tasawwuf*. Ingram's (2018) study of the Deobandi school is a vivid corrective to the conflation of shrine veneration and Sufism.

13. Faisal and I mostly spoke in English with a mix of Hindi and Urdu.

14. This temporal "splitting," in which true Sufis are relegated to a distant past whereas those in the present are seen as less authentic, is common throughout colonial discourse but also Islamic history (Ewing 1997, 41–64).

15. Lit., "People of house." The expression refers to the family of the Prophet.

16. Pilgrimage (Urdu: *ziyarat*) is a paragon of a cost-free expense, because not only does one gain from being present at the sacred destination but the effort, time, and opportunity cost invested in pilgrimage is itself edifying.

17. Gufran and I spoke in a mix of Hindi and English.

Works Cited

Badkar, Mamta. 2012. "More Indian Corruption Is Exposed in Massive New $39 Billion Land Scandal." *Business Insider*, March 27. https://www.businessinsider.com/india-land-scam-2012-3.

Bakhtin, Mikhail. 2004. "Forms of Time and of the Chronotope in the Novel." In *The Dialogic Imagination: Four Essays*, 84–258. Austin: University of Texas Press.

Clark, Quinn A. 2021. "Dīn and Duniyā: Debating Sufism, Saint Shrines, and Money in the Lucknow Area." PhD diss., Columbia University.

Ewing, Katherine. 1983. "The Politics of Sufism: Redefining the Saints of Pakistan." *Journal of Asian Studies* 42 (2): 251–68.

———. 1997. *Arguing Sainthood: Modernity, Psychoanalysis, and Islam*. Durham, NC: Duke University Press.

Ewing, Katherine, and Rosemary Corbett, eds. 2020. *Modern Sufis and the State*. New York: Columbia University Press.

Freud, Sigmund. 1913. *The Interpretation of Dreams*. Translated by A. A. Brill. New York: Barnes and Noble Books.

Green, Nile. 2012. "The Migration of a Muslim Ritual." In *Making Space: Sufis and Settlers in Early Modern India*, 33–64. New Delhi: Oxford University Press.

———. 2013. *Bombay Islam: The Religious Economy of the West Indian Ocean, 1840–1915*. Cambridge: Cambridge University Press.

Ingram, Brannon D. 2018. *Revival from Below: The Deoband Movement and Global Islam*. Oakland: University of California Press.

Keane, Webb. 2018. "On Semiotic Ideology." *Signs and Society* 6 (1): 64–87.

Maurer, Bill. 2006. "The Anthropology of Money." *Annual Review of Anthropology* 35:15–36.

Mitchell, Timothy. 1999. "Society, Economy, and the State Effect." In *State/Culture: State-Formation after the Cultural Turn*, edited by George Steinmetz, 76–97. Wilder House Series in Politics, History, and Culture. Ithaca, NY: Cornell University Press.

Muedini, Fait. 2015. *Sponsoring Sufism: How Governments Promote "Mystical Islam" in Their Domestic and Foreign Policies*. Palgrave Studies in Religion, Politics, and Policy. New York: Palgrave Macmillan.

Nayyar, Adam. 1988. *Qawwali*. Islamabad: Lok Virsa Research Centre.

al-Hujwīrī, ʿAlī bin ʿUthmān Sullābī. 2014. *The Kashf al-Mahjūb: The Oldest Persian Treatise on Sufiism*. Translated by Reynold A. Nicholson. Havertown, PA: Gibb Memorial Trust.

Pearson, Anne Mackenzie. 1996. *"Because It Gives Me Peace of Mind": Ritual Fasts in the Religious Lives of Hindu Women*. Albany: State University of New York Press.

Prime Minister's High Level Committee. 2006. *Social, Economic, and Educational Status of the Muslim Community of India: A Report*. New Delhi: Cabinet Secretariat, Government of India.

Srinivas, Tulasi. 2018. *The Cow in the Elevator: An Anthropology of Wonder*. Durham, N.C: Duke University Press.

Turner, Victor. 1967. "Symbols in Ndembu Ritual." In *The Forest of Symbols: Aspects of Ndembu Ritual*, 19–47. Ithaca, NY: Cornell University Press.

Chapter 10

On Wondrous Moments as the Basis for a Swaminarayan Ethics of Sociality

Hanna H. Kim

Introduction

My daughter and I sat in the sabha mandap [meeting place]. It was too crowded; we got up and walked to go outside. We saw Bapa's [Pramukh Swami Maharaj] sister [Ganga Ba], protected by women. She was surrounded by them and they can yell at you. I don't know, but I bent down to touch her feet. And, I said, "Kampala mandal says Jai Swaminarayan to you." She placed one hand on my head, the other on my daughter's head, and moved her hand down our hair, down our back. We were so happy. We received such joy that we were both crying. And, I thought, this must be the feeling that [my husband] has when Bapa touches him and he cannot explain what he feels. . . . I remember this every day, all the time, and it gives me such a feeling [goose bumps, gesturing to forearm].

—Swaminarayan devotee from Kampala, Uganda[1]

If there is any doubt that a wondrous moment is one that stands out from the usual—could it be a miracle or is it a trick—it is the unambiguous affective response that a wonder event immediately provokes that dispels doubts of such instances being only imagined. These moments are also ones where a disruption has made possible a reshaping of some dimension of the wonder-experiencing subject. Clearly wonder involves an affective component, a somatically registered response, that prompts a sensation more joyful than unwanted and these reactions are intimately connected to the context in which they have occurred. For the observer, wonder, upon close examination, is a notable event perhaps only upon having some understanding of the assemblages of discourses and relations from which it has emerged. How else to appreciate why a disruptive incident has resulted in a kind of subjection that is welcomed despite some aura of puzzlement over its occurrence. Would all people encountering the same event respond in affectively similar ways and, if not, why not, we would need to ask. For example, who is Pramukh Swami Maharaj, and is there a significance to being touched by his hand on one's head? Why should a touch by the sister of Pramukh Swami have a dramatic effect on two women? What does the recollection of a wondrous moment do? Can a strong connection be made between the experience of subjection to wonder and an orientation to living that is more attuned to and embracing of others? Does the wonder effect have to be anchored to a discourse in order to retain its affective impact? Can a wonder experience, in other words, be detached from any discursive foundation and still be memorable in a goose-bump kind of way?

In this chapter, to narrow the field of questions that wonder moments stir up, the question that I shall try to answer is, Can the affective state of wonder be the basis for an ethics of sociality? From a close look at wonder events that are connected to the Hindu devotional community known as BAPS Swaminarayan Sanstha, I reexamine these moments of surprise that, by their retelling, reaffirm a sense of something that guides the self and future decision-making and actions. Setting aside reasonable questions of whether a single affective response might be the basis for understanding behavior, I consider how a close focus on the experiencing of wonder can guide the subject and ethnographer to productive ends, ethically and ethnographically. This is one analytical strategy to gain some understanding of religious subjectivity. If wonder begets something, then tracing wondrous moments from their experiencing to their interpretations can show the relationships and connections to discourses and ontologies that figure in these wonder explanations.

For those of us puzzling through the equation of affect and religious subjectivity, it seems that there is an analytical path that navigates between ontological determinism and materialist explanations. Finding this path through a focus on affect and the assemblages that support its interpretation might contribute to an ethnography of religious subjectivity that is reliant on understanding linkages and relationships rather than reducing affect to the rational cognitive or the impressionist ephemeral. From first-person accounts of experiencing wonder collected during the course of long-term fieldwork on the BAPS Swaminarayan community in India, I am focused on the experience and aftermath of an encounter with wonder that lead to an ethics of sociality. It is the connections to others that end up guiding how to live in the world that I am calling an ethics of sociality. I argue that the interpretation of wonder, while particular to an individual, is also informed by discourses that contribute to the perceived significances of an "enchanted" encounter. This chapter looks at the trajectories of interpretation, as offered by my interlocutors, as they make sense of specific experiences and, in turn, reexamine their own selves in relation to others with whom they live, work, and spend time. For the anthropologist as much as her interlocutors, wonder moments are rich ethnographic sites, calling for interpretation and requiring multiple lenses to bring their significations into focus.

Matei Candea observes that the anthropological fieldsite "is a device for producing the unexpected" (2013, 15). To focus on wonder is to increase, if such can be measured, the amount of attention for the unexpected, and thereby provide opportunities for both ethnographer and interlocutor to trace the connection between remembered incident and the production of subsequent insights. For ethnographer and interlocutor alike, the interpretation of wonder is informed by already existing discourses as well as accumulated experiences. In following the discursive trail initiated by a wondrous moment, from recollection to subsequent actions, this chapter aims to show that an experience of wonder can foster an ethics of sociality, one that is not sui generis but, in its genealogy, conveys the power of certain discourses to achieve something. The experiencers of wonder are seeking answers and finding them in the BAPS Swaminarayan devotional tradition. I further suggest that exploring the experiencing of wonder, whether tangentially or explicitly tied to religious scaffolding, leads to a more granular appreciation of enchantment in the making of social and ethical selves. Dwelling on wondrous moments would seem to point in this direction, one where an ethics of sociality is dependent on one's conduct toward others as much as it rests on the desires of the autonomous self.

This chapter begins with a brief introduction of the BAPS Swaminarayan community. Then follows three narratives that have caught both my interlocutors' and my attention. These narrative descriptions of experiencing something unexpected offer the ethnographic grounding for mapping wonder events to an ethics of sociality informed by BAPS discourses.[2] The chapter concludes with a discussion of the anthropology of wonder as an ethnographically productive and portable strategy for exploring attachments and relationships in South Asia and elsewhere.

BAPS and the Swaminarayan Ground for Wonder Experiences

BAPS or, formally, Bochasanwasi Shri Akshar Purushottam Swaminarayan Sanstha, is a transnational Hindu devotional community whose followers, temples, and activities have expanded much beyond its origin in western India.[3] Founded in 1907 in today's Gujarat State, BAPS's headquarter is in Ahmedabad, Gujarat, and from here the activities of the global Swaminarayan community are coordinated. This rationalized system, which today includes over one thousand temples and centers, is overseen by the BAPS guru, and beneath him in hierarchy, the approximately one thousand *sadhus* (monks) and active lay volunteers.[4] The guru is always in the form of a living sadhu who has no fixed residence. According to BAPS *upasana* or the theological foundation of Swaminarayan *bhakti* (devotionalism), Swaminarayan followers rely upon and need the guru to guide their devotion of the ultimate principle who is Bhagwan Swaminarayan, or Lord Swaminarayan (Kim 2013).[5] The current BAPS membership, according to its own accounting, is about one million *satsangis* (devotees) and most are Gujarati in origin or heritage.

Since its beginning, BAPS has used temple construction or built forms as a primary means to signal its upasana as distinct from the original Swaminarayan community from which it separated (Kim 2012, 2021). BAPS *mandirs* (temples) contain the *murtis* (iconic forms) of Bhagwan Swaminarayan and the first BAPS guru in the central shrine or *garbha griha* with the murtis of all other BAPS gurus (*guru parampara*) displayed in pictorial or carved forms in adjacent areas in the mandir. Outside BAPS stone-carved temples, there are also individual *sinhasana* or throne-like shrines for guru parampara. Murtis in BAPS offer a material expression of this community's devotional emphasis on the distinct and separate ontological categories of the Akshar guru in relation to the category of Purushottam, the ultimate existential entity, who is Bhagwan.[6] The particularities of this relationship are connected to Swaminarayan ontological objectives, namely, for devotees to attain *moksha*, or freedom from birth and rebirth, and then be able to offer eternal devotion to Bhagwan as a released *jiva* (or *atma*), the eternal self. This objective is only possible through the guidance of the Akshar guru who is the ultimate ideal devotee and the penultimate existential reality wherein the power of the ultimate reality, Purushottam, resides. Serving the guru and seeking to please him through devotional practices that include *seva* (volunteered devotional labor) constitute an important practice in BAPS bhakti. Satsangis want to offer seva to Guru, for in doing so they are honing their corporeal selves according to the model that exists before them, and reaching closer to their devotional objectives to attain moksha. It is the capacity to orient oneself to the guru and to serve his needs as much as observing one's guru doing so for God that yield knowledge about the eternal self, the jiva, as separate from the transitory corporeal self. This relationship of satsangi to seva is thus one that rests on an attraction to the assemblage of guru, seva, and Swaminarayan ontological categories: satsangis are those with a desire to train the corporeal self to achieve the Swaminarayan ontological goal of serving Bhagwan eternally. In this devotional schema, the living guru is the model for an ethical framework for living, one that can guide satsangis in daily living for their future objective. In BAPS bhakti, devotees are those who accept this explicit connection between an emotional attachment and relationship to the guru as a necessary precondition and means for knowing, acting, and living in the world and, ultimately, for serving Bhagwan Swaminarayan eternally as a released *atma*.

In bodily postures, demeanor, and ritual performances, the BAPS guru exemplifies those devotional postures that satsangis would wish to acquire. Since the guru is oriented toward serving Bhagwan Swaminarayan in every waking moment, this is the ideal posture that satsangis wish to emulate while living in the world. And it is through the readily available technology for self-disciplining, seva, that satsangis can aim to craft a self that is like the guru, but, according to Swaminarayan upasana, never identical to guru or to God. Through seva, satsangis harness the postures of serving, of being expansive toward others, and of working toward a desired outcome tied to their own devotional aims (Brahmbhatt 2014; Kim 2013). There is an inherent sociality built into this devotional labor: the *sevak*, or one offering seva, is working within a community and toward the success of a BAPS project while hoping to shape the corporeal self into an ideal devotee. Those offering seva are thus primed to detect possibilities of their own transformations. When something unexpected and surprising does occur, it is the affective response that signals a need for self-examination. In these moments, where wonder and puzzlement and BAPS upasana converge, satsangis and anyone else present, have the option to consider the surprise as somehow connected to BAPS or to some other discursive assemblage. For those moments that transform into narratives of wonder connected to BAPS, these are recognized to be *prasangs*, or stories, that are made possible by guru and God. In this way, wonder events and the prasangs they catalyze contribute to the discursive ground on which an ethics of sociality emerges. Satsangi or not, for those who resolve the experience of wonder through BAPS discourses, there is an enhanced attunement of the self to others. To those who are devotees, a wonder event can become the basis for the making of an ideal devotee. This is the logic of serving the guru whereby supporting others can produce self-transformations that expand rather than shrink the arc of possibilities for one's own everyday living.

Narratives of Wonder

The research that prompted my exploration of wonder as generative of new relations of the self and therefore an ethics of sociality did not begin with this purpose. As part of a project to understand the devotional significance of the Swaminarayan Akshardham temple complexes, in January 2016, I travelled to Pindwara, an area in southwest Rajasthan known for its stone cutting factories and carving workshops.[7] There I visited sites where stone workers were working on BAPS temple projects. Between 2014 and 2020, in the month of January and during summers, I visited the Gandhinagar and New Delhi Akshardham complexes, speaking with BAPS senior administrators, volunteers, and visitors. I also visited the Robbinsville Akshardham campus in New Jersey for ritual events and inaugural openings of different phases of this mega temple complex. Robbinsville is the location of guru Pramukh Swami Maharaj's last visit to the United States in August 2014. During this time Pramukh Swami participated in the groundbreaking rituals at the specific areas where murtis of Bhagwan Swaminarayan and the BAPS guru lineage will be installed in the Akshardham *mahamandir*, the main edifice in this temple complex.

The narratives of wonder that appear in this chapter come from my fieldwork notes. These are specific incidents that I have found myself trying to understand, and each was narrated by interlocutors and shared with me in the course of talking about their relationship to the New Delhi Akshardham complex. These include narratives shared by a foreman at a stone-carving workshop in Pindwara; a volunteer at the New Delhi Akshardham who referred to herself as "Swaminarayan by marriage"; and a doctor who went to New Delhi Akshardham for family reasons and ended up becoming a volunteer and satsangi. While talking about a remembered moment, it is each narrator's recollection of a personal affective response and its aftermath that I have subsequently noted to be an experiencing of wonder.

Tulasi Srinivas (2018) in her call for an anthropology of wonder recognizes that delightful surprises in the context of ritual performances provide relief from the anxieties connected to uncontrollable societal changes. Srinivas focuses on two priests in a Bangalore neighborhood whose creative ritual interventions offer distraction from the encroachment of the unwanted. The priests' wonder moments are ones that they have consciously created and, while unfolding in the space of ritual, they allow for the suspension of time. Such wonder moments, Srinivas sees as the "point of the ritual" rather than, following Victor Turner, the moment that precedes the reincorporation of ritual participants back into the uncertainties of the everyday (5). Wonder, in this framing, is a deliberate temporal and ritual space that provides a short trip outside the ordinary for those who have participated in the ritual event. At the conclusion of the ritual, with the wondrous experience coming to an end, the assembled audience returns to the mundane, still buoyant from the suspension of time. Here, the affective dimension of wonder that has been provoked by creative priests allows for temple-goers to feel sensations that stand in contrast to their everyday lives. In the examples of wonder below, the narrators are not the audience of a consciously created moment of surprise that elicits joy. Rather, each of the three narrators recalls a memory where sensory responses and emotions emerge from a specific moment. The consolidation of affect within a specific event then contributes to a response on the part of the narrator that disrupts the usual. This something transformative is not ignored but becomes the basis for a new understanding of the self in relation to others. I am interested in these narrators' interpretations of their sensorially memorable incidents and their subsequent personal transformations. Furthermore, I explore what discourses, in particular, support the interpretations of "what happened."

Akshardham is arguably itself a creation intended to provoke wonder. BAPS's motivations are thus relevant to understanding the assemblage of discourses, meanings, and connections that inform individuals' wonder experiences (Kim 2016). From the stonecutter turned foreman whose labor contributed to the making of Delhi Akshardham to the volunteers who are working there, this temple complex invites interactions—between volunteers and visitors most obviously, but also with the site itself. The vastness of the complex as well as the stories of its creation are integral to the experiencing of this site, especially for satsangis. Hence Akshardham is variously implicated in their experiencing of this place, its creators, workers, and visitors. It is instances of sensorial surprise that my interlocutors chose to reflect on and that offer material to think through how and why an encounter with wonder can be connected to an ethics of sociality. These accounts did not include the usage of "wonder" in English, Hindi, or Gujarati. Rather, the dimension of wonder was evident from the mode of narration, from vocal tone and body language. Significantly, for each interlocutor, the remembered sensations of the wonder moment are translated into decisions and actions that affect the narrator and others whose lives are connected with the narrator. It is this side of the wonder equation that wants for further analysis: How does the somatically absorbed wonder become translated into new ways of relating to others? Do such moments exist if there is no commitment to the discursive ground on which they can become anchored? For the three narrators, the role of BAPS is connected to their wonder encounters and aftermath decision-making. Is it possible that, for some, BAPS provides a model for self-examination and living within society that transcends its highly specific ontological objectives? For all three interlocutors, it is an encounter with BAP's discourses on guru, seva, Akshardham, and other BAPS ideals that sets in motion a change in their orientation to their own selves, and, by extension, their relation to others.

THE PACKING-CRATE DOOR

In the summer of 2014, I visited several stone workshops, all sites where the cutting, carving, polishing, and packing of completed stone pieces for BAPS temples and the Robbinsville Akshardham were underway. Upwards of seven thousand men from the local area were working in the stone workshops at the time of my visit. I was accompanied by a research assistant and the owner of the largest stone production factory involved in producing carved stone for BAPS *shikharbaddha* temples (temples with spires) and Akshardham temple complexes. In each workshop, I saw local Rajasthani men working alone or in groups, creating with hand tools the individual marble, limestone, and sandstone carvings that would eventually come together, jigsaw like, to form the stone-carved temples that are distinctive to BAPS. Few of these men, according to the factory owner, come from the traditional stone-carving communities. Rather, they had been recruited from nearby villages and trained to become artisans. From the Swaminarayan perspective, given that Delhi Akshardham had required eleven thousand stone craftsmen, working every day of the week in shifts, for five years, the craftsmanship of stone carving is being revived in this region of southwestern Rajasthan; and the economic stability of families are improving as men are earning steady wages. Some of my interlocutors added that social and family problems associated with smoking and drinking, both proscribed in BAPS, have also decreased, as workers hear about "anti-addiction" messages while working for satsangi employers.

In the afternoon of one visit to an open-air carving workshop, I was invited to visit Dhanraj's home.[8] Holding the position of foreman, Dhanraj had risen from the rank of stone carver to foreman, managing hundreds of artisans. His leadership skills had been noted from his time working on the construction of Delhi Akshardham. When I arrived at Dhanraj's home, his children and wife, with her face covered, came out to greet us. The home was tall in height, made of concrete and bricks and outfitted with outdoor shelves built into concrete niches on either side of the front door. One set of shelves held shiny water pots, cooking vessels, and steel dishware. The foreman gestured to a *jhumpadi* (hut), a dilapidated low-height building with old curling roof tiles of mud and cow dung, just across from the *pakka* (solid-built) house. "This," he said, "is where we used to live, all of us. Our life has changed because of Akshardham, Pramukh Swami, and the work we have been given." The foreman asked me to look more closely at the wooden door to the jhumpadi. He and his children waited as I walked over to take a look. In a quiet voice, Dhanraj explained how this wood is very precious to him. "It comes from the packing crates that carried the carved stone from the workshop [in Rajasthan] to the place of Delhi Akshardham." Dhanraj narrated how he had seen the wood from the crates pile up; he wanted to have some part as a reminder of his role in building Akshardham. He decided to ask [a sadhu in charge] and he received permission to take a part of the packing crate wood. He described with a reserved but noticeable emotion that he was surprised at receiving the wood.

Though he has a solid new home, Dhanraj said, "I will not demolish the jhumpadi." This small hut is a material reminder of what he has achieved from his stone cutting employment, a skill that he did not previously have. The wooden door is more than a souvenir. For Dhanraj, it is a reminder of the genuineness of Pramukh Swami Maharaj's interest in the stone workers. This guru of BAPS, a leader of a large religious group, and the sadhus under the guru had recognized Dhanraj's skills, work ethic, and self-discipline.[9] Dhanraj further adds, "This is what Pramukh Swami has given to me and to my family." At this point, my research assistant asked if the foreman is Swaminarayan satsangi. "No," he said. "I am not, but I do not drink or smoke anymore. And, I have asked that anyone who comes to my home, the villagers, also observe this practice." And he reiterated his immense respect and love for Pramukh Swami, someone whose gestures and actions were truly generous and with no prejudice toward those with less. His wife, who had until then remained at a distance, came forward as her children and husband arranged themselves for a photograph before their former home, the one with part of a packing crate that is now a treasured door.

An Influencer's Gift

Since its opening in November 2005, the Delhi Akshardham temple complex has attracted attention. For some critics, it stands as a magnifier of middle-class aspirations, leisure pursuits, and upwardly mobile aesthetics (Brosius 2010; Srivastava 2009). These perspectives do not align with those of BAPS devotees, for most of whom the entire complex is an expression of their guru's devotion to his predecessor guru; Akshardham is also a materialization of satsangis' seva, or volunteered support that confirms their devotion to guru and to Bhagwan Swaminarayan. Within the Akshardham mahamandir, the murti of Bhagwan Swaminarayan is the central focus. For daily visitors and the tens of thousands who visit during holiday times, the smooth management of the complex, including security and crowd and traffic control, points to a highly efficient organization.

As for the hundreds of satsangis who are "doing seva" at Akshardham, their presence is visible owing to their uniforms and identification cards on a lanyard. What is less evident is that nearly all of Akshardham's staff are working without payment. They are at Akshardham to serve their guru and to cultivate their sentient selves into a BAPS ideal self, one that would gain admission to *dham*, the home of Akshar and where released eternal selves reside beyond the material and visible world.[10] The connection between the Akshardham mahamandir as the place of Bhagwan Swaminarayan on earth and the Akshardham beyond where Bhagwan can be eternally served is one that satsangis would recognize. Not surprisingly, the opportunity to offer seva in an Akshardham site is one that satsangis very much prize.

For the Swaminarayan tour guides who take around a prearranged group of guests, many shared with me their enjoyment of meeting people from around the world and having discussions about religion, Hinduism, and culture.[11] One guide, Rupa, originally from a neighboring state to Gujarat, was working as a full-time volunteer in the "Ladies PR," or public relations department. Rupa "became Swaminarayan by marriage," and with her husband, who is a Swaminarayan devotee, she and her family had, by January 2016, lived over nine years in the nearby housing provided for Delhi Akshardham volunteers. Rupa described her seva as "guiding and assisting VIP women guests during their visit of the Akshardham temple campus." She offered to share a prasang about Akshardham with me:

> One time, while I was taking people around, there was a lady, one with a big *chandalo* [forehead mark], messy green sari, and *rudraksha* beads who was nearby the group [I was leading]. . . . She was just following my group. At the end of my tour, she caught hold of me and I was afraid. The lady said that she wanted to have influence on me [*prabhāvita karne ke liye*]. She said that she tried to "apply" her power and that whenever she does this, a person becomes unconscious for 5–7 days. But today, she tried to influence me and she said that she could not do anything to me. "Though I am an expert, I could not do anything to you. I saw a kind of light around you; from the same image of the blessing [showing *mudra* or hand position] of Bhagwan Swaminarayan [in Akshardham]." The lady said, there is a "circle of protection around you." I told her, with my voice shaking, that in this place [Akshardham],

can you please take the decision not to abuse your powers. I told her that she could speak with my supervisor and she agreed and I brought her to him. My supervisor took her to lunch. My supervisor said to the *tantri* [practitioner of tantra] that "since you have the kind of power then you should use this power for something good." According to my supervisor, she said, "I have decided that I will not use this power for ill purposes."

Later . . . it dawned on me that if Pramukh Swami Maharaj [guru at the time] can protect me in such a way, then I would do the seva of Akshardham and he will look after me. Then, I had all the strength and power to do seva. And, I feel every minute that he is looking after me. And problems that I have in the house, with activities, I pray to him and I receive peace.

In January 2021, I asked one of my Akshardham research contacts to confirm some details of what Rupa had shared with me five years earlier.[12] Her narrative as well as that of her supervisor remained the same. Rupa did add, "[the experiences at Akshardham] have changed me. And, now I do my seva without thinking that this is not for someone of my community [in reference to her caste background]. I had some ego. I used to feel that in my community, other people do our seva."

There Is Such a Thing as a Free Lunch

Dr. Aggarwal impressed me when I met him on the Akshardham campus on Republic Day, 2016, and he lightheartedly shared that he had learned the Gujarati language in four days. I was curious how a non-Gujarati had come to be a dedicated physician volunteer in Akshardham. Dr. Aggarwal said that when he came to Akshardham in 2005 he was not a satsangi. He shared the following prasang: "I came voluntarily to visit Akshardham. My son got admission in [college], and for that we did some puja here in mandir in Akshardham. We did a big puja. Two hundred friends came and all had lunch here. And, I asked someone, where do we make the payment [for the lunch]? Where do I leave this 25,000 rupees payment? I was told, 'when you walk out, just make the payment in one box that is there.'" This response, one that rested on trust, shocked Dr. Aggarwal. As he recalled this incident, he shook his head and conveyed through his facial expression that the response did not make sense to him. "In this city, there is 2,000 rupees per plate for a marriage party in a hotel. Here [in Akshardham], there was no advance payment. And, it was even my suggestion to give 25,000 rupees! I felt that the trust they have put in me, it was just—[looking for a word] just super!" Dr. Aggarwal said he was asked, "You can do some seva here? So, I said, ok."

> The head doctor made so many accommodations for me . . . and let me tell you frankly, I found there was no need of me. There were already 50 doctors here! There was little work. So, he [guru] brought me here for my salvation only. Not for work. I feel that even now. I feel that I am here for myself. Every time, I come for enjoyment!
>
> I brought a friend here . . . a psychiatrist. "How is it that every day you come here," he asks. I asked him, "How does it happen that I get this high?" He said, "The vibrations are very strong, these stone have vibrations that are very strong. This, I have felt in two places, in Akshardham, visited by crores of people, and in Jama Masjid. The people who have offered prayers, these get stored in the stones. And, those who visit get the benefit of vibrations."

With an expression of incredulity, Dr. Aggarwal then acknowledged the satisfaction that he and eventually his whole family have experienced as they became more involved in BAPS and became dedicated satsangis. He pointed out that owing to his busy medical practice and volunteering in the Akshardham medical department, he became "a satsangi through *pravachans* [discourses] only." Thus, without the "benefit" of going to *sabha* or mandir gatherings, Dr. Aggarwal absorbed the teachings of BAPS. Through his "medical seva" at Akshardham, he notes that he has guided those who have visited him to have healthier habits such as not smoking. He attributes his patients' attitudinal changes and the "cold turkey" or "leaving off of tobacco" to Pramukh Swami Maharaj and Bhagwan Swaminarayan's presence in Akshardham. How else to explain that someone with addiction could just quit after one conversation! Dr. Aggarwal enthusiastically observes that from being in Akshardham and serving others, he is serving himself. "When your profession and your hobby become one . . ." as he smiles broadly and radiates a noticeable contentment.

Wonder as a Fieldsite for Knowledge Production

Where is wonder in these three narratives? Each narration conveys an affective description of surprise, of an experiencing that leaves an imprint: each narrator comes to a realization of abilities and being able to guide others; of acquiring tolerance toward others; of living with the desire to help oneself and others. These moments, arising from a particular time and context, have made an impression on each narrator, but they have also directed each to consider the subjectivity of others in the course of their everyday life. The moment when Dhanraj, the stone factory foreman is granted permission to have a portion of a wooden crate is a small one. Yet, this surprise connects Dhanraj to moral systems, relationships, and discourses that are significant. He has adopted habits and bodily discipline as well as ideas about what behaviors he no longer wishes to permit in his family home; he is recognized and respected by BAPS; he and his family are able to achieve a higher degree of economic stability. Beginning with a wonder incident, Dhanraj's affective responses motivate him to act in certain ways. These actions can be tied to an ethics of sociality, an orientation to others that is also present in the narratives of Rupa and Dr. Aggarwal.

The wonder moment for Dhanraj is amplified by his respect for Pramukh Swami Maharaj, the guru who spearheaded the Delhi Akshardham project, and to whom Dhanraj attributes his family's improved circumstances. "This is what Pramukh Swami has given to me and to my family," Dhanraj shares, as we stand in the space between his old home and his new one. There is a connection that we can draw between his employment in a BAPS project and his subsequent decisions that fit into a larger assemblage of BAPS discourses on moral teachings. I would argue that Dhanraj's expanded options, including the construction of a larger and solid home and the attainment of a supervisory position over stone artisans, is facilitated by his interaction with BAPS sadhus and others who have treated him with compassion and respect. The Swaminarayan discourse on shaping the corporeal self into the ontological form that would support release from samsara may not be Dhanraj's personal objective. Nevertheless, Dhanraj's adopted personal habits suggest that he has been influenced by BAPS's attitudes about how to live and behave toward self, family, and others. Perhaps more notably, while Dhanraj has not become a devotee, BAPS offers him an ethical framework that influences his relationships with others. BAPS morality is situated with an ethics that rests on doing for others in order to attain one's own desired objectives. While this ethical stance supports a devotional goal, in practice, satsangis' whose behaviors are deemed merit-worthy are those who set aside their desires in order to help others. This ethics of sociality, albeit undergirded by BAPS bhakti, is the one that Dhanraj has absorbed. The packing crate door to Dhanraj's jhumpadi is a material reminder of the relationships that have mattered and the relationships that, looking ahead, expand his ability to help fellow stone workers and in turn support his capacity to reach his own and his family's goals.

For Rupa, Delhi Akshardham volunteer, it is an encounter with someone of whom she did not particularly approve that results in her self-examination of her fears, areas of intolerance, and skepticism of seva. When Rupa learned from the lady in the "messy green sari," that she is protected by Bhagwan Swaminarayan, this wonder moment contributes to Rupa's personal transformation. She does not disguise her surprise that, despite some ambivalence to doing seva in Akshardham, it was the encounter with the "tantri" that dislodged her feeling that "this [doing seva] is not for someone of my community." Rupa's self-discovery that seva takes precedence over caste tradition emerged only after she met the tantric practitioner. A more long-term consequence of her wonder moment is Rupa's self-acknowledged ability to better manage domestic and other situations that arouse frustration or anxiety. As she tells me, by praying to Pramukh Swami Maharaj, she is able to feel "peace," or a quality of calm. As a satsangi, Rupa's prasang highlights the role of the living guru and his centrality to her understanding of who should serve whom. Rupa's decisions and actions following her wonder moment are thus connected and informed by Swaminarayan teachings. Perhaps too, the woman in the green sari experienced some kind of wonder when her self-described "power" had been defeated. Could this "tantri," as Rupa called her, reconsider her ability to render someone unconscious? For Rupa, who did not ignore the tantric practitioner, the encounter initiates a greater clarity about helping others through seva and that doing so facilitates the shaping of one's own self into a desired ideal.

In his telling of how he became involved with BAPS and eventually became a satsangi, Dr. Aggarwal began with a moment that caught his attention: the trust that BAPS monks and sevaks accorded him despite not knowing him. His response to the casual request that he drop off monies for a catered lunch into a donation box was astonishment. Then when he agreed to return to Akshardham for volunteer medical work, he discovered how being in the temple complex had an enormously positive effect on him. Dr. Aggarwal marvels that he has received much more than he has actually given in his seva. He wonders if the request for him to volunteer was really a means for him to experience self-transformation. As a new BAPS devotee, Dr. Aggarwal has shared his enthusiasm for BAPS with family, friends, and patients. From his initial surprise at how BAPS treated him with trust, Dr. Aggarwal has become an effective exemplar of self-transformation. His admission of being in a constant state of "high" owing to his contentment from being in BAPS has had a beneficial impact on others, a number of whom, as he shared, are "leaving off" their "addictions" upon hearing his own story about becoming a devotee. Dr. Aggarwal's interest in BAPS began before he was aware of its devotional teachings and moral moorings. Without this knowledge, he nevertheless was motivated toward an ethics of sociality, of being among and within the BAPS community of volunteers at Akshardham while providing medical service for visitors. From affect to motivated action, the tracing of Dr. Aggarwal's remembered wonder moment points to the productive connections between a feeling sensation and what Bennett describes as an "energetic" ethics, or an ethics that recognizes the capacity of affect to stir up a strong bodily response (2001, 131–58). Dr. Aggarwal's infectious enthusiasm for BAPS bhakti is generative. He welcomes colleagues and friends and the anthropologist for conversation. He has inspired patients and his family to become satsangis. His is an "energetic ethics" grounded in a sociality and including both pragmatic and guru-inspired sources.

The wonder moments in the lives of Dhanraj, Rupa, and Dr. Aggarwal were unanticipated and not intentionally created by anyone. For each, it is their individual affective reactions that prompt a connecting of something wondrous to something else. From a satsangi perspective, these moments of wonder are not necessarily random, for such occasions prompt, as with Dr. Aggarwal, a more sustained engagement with Swaminarayan bhakti. Dhanraj's, Rupa's, and Dr. Aggarwal's responses can all be illuminated by connecting them to the relevant BAPS discourses on guru, seva, and Swaminarayan moral teachings, including those on compassion for all and service toward others. We can map the connections between BAPS bhakti as the source of moral discourses and strategies for living; and, as well, BAPS bhakti is the basis for accepting the living guru as a model for living in the world. Bennett writes, "Moral codes . . . remain inert without a disposition hospitable to their injunctions, the perceptual refinement necessary to apply them to particular cases, and the affective energy needed to perform them (2001, 131). BAPS offers, for the three narrators in this chapter, the various means by which an affective energy is rallied, interpreted, and then activated. BAPS bhakti and its assemblage of discourses, including those on seva and guru, provide the basis for action as well as the interpretive means to understand incidents, whether wondrous or less so.[13]

For those who have encountered BAPS through personal experiences of wonder and awe, there is a sense that, thereafter, nothing can be the same from this moment of encounter onward. The really realness of these wonder experiences therefore offers sufficient motivation for living in a particular way. In their effective orienting of each narrator to a sociality that radiates outward from the self, these experiences suggest that wonder can be a basis for an ethics of sociality, of living among and with others in order to sustain a desired way of being. What makes the stories of Dhanraj, Rupa, and Dr. Aggarwal so compelling, I feel, is their very material anchoring to a spatial and temporal context alongside a singularity specific to each individual's affective response. In these moments of something deeply felt, these individuals experienced what Bennett describes as "the overall effect of enchantment"—"a mood of fullness, plenitude or liveliness, a sense of having had one's nerves or circulation or concentration power tuned up or recharged" (2001, 5). From these episodes, one becomes energized—literally, as Bennet writes, with an "energetic ethics," that informs subsequent actions and decision-making. In effect, the affective experience of wonder is attached to a scaffolding that supports and guides "how to act" (131–58).[14] This is the ethical framework for a sociality where the agentive self who is located in relation to others acquires the knowledge or insight to steer, and in what direction, and with whom, an affirming way of life. Being "enchanted," to use Bennett's term for the state of wonder, establishes a basis for reckoning what comes afterward: the before is acknowledged, but it is what happens after the enchantment that now demands attention. In the cognitive toggle between pre– and post–wonder experience, the experience of subjection to wonder puts into relief an attitudinal shift, or an aesthetic reset, that emerges post-wonder and becomes the engine for action. Such a shift, clearly, does not have to result in becoming Swaminarayan. This is one option, and a powerfully compelling one for some. Regardless, the productivity of being enchanted is aligned with the agentive self's capacity to decide how to respond and what to do next. If there were no sensorially significant moment to savor, for both interlocutor and ethnographer, the ethnographic record would then resolve this as a case of negative knowledge production or just a case of "nothing happened."

Experiences of wonder may, irrespective of one's relationship to Hindu devotional discourses or another knowledge system, contribute to a mode of knowing that is affirming.[15] And, though some might suggest that such an affirmative trajectory ignores the entangling of material realities and loci of power, the experiences of Dhanraj, Rupa, and Dr. Aggarwal demonstrate how the affirming, when connected to an ethical framework, provides an energizing basis by which to navigate the daily or unexpected. If an experience of wonder can be translated into an ethics of sociality, this rehabilitates not just the significance of the affective in knowledge production: it widens the space to consider how and when the affective can be steered into productive actions that are more inclusive and generous. Such a use of affectively driven ethics does not foreclose an ethics that dwells on darker motivations or more exclusionary aesthetic choices.

The BAPS Swaminarayan Sanstha, while focused on the dissemination of its particular devotional teachings and ontological ideals, has succeeded in offering contexts, spaces, and opportunities where wonder can emerge. In BAPS, wondrous moments can happen to each individual who encounters the guru, Akshardham temple complexes, smaller scale temples, or attends public celebrations and festivals. For some critics, BAPS activities appear to be geared toward grabbing the attention of middle-class Gujaratis who are in search of a satisfying religion to ease their anxieties. When I mentioned this, one student said, with exasperation:

> Our only purpose is to work constructively in society, to live a better life, to use our energy in constructive, creative directions. . . . I am so happy, so happy but I also want to serve others so that they can lead a better life. It is one thing to write books, another thing to come up with concrete solutions to inspire people to lead a better life. You can bloody write hundreds of books, but how do you inspire people to live? (conversation in Ahmedabad, Gujarat, July 22, 2014)

Many of my BAPS interlocutors have asked with incredulity, why, if their guru is known to have a profound impact on people—such as promoting the renunciation of drugs and alcohol, celebrating vegetarianism, fostering positive changes in temperament, life goals, and the ability to manage fears and disappointments—"Why would this knowledge *not* be shared?"

The Ethics of Sociality by Way of an Anthropology of Wonder

Wondrous experiences leave an imprint that calls for interpretive strategies or ways to make sense of the affective happening and its aftermath. This is so for both the one who has been enchanted and the ethnographer. Since the somatic response rests in an agentive self who is not separable from an assemblage of discourses, it is these discourses that offer ways to position and analyze wonder encounters. This approach, while a necessary one, may not, however, sufficiently address the sensorial and subjective dimensions of a wonder encounter that, while fleeting, has left distinct and memorable sensations. It is the power in these post-wonder recollections to influence an orientation to living that calls for more analysis. In this understanding of self, the self both has agency and is positioned within structures and discourses of power. This self has the capacity to interpret wonder events but is nevertheless not outside of ideological and institutional structures. Thus, there is a theoretical conundrum: connecting a subjective experience and its interpretation to its discursive foundations potentially diminishes the experiencing of wonder from the self. There is no practical method to capture in totality the assemblage of discourses that intersect with a wonder experience; and there is no analytical gain in responding to these instances as separable from the assemblage of networks and relations connected to the self. Is there a path, less hermeneutical and more grounded in ethnography that focuses on a fragment of a fragment, namely, one affective dimension of a remarkable moment, and traces this fragmented but sensorially real moment to subsequent and specific actions? This is the project of this chapter, to focus, albeit briefly, on the affective dimension of a wonder encounter and to see what ethnographic and analytical insights emerge for both agentive subjects and ethnographers.

My interest is in understanding specific instances of how exposure to BAPS Swaminarayan discourses can offer the means to reify an affective experience into a playbook for living with equanimity and care for others. For Bennett, wonder as a response to enchantment can produce a "temporary suspension of chronological time and bodily movement" where the one who is enchanted can be "transfixed" in a particular moment (2001, 5). There is something joy-inducing in a moment that has striking purchase on the corporeal, assuming that such an occasion is not a violent or unwanted one. A consequence of having been sensorially affected by an unexpected and surprising event can, and did for my interlocutors, engender a revision of a subject's orientation to living. It is this repositioning in relation to others that I am calling an ethics of sociality: this is an ethical stance of recognizing oneself in relation to others and of consciously aiming to live with equanimity among others. The rules and codes of behavior, or the dimension of morality, for how to live are not necessarily universal. For the Swaminarayan community, there are clear moral dispositions, supported by BAPS devotional ideals and ontological categories. The puzzle is the case where, whether or not one is a BAPS devotee, an enchanting experience emerging from within the space of BAPS supports an ethical orientation toward others irrespective of a subject's adherence to certain moral codes. Is it possible that a memorable affective moment associated with a Hindu devotional community can become the basis for an openness to consider new relations and engagement with others, whoever they may be?

The anthropology of wonder, as outlined by Srinivas, is a practical methodology and accessible framework for approaching precarious lives through ritual practices. Srinivas's ethnography *The Cow in the Elevator* (2018) offers data abounding to confirm that moments of "fracture" that startle, amaze, and twinkle can support ritual practitioners in sustaining ways. This connection between ritual, moment of rupture, and the embodied sensation of wonder is surely transportable to other spaces and geographies. This is a portable paradigm, inviting anthropologists and others to look more closely at the connections between wonder and ritual. Outside the domain of ritual practice, if we pay attention to the generative domain of wonder, we can surely discover it in our fieldsites, in the visual, the sensory, and the aesthetics of contemporary life in India and elsewhere. We can aim to better appreciate how the wondrous catalyst can emerge from anywhere and has relational repercussions for the self that go beyond the self. The very affirming capacities of experiencing wonder can be, as evidenced by the choices made by Dhanraj, Rupa, and Dr. Aggarwal, the basis for actions that affect oneself in relation to others. Wonder prompts a bodily reaction. What happens next is ontologically and discursively informed but not reducible to either ontology or the material, or Hindu discourses: what happens next is the transformation of an affective experience, via multiple discursive networks, into a way of living with others.

In BAPS, the knowing of oneself in relation to others is possible when the affective and the domain of knowledge production are not upheld as hierarchically separate. To choose to serve the guru is to choose a subjugation of the self that is not self-denial or self-erasure but a recognition that the present self can be reshaped according to existing ontological categories. Through seva, devotional practices, and the desire to please the guru, satsangis seek to strip away the elements of the corporeal self that stand in the way of the goal, moksha. This ontological goal, while coming at the end of biological life, is nevertheless one toward which the self can proceed with enjoyment rather than fear. The process of living can thus be conceptualized and experienced as opportunities to experience moments of wonder. The connection between experiencing wonder and moving toward an ethics of sociality is, for the satsangi, an organic one where the guru provides the quintessential model for how to act. Seva as an offering to the guru connects the actions of volunteered labor to an expectation that the self is reshaped from its existing contours into another kind of desired eternal self, the atma. The paradox here is that, in order to acquire the knowledge of the self as atma, there is the hard work of living among and within a community of others.

As Srinivas and her ethnographic material make vividly clear, in the context of anthropology in South Asia, wonder moments beckon both interlocutor and ethnographer to make sense of the unexpected. For the ethnographer, wonder moments allow for an overdrive thick description for how else to capture, in words, the somatic experience of others. Reducing this experience to the ontological will reveal the limits of this approach. And focusing on the material conditions of the experience is no less adequate. The anthropology of wonder can be critiqued for placing emphasis on the affirmative; yet this is also an anthropological strategy that rests firmly in the ethnographic. To appreciate the aftermath of wonder is to focus on the ethnography and to discern what has been activated, enabled, and how. As one satsangi shared, "BAPS just doesn't teach you how to be an ideal human being—it teaches how to maintain ideal relationships . . . in society" (conversation in Shahibaug Swaminarayan Mandir, Ahmedabad, Gujarat, January 18, 2016.). This succinct assessment sums the potential of Swaminarayan religious subjectivity to navigate a distinct tension: the self who is engaged in certain technologies of self-cultivation is nevertheless reliant on a community of others who are pursing the same as well as those who are not. Wonder moments can break this tension and allow others to enter into the suspension of the usual, the unanticipated. In its disruptiveness, wonder opens up an arena for considering options for the self that exist in relation to others. The contingency of religious subjectivity is thus acknowledged but, as well, the range of possibilities for interpretation invite more ethnography. Wonder, in an energetic and welcome twist, is good for the sociality of anthropology.

Notes

The research for this chapter was partially funded by an Adelphi University Faculty Development Grant (2016–17). An earlier version of this material was presented at the 2017 Association for Asian Studies Annual Conference, Toronto, Canada. My thanks to the audience for its questions and to John Cort and Brian Hatcher for their comments. In BAPS, I owe special thanks to Sadhu Ishwarcharandas, who facilitated my trip to Pindwada, Rajasthan. I also thank my research assistants and the indefatigable trio of Dr. Janak Dave, Dr. Neeta Shah, and Ms. Meena Bhavsar. I thank too the numerous devotees who contributed in so many ways to support my fieldwork. All interpretations remain my own.

1. This *prasang*, or story, was shared on January 22, 2016, at the Swaminarayan Mandir, Ahmedabad, Gujarat. Pramukh Swami Maharaj, was guru of BAPS from 1971 to 2016.

2. See Mattingly (2014) on the analytical device and metaphor of the "moral laboratory" wherein interlocutors experience something that provokes a reexamination of how to navigate one's way in difficult situations. Mattingly directs her focus to a "first person virtue ethics" that she connects to "the revival of Aristotle in Anglo-American moral philosophy" (37). Though beyond the discussion in this article, it would be tremendously productive to compare the analytical purchase of focusing on wonder and its discursive after effects with Mattingly's emphasis on the interpretation of enunciated narratives (a neo-Aristotelian virtue ethics) as the ground from which the self interprets, decides, and ultimately finds a way to live in the world.

3. BAPS shares historical connections to the early nineteenth-century movement founded by Sahajanand Swami (1781–1830). The antecedent Swaminarayan community has a religious hierarchy that does not involve a guru or guru lineage. This is one significant difference between the original and BAPS Swaminarayan movement. See Williams (2001) for background on the older Swaminarayan community. This chapter focuses on BAPS, and my usage of

"Swaminarayan" herein pertains only to the BAPS community. BAPS, BAPS Swaminarayan, and Swaminarayan are used interchangeably.

4. The BAPS (n.d.) website lists "more than 800 mandirs and 3,300 centers."

5. Non-English terms are italicized on first use. Proper nouns and guru remain unitalicized.

6. See Sadhu Paramtattvadas *Introduction to Swaminarayan Theology* (2017) for an accessible text on the metaphysical entities in Swaminarayan bhakti and their ontological significances.

7. Since 2005, BAPS has opened large temple complexes known as "Akshardham." The two completed Akshardham complexes are in Gandhinagar, Gujarat, and Noida, New Delhi, and are major destinations for tourism. The Akshardham complexes in India will be joined by one that is under construction in Robbinsville, New Jersey.

8. The names and identifying factors have been changed or omitted for all informants with the exception of the BAPS guru (Pramukh Swami Maharaj, 1921–2016), sadhus, and lay officials.

9. Pramukh Swami hosted a celebration of thanks to recognize the thousands of stone workers who constructed Delhi Akshardham.

10. Entry to the Gandhinagar and New Delhi Akshardham temple complexes in India is free, as is admission to the central "Akshardham" temple and monument. The exhibitions, movie theater (New Delhi Akshardham only), and evening "water show" require purchased tickets.

11. The New Delhi Akshardham has numerous buildings, including exhibition halls (with one featuring a boat ride that travels through a BAPS interpretation of Indian history), large-format movie theater, bookstore, and extensive covered-walkways. Visitors can eat at a popular vegetarian canteen and spend an evening at the outdoor water show, a multimedia program including laser lights, water, and sound. The Gandhinagar and Delhi Akshardham complexes also have a research center with facilities to support scholars.

12. This conversation was facilitated by Dr. Janak Dave from AARSH, the research center at Delhi Akshardham (January 7, 2021). Dr. Dave confirmed that the PR Supervisor "had taken the lady [in the green sari]" to the Akshardham bookstore after lunch and gifted her with books on Bhagwan Swaminarayan.

13. See Bhatt (2019) for ethnographic examples of BAPS satsangis trying to understand the unwanted and less than ideal events that have impinged on their lives.

14. Enchantment for Bennet is an affective state that can produce an ethical framing of how to live. Saraka (2003) positively summarizes this rehabilitative stance but critiques Bennett's affirmative orientation as one that, in pursuit of the enchanted moment, overlooks the material and sobering realities connected to the enchanted event.

15. By affirming, this is not intended to suggest that affective experiences engender only a positive outcome. There are darker outcomes though these are not the focus of this chapter; neither is it the choice of Bennett to dwell on the negative trajectories of an affectively driven ethics. See Saraka (2003) for a critique of this absence.

Works Cited

Bennett, Jane. 2001. *The Enchantment of Modern Life: Attachments, Crossings, and Ethics*. Princeton, NJ: Princeton University Press.

Bhatt, Kalpesh. 2019. "Dynamics of Hope: Secular and Religious Apprehensions in the Swaminarayan Hindu Tradition." *Ethnos* 86 (3): 426–43.

Bochasanwasi Shri Akshar Purushottam Swaminarayan Sanstha. n.d. "Global Network of BAPS." http://www.swaminarayan.org/globalnetwork/index.htm.

Brahmbhatt, Arun. 2014. "BAPS Swaminarayan Community: Hinduism." In *Global Religious Movements across Borders: Sacred Service*, edited by Stephen M. Cherry and Helen R. Ebaugh, 99–122. Farnham, UK: Ashgate.

Brosius, Christiane. 2010. *India's Middle Class: New Forms of Leisure, Consumption and Prosperity*. New Delhi: Routledge.

Candea, Matei. 2013. "The Fieldsite as Device." *Journal of Cultural Economy* 6 (3): 241–58.

Kim, Hanna H. 2012. "The BAPS Swaminarayan Temple Organisation and Its Publics." In *Public Hinduisms*, edited by John Zavos, Pralay Kanungo, Deepa S. Reddy, Maya Warrier, and Raymond Brady Williams, 417–39. New Delhi: Sage.

———. 2013. "Swāminārāyaṇa Bhakti Yoga and the Akṣarabrahman Guru." In *Gurus of Modern Yoga*, edited by Ellen Goldberg and Mark Singleton, 237–60. New York: Oxford University Press.

———. 2016. "Thinking Through Akshardham and the Making of the Swaminarayan Self." In *Swaminarayan Hinduism: Tradition, Adaptation, Identity*, edited by Raymond B. Williams and Yogi Trivedi, 383–401. New Delhi: Oxford University Press.

———. 2021. "Remembrances of Gurus Past: Reading the *Smṛti Sthāna* in the Sarangpur BAPS Swaminarayan Temple Complex." *Journal of Hindu Studies* 14 (1): 1–27.

Mattingly, Cheryl. 2014. *Moral Laboratories: Family Peril and the Struggle for a Good Life*. Oakland: University of California Press.

Paramtattvadas, Swami. 2017. *An Introduction to Swaminarayan Hindu Theology*. Cambridge: Cambridge University Press.

Saraka, Sean. 2003. Review of *The Enchantment of Modern Life: Attachments, Crossings, and Ethics*, by Jane Bennett. *Culture Machine*. https://culturemachine.net/reviews/bennett-the-enchantment-of-modern-life-saraka/.

Srinivas, Tulasi. 2018. *The Cow in the Elevator: An Anthropology of Wonder*. Durham, NC: Duke University Press.

Srivastava, Sanjay. 2009. "Urban Spaces, Disney-Divinity and Moral Middle Classes in Delhi." *Economic and Political Weekly* 44 (26–27): 338–45.

Williams, Raymond Brady. 2001. *Swaminarayan Hinduism: An Introduction*. Cambridge: Cambridge University Press.

Chapter 11

"Guruji Rocked . . . Duniya Shocked"
Wondertraps and the Camerawork Guruship of
Dera Sacha Sauda Guru
Dr. Saint Gurmeet Ram Rahim Singh Ji Insan

JACOB COPEMAN AND KOONAL DUGGAL

On January 25, 2017, at the headquarters of the Dera Sacha Sauda (DSS) devotional order in Sirsa, Haryana, the order's present guru, Dr. Saint Gurmeet Ram Rahim Singh Ji Insan, made his grand entry on an army tank before an audience of tens of thousands of devotees (see fig. 11.1).[1] As the guru progressed forward toward his fan-devotees, "wonder prompts" were delivered via loudspeaker: "Rockstar!" "You can shout! You can enjoy!" "Amazing! Amazing!" User comments beneath the YouTube video of the event repeat terms such as "fantastic," "fabulous," "incredible," "awesome," "powerful," and "superb entry." Other comments include: "Wow that's a full-scale model of tank"; "Grand people Grand works Grand entries"; and "woooow wonderful papa Jaan"; accompanied by a host of emojis—a showering of kisses and love hearts—expressing the perfection of the spectacle.[2]

The tank was a one-off, but his grand entry was not: the serial novelty of the guru's entrances ensured that novelty itself had become the norm. YouTube videos disclose that DSS *satsangs* (devotional gatherings) had become no ordinary *satsangs*. The guru variously entered on modified bikes, cars, and tractors (the latter a nod to his "rural chic"—he hails from a family of Jat landowner-cultivators and possessed, at least initially, a predominantly rural follower base, with the DSS owning vast swathes of agricultural land around Sirsa, apparently barren until his divine intervention); on some occasions mechanical cranes were employed to create the impression of him descending from the sky or heaven; on others he would be made mechanically to elevate into the devotional arena from underground. If such techniques for the production of awe and surprise in the grand entrance of the guru had been integrated from Bollywood films and live rock and pop concerts, these were roles that he had also already begun to perform. Indeed, given that the DSS was already what we call a "devotion of attractions," it wasn't a complete surprise—indeed it seemed fitting—when rumors of the first instalment of his feature film franchise in which the guru would play himself surfaced in 2015.[3] Clearly, deployment of modern technological effects and other creative strategies such as his grand entries have played a key role in the production and expansion of his roles and reach.

Figure 11.1. Guru enters on army tank. *Source*: Screenshot from the video titled "Gurmeet Ram Rahim Singh's GRAND Entry on Tank at Hind Ka Napak Ko Jawab Trailer Launch," on YouTube channel of Bollywood Hungama (https://www.youtube.com/watch?v=MkJDnrTpuF0&t=178s).

In particular, his entries in modified vehicles became a kind of trademark, setting him apart from other gurus. Consider the case of Jaggi Vasudev, popularly known as Sadhguru, whose adventurous, "sporty" persona—in particular his fondness for motorbikes—is another such trademark. One video of him riding a motorbike with another popular guru (Hindutva yogi Baba Ramdev) sitting behind him—captioned "Biker Dudes"—became wildly popular in the public domain. We see increasing use of terms belonging to modern urban lingo—rockstar, bling, dude, and so on—that define these diverse gurus in ways that emphasize their "being at home" in India's post-liberalization era and that seek to attract millennials. The DSS guru, however, is far more cringe-inducing to elite Indian sensibilities than the other two gurus just mentioned: we have mentioned his association with the rural; he is also a guru mired in scandals, including accusations that he had four hundred male devotees castrated. After his imprisonment for rape in 2017, elite disapproval of the DSS as vulgar medieval residue and obstacle to development was ubiquitous—often expressed in a trope of "more in sadness than in anger": "this is why education is more important in our country"; "Such people have no place in developing India"; "India cannot develop till the time these babas have unnecessary control or influence on Hindus and politics of the nation"; "Is this 21st century India??"; "Damn it what will be the future of India." Or, as a comment posted on the Reddit r/India forum succinctly put it in reference to devotee-police clashes following the guru's conviction: "Feels like old r/india."[4] All the same, like Ramdev and Sadhguru the DSS guru is supremely at ease before the camera; his guruship, as we shall see, is a *camerawork guruship*.[5] When asked in an interview about his rockstar persona and penchant for wearing fashionable blingy attires, the DSS guru explained that it formed part of an attempt to make his teachings and welfare measures attractive to young people who, drawn to the DSS, will refrain from taking drugs.[6] If this suggests that the guru's adventurous masculine acts were necessary to keep the devotional economy in circulation, it is also (appropriately enough) a classic Bollywood trope, with otherwise suspect acts of self-indulgence and ostentation coming to be sanctioned and recognized as virtuous in the narrative if they can be "demonstrated to be socially useful and out-reaching rather than inward-turning" (Vanita 2002, 155).

Our argument in this chapter is that the DSS guru achieves wonder effects in three principal overlapping ways. These are through the projection of himself as (1) an inclusive, expandable unity; (2) temporarily inhabiting (dashing in and out of) different forms and identities; and (3) the embodied mixing together or unity of opposites (here we can speak of the "schismatic guru"). We shall draw on and extend the work of Nigel Thrift (2008, 2012) on tactical manipulations and the exploitation of potential, Alberto Corsín Jiménez (2013, 2018) on aggrandizement and traps, the philosophical elucidation of wonder provided by Mary-Jane Rubenstein (2008), and our own previous and ongoing work on the different *methodologies of presence* employed by gurus.[7]

It is because we are in agreement with Mary-Jane Rubenstein's differentiation of wonder that we use the term "effects of wonder" advisedly. Rubenstein (2008, 21) distinguishes between two kinds of wonder: one mode of wonder "gives birth," produces "aporetic vertigo" (25), and is marked by radical incompleteness (26). Such wonder comprises an "open sea of endless questioning, strangeness, and impossibility" (21). The other mode of wonder contains no such "wondrous openness" (25). Instead, it is a wonder that "relentlessly seek[s] out new marvels to calculate, comprehend, or possess" (25)—it is appropriative and produces assent through stupefaction. It is not that calculation or rigorous argument is inimical to the first mode of wonder, but rather that "there is an irreducible difference between a rigorous, investigative thinking that sustains wonder's strangeness and a rigorous, investigative thinking that endeavors to assimilate that strangeness" (25–26). Indeed, let us now follow Rubenstein in clarifying what already may be evident; namely, that the second mode of wonder is not wonder at all but precisely a retreat from it (21). Proceeding from this, we argue that the DSS guru has successfully generated a series of effects of wonder that bear affinity with the second mode of wonder described here—the wonder that is not wonder, or that is "anti-wonder." There is no aporetic vertigo in the cases we consider in this chapter—everything is reduced to one person. It is a wonder of the "excessive subject" (Thrift 2012)—one that is totalizing, seeking continual expansion and possession. It "keeps [one] chained in stupefied assent to [that which is] 'self-evident'" (Rubenstein 2008, 21). It displays not the "frightening indeterminacy" (24) of the first mode but only effects of wonder that "uncontain" the guru's personality the better to "contain" the other; that expand it the better to enfold (possess, appropriate) all subject positions and attention.

Such a language of enfolding and possession suggests our next analytical move, which is to suggest that wonder is staged as a trap: the

DSS generates wondertraps. We do not seek to portray devotees as pitiable, hapless, and hoodwinked. Much has been offered back to them by the guru and the DSS even as they have been trapped by wonder: most prosaically, there are the free health and social services made available to them by the DSS. More profoundly, there is a sense of participating in the personality of the guru, which takes on the form of a kind of community. The DSS guru mobilizes his devotees to conduct social welfare schemes on a massive, world record breaking scale.[8] Devotees, in forming part of the guru's enlarged sense of personality, have been able to assume the role of givers in meaningful ways—embodied in the guru's extended personhood, they give outwards to society in the same movement in which they give to the guru,[9] allowing his name to travel and kingly charisma based on excessive giving to grow. In one way, the guru's gift to his economically disadvantaged devotees is to enable them to become givers, too. Here we can consider the etymology of *bhakti*, "bhaj": "to participate." Devotees experience a sense of participation, too, in the guru's high-profile media adventures (a million devotee-extras are reported to have appeared in the guru's first feature film) and role uptake. This is to say that the guru's effects of wonder and explosion of subject positions have required devotee buy-in (Thrift 2012)—a degree of mutuality inheres in the entrapment (Corsín Jiménez and Nahum-Claudel 2019, 2; Lucia 2018, 980).

But they are traps nonetheless. The reason for escalating the quantity and diversifying the nature of devotional attractions is to produce a heightened "devotional grip." Effects of wonder, or wondertraps, require devotional labor that in turn can be put to work to produce more wondertraps, and so on. Devotees become complicit in the predation of more devotees. Consider the modal reciprocity of entrapment and wonder. Corsín Jiménez (2018, 75) writes that "traps capture, caution and captivate; they provoke wonder, suspension and elicitation." Traps provoke wonder. From the other side, Tulasi Srinivas (2018, 113) writes of how the technicolor "wonders" of Bangalore's early twenty-first-century temples "fascinated, compelled [and] entrapped" spectators. Wonder provokes entrapment. We conceptualize, then, a predatory wonder, or wonder as predation—but in a manner that leaves room for mutuality and love; or put differently, devotional buy-in. We paraphrase Gebauer and Wulf (1996, 213) on seduction: seduction depends on lending form; the guru-seducer's weapon, here, is an image. As soon as the object of seduction—the devotee—becomes fascinated by this image, she falls under the power of the seducer. But only because the object of seduction herself desires does she let herself be seduced.

Exaggeration Procedures

Like other devotional movements with their origins in the north Indian *sant* heritage—"the creed of the saints, a tradition associated with such figures as Kabir and Nanak" (Babb 1986, 17)—the DSS, founded in 1948, is an avowedly social reformist spiritual organization that aims, according to its official website, to "save people from the complex ties, malpractices and superficial rituals that had been afflicting religion."[10] Its teachings do not markedly differ from other devotional orders that have their origin in the north Indian *sant* heritage. Common to most of these orders is *guru-bhakti*—devotion to a living spiritual master, devotee constituencies made up of both Hindus and Sikhs, an emphasis on the recitation of sacred words, a conception of transcendence as being open to all in this birth regardless of caste or gender, a social reformist agenda, and a set of teachings genealogically derived from a family of nonsectarian *sants*, or saints, which began to emerge in the medieval period. Distinctions between Hindus and non-Hindus and indeed distinctions of caste and other internal differentiations of "community" tend to be downplayed in favor of shared devotional attachment to a spiritual master. DSS teachings emphasize the importance of reciting sacred words (*ram nam*) for the achievement of transcendence, abstaining from alcohol and meat, faithfulness in marriage, and refraining from lying or making religious offerings of money. In tension with the high-profile adventures of the present guru, official DSS teachings propound a strong anti-"show-off" message: "Dera Sacha Sauda does not believe in any kind of false practices, false pretensions, misguidance or any kind of show off which has nothing to do with spiritualism and those ritual practices which take you away from your real goal."[11] The paradox here is not insignificant. We will suggest that such mixing of opposites—aversion to spectacle while conspicuously engaging in it—can be key to the generation of wonder effects.

In our discussions with devotees in Sirsa, they repeatedly drew attention to the absence in the DSS of distracting "rituals" (*rasmen*), something they saw as one of the movement's key defining features. Instead, they argued, it is through the more direct method of *guru-bhakti* that spiritual progress results. The movement's professed aversion to ritual and "show off" (*tamasha*) situates it in a reformist tradition that has been determined to undermine "superstitious ritual." All this is fairly standard for this devotional milieu. What does set it apart—quite dramatically—from comparable *sant* orders are innovations introduced since the accession to the guruship of Gurmeet Ram Rahim Singh Ji Insaan in 1990.

It is by way of the novel directions introduced under his leadership that the DSS has achieved distinctiveness and, it must be added, notoriety: for the DSS has in recent years come to possess a very particular relationship with excess. Its leaders and devotees alike understand the movement to be on a very special mission, its guru a figure of the stature of Krishna or Jesus. It seeks massive expansion. When we first began research on the DSS in 2004, it claimed to have one to two million devotees; by 2018 it claimed sixty million.[12] Excess of all kinds: a ramping up of the celebrity status that other spiritual leaders have sought and achieved, which "casts believers as spectators" (Meyer and Moors 2006, 9), is frequently achieved through adept harnessing of new media forms; but there are also the world record–breaking spectacles of "service" inspired by, or achieved because of, the blessings of the guru—such as most blood pressure readings and diabetes screenings in a single day and highest number of people sanitizing their hands simultaneously. More whimsical and fantastic are the records achieved for largest display of oil lamps (150,009), largest finger painting (3,900 m^2), and largest vegetable mosaic (185,807 m^2) (Roy 2017). The hand sanitization record that the guru inspired is now taken as proof that he had foreknowledge of the COVID-19 pandemic; they evidence him seeking to equip and prepare humanity for what would befall it.[13] Further, we learn from the guru's personal website (https://www.saintdrmsginsan.me) that under his guidance "more than 115 humanitarian works are being conducted and also 55 world records are registered on his name." In light of this, "world record university London has decided to grant Him [a doctorate] degree."[14] Therefore, "from [January 25, 2016] onwards Revered Saint Ji will be addressed as Saint Dr Gurmeet Ram Rahim Singh Ji Insan." Thus it is the guru who is credited for the world records his devotees perform. Moreover, there is an evident slippage between attainment of world records and the production of miraculous results, with the former standing in for but also suggesting the latter. The labor of such wondertrap miracles is performed, of course, by devotees; DSS followers are responsible for the miracles they attribute to their guru. The participatory production of such miracles and wonder effects is ideologically denied by both the movement's literature and by devotees themselves.

The DSS has also experimented with a hyperpatriotic brand of guruship that in some ways aligns with, yet is not completely reducible to, Modi's Hindutva agenda: massive provision of blood for Indian soldiers, annual Mega Cleanliness Campaigns in association with Modi's Swachh Bharat Abhiyan,[15] and the steroidal nationalism of the guru's feature films. His grand entry astride a tank was consistent with this overall schema, with its staging at the time of India's Republic Day (January 26), a day known for exhibiting the nation's "unity in diversity" and military might, with marching armed regiments and displays of tanks, missiles, and fighter jets. The event—and also the film *Hind ka Napak Ko Jawab: MSG Lion Heart 2* (2017), which thrust the guru into heroic, militaristic, border-defending scenarios[16]—merged *desh-* and *guru-bhakti* in support of the hypernationalism currently dominating contemporary Indian politics. Meanwhile, the guru lent his support to the Bharatiya Janata Party (BJP) in the 2014 Lok Sabha and 2015 regional assembly elections.[17] However, rather than transparent backing of and ideological alignment with the Hindutva agenda, the endorsement should be understood, at least partly, in terms of sheer opportunism. For as we have already intimated, serial serious criminality—rape, murder, castration of devotees, expropriation of land—apparently has been another of the DSS guru's modes of excess, and he has seemed to bestow his political endorsements as a means of seeking protection against mounting charges. Indeed, his *dera* operated as something in between a "little fiefdom" (Singh 2017) and a "temple racket" (Michelutti et al. 2018, 158), in which he operated with kinglike extralegal impunity (see Lucia 2018 on the authoritarian structure of guru-disciple relationships; we note also that one of his titles is Maharaj and that his close kin are known as "the royal family").[18] His grand entry on the tank provided a strange reflection of exactly this, for riding a modified vehicle is in violation of Indian law; specifically section 52 of the Motor Vehicles Act, amended in 2000, which grants exceptions only on conditions of permissibility from legal authorities. The exceptional, extralegal, nature of his grand entries in modified vehicles not only reproduced his sovereign figure, but underscored his status as someone apparently beyond the laws of the land. However, if his previous support for the Congress had afforded him a measure of protection, the political winds were such in 2014 that strategic alignment with the ongoing populist politics of the BJP came to make sense. It "worked" for both parties up to a point—the BJP made gains in the guru's regions of influence (parts of Punjab, Haryana, Rajasthan, and to a lesser extent Delhi) and in government it ensured that his first feature film *MSG: Messenger of God* was released, despite the Censor Board's initial ban on it, a subplot that we discuss further elsewhere (Copeman and Duggal 2023). Eventually, however, the quantity and gravity of the charges against the guru outweighed the protection the BJP was willing or able to give him, and in 2017 the guru was sentenced to twenty years in prison for the rape of two *sadhvis* (female ascetics), while, in 2019, he was convicted for the murder of an investigative journalist and sentenced to life imprisonment. He faces further charges.

This explains the wistful nature of some of the devotee comments on his online videos: "Dr MSG The Great miss you; "You are, you were and you will be my love charger forever"[19]; "Happy incarnation day Papa Ji. Miss you Papa Ji. Come soon Papa Ji"; "MSG PAPA JI AAJO JI" (Papa MSG come); "Msg love *Pita Ji jldi aao ji pita ji jldi aao ji jldi aao ji pita ji jldi aao ji*" (come soon come soon come soon); "*Ve aaja mahi, aaja ve, ve aaja mahi, aja ve*" (come beloved, come, come beloved, come); "finally *pita g Da khatt aa hi gya, pita g ne ishara v. Kiya ha ki jaldi ayega*" (pita ji's letter has arrived, pita ji has hinted that he will come soon); "Sole soothing melody made me to miss more to my MSG papa"; "Miss u a lot Pita g. Plzz come back we alone without you"; "Waiting for saint MSG, *jaldi aajo*" (come quickly); "A lot of wait my lord Papa"; "*Ao jao dharti rakshak ji*" (come earth protector).[20]

Indeed, his arrest and imprisonment marked the moment he became a kind of virtual guru (cf. Lucia 2023): imprisoned though he now was, he remained available to his devotees via his prior recordings on video-hosting platforms such as YouTube, which attain renewed importance as an archive of wondrous effects for keeping the devotion of attractions intact. An instance of the affective mobilization of the media archive of the guru was seen on the incarnation day of DSS founder guru Shah Mastana Ji in 2018, a year after the present guru had entered prison: "A recorded video of Saint Gurmeet Ram Rahim Singh Insan was played [to attendees], making devotees nostalgic and filled with devotion."[21] The following year, on the occasion of the DSS's Foundation Day, "the congregation program started with the playing of recorded Satsangs of Guru Ji and the followers were absorbed in the sermons and motivational teachings rendered on screens."[22] In 2017, after his imprisonment, media speculation centered on possible candidates to succeed him and on whether the DSS could survive the guru's downfall at all. But at the time of writing he remains enthroned, prisoner or not. Have devotees lost faith in him? This is difficult to gauge, but not according to our contacts and devotee comments on YouTube. The charges were well known for decades before his eventual imprisonment, during which time the devotee base expanded dramatically; and, indeed, scandals and exposés concerning gurus seem rarely to unseat them—rather, they are often taken by devotees as tests of their devotion, potentially leading to its intensification (Gold 1987; Lucia 2023).[23] The DSS guru's criminal convictions could not be graver, yet one cannot write him off. As we write this in August 2022, he is on parole, residing in Bhagpat, near Delhi. He has periodically sought parole ever since he was first imprisoned—for family reasons and in order to cultivate his fields, say his requests—and since early 2022 it has been granted several times. Various political parties continue to vie for the support of his followers: it is easy to think of what those followers, and indeed the guru himself, might demand in exchange (see Sood 2019). David Graeber's (2008) definition of charisma as the ability to do things you are not supposed to do and get away with it could not be more apt in this case.

As will be apparent, the DSS presents a devotion of the gigantic and the exaggerated (Corsín Jiménez 2013, 77).[24] Its claim to possess sixty million devotees may be wildly inaccurate. But still, there is a story worth telling here. How does someone who twenty years ago was an obscure provincial guru come to achieve such an escalation of presence, devotees, and national and international fame? We suggest that effects of wonder lie at the heart of the story, and our task in this chapter is to try to determine how they are generated. We earlier suggested a notion of a devotion of attractions. Famously, Tom Gunning (1990) coined "cinema of attractions" to refer to the dominance of special effects and technological wonders over narrative coherence in early cinematography. Whatever the value or coherence of DSS teachings may be, they have tended to be completely eclipsed—in devotional practice, reportage, and scholarship—in part no doubt by the politics of caste and electoral alliances associated with the movement, but most of all by the sheer escalating spectacle of the guru himself. The message of his guruship progressively came to be outdone by the command "See!"; by devotional novelties; by his ability—like that of the cinema of attractions—to show but far less to tell. He has always enacted a camerawork guruship: when we spent time at his ashram in 2004, we met sadhus whose sole job they described as "photograph *seva*"—on excursions he was constantly accompanied by at least two cameraman *sadhu*s. The results were published in the organization's newspaper, *Sach Kahoon*, and official press releases; meanwhile, his *satsang* addresses were recorded and distributed in the form of video CDs (they were also streamed into the waiting rooms of the DSS-run clinics we visited). The intermediality of his guruship has since escalated, with his diverse modes of performance gaining traction across various mediums at various levels.[25] Whether at his *satsang*s or pop concerts (the line between them came to be blurred), film cameras perennially hovered above devotee-audiences and the stage, where crew members with camera cranes and video dollies could be witnessed recording these events for simultaneous live telecast on the DSS website and elsewhere. In 2014 the guru's *101 Ru-b-Ru Night* concert at Delhi was live telecasted by six television channels (ETC Punjabi, Zee Jagran, Sadhna, 4Real News, Sanskar and Sarv-Dharam Sangam). Footage from such concerts was then edited with graphics and special effects for use in music videos; for example, his song *Love Charger*, released in 2014 by leading music video channel Vevo (fig. 11.2). The devotional congregation as shooting event made full use of the *bhakt*-spectator crowd; for example, the song *Mein Tujhe Bhool Jau—Never Ever*, which he performed in his first cinema release *MSG: Messenger of God* (2015), features a climax sequence showing the guru performing live in concert among just such a crowd (the 1.3 million devotees who reportedly acted as extras in the film surpassed another world record). Images from such events would later feature in various printed, digital, and virtual platforms across different mediums of communication, distribution, and consumption. We see how the different "modes of exhibition" (Gunning 1990, 65) afforded by the polymedia landscape the DSS was alive to facilitated the expression of the guru's persona(s) in more and more dimensions.

Exceptional though some of this might appear, it is important not to overstate the case. The DSS's devotion of attractions does not exist in a vacuum—we can think of the larger burgeoning landscape of "Disney divinity" (Srivastava 2009) it belongs to and of multiple past and present instances of guru-focused excess and theatricality; and, certainly, many other gurus, too, have proliferated their roles and wider presences well beyond the bounds of the ashram.[26] Precedents exist for many of the "unusual" maneuvers of the DSS guru. Yet, for all that, the DSS guru's experiments in wonder should be acknowledged as novel and innovative

Figure 11.2. Gurmeet Ram Rahim Singh Ji Insan performing on stage with psychedelic effects projected on background screen in "Love Charger" music video. *Source*: "Saint Gurmeet Ram Rahim Singh Ji Insan—Love Charger," on YouTube channel DeraSachaSaudaVEVO (https://www.youtube.com/watch?v=Q48tagwurUw).

insofar as a large enough quantitative shift becomes a qualitative one. For this alone they deserve investigation, but also because the very hyperbole of the DSS guru's devotion of attractions can help us to comprehend more general aspects of the production of wonder; his case affords, in other words, the technicolor disclosure of (certain and more mundane?) techniques of guruship.

This chapter thus seeks to provide a provisional account of the DSS guru's experiments in wonder—for the DSS guru has indeed succeeded in generating effects of wonder, as evidenced in the comments from devotees that we disperse throughout this chapter and by growth in follower numbers. These comments are predominantly "user comments" below the line of YouTube music videos featuring the guru in spectacular pop-star mode. Hence they hold a particular sense of immediacy: devotees are either watching or have just watched the videos they offer comments on. At the same time, the comments contain rhetoric that undoubtedly is prompted by official DSS "talking points." For instance, official DSS literature makes much of the guru's "versatility," which is also a notable feature of devotees' praise for their guru as found in user comments. Such comments, in other words, are an interesting mixture of the scripted and the unfiltered immediate. We turn now to some accounts of the guru's wonder effects.

Pop Star

One mode of the guru's expansion and proliferation of presence is his pop stardom. In 2012 he released his first self-composed album of devotional melodies. Since then, he has embraced mainstream rock and pop music. Indeed, his singing is a central point of attraction among his followers (and also a matter of great curiosity to nonfollowers). This has led to additional personas and appellations, such as "Rock-star Saint" and "Love Charger Baba," used by both the popular media and his followers. The massive rock concerts he stages both connect with and depart from the more traditional form of *satsangs*, thereby expanding our normative understanding of congregational religiosity. Departing from the daily delivery of spiritual discourses in his *Ruhani Majlis* (sacred gatherings), but at the same time reproducing them in another form, he now became the Rock-star Saint who was able to perform in various genres such as bhangra, pop, hip-hop, and rap, and also in various languages, thereby finessing the expansion of his spiritual enterprise.[27] These languages—Hindi, Punjabi, Haryanvi, Rajasthani, and English—are the languages of the north Indian states where the major base of DSS followers is located, and also where the guru performed a remarkable series of 101 *Ru-b-Ru* (face-to-face) rock concerts in 2014.

The final concert, which took place at the Ramlila grounds of the national capital on April 27, 2014, was advertised as follows: "After 100 successful divine musical nights, Revered Saint Gurmeet Ram Rahim Singh Ji Insan is all set to rock the capital of India. . . . Main highlights of the event will be Live concert by Revered Guru Ji on songs written & composed by HIMSELF, cultural program and face-to-face interaction with Guru Ji. . . . The event will be a fusion of spiritual and modern music and enlighten every heart with bliss and ecstasy, never experienced."[28] A DSS blog described how at the concert

> a sea of people converged . . . to celebrate the name of God, and lose themselves in Divine music, creating a history of sorts. The melodies of Guruji, the thunderous applause of the spellbound audience seemed to have frozen time in its tracks. Over

50 million viewers, across the world, enjoyed a live telecast of the program, and learnt more about 101 programs of social welfare initiated by the Guruji. . . . It seemed that the earth and the sky joined hands to dance to the melodious music and throbbing beats of Guruji's compositions. . . . It seemed like a celebration of life, everyone expressing joy his own way. Some clapped, some hooted, others broke into a jig, waved handkerchiefs, or released balloons in the sky. . . . Religions faded into oblivion, as Hindus, Sikhs, Muslims, Christians mingled with each other, dancing together in ecstasy.[29]

The event was titled 101st Wonder Kohinoor Diamond Jubilee Masto Mast Ruhani Ru-b-Ru Night. The name of the concert series, *Ru-b-Ru* (face-to-face), foregrounds the "directness" of the performance, while the word "Wonder" is juxtaposed with "Kohinoor Diamond." One of the world's largest cut diamonds, the Kohinoor is currently in the possession of the Queen of England. Famously taken from India by British colonizers, it remains the subject of contestation between the two countries. As a brand name, Kohinoor denotes premium-end products and authentic quality; for example, Kohinoor Authentic Platinum Basmati Rice. Its symbolic sequestration by the "baba of bling" seemed appropriate enough. Indeed, the stage consisted of a large-scale replica of the diamond, with the guru's throne placed at its head: "The stage was like a diamond, 16 feet high. How the diamond stage was firmly stationed was another mystery. Its narrow tip rested on the ground and the broad end rose all the way up. Later, the engineers revealed to Saying Truth, that they had failed to come up with a suitable structure design since a top-heavy stage would have been unstable."[30] The impossible became possible, in other words, due to the guru's visionary guidance and design. There were, in addition, a revolving stage, fireworks, dazzling rotating spotlights and psychedelic projections on a massive screen. Dancers and acrobats were brought in from Africa and Indian reality television shows like *Dance India Dance* and *India's Got Talent*. The guru's costume changes apparently were limitless.

The gigantic stage backdrop was decorated with symbols and figures popularly associated with the world of fantasy and the cosmos, such as mountains, fairies, conches, swans, unicorns, golden stars, moons, and glittering water flowing out of mountains, borrowed from the aesthetics of mass produced bazaar or calendar art.[31] In such art, scenic landscapes indexing "freshness, fecundity and plentitude" (Jain 2002, 46) are markers of auspiciousness. Here, then, the guru is center stage locus of auspiciousness, plentitude, and fulfillment of desired hopes. The usage of material objects associated with shine and dazzle conjure divine radiance as "they imitate the sky, dazzling like the golden sun, '*suryan polle*,' and the diamond-like stars, a cosmological metaphor overflowing with wonderment and beauty. As in Vedic alchemy, gold is illuminating and cosmic; it radiates divine energy and power" (Srinivas 2018, 112). The aesthetics of bling embodied in the DSS guru and his spectacular concerts not only create wonder effects but also the desire for fulfillment of the hopes of followers in his depiction as a desirable, aspirational figure capable of fulfilling the aspirations of followers.

Fashion Icon

Consider the cover image of DSS publication *Spiritual Fusion: Fashion—the Revolutionary Era*, which presents the guru as a fashion icon. The image depicts the camera itself as a stage set for the DSS guru, who himself sits before a camera. The overbearing presence of the camera not only foregrounds the significance of photography, film, and video within DSS visual culture, but also meta-reflexively depicts how the guru's image "rests" on the (stage and throne-like) form of the camera and its function (see Duggal 2015, 164). Having oneself enthroned on the machine of one's image production places in tandem the desirable eye of the camera and the desired subject; captured is not only the eye of the camera but also that of the viewer. 'The frontal desirable (*darshanic*) eye of the camera functions as a vehicle of the guru's eyesight, looking straight onto the viewer's face, which also renders the viewing subject a desired (to be photographed [wondertrapped]) subject' (Duggal 2015, 164). Who desires who? The devotee desires the guru, as is convention. But what is the guru's desire? For devotees? For more and more versions of himself? These things are not necessarily isolable: since those "more and more" versions always contain his devotees, his (and their) desire is also for more and more versions of his devotees. If they contain one another then mutual desire is simultaneously self-desire. This reflects our earlier point that, if the guru is glorified, so are his devotees, to the extent that they participate in him. The power of the guru, enacted through vision, is fascinatingly poised: if conventional narrative cinema invisibilizes spectators—rendering them almost voyeurs—in the cinema of attractions "the attraction does not hide behind the pretense of an unacknowledged spectator" (Gunning 1993, 44). The DSS guru, similarly, gazes back at his devotees. The relationship established through the gaze is neither a Foucauldian one of power-knowledge nor the simplistic obverse, tapping power by making oneself seen by others (in the right way). Rather, it tells of the *complicity* (43)—what we earlier termed the mutual entrapment—that characterizes the guru-devotee relationship.

Consider also his dress. His "spiritual style" reflects the DSS's claim to be the "Confluence of all Religions," with his sartorial choices seeking to contain all heterogeneities—different religions, regions, caste, cultures, and traditions—in a kind of collective image. Similar to Swami Vivekananda's studio portraits, the DSS guru engages in the "conscious production of self-image for the other," becoming "both a spokesman and that of which he speaks" (Prasad 2014, 575–76). In the case of Vivekananda, we see a resolve in "the way[s] I want others to see me" (576) and also a struggle for self-image whereby he could become a particular iconographic form through which he is still identified and remembered in the public imagination. However, in the case of the DSS guru, stabilization of image is not the point—it is the act of experimentation, the desire to expand, include, and modify styles of attire from different cultural traditions that is foregrounded. The aspiration to continuously re-present himself through renewed sartorial self-imaging—his "unique heterogeneity"—is itself the identity.

On the one hand every image of him in new attire depicts him in a novel form (*roop*). On the other, this form is temporary and incomplete—which leads to further possibilities of exploration. Such heterogeneous representations function as highlights in the guru's spiritual functions, such as in the form of massive hoardings representing him in *naye-naye paridhano ke akarshak andaz*[32] (the unique attractive traits of his new-new attires), and in his spiritual concerts. Such image-making suggests he can only be grasped through the totality of all of these images. The inconclusiveness of his representations also offers choice (Warrier 2003) to his followers—they can pick out whichever image-form they wish to connect with. Curiosity is maintained: What image will come next? In the afterlife of these *ruhani mehfils* (evenings of spiritual entertainment) other means for circulation of his image include studio portraits in printed materials (hoardings, magazines), video performances, and most recently feature films (Copeman and Duggal 2023).

In the period of colonial modernity, writes Madhava Prasad (2014, 577), "while other secular middle-class customers went to the studio for family photographs embellished with English props, the spiritually minded too seem to have found in the studio the right settings in which to try out their newfound self-images." Prasad is concerned here with the studio portraits and image-making practices of Ramakrishna and Vivekananda. In the case of images of the DSS guru, the studio setting, with its painted backgrounds and props, is replaced by digitally manipulated (photoshopped) versions of the same. Photomontage background effects transport the guru into settings such as that of a European palace, or equally take him to freezing north pole–like locales; and, digitally manipulated though they are, the various postures adopted of standing, sitting, and kneeling remain inspired by more traditional studio photography.

This aesthetics of variety—the guru placed in various settings and styles of attire and pose in photoshopped photomontage—is gathered and anthologized in the aforementioned collector's item *Spiritual Fusion: Fashion—the Revolutionary Era*. A six-volume set akin to an album or catalogue, it is designed for a certain kind of class consumption. Though expensively priced at 1,500 rupees—with superior printing quality synonymous with high-end fashion magazines—it nevertheless forms part of the guru's broader attempt to scale up his presence beyond and across domains and registers: spiritual, musical, film, and now fashion model and icon. Despite its sophistication, however, the publication retains the aesthetic imprint of the cheaply available photomontage calendars of roadsides, bazaars, and framing shops. It presents broad bases of referentiality, with local, folk/regional, and rural chic modes of attire and picture composition finding their place alongside images that place the guru in urban, world-wrapping settings.

The DSS's hybrid stylizations are frequently seen by nonfollowers as a derivative form of aesthetic such as "kitsch." He is the bejeweled and flashy "guru of bling." Ashis Nandy (2015) argues that non-elite gurus like Ram Rahim "are not drawing from ancient spiritual traditions; they have no access to those traditions. They are imitating spirituality as it is reconstructed in popular culture." For Nandy, "the gaudiness one sees is a result of this tension. . . . It is a borrowed aesthetic: you are trying to break into some of the glamour you see around, but you can't get the pitch right." From the point of view of nonfollowers and elites, Nandy has a point—but *only* from that point of view. Controversial spiritual master Osho née Rajneesh (1931–90) wore jewels, too (Kakar 2008,

14), but one should not forget the difference between the two. If Osho delivered sophisticated Zen and Nietzschean-style discourses wearing Rolex watches having arrived by Rolls-Royce and cultivated a "class" of elite followers, the DSS guru is generally considered to be gaudy and crass (for one critic exhibiting a "cringing parade of crazy costumes" [Roy 2017], to take just one example), and for his decidedly non-elite followers—for whom he is "Rockstar Pita Ji" and "Our Honey Singh"[33]—the pitch is just right; that is to say, it works. Neither are DSS aesthetics derivative in any simple sense. Rather, they frequently express a novel conjunctural aesthetic language. The heterogeneity of the associations he draws into himself move beyond derivativeness or copy; he is a kind of embodied remix (Lessig 2012, 164).

The guru as embodied remix can create controversy and lead to confusion—as when he was subject to bans and assassination attempts following a notorious occasion in 2007 when he dressed up as Guru Gobind Singh.[34] He was then accused by mainstream Sikh organizations of seeking to pass himself off as the revered final living Sikh master.[35] He was in a way, but only temporarily—it was just another of his "unique attractive . . . new-new attires." He no doubt did lift ritual and sartorial elements from the Sikh tradition, but soon enough he was dressing up as other iconic figures; he is a guru who lifts the auras of others, quickly moving on, continually remixing himself. The temporariness of the inhabitation allows for deniability, while begging the question "What next?" and enhancing the acceleration effects of the movement. Perhaps it was the depthlessness of the appropriation more than anything else that offended mainstream Sikh sentiments. An abiding image for us derives from an unofficial film made in response to the DSS guru's mediatized actions—smartphone footage uploaded onto YouTube shows orthodox Sikhs throwing their *chapal*s (sandals) at TV screens depicting him.[36]

The DSS guru achieves wonder effects (and on occasion consternation), then, through temporary inhabitation of different forms and identities. This is a guru who never stands still. As one devotee, who having only just watched the "wonderful amazing superb . . . awesome" Love Charger video starring the guru, put it rather curtly: "now waiting for something new."[37] For Roy (2017), MSG similarly provided the "curious hook of 'What next and how much bigger . . .'" Writing of contemporary trends in the qualification of commodities, Thrift (2012, 151) points to the "art of building attachments, of continually restarting the work of association. The overall goal is to produce, often for only the briefest of moments, a kind of secular magic by forming collectives, temporary gestalts to use Merleau-Ponty's filmic description, which have pull through their 'whatever singularity,' an internally plural collectivity understood as that which has an 'inessential commonality,' a solidarity that in no way concerns an essence." Indeed, the brevity of the guru's prolific associations (their "inessentiality"), as we have noted, disarms potential claims of appropriation while simultaneously forming the association nonetheless; it also contributes to the excitement. The filmic nature of Merleau-Ponty's description is apt, for film affords the guru's diverse images a flickering momentariness that contributes to generating these sorts of (non)association. Such experimental traversal of difference might seem to be for him only; yet he also provides access points for his devotees inasmuch as they form part of the collective personhood enacting the traversal.

His name itself is also used to build an ecology of associations and embodied remix. A guru of novel forms (*roop*) and temporary possession, his name's expansive instability is not dissimilar to, is even a form of, his "unique attractive . . . new-new attires"—the ever-changing nature of which suggests his ungraspability. When we first became interested in the DSS in 2004 his official name was Gurmeet Ram Rahim Singh, though devotees would also call him Hazoor Maharaj or simply Pita Ji. His official title, in combining names from Sikhism, Hinduism, and Islam, advertised the movement's professed secularism, and also the guru's claim to be the embodied confluence of those faiths. It had already been expanded from plain Gurmeet Singh; the insertion of "Ram" and "Rahim" acting to "brighten the halo around his syncretic claims, with an eye at perhaps broadening the base of his clientele from varied religious affiliations" (Singh 2017, 21). But the already spacious name wouldn't stay still or contained. By 2016 his name was recorded in film credits as Doctor Saint Gurmeet Ram Rahim Singh Ji Insan. We have discussed the adoption of "Doctor." The name "*Insan*"—"Human"—was adopted in 2007, since when all baptized devotees have been expected to shun their family names and take this name instead. His name will not stand still—restless and tumescent, constantly spilling over, enfolding (possessing) numerous religious identities and indeed all of humanity (*insan*). (And this is just his official name: Rockstar Saint, Baba of Bling, Dr MSG, and Lionheart are only some of the unofficial ones.)

In one of Claude Lévi-Strauss's most famous reflections on names he says:

At one extreme, the name is an identifying mark which, by the application of a rule, establishes that the individual who is named is a member of a preordained class (a social group in a system of groups, a status by birth in a system of statuses). At the other extreme, the name is a free creation on the part of the individual who gives the name and expresses a transitory or subjective state of his own by means of the person he names. But can one be said to be really naming in either case? The choice seems only to be between identifying someone else by assigning him to a class, or, under cover of giving him a name, identifying oneself through him. One therefore never names: one classes someone else if the name is given to him in virtue of his characteristics and one classes oneself if, in the belief one need not follow a rule, one names someone else "freely," that is, in virtue of characteristics of one's own. And most commonly one does both at once. (1966, 181)

The guru's name is an extreme example of the name as a free creation of the individual, albeit he does not name another but himself. On the one hand his name seems not to comply with Lévi-Strauss's schema—its expansiveness and instability make it seem unclassifiable. Boundary-crossing, it is an example of what we have called elsewhere a both/and name (either/or names, conversely, seek to reduce identity to singularity; neither/nor names seek to evade all identity).[38] On the other hand, the guru's name is classificatory in a negative sense in classifying his very unclassifiability. It points to his inability to be pointed at (Das 2015); that is to say, his ungraspability. His name is also a kind of story (Ingold 2011) or document of history (Brink-Danan 2010), with changes to it chronicling the different stages of the guru's encompassment of subject positions—the way in which he includes in order to extend. The DSS guru is not alone in engaging in such promiscuous inclusivism or "trapping" of difference; the guru-scape is replete with instances—for example, Sathya Sai Baba's prolific associational additions (Srinivas 2010). It is the extent and intensity of the DSS guru's remixing—and to some degree the novelty of the tools he employs (e.g., attires, medias, names)—that singles him out.

Amanda Lucia (2014, 244–45) has questioned our earlier conception of uncontainability (or "including in order to extend") as a heuristic for comprehending the varied methodologies of presence employed by different orders of provincial, national, and global guru in India's recent history. For Lucia, it can appear to amplify the stories gurus tell about themselves, endorsing their own self-narrativization.[39] We welcome the critique, which is mostly persuasive and certainly nuanced; indeed, elsewhere Lucia provisionally endorses an analytic of uncontainability (e.g., 2021, 2022) with the proviso that it be recognized as a "constructed reality" (Lucia 2014, 245). Since we enormously admire Lucia's work, and perhaps also run the risk of reenacting here some of the modes of analysis she is disquieted by, we briefly respond: no doubt, in the earlier work, we did not say what we wanted to say clearly or often enough, for our interest has been precisely in gurus' means of producing ("constructing") effects contributive to their seeking to be other than, or more than, they are. In the present instance, these effects are wonder effects that in turn feed into other effects such as expansion of the movement. One has to admit that the associative labor engaged in by gurus has often been quite successful—the form of subjecthood that we have called an inclusive singularity is in many cases a sociological reality.[40] While we do not necessarily concur that the analysist's job is to "challenge" guru self-narrativizations (245)—though no doubt there are occasions where this is called for (e.g., Lucia 2018; McCartney 2018)—we agree with Lucia that the analyst must take care to go beyond breathless description of these and acknowledge that our previous analyses might not have achieved the right balance in this respect. Even so, we maintain that our purpose here and elsewhere has been to give an account of how the associative labor process operates and of the logics informing gurus' varied methodologies of presence. Here, for instance, we have examined an onomastic means of progressive other-incorporation that couples together techniques of expansion and instability, and also how an aesthetics of variety produced through studio portraiture, choice of attire, and remix can contribute to the production of effects of incorporative ungraspability. The effects were not divorced analytically from their means of production; moreover, we have highlighted those instances where these processes find their limits.[41]

Reflection: Camerawork Guruship and *Bhakti* at the Speed of Light

We return now to our provisional schema of the guru's wonder effects, wondertraps, and methodologies of presence, suggesting an analogy between the DSS guru and the pop star Madonna—and not only because the former, too, became a pop star. For decades Madonna fascinated publics, including scholarly ones, for "exploding boundaries" and for her experiments in identity (Kellner 1995, 263)—her own brand of uncontainability. But if she symbolizes "experimentation, change, and production of one's individual identity," she does so as part of a high-level marketing strategy. Similarly, the guru's camerawork guruship—experimentation with genres, styles, and technologies and varied appeals to our visual senses—lies at an intersection in which desire is created in the spectator-devotee and the guru is created as a desirable figure. Comparable to Madonna, he is deeply invested in fashion and its offering of "choices of clothes, style, and image"; the "perpetual innovation" (264) and restlessness that are its hallmark are in tune with and augment his own cultivated instability of presence—his dashing into and out of associations; and if, for Madonna, "her sometimes dramatic shifts in image and style suggested that identity was . . . something that one produced, and [could be] modified at will [such] that one's appearance and image helps produce what one is," the guru's not dissimilar shifts in image and style might take on a heightened significance in a land of ascribed caste and religious identities. For instance, his projection of caste (Jat) pride in the film *Jattu Engineer* (2017), in this view, might be understood as just another performance—one that questions the essentiality of the identity it imitates. Not only caste essence but also that of the "true guru" are disclosed as production techniques via the hyperbole of his dressing up, which like the relation of drag to "proper" gender (Butler 1998, 722), enacts the structure of performance and impersonation by which guruship very frequently is assumed. Of particular relevance is how Madonna's "marketing strategies successively targeted different audiences. While she appealed to young teenage girls in her early work, she quickly incorporated minority audiences with her use of Hispanic and black figures and culture in her videos and stage performances" (Kellner 1995, 277). Similarly, we have seen how the guru's progressive role expansion (e.g., in order to attract youthful devotees) was designed as a means of "successively incorporating different audiences into [his] orbit" (277). Also in common is their embracement of contradictions (and profiting from them) (278), aesthetics of shock, excess, and tastelessness (284) and appropriative "trapping" of difference. In their different ways, the two figures continually seek to go beyond themselves (283). Like Madonna in regard to the category "pop star," Ram Rahim seemed to push the category of "guru" beyond previous boundaries, subverting established rules, conventions, and limits and "always trying to develop something new" (285). His devotion of attractions—grand entries, live concerts, "new-new" sartorial avatars and films—portray different modes of (ever growing) bigness and incorporative agency achieved through modern technology, varying from the digital camera and revolving stage to cranes and cinema screens, and across multiple platforms of production, dissemination, and consumption. Thus developed the guru's schismatic, trap-laden effects of wonder.

The early history of photography is replete with instances in which potential subjects of the new technology sought to evade "capture" by the photographic lens (Pinney 2011). The DSS guru's camerawork guruship consists of beckoning the camera to himself in repeated enactments of self-capture, the better to distribute many and varied visual self-iterations across time and space in the cause of viewer-devotee captivation through bedazzlement. We have seen how the embodied two-way visual exchange of *darshan* remains significant but also is not the only scopic register at stake in the process. At least as important in his camerawork guruship is the production of views that "confound the eye through bedazzlement [and] inscrutability," with "clothing, gesture, and jewellery—the way such objects shine, move, and conceal"—operating not "simply as accessories to the main spectacle" (Dinkar 2021, 77) but central to the production of nonreciprocal modes of captivation through bedazzlement. His is not the only camerawork guruship, of course. We referred earlier to photographic portraits of Vivekananda, and it is worth emphasizing the keen interest he took in these portraits, their evident captivating power, and connectedly the significant role they played in popularizing the Ramakrishna Mission (Beckerlegge 2012). The magnetic pull of photographs of Ramana Maharshi (1879–1950), glimpsed on posters or book covers in an array of global locations, have caused hitherto completely unaffiliated observers to travel directly to his ashram in Tamil Nadu (Chowdhuri 2023), which itself is an "ashram of photographs."[42] Evidently, the DSS guru is far from alone in pursuing a guruship within the photographic frame.

Yet there are several distinguishing features. First, is the DSS guru's uniquely intense embrace of the "exorbitant flow" (Pinney 2019, 205) of photography; a kind of Benjaminian espousal of the camera's ability to create "disruptive cutoffness, its surrealistic potential to create new revolutionary alignments [and] destabilize the familiar reality to which ordinary human vision binds us" (205). His "revolutionary era" fashion photos, in particular, create Benjaminesque unfamiliar alignments and associations. Pinney contrasts the type of photography valorized by Benjamin with the "sensual plenitude" of digital photography, which allows an image to be "everywhere at once, accessible from any point in the network establishing a regime of intoxication and plenitude through its rapid multiplication and profusion" (Rubenstein and Sluis 2013, 30). But, of course, this too perfectly accords with the DSS guru's own desire to be everywhere at once. The guru's surrealistic fashion shots are also subject to—and this is precisely the point—intense intermedial maneuvers, as they partake, in particular, of digital photography's "rolling frontier of superabundance" (Pinney 2019, 208), spreading within and beyond devotee WhatsApp groups, intoxicating viewers, and augmenting a guruship of profusion. The second difference is suggested by the first: if Ramana Maharshi's acquiescence to devotees who repeatedly wished to photograph him indicated a kind of self-denial—a surrender to the will of the photographer; a kind of "unselfing" (Chowdhuri 2023)—the DSS guru's relationship to the camera could not be more different. Camerawork is employed as a set of practices of self intensification/extensification—further means of intensifying the intensity of his guruship, enacting self-multiplication, and pursuing a mode of visually heterogeneous omnipresence that might stand (in) for omniscience. Photography, it has been argued, resists totality and a sense of the absolute on account of its birth at a time of secular modernity that it mirrors and takes forward (Taminiaux 2009,12). Moreover, its constant dissemination allies it with the familiar and mundane; that is to say, the non-ultimate (12). In truth, many cases, including Western ones, could probably be marshalled to question such claims. The DSS guru's camerawork guruship—in which constant dissemination of "new-new" images forms part of an exaggeration process that "throws human concepts up to the heavens and believes with 'hyperbolic naivety' that they could be objectivized there" (Sloterdijk 2017, 167)—enables us to see clearly enough how photography can be recruited into the pursuit of a totalizing fantasy.

Further, it is worth briefly dwelling on how the different temporalities enfolded in the DSS contribute to its production of wondertraps. The guru's instability of presence that we just highlighted in reference to restless "fashion" is a feature of the temporary inhabitations (of associations, identities) that we have pointed to as a driver of wonder effects. The "dashing" nature of the guru's associative labor marries well with—participates in—the movement's culture of rush. From the miracles generated via time compression, to the release of four guru-starring feature films in two years, and so on, this is *bhakti* at the speed of light. The "new-new" attires and, if we may, "what nextness" of the order, find expression in the title of the compilation of portraits of the guru discussed earlier: *Spiritual Fusion: Fashion—the Revolutionary Era*. Devotee comments similarly refer to "total revolution in music"; "never seen in the history of movie industry."[43] Devotees exhibit a perception of their being permitted entry into a world of "the never having been done before." Their vital participation in the accomplishment of world records is the most literal manifestation of this. However, if these temporalities of revolution, brevity, and rush seem to recall those of the cinema of attractions, a further critical temporality embodied by the DSS makes the connection explicit, for, as with its cinematic forbear, "rather than a desire for an (almost) endlessly delayed fulfilment and cognitive involvement in pursuing an enigma," the devotion of attractions "arouses a curiosity that is satisfied by surprise" (Gunning 1993, 44). The basic temporality of attractions, argues Gunning, is "that of the alternation of presence/absence that is embodied in the act of display" (44). We can think here, in particular, of the guru's grand entries as just such an "intense form of present tense": appearing "out of nothing" astride an army tank, descending from the sky, or elevated from below, his varied realizations of presence from absence take the form of "staccato jolts of surprise" (or "sudden burst[s] of presence") (45). Does this engender wonder? For Descartes, value-free, "wonder simply prompts us to focus our attention on whatever has taken us by surprise"; while, for Heidegger, awe is always renewed by the surprise conditioning it (Rubenstein 2008, 38, 111). But the wonder the philosophers were considering was a wonder that keeps questions open. The surprising realizations of the guru, on the other hand, produce something else: an astonishment that captivates (takes captive) and brooks no questions at all.

We have followed Rubenstein in understanding wonder as a quality that eludes rather than possesses us. As she puts it, "mastery that proceeds by means of certainty and exceptionless appropriation" is "inimical to wonder" (2008, 25). Following from this, we can see that if the DSS guru generates wonder it is in the mode of *possessive wonder* (where what is possessed ranges from devotees to subject positions, identities, attention, and more). For Rubenstein, as we have seen, such possessive wonder is not wonder at all, for it seeks to assimilate encountered strangeness rather than sustain it (26). This clarifies our use of the term "wonder effects." We have described a kind of toolkit for the relentless production of such effects, which fix and "trap" spectators; for, undoubtedly overwhelming as devotees' experiences have been, the open multiplicity of such marvels is always assimilated to, or reduced back down to, one figure of possession—as one devotee put it, "pitaji u are the only one who is all in one."[44]

Devotee comments that appreciatively call attention to the guru's all-in-oneness are, as we have mentioned, in part DSS-scripted talking points. The *Hind Ka Napak Ko Jawab* movie trailer highlights the "42 Spectacular Roles [performed in its realization] by Dr. MSG Insan": direction, action, music, stunts, special effects, makeup, costume design, and more; while the guru's own website declaims his remarkable "versatility" and "multi-talented" personality—he is "Spiritual Saint; Writer; Musician; Director; Scientist; Feminist; Youth Icon; etc."[45] Despite this, it is evident that his all-in-oneness inspires awe in devotees: "You, your voice, your music, your lyrics, your walk, your talk"; "Never seen so many varieties in a single album"; "HE is an all-rounder"; "to have so much in one person is more than a miracle"; "HE will be the only man in Bollywood who is so versatile."[46]

"All in one" phraseology is, of course, inspired by commodity labeling and advertisements, and its usage to describe the DSS guru should be understood as "more than an analogy": "all in one" is indeed his marketing strategy. The logic and phenomenon are not novel. The expansive, encompassing qualities of "guru personhood" across time and space have been well documented. The "all in one" phrase marks a quality of excessive subjecthood common to many a guru who contains many. It is the pitch, scope, and explicitization of the case described here that cause it to be distinctive: the very "constitutive excess" (Mazzarella 2010, 727) of the DSS guru and his propensity to enfold, trap, and possess. The commodity derivation of the "all in one" phrase points, appropriately enough, to the guru's simultaneous borrowing from and participation in techniques of what has been called "full-palette capitalism" (Thrift 2008, 30). Such a full-palette guruship, similar to contemporary trends in the extraction of value, "relies on a series of practices of intensification" and "extensification" (30), since his approach has been to construct himself as "resonating" in many sensory registers at once, increasing both the range of appeal and its stickiness (what we might call devotional grip) (39). This partly develops from the combining of commodity and wonder logics.

Scholars frequently suggest that "coincidence" or "mixing-up of opposites" are key provocations of wonder (Rubenstein 2008, 18). Connectedly, Steven Shaviro (2006) has discussed recently honed marketing techniques which propose that products should simultaneously fulfil contrary and seemingly mutually exclusive desires, thereby covering the range of possible consumer dispositions. In his novel *The Savage Girl*, Alex Shakar (2002, 60–61) introduces the idea of paradessence, short for "paradoxical essence." It refers to depictions of commodities by marketers: "Every product has this paradoxical essence. Two opposing desires that it can promise to satisfy simultaneously." Paradessence is the "schismatic core, [the] broken soul, at the center of every product" (60). For instance, "coffee promises both 'stimulation and relaxation'; ice cream connotes both 'eroticism and innocence,' or (more psychoanalytically) both 'semen and mother's milk.' . . . The paradessence is not a dialectical contradiction; its opposing terms do not interact, conflict, or produce some higher synthesis" (Shaviro 2006, 12). As Shakar (2002, 179) puts it, the paradessence is a matter of "having everything both ways and every way and getting everything [one] wants." Shaviro points out that Shakar's concept of paradessence, initially proposed as a kind of "model of" contemporary "postironic" advertising culture quickly evolved into a "model for" it. One marketing "guru," speaking at a United States conference of advertising executives, explicitly drew on *The Savage Girl* in declaring, "It is the things that can promise two, mutually exclusive things that thrive."[47]

The DSS guru similarly embodies the coincidence of opposites. We suggest this embodiment contributes to his generation of wonder effects. Let us return to Graeber's (2008) pithy conception of charisma as doing what you are not supposed to do and getting away with it. An individual's simultaneous repudiation and enactment of *tamasha* and ostentation might lead, for one with little or no charisma, to accusations of hypocrisy. For the guru's followers at least, it only enhances the effect of wonder—his all-in-oneness is underscored. "Having everything both ways and every way" might be his official slogan. His paradessence is of a piece with his all-encompassing sovereign presence: capaciously embodying contrary and seemingly mutually exclusive principles and desires, he covers the range of possible devotee dispositions. Without interaction or synthesis between the opposing principles, he embodies and projects both transcendence of caste (the name Insan, human, borne by him and his followers, was explicitly instituted as a means of transcending and invalidating *jati*) and caste pride (as in his film *Jattu Engineer*). Army tank driver and stockpiler of weaponry (see Copeman and Duggal 2023), the guru of MSG nonetheless celebrates—and seeks to claim affiliation with—"Gandhi's message of winning one's opponent through non-violence" (Roy 2017). In the same film he "addresses himself as fakir, but is seen in elaborate never-repeating costumes that feature some [of the most] heady imaginations with bling that you would ever see" (Roy 2017). The paradessence of the guru inscribes a devotional world in which one does not know negatives. Contraries are not commensurated but simply contained, "all in one."

We have described the coimplication of entrapment and wonder, and how devotee labor is frequently required to set the wondertraps via which the replenishment and augmentation of the same labor supply is accomplished, which in turn enables more wondertraps to be set. At the same time, a model of predatory wonder must be balanced out by recognizing the degree of mutual complicity, or devotee buy-in, that inheres in it. Devotees "travel with" the guru, partaking of the personality they expand—a kind of love relationship with one's own expanded sense of self. While we have seen how "storage" of the virtual guru in the online archive can help to sustain the devotional relationship and production of wonder effects, more work is required on how this relationship may have been affected after the guru was imprisoned in 2017. Given the rush and revolution of the previous years, it is easy to imagine how—archival resources notwithstanding—the new devotional temporality of sudden stillness and quiet might have been a very unsettling one indeed for devotees.

Notes

The research for this chapter was made possible by the support of a Leverhulme Trust Research Project Grant (RPG-2018-145). We thank fellow project team members Arkotong Longkumer and Neelabh Gupta for very helpful feedback. The authors contributed equally to this chapter.

1. The Hindi word *duniya*, in the title of this chapter, means "world."

2. See the YouTube video "Sant Gurmeet Ram Rahim Singh Makes a Grand Entry at Hind Ka Napak Ko Jawab Trailer Launch" (https://www.youtube.com/watch?v=DyoEbSUDYBc).

3. See Copeman and Duggal (2023) on the guru's MSG feature films and the DSS's wider "devotion of attractions."

4. "rIndia" from the name of the Reddit discussion forum (r/India) in which the comment was made (see http://.reddit.com%2Fr%2Findia%2Fcomments%2F6w4fsn%2Fyou_and_i_created_the_dera_sacha_sauda_read_what%2F).

5. We continue to use the present tense, despite the DSS guru's imprisonment. This is because it is far from clear that his story is over. As we write this in July 2022, the guru has been released on parole for a limited time. He was also released briefly earlier in 2022. These facts may not be unconnected to forthcoming Haryana state elections

6. *Mumbai Mirror*, October 14, 2015.

7. See, in particular, Copeman and Ikegame (2012) and Copeman, Duggal, and Longkumer (2023).

8. See Copeman (2009) on gurus and the surpassing of world records, and also Kim (2010).

9. Please see discussion in Copeman (2009).

10. From an official Dera Sacha Sauda website (http://www.derasachasauda.in/index.html), as consulted in 2008.

11. From an official Dera Sacha Sauda website (http://www.derasachasauda.org), as consulted in 2008.

12. Official DSS press release, PR Newswire, November 27, 2018.

13. *Times of India*, April 5, 2020. See Srinivas (2010) and Copeman (2009) on gurus and prophecies.

14. From an official Dera Sacha Sauda website (https://www.saintdrmsginsan.me/degree-of-doctorate/#:~:text=On%20the%20auspicious%20occasion%20of,Ram%20Rahim%20Singh%20Ji%20Insan), as consulted in April 2021. Not much public information is available concerning the World Records University. Its website (https://worldrecordsuniversity.co.uk), consulted in April 2021, described it as "an autonomous university formed by the conglomeration of Record Books around the World. Its associates include Asia Book of Records, Vietnam Book of Records, Indo-China Book of Records, India Book of Records, Nepal Book of Records, World Records Union, World Creativity Science Academy, and Indo-Vietnam Medical Board. World Records University is the only university offering an honorary Doctorate to Record Holder's / breaker's Community. The degree is awarded to those who have demonstrated an Honoris Causa, or cause to be honored. This program is offered only to a select group of highly accomplished individuals specially who have made a world or a national record."

15. Clean India Mission: Modi launched the mission on Mahatma Gandhi's birth anniversary (October 2) in 2014 to promote cleanliness and hygiene with a particular emphasis on ending open defecation.

16. The DSS guru's fourth film, *Hind ka Napak Ko Jawab: MSG Lion Heart 2*, was released in February 2017. It starred the guru as the main protagonist, Sher-e-Hind, with a plot based on the real-life Uri attack, committed in Indian-administered Jammu and Kashmir in September 2016, reportedly by armed terrorists supported by Pakistan. India retaliated with a much-debated surgical strike across the Line of Control in Pakistani-administered Kashmir. Subverting *Pakistan* (land of the pure) by naming it *Napak* (unholy or unhallowed), the film depicts India and Pakistan in binary terms of good versus evil. Fittingly, the guru's grand entry atop a tank was also an event meant for launching the film's trailer. One of the loudspeaker wonder prompts ran: "*Hind ka Napak ko Jawab dene ke liye taiyar hai Sher-e-Hind*" (Lion of India is ready to reply back to evil/unholy forces).

17. It is not only caste leaders, but also gurus, who are vital "container actors" at election time (Ikegame [2012] has shown that the categories of guru and caste leader are perfectly capable of collapsing into one). Gold (2012) refers to the Indian media's coinage of the term "Ballot babas" to describe the phenomenon, the assumption being that the recruitment by political parties of consummate "inclusive singularities" constitutes simultaneously the recruitment of those whom they contain (their followers) (see also Chatterjee [2004, 50] on the state's engagement with governed populations through their "natural leaders").

18. Though eventually prosecuted, there had seemed to be impunity, with charges of rape and murder in legal paralysis for decades.

19. Comments on the YouTube video "Saint Gurmeet Ram Rahim Singh Ji Insan—Love Charger" (https://www.youtube.com/watch?v=Q48tagwurUw).

20. Comments on the YouTube video "Guru Da Pattar, MSG Cover Melodies" (Youtube.com/watch?v=xB_LiG-yOfE).

21. Official DSS press release, PR Newswire, November 27, 2018.

22. Official DSS press release, PR Newswire, May 2, 2019.

23. See Copeman and Ikegame (2012).

24. The section heading—also on exaggeration—is a borrowing from Sloterdijk (2013).

25. That is to say, interaction and crossing over between different media forms.

26. See Copeman and Ikegame (2012).

27. See Copeman and Duggal (2023) on use of cinematic dubbing in the guru's MSG movies to reach hitherto inaccessible audiences and so further "scale up" the movement.

28. Quotation from the article "Celebration of 101st Wonder Diamond Jubilee Masto Mast Ruhani Ru-B-Ru Nights," published on an official Dera Sacha Sauda website (https://www.derasachasauda.org/celebration-of-101st-wonder-diamond-jubilee-masto-mast-ruhani-ru-b-ru-nights/), as consulted in April 2021.

29. Quotation from the article "101st Blast Kohinoor Diamond Jubilee" published on an official Dera Sacha Sauda website (https://www.sachishiksha.in/101st-blast-101st-kohinoor-diamond-jubilee/), as consulted in April 2021.

30. Quotation from the article "101st Blast Kohinoor Diamond Jubilee" published on an official Dera Sacha Sauda website (https://www.sachishiksha.in/101st-blast-101st-kohinoor-diamond-jubilee/), as consulted in April 2021.

31. See images accompanying the article "Thousands Swayed at The 101st Wonder Kohinoor Diamond Jublee Masto Mast Ruhani Rubru Night," published on an official Dera Sacha Sauda website (https://www.derasachasauda.org/thousands-swayed-at-the-101st-wonder-kohinoor-diamond-jublee-masto-mast-ruhani-rubru-night/), as consulted in April 2021.

32. Such terms for defining the uniqueness of the guru's attire are found in the DSS publication *Sachi Shiksha*, June 10, 2014.

33. An extremely popular Punjabi rapper and singer, Yo Yo Honey Singh has gained notoriety for offensive lyrics that glorify violence and misogyny.

34. See Copeman and Banerjee (2019, ch. 6).

35. The DSS guru responded by claiming that his attire was inspired not by the iconography of Guru Gobind Singh but rather by that of the Mughal tradition (see Duggal 2022).

36. See the YouTube video "sacha sauda 1" (http://www.youtube.com/watch?v=dXnLjBGf5SI).

37. Comments on the YouTube video "Saint Gurmeet Ram Rahim Singh Ji Insan—Love Charger" (https://www.youtube.com/watch?v=Q48tagwurUw).

38. Copeman (2015).

39. See Copeman and Ikegame (2012).

40. Copeman and Ikegame (2012, 307).

41. See Copeman and Ikegame (2012, 325); further, in our work on the DSS guru's feature films we discuss an unsuccessful series of visits by the DSS guru, outside of his north Indian stomping ground, to Kerala (Copeman and Duggal 2023).

42. See Copeman, Duggal, and Longkumer (2023).

43. Comments on the YouTube videos "Saint Gurmeet Ram Rahim Singh Ji Insan—Love Charger" (https://www.youtube.com/watch?v=Q48tagwurUw) and "Never Ever (Remix)—Full Video Song—MSG" (https://www.youtube.com/watch?v=lN5YXmIz2QI).

44. Comment on the YouTube video "Saint Gurmeet Ram Rahim Singh Ji Insan—Love Charger" (https://www.youtube.com/watch?v=Q48tagwurUw).

45. Quotation from the homepage of an official Dera Sacha Sauda website (https://www.saintdrmsginsan.me/), as consulted in April 2021.

46. Comments on the YouTube videos "Saint Gurmeet Ram Rahim Singh Ji Insan—Love Charger" (https://www.youtube.com/watch?v=Q48tagwurUw) and "Never Ever (Remix)—Full Video Song—MSG" (https://www.youtube.com/watch?v=lN5YXmIz2QI).

47. Web source consulted in April 2021, which no longer exists (http://www.pattern-recognition.se/blog.php).

Works Cited

Babb, Lawrence A. 1986. *Redemptive Encounters: Three Modern Styles in the Hindu Tradition.* Berkeley: University of California Press.

Beckerlegge, Gwilym. 2012. "Media Savvy or Media Averse? The Ramakrishna Math and Mission's Use of the Media in Representing Itself and a Religion Called 'Hinduism.'" In *Public Hinduisms*, edited by John Zavos, Pralay Kanungo, Deepa S. Reddy, Maya Warrier, and Raymond Brady Williams. Delhi: Sage.

Brink-Danan, Marcy. 2010. "Names That Show Time: Turkish Jews as 'Strangers' and the Semiotics of Reclassification." *American Anthropologist* 112 (3): 384–96.

Butler, Judith. 1998. "Imitation and Gender Insubordination." In *Literary Theory: An Anthology*, edited by Julie Rivkin and Michael Ryan. Oxford: Blackwell.

Chatterjee, Partha. 2004. *The Politics of the Governed: Reflections on Popular Politics in Most of the World.* New York: Columbia University Press.

Chowdhuri, Yagna Nath. 2023. "Envisioning Silence: Ramana Maharshi and the Rise of Advaitic Photography." In *Gurus and Media: Sound, Image, Machine, Text and the Digital*, edited by Jacob Copeman, Arkotong Longkumer, and Koonal Duggal. London: UCL Press.

Copeman, Jacob. 2009. *Veins of Devotion: Blood Donation and Religious Experience in North India.* New Brunswick, NJ: Rutgers University Press.

———. 2015. "Secularism's Names: Commitment to Confusion and the Pedagogy of the Name." *South Asia Multidisciplinary Academic Journal* 12. https://doi.org/10.4000/samaj.4012.

Copeman, Jacob, and Dwaipayan Banerjee. 2019. *Hematologies: The Political Life of Blood in India.* Ithaca, NY: Cornell University Press.

Copeman, Jacob, and Koonal Duggal. 2023. "The Total Guru: Film Star Guruship in the Time of Hindutva." In *Gurus and Media: Sound, Image, Machine, Text and the Digital*, edited by Jacob Copeman, Arkotong Longkumer, and Koonal Duggal. London: UCL Press.

Copeman, Jacob, Koonal Duggal, and Arkotong Longkumer. 2023. "Gurus and Media: An Introduction." In *Gurus and Media: Sound, Image, Machine, Text and the Digital*, edited by Jacob Copeman, Arkotong Longkumer and Koonal Duggal. London: UCL Press.

Copeman, Jacob, and Aya Ikegame. 2012. "Guru Logics." *HAU: Journal of Ethnographic Theory* 2 (1): 289–336.

Corsín Jiménez, Alberto. 2013. *An Anthropological Trompe L'Oeil for a Common World: An Essay on the Economy of Knowledge.* Oxford: Berghahn Books.

———. 2018. "Spider Web Anthropologies: Ecologies, Infrastructures, Entanglements." In *A World of Many Worlds*, edited by Marisol de la Cadena and Mario Blaser, 53–82. Durham, NC: Duke University Press.

Corsín Jiménez, Alberto, and Chloe Nahum-Claudel. 2019. "The anthropology of Traps: Concrete Technologies and Theoretical Interfaces." *Journal of Material Culture* 24 (4): 1–18.

Das, Veena. 2015. "Naming beyond Pointing: Singularity, Relatedness and the Foreshadowing of Death." *South Asia Multidisciplinary Academic Journal* 12. https://doi.org/10.4000/samaj.4005.

Dinkar, Niharika. 2021. "*Tirchhi Nazar*: The Gaze in South Asia beyond *Darshan*." *South Asian Studies* 37 (2): 77–88

Duggal, Koonal. 2015. "Crossing Religious Boundaries: Representation, Caste, and Identity in Contemporary Punjab." PhD diss., English and Foreign Languages University, Hyderabad.

Duggal, Koonal. 2022. "The 'Vexed' Status of Guru Images: Visuality, Circulation and Iconographic Conflict." *South Asian Popular Culture* 20 (1): 97–117.

Gebauer, Gunter, and Christoph Wulf. 1996. *Mimesis: Culture, Art, Society*, translated by Don Reneau. Berkeley: University of California Press.

Gold, Daniel. 1987. *The Lord as Guru: Hindi Sants in the North Indian Tradition*. Oxford: Oxford University Press.

———. 2012. "Continuities as Gurus Change." In *The Guru in South Asia*, edited by Jacob Copeman and Aya Ikegame, 241–54. London: Routledge.

Graeber, David. 2008. Discussant comments at "Economies of Fortune" conference, University of Cambridge.

Gunning, Tom. 1990. "The Cinema of Attractions: Early Film, Its Spectator and the Avant-Garde." In *Early Cinema: Space, Frame, Narrative*, edited by Thomas Elsaesser, 56–62. London: British Film Institute.

———.1993. " 'Now You See It, Now You Don't': The Temporality of the Cinema of Attractions." *Velvet Light Trap* 32 (Fall): 71–84.

Ikegame, Aya. 2012. "The Governing Guru: Hindu *Mathas* in Liberalising India." In *The Guru in South Asia*, edited by Jacob Copeman and Aya Ikegame, 46–63. London: Routledge.

Ingold, T. 2011. *Being Alive: Essays on Movement, Knowledge and Description*. Abingdon, UK: Routledge.

Jain, Kajri. 2002. "More Than Meets the Eye: The Circulation of Images and the Embodiment of Value." *Contributions to Indian Sociology* 36 (1–2): 33–70.

Kellner, D. 1995. *Media Culture: Cultural Studies, Identity and Politics between the Modern and the Post-modern*. London: Routledge.

Kim, Hanna. 2010. "Public Engagement and Personal Desires: BAPS Swaminarayan Temples and Their Contribution to the Discourses on Religion." *International Journal of Hindu Studies* 13 (3): 357–90.

Lessig, L. 2008. *Remix: Making Art and Commerce Thrive in the Hybrid Economy*. New York: Penguin.

Lévi-Strauss, Claude. 1966. *The Savage Mind*. Oxford: Oxford University Press.

Lucia, Amanda. 2014. *Reflections of Amma: Devotees in a Global Embrace.* Berkeley: University of California Press.

———. 2018. "Guru Sex: Charisma, Proxemic Desire, and the Haptic Logics of the Guru-Disciple Relationship." *Journal of the American Academy of Religion* 86 (4): 953–88.

———. 2021. "The Global Manifestation of the Hindu Guru Phenomenon." In *The Routledge Handbook of South Asian Religions*, edited by Knut Axel Jacobsen, 413–27. Abingdon, UK: Routledge.

———. 2022. "The Contemporary Guru Field." *Religion Compass* 16 (2): 1–15.

———. 2023. "Flooding the Web: Absence-Presence and the Media Strategies of Nithyananda's Digital Empire." In *Gurus and Media: Sound, Image, Machine, Text and the Digital*, edited by Jacob Copeman, Arkotong Longkumer, and Koonal Duggal. London: UCL Press.

Mazzarella, William. 2010. "The Myth of the Multitude, or, Who's Afraid of the Crowd?" *Critical Inquiry* 36 (4): 697–727.

McCartney, Patrick. 2018. "Downward Facing Dogs, Core Indian Values and Institutionalised Rape of Children." *Sociology International Journal* 2 (6): 748–52.

Meyer, Birgit, and Annelise Moors. 2006. Introduction to *Religion, media, and the public sphere*, edited by Birgit Meyer and Annelise Moors, eds. Bloomington: Indiana University Press.

Michelutti, Lucia, Ashraf Hoque,, Nicolas Martin,, David Picherit, D., Paul Rollier, P., Arild E. Ruud, A. E., and Clarinda Still, C. 2018. *Mafia Raj: The Rule of Bosses in South Asia.* Stanford, CA: Stanford University Press.

Nandy, Ashis. 2015. "There's a Reason Indians Love Radhe Maa. And It's Not Superstition." *Catchnews*, August 13. http://www.catchnews.com/india-news/there-s-a-reason-indians-love-radhe-maa-and-it-s-not-superstition-1439445272.html.

Pinney, Christopher. 2011. *Photography and Anthropology.* London: Reaktion.

———. 2019. "Digital Cows: Flesh and Code." In *Photo-Objects: On the Materiality of Photographs and Photo Archives*, edited by Julia Bärnighausen, Costanza Caraffa, Stefanie Klamm, Franka Schneider, and Petra Wodtke, 199–210. Max Planck Research Library for the History and Development of Knowledge. http://mprl-series.mpg.de/studies/12/.

Prasad, Madhava M. 2014. "The Struggle to Represent and Sartorial Modernity: On a Visual Dimension of Indian Nationalist Politics." *Inter-Asia Cultural Studies* 15 (4): 572–88.

Roy, Piyush. 2017. "The Barred Baba of Bling." *Orissa Post*, September 3–9.

Rubenstein, Daniel, and Katrina Sluis. 2013. "The Digital Image in Photographic Culture: Algorithmic Photography and the Crisis of Representation." In *The Photographic Image in Digital Culture*, edited by Martin Lister, 22–40. Abingdon, UK: Routledge.

Rubenstein, M. J. 2008. *Strange Wonder: The Closure of Metaphysics and the Opening of Awe*. New York: Columbia University Press.

Shakar, Alex. 2002. *The Savage Girl*. New York: Perennial.

Shaviro, Steven. 2006. "Prophecies of the Present." *Socialism and Democracy* 20 (3): 5–24.

Singh, Santosh K. 2017. "Deras as 'Little Fiefdoms:' Understanding the Dera Sacha Sauda Phenomenon." *Economic and Political Weekly* 52 (37): 20–23.

Sloterdijk, Peter. 2013. *You Must Change Your Life*. Cambridge, UK: Polity.

———. 2017. *Not Saved: Essays after Heidegger*. Cambridge, UK: Polity.

Sood, Jyotika. 2019. "With Gurmeet Ram Rahim in Jail, Dera Followers Are Unsure of Which Party to Support." *Outlook*, March 29. https://www.outlookindia.com/magazine/story/india-news-bling-babas-offline-army/301369.

Srinivas, Tulasi. 2010. *Winged Faith: Rethinking Globalization and Religious Pluralism through the Sathya Sai Movement*. New York: Columbia University Press.

———. 2018. *The Cow in the Elevator: An Anthropology of Wonder*. Durham, NC: Duke University Press.

Srivastava, Sanjay. 2009. "Urban Spaces, Disney-Divinity and Moral Middle Classes in Delhi." *Economic and Political Weekly* 44 (26–27): 338–45.

Taminiaux, Pierre. 2009. *The Paradox of Photography*. Amsterdam: Rodopi.

Thrift, Nigel. 2008. *Non-representational Theory: Space, Politics, Affect*. London: Routledge.

———. 2012. "The Insubstantial Pageant: Producing an Untoward Land." *Cultural Geographies* 19 (2): 141–68.

Vanita, Ruth. 2002. "*Dosti* and *Tamanna*: Male-Male Love, Difference, and Normativity in Hindi Cinema." In *Everyday Life in South Asia*, edited by Diane Mines and Sarah Lamb, 146–58. Bloomington: Indiana University Press.

Warrier, Maya. 2003. "Processes of Secularization in Contemporary India: Guru Faith in the Mata Amritanandamayi Mission." *Modern Asian Studies* 37 (1): 213–53.

Conclusion

The Worlds of Wonder

TULASI SRINIVAS

Hannah Arendt reminds us, "What begins in wonder ends in perplexity and thence leads back to wonder" (Arendt 1978, 165–66). And if wonder was our beginning, it returns to us at the end, turning us back, ever more mysteriously, yet inevitably, to curiosity. But rather than seeking closure, we have boldly followed wonder as it led to further interrogation.

The ethnographies within this volume demonstrate that whereas curiosity entails an effort to understand events or objects in their component parts, wonder is the experience of contemplating how the various parts relate to a greater whole (Fuller 2006, 8–9).

Wonder in this whole sense that is felt and provoked by Tamil marulaadis, invested in graveyard ritual of the Thirunankai, in the shrine of healing goddess in Rajasthan, or the Sufi shrines and performances, offers the unknown and ineffable that is at the center of our quest. Such wonder, as the contributors have demonstrated, inheres in sites as varied as Kuchipudi dance guising, in Dera Sacha Sauda and Swaminarayan satsang gatherings, and in fantasy literature and weird tales, and unsettles our established thinking about practices and meanings. The ethnographies and ethnohistories of wonder in South Asia in the previous pages have unlocked how various groups have provoked, engaged, and understood wonder. They also indicate that wonder as a quest in never wholly fulfilled, its curiosities mounting with every provocation.

Let me add that while it may appear that the various chapters deal with sites and topics that are quite disparate, all of them have in common the curiosity about the subject, the pursuit of wonder, and the creative engagement with it. We didn't set out to do this programmatically. Rather, as we looked back at what we had said and argued, we were struck by what these works had in common; their approach to the subject of wonder tends to be allusive, interpretive, and metonymic, moving from idea to idea, from text to text, or site to site, from question to meaning in creative itinerations. Indeed, then what our contributions sediment around is that the questions of meaning with regard to wonder are not problem questions that are usually raised, but questions of mystery.

This profound ungraspable nature of wonder has proved very productive for us. Our objective was never to resolve wonder and provide a singular encompassing answer as to what it *is*, but to hint at the many open-ended facets of wonder, to think about what it *does* in the world. Our ambition was to demonstrate that when we take wonder seriously, both as a force for our interlocutors and as a theoretical apparatus, our studies of various phenomena are enriched, bringing new horizons into view. If we understand wonder to be "good to think with," it gives wonder certain power beyond itself and its provocation to explore the histories, politics, aesthetics, and ethics of our world.

The cultural anthropological questions that this book drew inspiration from and lead back to are: Are certain forms of wonder specific to certain cultures? Are certain people more primed to be sensitive to wonder than others? And this in turn leads to the other quintessential question in cultural anthropology: Is there something universal or particular about how we experience and evoke wonder? Is our current age dominated by specific kind of wonder? Or a lack of it?

Indeed, throughout this book the attempt has been to offer an invitation to think about wonder in toto as an analytical tool and theoretical invitation, as broadly, comparatively, and robustly as possible. But the authors also hoped that through these South Asian examples, these non-Western illustrations, they could offer a way to decolonize our thinking on wonder itself, drawing it outwards from Western philosophy to illuminate other corners of the world.

So the ethnographies and ethnohistories in this volume coalesce around the an Other sense of wonder that lies in, as Pieper argues, "making it possible, and indeed necessary, to strike yet deeper roots" (1963,

102). And, indeed, this call for "deeper roots" is what this volume is responsive to. The contributors see South Asian culture and society in its multiplicities as offering a possibility to consider these deeper roots. Through their contributions, spanning disciplines, cultures, sites, time periods, geographies, and areas of interest, we can understand wonder as serving an intellectual and speculative function, part of a structure of thought, imagination and affect.

The inexplicability of wonder that the previous pages draw out cast seemingly durable and unquestionable theories about the way things are and should be into radical doubt. Doubt is useful to pry open the joints of what we do and how we assign meaning to these practices and ontologie. The chapters in this volume argue that that doubt should be considered a positive value, not simply a state that must be rectified with clear answers. That doubt is more important than certainty in the realm of understanding that which is unseen. If we consider some alternatives to "I know" we come to "I wonder," and then uncertainty becomes a space of possibility and inquiry rather than a mistaken refusal to accept a definite answer.

Wonder enables the focus on this flux, this indefiniteness, this rupture, offering the possibility of creating a new understanding of certain experiences, charging them with ontological significance, because they "transform our knowledge of what is by awakening us to realities of which we would otherwise be oblivious" (Miller 1992, xii). Wonder reveals the extraordinary in and through the ordinary, and is therefore crucial to the task of reimagining political, religious, and ethical terrain. And the contributions in the previous pages when read together, tell us as much about ourselves and our need for wonder as a positive force to break the tedium of life, as they do about wonder itself.

What we have learned through these ethnographies of wonder in South Asia is that part of the phenomenology of wonder is that wonder reveals something, but only partially. That larger whole, similar to the many worlds that South Asia itself reveals, is a multiverse of possibility. Pieper says that "wonder signifies that the world is profounder, more all-embracing and mysterious than the logic of everyday reason had taught us to believe" (Pieper 1963, 102). Wonder thus points to the transcendent, the more than human, the cosmic, the frightening and the awe inspiring.

In this way, wonder allows us the larger perspective; to see our own lives and their entanglements in this world more clearly. The ethnohistories and ethnographies in this volume demonstrate how entangled we are and how much we wait for wonder to break us free, to "surprise our souls" (Dalston and Park 1998, 6). Entanglements and relationalities form the ground of our lives. Assembling ethnographies of wonder enables us to imagine a different set of answers, answers that emerge from the pursuit of life and its meaning in the everyday.

As wonder breaks the ground of the everyday, as it causes an ontological disruption, it enables us to appreciate the entanglements we find ourselves in, to afford them some compassion, and to also hope to somehow break free of them. This collective hope, what I termed "radical social hope," is writ large through this volume in ways large and small (Srinivas 2018).

And through this volume what we hope the reader will take away is that wonder, particularly in its inhabitation in South Asia, enables a creativity both spatially and temporally, to negotiate our relationship to our past and futures through acts of imagination. It allows for us to imagine a different horizon, a future anterior. What this volume undeniably demonstrates is through wonder we recognize that not only is another world possible—it exists.

Works Cited

Arendt, Hannah. 1978. *The Life of the Mind*. San Diego: Harcourt.
Dalston, Lorraine, and Katharine Park. 1998. *Wonder and the Order of Nature, 1150–1750*. New York: Zone Books.
Fuller, Robert C. 2006. *Wonder: From Emotion to Spirituality*. Chapel Hill: University of North Carolina Press.
Miller, Jerome A. 1992. *In the Throe of Wonder: Intimations of the Sacred in a Post-modern World*. Albany: State University of New York Press.
Pieper, Josef. 1963. *Leisure: The Basis of Culture*. New York: Random House.
Srinivas, Tulasi. 2018. *The Cow in the Elevator: An Anthropology of Wonder*. Durham, NC: Duke University Press.

Contributors

Amy L. Allocco is Professor of Religious Studies at Elon University, where she is also the founding director of the Multifaith Scholars program. Allocco is an ethnographer of South Asian religions whose research focuses on vernacular Hinduism, especially contemporary Hindu ritual traditions and women's religious practices in the South Indian state of Tamil Nadu, where she has been studying and conducting fieldwork for more than 20 years. Allocco's publications to date have concentrated primarily on South India's snake goddess traditions and the repertoire of ritual therapies performed to mitigate *nāga dōṣam*, a malignant horoscopic condition that causes delayed marriage and infertility. In 2018 SUNY Press published her co-edited volume, titled *Ritual Innovation: Strategic Interventions in South Asian Religion* (with Brian K. Pennington). Allocco's book project, *Living with the Dead in Hindu South India*, delineates the repertoire of ritual relationships that Hindus maintain with their dead kin and analyzes the ceremonies to honor deceased relatives called *pūvāṭaikkāri* ("the woman wearing flowers"). Her work is animated by interests in the forms of religious change inspired by the new social and economic realities that characterize a globalizing South Asia, as well as narrative, everyday religion, and gender in urban India.

Quinn A. Clark is a Lecturer in the Religion Department at Columbia University and the MA Director at Columbia's South Asia Institute. Quinn received his PhD from Columbia's Religion Department where completed a historical ethnography of religious Muslim life in north India, the research for which he completed as a Fulbright Fellow (2018–2019) in Lucknow. He has received various Foreign Language and Area Studies (FLAS) fellowships and grants from the American Institute for Indian Studies for the study of Hindi and Urdu. He lives, works, and teaches in New York City where he is completing a book project on sacred real estate, the shrines of Muslim saints, and the religio-political Muslim life in neoliberal north India.

Jacob Copeman is Research Professor (Investigador Distinguido Oportunius—GAIN) at the University of Santiago de Compostela, and Senior Researcher (CISPAC). He is coauthor of *Hematologies: The Political Life of Blood in India* (Cornell University Press, 2019) and author of *Veins of Devotion: Blood Donation and Religious Experience in North India* (Rutgers UP, 2009). Amongst his coedited volumes are *Gurus and Media: Sound Image, Machine, Text and the Digital* (UCL Press, 2023), *An Anthropology of Intellectual Exchange: Interactions, Transactions and Ethics in Asia and Beyond* (Berghahn, 2023), *Global Sceptical Publics: From Non-religious Print Media to "Digital Atheism"* (UCL Press, 2022) and *The Guru in South Asia: New Interdisciplinary Perspectives* (Routledge, 2012). He is currently Principal Investigator of the ERC project "Religion and Its Others in South Asia and the World: Communities, Debates, Freedoms."

Koonal Duggal is Research Fellow in Social Anthropology at the University of Edinburgh. He is currently working on a research project, funded by the Leverhulme Trust, titled "Gurus, Anti-gurus and Media in North India." He completed his MA in Art History and Aesthetics at the Maharaja Sayajirao University of Baroda and has a PhD in cultural studies from the English and Foreign Languages University, Hyderabad. He is coeditor of *Gurus and Media: Sound, Image, Machine, Text and the Digital* (UCL Press, 2023), author of the article "The 'Vexed' Status of Guru Images: Visuality, Circulation and Iconographic Conflicts" (2022), coauthor of "Gurus and Media: An Introduction" (2023), and "The Total Guru: Film Star Guruship in the Time of Hindutva" (2023).

William Elison is an Associate Professor in the Department of Religious Studies at the University of California, Santa Barbara. He specializes in the study of religion in South Asia—specifically, modern India—from an ethnographic perspective. His research purview includes cities, especially Mumbai; Indian visual culture, especially Hindi popular cinema ("Bollywood"); Adivasi (ST or "tribal") communities; and questions of subalternity. Recently he has been drawn to the methodological and creative possibilities of ethnographic fiction. He is the author of *The Neighborhood of Gods: The Sacred and the Visible at the Margins of Mum-*

bai (Chicago, 2018), and a coauthor (with Christian Lee Novetzke and Andy Rotman) of *"Amar Akbar Anthony": Bollywood, Brotherhood, and the Nation* (Harvard, 2016).

Ann Gold is the Thomas J. Watson Professor Emeritus of Religious Studies and Professor of Anthropology at Syracuse University. She is a scholar of the religious mores of Rajasthan. Her more than 20 books and award winning essays mark her as the premier scholar in the field of local religion and pilgrimage.

Jazmin Graves Eyssallene is Assistant Professor of African American and African Diaspora Studies at the University of North Carolina at Greensboro. She completed her doctoral research in the Department of South Asian Languages and Civilizations at the University of Chicago. Her dissertation, "Songs to the African Saints of India," centers on the Sidi (African Indian) Sufi devotional tradition of Gujarat and Mumbai. Jazmin's work has been published in the *Journal of Africana Religions*. She has also co-edited a three-volume series, *Afro-South Asia in the Global African Diaspora*. In 2018, Jazmin was named one of the MIPAD Global Top 100 Most Influential People of African Descent Under 40.

Mary Hancock is Professor Emerita in the Departments of Anthropology and History at University of California, Santa Barbara. She is an anthropologist of South Asia, with particular interests in urban south India. Her research specialties include spatial studies, cultural memory, gender, and religion. She is the author of *Womanhood in the Making: Domestic Ritual and Public Culture in Urban South India* (Westview, 1999) and *The Politics of Heritage from Madras to Chennai* (Indiana, 2008), as well as numerous chapters and articles, published in journals that include *American Ethnologist, Modern South Asia, Environment and Planning D: Society and Space, Material Religion, Journal of the American Academy of Religion,* and the *International Journal of Urban and Regional Studies*.

Harshita Mruthinti Kamath is Visweswara Rao and Sita Koppaka Associate Professor in Telugu Culture, Literature and History at Emory University. Her research focuses on the textual and performance traditions of Telugu-speaking South India in conversation with theoretical discourses on gender and sexuality in South Asia. Kamath's monograph, *Impersonations: The Artifice of Brahmin Masculinity in South Indian Dance*

(University of California Press, 2019) analyzes gender impersonation in the Telugu dance style of Kuchipudi. She has also co-translated the sixteenth-century classical Telugu text *Parijatapaharanamu (Theft of a Tree)* with Velcheru Narayana Rao, which was published as part of the Murty Classical Library of India (Harvard University Press, 2022). With Pamela Lothspeich, she published an edited volume, *Mimetic Desires: Impersonation and Guising Across South Asia* (University of Hawai'i Press, 2022).

Hanna H. Kim is Professor and Chair of Anthropology at Adelphi University. Her research interests include the anthropology of religion, religious subjectivities, and definitions of the good life. Her long-term fieldwork on the BAPS Swaminarayan Sanstha is the basis for the book, The Globalisation of a Modern Hindu Community: Ethnographic Chronicles on the BAPS Swaminarayan Sanstha (Routledge, forthcoming).

Amanda Lucia is Professor of Religious Studies at University of California-Riverside. Her current research focuses on sexual abuse in guru-led religious communities, with emphasis on guru celebrity and media discourses on scandal. She is also crafting a body of research focused on the Kumbh Melā, the largest religious gathering in the world. Her forthcoming book, *White Utopias: The Religious Exoticism of Transformational Festivals*, uses in-depth ethnography to investigate the intersections of whiteness and religious exoticism among "spiritual, but not religious" (SBNR) communities in transformational festivals, such as Bhakti Fest, Wanderlust, Lightning in a Bottle, and Burning Man. Her first book, *Reflections of Amma: Devotees in a Global Embrace* (2014) focused on transnationalism and gender in a global guru movement. Broadly, her research engages modern, global Hinduism by focusing on religious migrations, movements, and adaptations in the dialogical exchange between North America and India. She holds a BA in Religion and India Studies from Indiana University and an MA and PhD in the History of Religions from The University of Chicago. Her articles have been published top ranking journals, including the *Journal of the American Academy of Religions, History of Religions*, the *International Journal of Hindu Studies*, and *CrossCurrents*.

Tulasi Srinivas is Professor of Anthropology, Religion and Transnational Studies at the Marlboro Institute of Interdisciplinary Studies at Emerson College, and a Visiting Professor at the Women's Studies in Religion program at the Harvard Divinity School. Srinivas' research has been supported by prestigious fellowships at the Kate Hamburger Kolleg, Germany, the Radcliffe Institute of Advanced Study, Harvard University and the Luce-ACLS, and by the NEH and the Templeton Foundations. She has written and edited three award winning monographs: *Winged Faith: Rethinking Globalization and Religion Through the Sathya Sai Movement* (Columbia 2010), *Curried Culture: Globalization, Food, South Asia* (University of California Press and OUP India 2012) and *The Cow the Elevator: An Anthropology of Wonder* (Duke University Press and OUP India 2018) and dozens of scholarly articles. She is a fellow of the Royal Asiatic Society and her work has been featured on The Conversation, CNN, NPR, The Hindustan Times, The Times of India, The Revealer, The Harvard Divinity Bulletin, National Public Radio, and The Boston Globe.

Aniruddhan Vasudevan is a Cotsen Postdoctoral Fellow in the Princeton Society of Fellows and Lecturer in the Humanities Council & Anthropology at Princeton University. His current book project is an ethnography of thirunangai devotion to goddess Angalamman and the ethical life that revolves around this embodied attachment to the goddess.

Index

AARSH, 267n12
ABAP (Akhil Bharatiya Akhāra Parishad), 212–13
ABC, 98n3, 98n4, 98n5, 98n6, 98n7, 98n8, 98n9, 99n18, 99n24, 99n27, 99n28, 99n31, 99n32, 100
ABCFM (American Board of Commissioners for Foreign Mission), 82–84, 98n3, 98n4, 98n5, 98n6, 98n7, 98n8, 98n9, 98n15, 99n18, 99n24, 99n27, 99n28, 99n31, 100
Abhinayadarpana, 136, 142n12
ability, spiritual, 113–14
Abingdon, 303–4
ABP News, 213, 217
Abrahamic traditions, 23
abundance, 14, 175, 223–43
    infinite, 15, 226, 234, 240
accusations, 217n10, 273, 297
acts, 78, 86, 90–91, 231, 238, 240, 258, 265, 273, 286, 295
adavu, 128, 137
adbhuta, 7, 134, 139
adbhutarasa, 184, 194
addictions, 257, 260
Adivasi, 312
administration, 31, 49, 209, 211, 215, 239
    colonial, 61

admission, 256, 260, 267n10
adorn, 173, 218
adventurers, 71
aesthetics, 9, 12–13, 134, 137–39, 142n11, 143, 284–85, 287, 291–92, 308, 312
    brahminical, 138
    feminine, 140
    gendered, 140
    mobile, 254
    traditional, 142n17
Affirmation, 165
afflictions, 33, 181
Africa, 61, 115–16, 284
African ancestry, 12, 105
Africana Religions, 121, 313
African conceptual frameworks, 106
African Diaspora, 119n1, 120–21
African Elites, 121
African Heritage, 116, 120
African ideological frameworks, 12
African Indians, 120–21, 312
African Rifai Sufi, 12, 105
African Sufi Ancestor-Saints, 121
Afro-South Asia, 121, 313
Agamas, 92
age, 4, 73, 77, 100, 110, 128, 194, 212, 308
agency, 22, 93, 226, 263
Aggarwal, 256–62, 264

317

aghora rupam, 181, 187
Aghorıs, 195
ahi snān, 197, 211, 216
Ahmed, 82, 100, 126, 131–32,
    139–40, 141n9, 142n16, 142,
    186, 193
Ahmedabad, 109, 113, 119n12, 121,
    248, 262, 265, 266n1
air, 33–34, 72, 167, 177, 181, 208,
    211, 238
Ajmer, 11, 23
Akhār, Juna, 202, 216n8
Akhil Bharatiya Akhār, 212
Akshar, 255 Akshardham
    mahamandir, 254–55
Akshardham temple complexes, 253,
    262
Akshar guru, 248–49
Alam-e-ghaib, 237
alankaram, 173, 190n10
alcohol, 49, 263, 276
Alf Hiltebeitel, 191n13, 195
Algernon, 66–67, 69–70
Allah, 107
Allahabad, 197, 199–200, 218–19
All-India Dance Seminar, 135
altars, 52, 224
alterity, 5–6, 97, 195
Altman, 45, 62, 77, 79–80, 100
amavasai, 170
amazement, 1, 4, 6, 8, 24, 208
Ambedkar, 132
ambivalence, 195, 240, 259
American Institute, 163, 188, 312,
    315
American Oriental Society (AOS),
    90–92, 99n25, 99n29, 99n30,
    101
American Protestants, 80–81, 95
Amirthalingam, 192n17, 193
Amma, 107, 160, 304, 314
Amman, 148, 155, 158, 171

Ananda Kentish Coomaraswamy,
    142n12
ancestor-saints, 105–6, 116, 118
Anderson, Rufus, 98n4, 98n8, 98n9
Andhra Pradesh Sangeeta Nataka
    Akademi (APSNA), 135–36
Andover Theological Seminary, 83
Angalamman cults, 151, 191n13
Angalamman worship, 147, 151–52,
    154–55, 157
Angalaparameshwari, xi, 167,
    169–72, 179, 181–82, 186–88,
    191n12, 192n14
  the pride of, 182
Angalaparameshwari temple, 168,
    175, 188–90, 189n3, 190n10,
    192n15
Angali, 177, 181, 189n1
anthropology, 6, 9, 17, 21, 166,
    195, 228, 243, 265–66, 303–4,
    312–14
  cultural, 8, 308
anthropology of money, 228
anthropology of religion, 227, 241, 313
anthropology of wonder, 7, 96, 144,
    146, 166, 243, 248, 251, 263–65,
    269, 305, 310, 314
Anti-caste, 166
anti-elite, 224, 226
antiquity, 92, 142n11, 199
anxieties, 88, 234, 251, 259, 262
aporetic vertigo, 15, 274
aporia, 3, 69
appeal, 87, 107, 135, 138–39, 149,
    226, 296
ārati, 206, 211
archive, visual, 50
Ardhanarishvara
  character of, 126, 129–30, 134
  performing, 132
  portray, 130
  role of, 125, 127

Ardh Kumbh Mela, 199, 210–11, 216n2, 220
Arendt, Hannah, 307
Armstrong, 99n18, 99n19, 99n20
artifacts, 58, 79, 82, 84–86, 88, 90–91, 98n4
Art of Living Foundation, 203, 206
Arumugam, 42n1, 42, 188n1, 193
asamyutahastamudra, 136
Asaram Bapu, 203
ascetics, 197, 199, 201, 208
  yogic, 201
ash figure, xi–xii, 174–75, 182–83, 187, 190n10
ashram, 281, 293
aspirations, 285–86
  juridical, 163n1
  middle-class, 254
assemblage, 23, 62, 68, 246, 249, 258, 263
associations, 46, 55, 116, 182, 225, 266, 273, 278, 288–89, 292, 294
astonishment, 2, 4–6, 8, 13, 16, 141, 145–48, 150, 154, 157, 159, 162–63
āstra, 135
atma, 249, 265
attachments, 149–51, 156, 163, 212, 248, 268, 315
  collective, 164n7
attractions, 38, 249, 281–83, 286, 295
attributes, 5, 50, 95, 187, 257, 278
  racialized, 81
  religious, 81
attunements, 112–13, 186, 208, 224
audiences, 124–25, 138, 140, 163n2, 168, 200, 206, 209, 266, 271, 292
auliya, 225–26, 230–32, 234, 237–38, 242n12
Austin, 144, 166, 195, 243, 315

authorities, 51, 53, 67, 136, 203
  legal, 278
  religious, 206, 226
  scholarly, 68
Ayodhya, 74, 212–13, 219

babas, 218, 273, 289
Babri Masjid, 212
Bakhtin, 234, 243
Bala Baldev, xii, 204
Balak Lokeshwara, 204
Balatripurasundari, 127, 141n3
Banas Basin, 23, 36
Bangalore, 1, 150, 203, 228, 275
BAPS, 248, 250, 252–55, 257–62, 264–66, 266n1, 266n3, 267n3, 267n4, 267n7, 268
BAPS discourses, 248, 250, 258
BAPS Swaminarayan, 267n3
Barbara Fields, 80, 101
barbarian, 11, 70–71, 73–74
barkat, 105
Baroda, 113, 119n18
Basu, 106–7, 111, 116, 119n1, 120
Bava Gor, 108, 112, 115
  medium of, 109–10, 112
bay, 66, 185, 229, 237
Bean, 62, 77, 80, 100
Beast, 48–49, 51–53, 56, 60, 67, 78
Beckerlegge, 293, 302
Beheroze Shroff, 106, 119n6
bekar, 230
Bellamy, 108–10, 119n9, 120
Bellamy's analysis, 109, 111
Benazzo, 217n11, 218
Bengal, 66, 83, 143
Bennett, 260–61, 263, 268n15, 268
Berkeley, 16, 42, 101, 120–21, 166, 194, 302–4
Bhagavad Gita, 2, 8, 16, 79, 101
Bhagwan Swaminarayan, 248, 250, 254–55, 257, 259, 267n12

bhakti, 8, 192n19, 248, 275, 291, 295
Bhakti Yoga, 268
Bharata, 134, 137
Bharatanatyam, 135, 138, 142n11, 142n15, 143–44
Bhatt, 267n13, 268
bhayankar, 42n2
Bhojuram Gujar, 21, 23, 27, 41, 43
Biblical, 49, 91
birth, 71, 249, 276, 290, 294
Blast Kohinoor Diamond Jubilee, 300n29, 301n30
blessings, xi, 14, 29, 106–7, 109, 115, 118, 202, 206, 236, 238
blood, 65–66, 72–73, 144, 167, 173, 177, 180, 185, 278, 302
bodies, 31, 34, 62, 72–73, 106, 108, 110–13, 124–26, 130–34, 137–40, 143–44, 167, 225–26
Body and Practice, 144
Bollywood, 296, 312
bommai, xi, 173–74, 176, 185
bones, 173–74, 183, 187
boundaries, 23, 38, 120, 135, 168, 183–85, 188, 225, 227, 229, 236–37
Brahma, 54, 143, 181, 190n8
Brahmbhatt, 249, 268
brahmin, 13, 128, 137–40
Brahminicide, 171, 188n1
Brink-Danan, 290, 302
Britain, 80, 102, 112
British Raj, 52, 54, 232
Brosius, 254, 268
brothers, 32, 39, 68, 127, 166
Butler, Judith, 131

Cailapati, 192n15, 193
Calcutta, 86, 143
camp, 36, 197, 202, 205, 207, 212, 217n12

Cantiracekar, 192n16, 193
capacity, 81, 84, 148, 150, 154, 158, 161, 169, 186–88, 259–60, 263
care, xiv, 15, 146–47, 152–53, 156–57, 215, 232–33, 263, 291, 314
career, 128, 130, 141n3
carnivalesque, 170, 208
Cartesian dualism, 10, 93
cash, 14, 223, 228, 238, 240
  deposit, 238
cash donations, 239
castes, 101–2, 128, 130, 132, 142n15, 143, 145, 169, 173, 236, 276, 280, 312
Caste Society, 194
categories, 14, 81, 83, 93, 158, 168, 183–84, 248, 292–93, 300n17
  ahistorical, 227
  analytical, 200
Catholic Orientalism, 102
Catlin-Jairazbhoy, 114–15, 117, 119n1, 119n3, 120n22, 120n23, 120n24, 120
celebrations, 15, 36, 108, 151, 267n9, 284, 300n28
cemetery, 174, 183, 185, 192n20
Ceylon, 80, 83, 92
character, 51, 53, 76n3, 128–30, 134, 229
charisma, 105, 109, 117–18, 275, 280, 297, 304
chatter, 127, 160
Chatterjee, 300n17, 302
Chaugnar, 65–68, 70, 73
Chavali Balatripurasundari, 141n2, 141n3
Chennai, 13, 126–28, 136–38, 163, 163n2, 166, 168, 189n2, 191n14, 192n14, 192n15, 192n20, 195, 313, 315
  north, 146–47, 152–53, 192n15

Chidanand Saraswati, 203–4, 206
chimera, 69, 216
China, 65, 77
Chinna Satyam, 125–28, 133,
    136–38, 141n4, 143
choreography, 127, 129, 133, 139
Chowdhuri, 293–94, 302
Christian conversion, 81, 95
Christian Imperialism, 80, 100
Christianity, 88, 95, 165n14, 194
Christian practices, 85, 90
Christians, 12, 80, 84–88, 90, 97,
    212, 233, 284
Christian Thought, 102
Christoph Wulf, 303
Chronotope, 243
Cinnamalaiyanūril Mārc, 193
circulation, 121, 146, 239, 261, 273,
    286, 303
city, 1, 13, 16, 58, 61, 71, 74, 150,
    210, 214, 231–32
    bustling temporary, 205
    largest, 210
    old, 230
Clark-Decès, 191n11, 193
class, middle, 149, 203, 205
cobra, 27, 29, 41, 42n8
codes, moral, 260, 264
coins, 67, 149, 167
    hard, 14–15
collection, 49, 82, 84–85, 91–92,
    95–96, 125, 127, 200
colleges, 87–88, 91, 256
colonial era, 200
colonialism, 54, 60, 165n14
    global, 61
commensurability, 93, 163n2
commercial economy, 225–27, 229,
    233–35, 237, 240–41
commitment, 21, 23, 146–49, 151,
    154, 157, 162–63, 252, 302
commodification, 201, 216

commodities, 288, 296–97
communalism, 224, 226
communication, 11, 40–42, 42n14,
    106, 108, 112, 115, 118, 119n12,
    119n17, 119n18
    verbal, 112, 114
communion, 171, 175
community, 13, 88, 90, 146, 148,
    150–52, 154, 158, 161, 164n6,
    256, 259, 275–76, 312, 314
    caste-based, 151
    marginalized, 163n1
    moral, 158
    religious, 224
    trans, 159
Conan, 11, 47, 70–75
concepts, 16, 22, 109, 112, 120,
    131–32, 134, 227, 241n3, 242n9,
    242n10
concerts, 99n23, 281, 283
Congregationalism, 88
Congress, 278
Conroy-Krutz, 80–81, 100
consciousness, 54, 232
consecration, 92, 112
Conservation, 193
construction, 51, 170, 200, 253, 258,
    267n7
contact, 126, 132–33, 138, 140,
    142n9, 180, 240, 280
Contemporary South India, 166, 193
content, 46–47, 52, 71, 75, 89
context, 12, 14, 105, 107, 118–19,
    119n5, 120n25, 132, 138–39,
    148–49, 187–88, 189n5, 190n8,
    191n13, 192n20
    social, 229
contradictions, dialectical, 297
contributions, 46, 144, 148, 303, 309
contributors, xiii, 5–6, 307, 309,
    311–15
control, 22, 110, 185, 199, 273, 300n16

controversies, 143, 237–38, 288
conundrum, 94, 96
conversations, 2, 9–10, 12, 182, 186, 189n1, 257, 260, 262, 265, 267n12, 313–14
conversion, 81, 85, 88, 93, 166, 212
Conversionary Christian Place-Making, 101
Coomaraswamy, 75–77
Coorlawala, 135–36, 143
Corbett, Rosemary, 242n7, 243
corruption, 225–27, 232, 236–37, 239
Corsi, Alberto, 274
COSAS, 101
cosmic, 285, 309
cosmological, 3
cosmopolitan, 137
Costanza Caraffa, 304
Cotton Mather, 83
counsel, 113, 115, 118, 206
Cow, 7, 17, 43, 102, 220, 227, 264, 269, 305, 310, 314
cow dung, 253
cow urine, 42n6
creation, 5, 54, 70, 95, 120, 137, 252
creativity, 8, 11, 24, 29, 31, 39, 126, 169, 215, 227, 310
creators, 70, 252
creatures, 61–62, 70
cremation ground, xii, 13, 167–87, 189n1, 191n10, 192n19, 193, 195
cremations, 183, 185, 189n4
crisis, 29, 51, 66, 304
critics, 60, 254, 262, 288
crowds, xii, 15, 179, 198, 203, 207, 213, 254, 281, 304
Cthulhu, xi, 54, 56–57, 60–65, 68–70, 78
cult, 57–58, 65, 116, 165, 181, 192n14, 194
cultivation, 8, 87, 90, 242n12

cultural analysis, 12, 83
Cultural Politics of Emotion, 131, 139, 142, 193
Cultural Studies, 303, 312
cultures, 6, 8, 16–17, 76, 82, 120–21, 231–32, 243, 286, 292, 303, 308–10
  popular, 83, 287
cures, 27, 31, 33–35, 40
curiosity, xiv, 4–6, 8, 11, 24–25, 27, 39, 41, 82, 85, 91–92, 95–96, 307–8
curse, 50, 53, 160, 171, 181–82
cycles, 87, 143, 199

Daksha's sacrifice, 182, 188n1
Dalai Lama, 216n7
Dalits, 142n17, 143
Dalston, 4, 16, 310
dandemulu, 136–37
Danell, 113, 120
dargah, 105, 111, 235–37, 241n2
darshan, 1–2, 36, 52, 54–55, 74–75, 86, 168–69, 203, 206, 293, 303
Daston, 95–96, 100
David Dean Shulman, 189n5
Davis, 80, 85–86, 99n29, 100n34, 101
decay, 132, 225
Decoloniality, 16
decolonize, 10, 308
decorations, 170, 185, 190n10
DeHart, 208, 218
deities, 1–2, 36, 40, 42n1, 49, 52, 74–75, 85–86, 92–94, 96, 149, 151–52, 156–57
  female, 52
  heathen, 86
  lineage, 170, 192n14, 194
  pagan, 55
  therioanthropomorphic, 48, 58
deity figures, 85–86, 93

Delhi, 102, 135–36, 164n9, 211, 216n4, 230–32, 269, 279–81, 302, 305
Delhi Akshardham, 252–55, 258–59, 267n11, 267n12
demon, 47, 72, 74, 137, 174, 225
demonetization, 235
demonization, 225
denomination, 99n23
Denton, 206, 210, 218
Deobandi school, 242n12
Descartes, 186, 295
description, 2, 42n12, 50, 76n3, 111, 113, 120n24, 186, 190n8, 303
Deslippe, 200, 218
destruction, 94, 169, 178, 187, 188n1, 191n13, 212
Devadāsīs, 144
devils, 73, 107, 225
devotees, 15, 86, 105–8, 112, 118–19, 161, 167–70, 172, 181–83, 187–88, 204–6, 237–38, 248–50, 275–82, 285–86, 288–89, 294–96, 298
devotion, 8, 13, 15, 145, 150, 158, 162, 248, 254, 276, 279–80
devotional music, 105, 114, 204–6, 223
Dev Ram, 31, 41
dhammal, 12, 105–6, 108, 110, 114–15, 117–18, 119n3
dhammal/goma, 114, 116, 118
Dhanraj, 253–54, 258–62, 264
dialogue, 47, 191n13, 201, 207, 217n12
diamonds, 284
diegesis, 53–54, 69, 74
difference, 5–7, 25, 74, 234, 266n3, 288–90, 292, 294, 305
dimension, 69, 84, 245, 252, 264, 281
affective, 251, 263
moral, 150

subjective, 263
unholy, 70
Dinkar, 293, 303
dir, 143, 219–20
disciplines, xiii, 4, 88, 139, 309
ascetic, 92, 203
discourses, 9–10, 13, 15, 112, 159, 183–84, 186, 241, 246–47, 252, 257–58, 261, 263
colonial, 242n14
media, 314
moral, 260
discovery, 4–5, 58
disenchantment, 3, 14, 79–97, 99n16, 101, 198
display, 59, 86, 169, 177, 182, 201–2, 211, 295
dispositions, 81, 227, 260
divine, 2, 4–5, 8, 17, 100n34, 106, 134, 141, 193, 206–7, 226
divine agency, 56, 87, 193
divine beings, 21, 100n34, 158
Divya Jyoti Jagrati Sanstan (DJJS), 205
domain, 29, 134, 227, 264–65, 287
donations, 82, 90, 150, 202, 233, 238–39
donning, 12, 130, 133, 137
dramas, 48–49, 125, 128, 191n13
Dravidian, 100, 163n1
dream, 36, 52–54, 56–57, 61–62, 66–67, 77n9, 243
dressing, 175, 191n10, 288, 292
drumming, 115, 117, 171, 173
DSS guru, 273–74, 281–82, 285–88, 290, 292–97, 299n16, 301n35, 301n41
DSS teachings, 276, 280
Dubey, 201, 217n9, 217n15, 218
duniyadars, 153–54, 158, 164n9
Dunsany, 55–57, 61, 77n10, 78
Durga, 53, 121

duties, 1, 32, 147
Dvaraka, 210
dwelling, 120, 122, 192n18, 294
dynamics, 118, 194, 238, 240, 268

East Asia, 46, 80
Easwaran, 2, 16
ecology, social, 87, 90
Economic, 143–44, 165, 218, 269, 305
economies of wonder, 14, 197–215, 217n9, 219
economy, 200, 210, 243
   expansive, 199, 209, 215
   monetary, 149
   moral, 148, 157, 164n12, 164n13, 165
   political, 226
ecstasy, 106, 109, 115, 118, 283–84
   euphoric, 223
ecstatic, 105, 114, 118
Edgar Rice Burroughs, 76n2, 77
education, 17, 48, 87, 91–92, 273
effigies, 174–75, 191n13
Egypt, 62, 116
Elephant God, 65, 78
elephant's head, 69, 75
Elison, 11, 75, 77
Ellen, 143, 193
Elsaesser, Thomas, 303
embodiment, 50, 84, 106–11, 114–15, 117–18, 158, 163n2, 297
   ecstatic, 12, 106, 111, 113
   symbolic, 108, 117
emotions, 2, 10, 120, 122, 131, 139, 142, 186–87, 193–94, 251, 254
enchantment, 3–4, 14, 198, 247, 261, 263, 267n14
enfolds, 5, 274, 296
engagements, 190n6, 210, 264
   affective, 186
   creative, 308
   tactile, 84

Engelke, 94, 101
enjoyment, 255, 257, 265
enlightenment, 3–4, 75
enslaved Africans, 81, 116
entanglements, 94, 302, 309–10
   political, 225
entertainment, 102
entrails, 160, 179, 192n18
entrapment, 15, 275, 298
entry, 56, 86, 97, 267n10, 273
environment, 32, 134, 313
envisioning, 4, 8, 81
epidemic diseases, 199
episodes, 23, 27, 144, 261
Erndl, 119n5, 121
escape, 34, 55, 59, 94, 132, 240
ethical framework, 249, 258, 261–62
ethics, 5–7, 9, 14, 153, 157, 163, 166, 259–60, 262, 268n15, 268, 308, 314
ethnographer, 6, 10–11, 15, 168, 246–47, 262–63, 265, 311
ethnographic, 184, 241, 263, 265
ethnographic approach, 10
ethnographic examples, 267n13
ethnographic fieldwork, 126
ethnographies, 6–11, 16, 246, 263, 265–66, 307–10
Ethnos, 16, 268
Europe, 4, 90, 95
event, 23, 27–28, 199–200, 211–12, 214–15, 217n11, 246, 248, 251, 264, 278, 281, 283–84
everyday life, 6, 8, 14, 168–69, 184, 188, 198, 227–28, 258
evocations, 8–9, 12, 201
Ewing, 234–35, 242n7, 242n14, 243
examination, 46, 155
exchange, medium of, 149–50
excitement, 4, 12, 289
exhibitions, 83, 200, 267n10
exit, 49, 123, 125, 170

Index

exotic, 12, 45, 62, 66, 79
expansion, 102, 199, 272, 283, 291
experience, 3, 5, 21, 23–24, 75,
    106–10, 145, 147–48, 184–85,
    187, 188n1, 190n9, 192n20,
    265, 307–8
  aesthetic, 134
  ordinary, 186
  sensory, 149
  subjective, 263
explanations, 34, 55, 68–69, 76n8,
    159, 162, 225
exploration, 4, 15, 22, 95, 250, 286
extension, 51, 89, 183, 212, 239, 252

faiths, 43, 162, 216, 218–19, 289
families, xiv, 2, 27–29, 33, 151,
    153–54, 156, 170–71, 176–77,
    184, 189n4, 190n9, 253–55,
    257–58, 260
  natal, 146, 151, 155–57
fantasy, 47, 49, 75, 284
FCHS Collective, 139, 142n16, 143
fear, 43, 51, 56, 85, 131, 187, 190n9,
    199, 259, 263, 265
feats
  ascetic, 206
  extraordinary, 211
  miraculous, 111
feeding, 66, 82, 177, 180
festival contexts, 169, 185, 187,
    189n5, 191n11
festival performances, 182, 188,
    191n14
festivals, 13–14, 146–49, 151–53,
    155, 158, 168–71, 173–74,
    181–82, 185–88, 188n1, 189n3,
    190n8, 191n12, 191n13
  annual, 148–50, 157, 189n2
fiction, 48, 54, 56, 77–79
fields, 21, 29, 60, 81, 101, 161, 163,
    186, 193, 246, 280

fieldwork, 23, 31, 38, 127, 132,
    141n2, 184, 188, 217n12, 225,
    233
Findlayson, 51, 53
flame, 52, 71, 171, 206, 208
Flaubert, 78
Flueckiger, 22, 42, 107, 120n21, 121,
    189n5, 193
Flueckiger, Joyce, 107
fluidities, 168–69, 183–85, 188
focus, 15, 105, 107, 145, 148–49,
    227, 233, 246–47, 263, 265,
    266n2, 268n15
  central, 254
  exclusive, 183
food, 51, 131, 170, 172, 176–77,
    181–82, 184–85, 190n8, 192n18,
    205–6, 237
foregrounds, 159, 163n1, 284–85
Foreign Languages University, 303, 312
forms
  ambivalent, 81
  derivative, 287
  devotional, 159
  hierarchical, 152
  sensorial, 151
Franckeschen Stiftungen, 194
freedom, 102, 155, 226, 249
function, 117, 203, 234, 285

Gabie Smith, 188
gajab, 22–23, 42n2
Gaji Pir, xi, 38, 40, 42n12
Ganesh, 45–47, 50–52, 62, 65, 74,
    76n2
Ganga, 52–53, 126, 197, 206, 214
Gautret, 217n19, 220
gaze, 173, 178–79, 228, 286
Geertz, 6, 16
gender, 125, 146, 159, 162, 165, 276,
    311, 313–14
  proper, 292

gender identity, 145, 163n1
genealogy, 3, 47, 95, 133, 247
generations, 13, 27, 29, 91, 136, 184
genres, 47, 73, 114–15, 118, 191n13, 283, 292
  prescribed, 92
geographies, 84, 264, 309
gesture, 55, 86, 89, 117, 132, 149, 157, 254, 293
  abstract, 226
ghar wapsi, 212, 219
Ghatiyali, xi, 24, 27, 30, 35–36, 42n7, 42
Ghosh, 142n10, 143
Global African Diaspora, 121, 313
Global Religious Movements, 268
goddess, xi, 13, 30–31, 36–37, 124–27, 129–30, 132–33, 145–49, 151, 153–63, 166, 168–75, 177, 179, 181–83, 185–88, 189n5, 193–95
  local, 187
goddess Angalamman, 13, 146, 154, 157, 159, 315
gods, 13–14, 21, 25, 39, 52–54, 60–61, 77–78, 84–85, 94, 101–2, 114, 226–28, 231, 235, 239–40, 249–50
Goldberg, Ellen, 268
goma, 12, 105, 114–16, 118, 122
Gospel, 89, 102
government, 21, 210–14, 236, 243, 279
governmental correspondence, 211
governmental policing, 200
government facilities, 229
government officials, 212
Government Press, 195
government servant, 38
government trucks, 214
grace, 31, 38–39, 41, 89–90, 93
  indwelling, 88, 95–96

Graeber, 297, 303
graves, xii, 117, 119n1, 119n7, 120n25, 121, 174, 176–77, 185, 232–33, 241n2
  decorate, 176
gravesites, 173, 176, 185
graveyard, 14, 168, 177, 179–80, 184, 192n20
Greek Myths, 3, 16
Greenblatt, 5, 16
Ground
  burial, 187
  burning/burial, 183, 185
  cremation/burial, 173, 185
groups
  local, 161
  sectarian, 197
  social, 290
guardians, 56, 173, 175, 194
Gufran, 236, 242n17
guides, 15, 207, 246, 248, 255, 258, 261
Gujarat, 12, 15, 105, 107, 109, 113, 120–22, 248, 255, 262, 265–66, 266n1, 267n7
Gulf States, 234, 237
gūmne, 207
gunas, 24
Gurmeet Ram Rahim Singh Ji Insan, xii, 277, 282
guru, 14–15, 203–7, 248–50, 254–58, 260–62, 265–66, 266n3, 271–83, 285–89, 291–98, 299n3, 299n5, 299n8, 300n17, 302–4
guru-bhakti, 276, 278
guru camps, 205, 207
Guru Gobind Singh, 288, 301n35
Guru Pramukh Swami Maharaj, 250
Gurus and Media, 302, 304

Habshi Amarat, 121
Haggis, 82, 101

hair, 125, 245
    human, 72
hal, 12, 106–13, 118, 223
Halloween, 67, 69
halls
    cinema, 211
    exhibition, 267n11
Hanuman, xi, 37, 49–53, 62
    real, 53
Haptic Logics, 304
Haqā'iq-i Hindı, 121
Haridwar, 216n2
Harivamsa, 184
Harp, Matthew, 142
Harrasowitz Verlag, 195
Hartmann, Nicolai, 16
Haryana, 271, 279
Hatcher, Brian, 266
haziri, 106–11, 113, 118
Hazoor Maharaj, 289
healing, 34, 38, 107–8, 115–16, 118, 121, 195
    bodily, 171
    miraculous, 234
healing shrine, 11, 23, 30, 33
health
    free, 275
    younger brother's, 127
heart, 15, 25, 73, 89, 169, 280, 283
heathens, 50, 77, 81, 83, 89, 100
Heena, 107–8, 110, 112, 119n13
hegemony, 61, 203
Heidegger, 295, 305
Henry Anthony Wilcox, 60
Henry David Thoreau, 101
hero, 48, 70, 73, 140
hierarchies, 14, 120, 202–3, 248
    racialized, 81
hijras, 152, 154, 156, 165–66
Hiltebeitel, 188n1, 190n7, 191n11, 191n13, 192n14, 192n18, 194

Hind Ka Napak Ko Jawab, 278, 296, 299n16
Hindoo, 66, 68, 77, 100
Hindoostan, 82, 89, 94, 97
Hinduism, 23, 45, 50–51, 80, 92–93, 96, 121, 165, 193–95, 212, 255
    global, 314
Hindus, 1, 12–13, 51, 53–54, 93–94, 201, 204, 207, 216n7, 242n13, 242n17, 273, 276, 283–84, 311–12
Hindustan, 12, 96
Hindutva, 218, 302
histories, 4, 6, 9–11, 119n1, 119n2, 131–33, 135, 138, 140, 142n9, 142n11, 143–44, 290–91, 313–14
Hoisington, Henry, 92, 99n31
Holbraad, Martin, 195
Holmes, 4, 216n4
holy bath, 197, 201, 215
    auspicious, 197
horizons
    imaginative, 7
    mental, 4
horror, 6, 12, 47, 51, 53, 65, 67, 82, 88–90, 96, 187
houses, 9, 58, 153, 190n6, 233, 253, 256
Howard, 48, 70, 73, 78, 200, 218
Howard Phillips Lovecraft, 48
Hsieh Ho, 66–67
Al-Hujwiri, 241n3
humanity, 143, 208, 277, 289
Hyderabad, 107, 120, 122, 126–27, 132, 137, 141n3, 143, 154, 303, 312
hyper-gurus, 204
hypernationalism, 278

IANS, 211, 218
IBTimes, 216n7, 218

icon, 57, 285, 287
iconography, 62, 74, 182, 301n35
  religious, 12
identity, 38, 40, 146, 151, 157, 162, 163n2, 286, 288, 290, 292, 294–95, 303
  individual, 292
  religio-ethnic, 226
  transgender, 152
ideology, 209
  political, 163n1
idols, 46–47, 50, 54–60, 62, 65, 67, 69–70, 73, 83–87, 94
Ikegame, 203, 299n7, 300n17, 300n23, 300n26, 301n39, 301n40, 301n41, 303
images, 47, 49, 72, 79–80, 82, 84, 87, 89–90, 92, 275, 285–89, 292, 294, 301n31, 302–4
immanent, 94, 97
Immerwahr, 80, 101
impersonation, 13, 143, 292, 313
impression, 83, 133, 142n9, 258, 272
imprisonment, 42n14, 273, 279–80
incarnation, 70, 76n4, 78, 93
India, 12, 45–46, 48–49, 61–62, 77, 79–84, 89–91, 96–97, 100, 115–16, 120–21, 165–66, 194–95, 219–20, 224–26, 234–35, 243, 283–84, 300n16, 312–15
  developing, 273
  neoliberal, 15
  urban, 311
Indian, 12, 45, 126, 133–35, 138–39, 143, 203, 205, 216n9, 284, 312
Indian economy, 227, 235
Indian government, 210, 212, 214, 224, 236, 239
information, 90, 106, 118, 120n22
Ingold, 16, 290, 303
Ingram, 242n12, 243
inhabitants, 55, 164n14

innovations, 143, 277
inquiries, 1, 10, 17, 57–58, 91, 95, 309
insan, 289
inspiring, 186, 309
instability, 149, 228, 290–91
intensity, 109, 112, 114, 131, 154, 168, 186, 203, 290, 294
interlocutors, xiv, 7, 14–15, 182, 184, 190n9, 241, 242n11, 247, 251–53, 262, 264–65
interpretations, 3, 15, 24, 169, 246–47, 251–52, 263, 266, 266n2
intersections, 211–12, 235, 292, 314
intervention, 55, 238
interwoven, 10, 182
intolerance, 14, 259
ishta deivam, 164n7
Islam, 121, 225, 231, 234, 243, 289
Islamabad, 243
Islands, Solomon, 6, 164n14, 166
István Keul, 101
Ithaca, 100, 166, 243–44, 302

Jacobsen, 203, 218
Jaggi Vasudev, 273
Jahazpur, 38–39, 42n12, 42n13
Jains, 96, 285, 303
Jaipur, 32, 35, 43
Jambur, 113, 119n17
James, 16, 102, 194
Janak Dave, 266, 267n12
Janzen, 115, 117, 121
jati, 128, 137, 184, 298
Jenny-Ann Brodin, 120
Jerome, 17, 310
Jeychandran, 119n1, 121
jholi, 118
Ji Maharaj, xii, 204
Jime, 274–75, 280, 302–3
jinn, 107
jiva, 249

Index

Johnson, Thomas M., 43
John Stratton Hawley, 121
joy
  collective, 115
  expressing, 284
Joyce Burkhalter Flueckiger, 141
Jyotika, 305

KAA (Kuchipudi Art Academy), 127–28, 136–37
kaaval deivam, 182
Kabir, 276
kaccha, 113
Kāl, 188n1
Kalakshetra, 136
Ankālamman cult, 181
Kali, 52, 181, 194
Kalla Nath, 27, 29, 41
Kalla Nathji, 29, 31
kalpavāsis, 197, 211
Kama Maclean, 199, 215
Kamath, 13, 126, 133–34, 137, 141n2, 141n3, 141n4, 142n13, 143
kapalam, 181
kapparai, xii, 173, 178, 190n8
kappu, 170
Karachi, 116
Kashf al-Mahjūb, 243
Kashi Annapurna Annakshetra Trust, 205
Kashmir, 300n16
Keane, 164n12, 164n13, 165, 242n9, 243
Kellner, 292, 303
Keune, Jon, 193
khadim, 223
Khanal, 213, 219
khilafa, 238
Khitai, 72, 74
kin, 61, 173
  close, 155, 278
  dead, 186, 311

King Gopi Chand, 42
kin groups, 185
kings
  hundred Kaurava, 1
  true, 237
kinship, 146, 152–53, 155–56, 164n8, 164n11
  natal, 156
  normative, 146
Kipling, 46–49, 51, 53–56, 60, 74, 76n3, 76n4, 76n5, 78
Kirin Narayan, 41
kırtan, 206–7
kitsch, 287
  postcolonial, 15
Klesh, 56
knowledge, 4–5, 8–10, 68, 75, 85, 88, 90–92, 99n26, 260–61, 263, 265, 302–4, 309
  dark, 72
  esoteric, 56
  modern, 61
  objective, 68
  scientific, 55
knowledge production, 258, 262, 265
Knut Axel Jacobsen, 304
kodumbavi pen, 191n11
Kothari, 159, 165
Krishna, 2, 5, 52–53, 121, 126, 133, 138–39, 143, 277
Krishna district, 13, 137
Krishna Mulvaney, 76n4, 78
krpa, 31
Kuchalwara Mataji, xi, 11, 23, 29–30, 32, 34–37, 41
Kuchipudi, 125–27, 130, 134–38, 140, 141n2, 144, 307, 313
  style of, 126, 136, 138
Kuchipudi village, 13, 128, 137, 142n14
kuladeivam, 170, 192n14
Kumar, 217n14, 219

Kumbh Mela, xii, 14, 197–201, 203–16, 216n2, 216n7, 217n9, 217n12, 217–20
Kumbh Mela Carnival, 219
Kumhar community, 32
kumkum, 171, 174
Kurukṣetra, 194

labor, 31, 81, 88, 91, 147, 151, 223, 252, 277
  associative, 291
  migrant, 231, 234
  volunteered, 265
laboratory, 68
  mad scientist's, 47
  moral, 266n2
labor supply, 16, 298
laity, 83, 207, 217n12
  promenading, 202
Lamb, Sarah, 305
land
  agricultural, 272
landscape
  aesthetic, 186
  enchanted, 56
  unpredictable, 226
languages, 35, 91, 93, 95, 100, 184, 231, 274, 283
  aesthetic, 288
  classical, 92
  local, 23
  pejorative, 93
  performative, 94
  regional, 135
Lascars, 51, 53, 59
Late Francis Wayland Thurston, 60
Lawrence, John, 83, 85, 98n3
leaders
  natural, 300n17
  spiritual, 277
Leavitt, 184, 194
Lecturer, 311

Lempert, 164n5, 165
lens, 8, 14, 22, 126, 133, 138, 201
  brahminical, 139
  casteist, 133
Lessig, 288, 303
Lévi-Strauss, Claude, 289
LGBTQAI community, 163n2
LGBTQ rights discourse, 159
life, xiv, 2–4, 6–8, 10, 15–16, 40, 42n4, 60–61, 127, 147, 179, 181, 188, 189n5, 309–10
  communal, 315
  contemporary, 264
  eternal, 192n18
  ethical, 3, 315
lifeworlds, transfeminine, 152
light, 13, 16, 22, 170, 177, 179, 184, 190n10, 191n14, 291, 295
līlās, 204, 207
Limbale, 143
liminality, 97, 164n10, 226–27
  intimate, 95
lineage, 38, 232
links, 5, 15, 55, 106, 115, 151, 164n9, 189n3, 190n8, 191n14
  missing, 47
Lister, Martin, 304
literary nexus, 47
Literary Theory, 302
living, 69, 72–73, 160, 168, 171, 183–84, 188, 190n6, 226–27, 230, 249–50, 252, 258, 260–61, 263–65
locales
  dispersed, 96
  romantic, 46
locality, 38, 120, 122, 154
location, 10, 138, 171, 216n2, 250
  featured, 89
  paradigmatic, 161
  real geographical, 59
  social, 146, 154

logic, 3, 10, 51, 93, 112–13, 118, 240, 250, 291, 296, 309
 consumptive, 198
 magical, 169
 neoliberal, 199
 temporal, 131
Lok Virsa Research Centre, 243
Lord Ganesh, 46, 48, 76n8
 elephant-headed, 11
Lourdusamy, 191n13, 192n17, 195
love, xiv, 14, 120, 131, 163, 225, 228, 232, 235–36, 239–40, 254
 eternal, 227–28
 first, 89
 sincere, 233
Love Charger, xii, 279, 281–82, 288, 300n19, 301n37, 301n43, 301n44, 301n46
Lovecraft, xi, 48, 54, 56, 60–65, 70, 75, 77n9, 77–78
 letter, 69
 outline, 64
Lubomír Ondrac, 192n20
Luce Irigaray, 16
Lucknow, 15, 224–25, 230–34, 236, 311
 old, 231
 real, 233

Mackenzie, Anne, 243
Maclean, 199, 212, 215, 216n3, 216n6, 217n16, 219
madness, 56, 72, 178, 187
Madras, 98n6, 195, 313
Madura, 86, 98n7, 98n8, 98n14
Madurai, 83, 91
 19th-Century, 101
Magh Mela, 199, 217n12
 annual, 216n2
magic
 ancestral Celtic stratum hosting, 56

 black, 181
 white, 73
magulman, 116
Mahabharata, 1, 184, 191n13
Mahābrāhman, 195
Maha Kumbh Mela, 210, 218
Mahamandaleshwar, 213
māhāmantra, 207
Māhānirvāni Akhār, 202, 213, 216n8, 217n12
Mahatma Gandhi, 299n15
Mai Misra, 105, 107–10, 112, 114, 116–17, 119n7, 119n19
Makbul Bava, 108, 114
Makirans, 17, 165n14, 166
Mala, 147, 152, 154–56
 chosen, 155
Malaiyanur, Mel, 181, 191n14, 192n15
Malaiyanūr, Mel, 181
mālās, 202, 207
Malleshwaram, 1, 141
management, 210
 smooth, 254
Mandi, 216n5
 toured, 200
mandir, 248, 256–57, 267n4
mangalarathi, 1
manifestations
 literal, 295
 local, 169
manifests, 41, 58, 146, 149, 169, 187
manipulations
 nimble, 126
 tactical, 274
Manmohan Ghosh, 142n12
Manoj Mishra, 214
mantras, 34, 92–93, 100n34
maps, 88–89, 203, 260
 attitudes, 51
marble
 individual, 253
 white, 26

marble couch, 72
Māriyamman, 195
marketing strategies, 292, 296
   high-level, 292
markets, 46, 116, 152, 165, 190n10, 232
   flower, 152
   foreign exchange, 235
Mark Singleton, 268
maruladi, 13, 145, 153, 163
Marvelous Possessions, 16
marvels, 6, 8, 95, 133, 228, 296
   divine commands, 224
   new, 274
   newer, 15
Mary Jane Rubenstein, 15
Mary-Jane Rubenstein, 274
Masi, 170, 176
Masilamani-Meyer, 192n17, 194
mass, 192n20, 199, 207, 215, 284
   dream-bound, 61
master
   ancient, 54
   colonial, 74
   spiritual, 276
master archer, 1
Masters of Disenchantment, 79–97, 99n16, 101
master's successors, 65
mastery, 51, 61, 114, 295
Mata Amritanandamayi Mission, 305
Matei Candea, 247
material, 76n1, 78, 82, 86, 90, 150, 156, 162, 252, 255, 261, 265–66, 267n14
   consecrated, 14
   raw, 49
Material Acts, 42
material body, 69
material care, 156
material expression, 248

material force, 229
materiality, 84, 87, 117, 165, 185, 304
   idolatry's, 96
   resplendent, 150
   sheer, 149
materialization, 254
material mediants, 97
material otherness, 2
material realities, 262
material witness, 66
Matthew Harp Allen, 142n12
Maulana Azad, 42n14, 43
Maurer, 228, 243
Māyā, 143
Mayana Kollai, xi–xii, 146–47, 168–72, 174, 176, 179–80, 182–88, 189n2, 190n6, 190n9, 190n10, 191n13, 191n14, 192n14, 192n15
   celebrate, 189n3
Mayana Kollai day, 169, 176, 185–86
mazar, 38, 241n2
maze, 1, 71, 179
   ethical, 2
Mazzarella, 296, 304
McCartney, 291, 304
McLeod, 119n1
McLeod, John, 121
Mead, Margaret, 5
Mecca, 234
Media, 5, 290, 302, 304
Media Culture, 303
Media Strategies, 304
Mediated Manifestations, 193
Medical Anthropology, 43
medicine, 31, 34, 41, 120, 160
medieval period, 276
mediums
   actualized, 114
   meaning-making, 229

musical, 117
uninitiated, 113
mediumship, 109, 114, 118
Meena Bhavsar, 266
Meenavar caste, 170
mehfil-e-sama, 237, 239
mela, 197–99, 208, 212, 215, 219
memories
  affective, 15
  cultural, 313
  fragmented, 115
  fuzzy, 27
  repressed, 49
Messenger of God, 279, 281
Metamorphosis, 16
metapragmatics, 146, 164n4
Methodists, 80
methodologies, 15, 264, 274, 291
  varied, 290–91
Meyer, Birgit, 304
Meyer, Eveline, 151, 161, 165n16, 169
Michel Lévy Frères, 78
Michel Ralph Trouillot, 9
Migrant communities, 45
militaristic, 278
Miller, Jerome, 5
mind, 3, 6, 16, 67, 74, 77, 90, 113, 152, 156, 243
Mines, Diane, 305
Mir, 121
miracles, 34, 224, 245, 278, 295–96
Misfortune, 43
Mishra, Mai, 115, 120
mission, 12, 80–83, 86–87, 89, 91–92, 97–98, 101, 299n15
missionaries, 49, 81–85, 87–88, 90–92, 95–96, 98n5, 99n23, 99n33
Missionary Herald, 90, 98n2, 98n15, 98n16, 99n17, 99n22, 99n23

missionary Orientalists, 94
mission narratives, 88, 90
mission practice, 12, 82, 84–85, 88
Mitchell, Timothy, 229
Mitchell's analysis, 229
model
  dominant, 241
  full-scale, 271
  quintessential, 265
model for, 297
model of, 297
modernity, 3, 10, 14, 54, 95, 120, 122, 144, 198, 243
  colonial, 287
  late-capitalist, 199
Modern Yoga, 268
modes, 8, 13, 145–46, 228, 236, 238–39, 274, 281, 283, 291, 293–95
  discursive, 187
  exoticist, 200
  felicitous, 158
Modi, 77, 211–12, 214, 218, 299n15
Modi's Swachh Bharat Abhiyan, 278
Moffat, Michael, 191n14
moksha, 249, 265
money, 14–15, 26, 34, 147–51, 153–54, 157, 162, 166, 223–43, 276
  donating, 90
  earning, 232
  transmit, 238
money-lender, 76n3
Monius, Anne E., 193
monster, 65, 72–73
monstrous, 52, 58
Moors, 277
Moral Laboratories, 268
mortals, 56, 193
Mosse, 194

mother, 27, 36, 117, 121, 128, 155, 172, 182, 240
   elderly, 35
movement, 6, 129, 131–32, 137, 275, 277, 280, 288–89, 291, 300n27, 303
   basic, 129
   devotional, 276
   early nineteenth-century, 266n3
   embodied, 133
   learned, 136
   religious, 313
   sliding, 132
   tracks Conan's, 70
mridangam, 123
MSG, 279, 281, 288–89, 298–99, 299n3, 300n27, 301n43, 301n46
mudra, 255
Muedini, 241n4, 243
mugarman, 115–16, 120n24
multivocality, 9, 106, 118, 120n25
Mumbai, 77, 105–6, 119n1, 119n4, 119n8, 119n11, 119n13, 121, 164n9, 194, 312
Mundakkanni Amman, 171
murder, 2, 278–79, 300n18
murtis, 46, 53, 74–75, 207, 248, 250, 254
music, 76, 120, 123, 133, 223, 237, 296
   melodious, 284
   modern, 283
Muslims, 15, 32, 38, 96, 212, 223–25, 234, 236, 284
   medieval, 224
Muslim saints, 38, 107, 109, 223–24, 312
Muslim Saint Shrines, 223–43, 312
Muthukumaraswamy, 191n13, 194
mutiny, 55, 102
mysterious, 3–4, 307, 309
mystery, 5, 17, 53, 64, 74, 92, 284, 308

Mythopoetics, 144
myths, 165n16, 165, 168, 181–82, 184, 188, 188n1, 190n7, 191n14, 194–95, 304
   animating, 175, 181

Nabokov, 164n3, 165, 181, 190n6, 190n7, 194
nafs al-ammarah, 224
nāgā bābās, 201–2, 211, 217n12
Nagarchi Pir, 113
nāgā sādhu, 208
Nahum-Claudel, Chloe, 303
nakli, 232
Nanak, 276
Nanda, 152, 165
Nandy, 287, 304
nangai, 163n1
Narayan, 42n11, 43
narratives, 10, 55, 89, 96–97, 161, 164n3, 168, 182, 247, 251, 258
   enunciated, 266n2
   mission-based, 82
narrator, 48–51, 56, 58–59, 69, 117, 251–52, 258, 261
   omniscient, 70
   reliable, 27
Nartanam, 141n2, 143
Nasik, 216n2
Nataraj, 159, 163n1, 166
Nathaniel, 166
Nathu Natisar Nath, 30
Nath yogis, 211
nation, 71, 224, 273, 278, 312
National Green Tribunal (NGT), 214
nationalism, 203
nature, 3, 11, 16, 40, 43, 93, 100, 182, 187, 275, 278
   constituents of, 24
   dashing, 294
   durable, 153
   ethereal, 240

ever-changing, 289
  ungraspable, 308
  wistful, 279
Nāṭyas, 135, 143
Natyashastra, 134–37, 142n10
Nayyar, 223, 243
nazar, 238–39
Nazir, 38, 41
Neeta Shah, 266
neighborhoods
  adjacent, 231
  next, 155
  surrounding, 171
neoliberal, 225, 227, 237, 312
network, 105, 161, 229, 263, 294
  multiple discursive, 265
New Age Channeling, 122
New Delhi, 143–44, 165, 194–95, 219, 243, 267n7, 268, 312
Newell, Samuel, 99n23
New Indian Express, 219
New Religions, 120
News Minute, 143
New York Times, 193, 218
nez, 274–75, 280, 302–3
ngoma, 115–18, 121
Nicholson, 243
Nidān, 193, 195
niece, 156
Nigri, Miri, 67–68, 77n9
Nirvana, 217n11, 218
Nithyananda, 216n8
Nithyananda's Digital Empire, 304
Noida, 120, 267n7
nonattachment, 201
non-Christian, 81
nondualism, relational, 10
Normativity, 305
North India, 11, 22–23, 223, 233, 240–41, 302, 311–12
North Indian, 22, 276
Norwegian, 59
NUJS Law Review, 165–66

Oakland, 143, 166, 219, 243, 268
object of wonder, 14, 96, 184, 199, 230
obligations, 146, 148, 155–56, 163
occasions, 90, 107–8, 185, 191n11, 195, 260, 264, 272, 279, 288, 291
offerings, 171, 173, 177, 179, 185, 188n1, 190n8, 230
  flower, 170
  nonvegetarian, 183
officers
  medical, 210
  retired army, 32
Old Testament, 84, 86
Olympian, 52
omniscience, 294
Ondrac, 194
online, 15, 78, 211, 218
ontological premises, 10, 13, 146, 158–59, 164n14, 165n14
ontologies, 10, 146, 159, 246, 264, 309
Opdal, 3, 17
opposites, 25, 240, 274, 276, 297
  mixing-up of, 297
order, 5, 16, 60, 68, 94, 100, 137, 271, 276–77, 291, 295
organization
  efficient, 254
  sending, 83
Orientalism, 46, 96, 99n26, 101–2, 201
Orientalists, 12, 91, 200
orientation
  affective, 95
  affirmative, 267n14
  ethical, 264
origin, 68, 86, 102, 144, 181, 248, 276
Orsini, 106, 120n25, 121
Oscillating Universe, 101
oscillating visions, 9

Osho, 288
Oslo, 59
Ostrander, Julia, 88, 99n18
otherness, 5–6, 96
outsiders, 193, 231–32
outwards, 202, 238, 261, 275, 308
　sloped, 65
overbearing, 285
Oxford, 16, 165, 218, 302–3

Paalam Publications, 166
padabheda, 137
padam, 140
padivilakku, 170–71, 173, 180
Padmabharathi, 155, 166
pagan monolith, 62
pagan practices, 84
Paik, 132, 143
pain
　bodily, 31
　medium associates, 111
　presage, 112
Pakistan, 116, 120, 224, 243, 300n16
Pali term, 11, 75
pambai-udukkaikkarar, 171
pandal awning, 153
　thatched, 150
Pandava brothers, 1
pandemic times, 22
Pandian, 22, 43, 192n16, 194
Pandiaraj, 188
Pankaj Jain, 194
Pankhurst, Richard, 121
panorama, 11, 22, 27, 40
paradox, 157, 228, 265, 276
parentheses, 42n3
Paris, 78, 195
Park, Katharine, 16, 95, 100, 310
Parmarth Niketan, 204–6
parrot, 17, 52, 160, 166

Parsis, 106, 121–22
participation, 12, 80, 186–87, 275, 295–96
parties, political, 212, 280, 300n17
Parvati, 129, 169, 181
　consort, 123
pās, 93
passages
　quoted, 42n3
　subterranean, 55
passions, 3, 5, 82, 88, 96
　new, 95
patients, 32, 42n6, 257, 260
Paush Purnima, 197
pavadai, 182, 192n18
Pavadairayan, 167, 169, 173–75, 182, 190n8, 192n14, 192n17, 192n18
payals, 207
Peabody Essex Museum, 77, 100
pedagogy, 82, 89, 97, 302
　sabbath school, 85
Peeples, Tim, 188
Pegāna, 56, 78
Pennington, Brian K., 193, 311
Penzoldt, Peter, 55
perceptions, 2, 75, 111, 162, 184, 295
　public, 215
performance, 106, 108, 110–11, 114–16, 118, 120, 127, 130, 134, 137–39, 143–44, 168–69, 188, 191n14, 292
　dance, 12
　tamasha, 132
　video, 286
　wondrous, 130
performers
　senior, 142n14
　showering, 238
　trans women, 13
perpetual innovation, 292

person, 15, 27, 32, 38–39, 51, 69, 79–80, 155, 161, 290, 296
  androgynous, 155
  nonhuman, 53
  transgender, 191n14
perspectives, 3, 10, 46, 53, 113, 254, 309
  competing, 9
perspective situates, 113
Perundevi, 195
Peter, 17, 77, 107, 122, 305
phenomena, 100n36, 192n14, 229, 296, 300n17, 308
  dual-staged, 111
Philadelphia, 43, 102
Philip, 218
Philippines, 61, 80
philosophers, 5, 295
philosophical elucidation, 274
Philosophical Papers, 17
photographs, 33, 65, 200, 254, 293–94, 304
  ashram of, 293
  circulated colonial-era, 200
Photomontage background effects transport, 287
photoshopped photomontage, 287
physical evolution, 70
Picasso, 76
Picherit, David, 304
Pieper, 3, 17, 308–10
Pierre, 305
piety
  ardent, 92
  conjoined, 89
  engendering, 82
pilgrimage, 24–25, 30, 95, 215, 218–19, 242n16, 312
Pilgrimage Studies, 217n12, 218
pilgrims, 24–25, 30–34, 36, 107, 197, 199–209, 211–16, 219

Pillai, 139, 143
Pillaiyar, 94
Pilot Baba, 203–4, 206, 216n8
Pinney, 293–94, 304
pir, 107, 223, 225–26, 233–34, 237–39, 241n1
pita, 279
plates, 205, 257
Platts, 110, 121
plenitude, 149–50, 261, 294
  sensual, 294
Pnina Werbner, 120
poetry, 4, 225
political agenda, 212
Political Weekly, 143–44, 218, 269, 305
politicians, 212–13, 233, 235–36
  extortionate, 226
politicization, 216, 242n7
politics, 9, 219, 225–26, 241n5, 243, 273, 280, 302–3, 305, 308, 312–13
  global, 241n4
  nationalist, 226
  populist, 279
Politics of Aesthetics, 143
Politics of Ethnography, 16
Politics of Sufism, 243
Polity, 305
pollution, 50, 168, 184
  ameliorate, 185
Polyani, Karl, 228
Pondichéry, 195
pongal, 184
Ponnamaravathi, 194
Ponniah, James, 188
pontoon bridges, 210
Poongaavanam, 160
Poor, Daniel, 98n8
Porterfield, 88, 98n15, 102
portraits, 62, 286, 293, 295
  photographic, 293

Portuguese Empire, 100n36, 102
posicionamento sobre, 219
possession, 12, 106–7, 119n5, 121, 180, 183, 195, 274, 284, 296
  collective spirit, 115
  temporary, 289
postcolonial nation-state, 165n14
Post-Earthquake Gujarat, 313
Post-modern World, 17, 310
postures, 135, 140, 230, 249, 287
  ideal, 249
  seated, 140
potentiality, 198, 208
potent levels, 113
power, 34, 41, 43, 51, 53, 60, 62, 86–87, 99n26, 100, 140, 223–24, 255–56, 262–63, 285
  blessing, 238
  captivating, 293
  concentration, 261
  demonic, 95
  irresistible, 61
  metaphysical, 231
  panacean, 226
  proselytizing, 205
  satanic, 84
  spiritual, 113
  wondrous, 93
pozhappu, 152
Practical History, 17
practices
  ascetic, 197
  casteist, 126
  commonplace, 201
  cultural, 159
  devotional, 15, 118, 148, 249, 265, 280
  discursive, 148
  ethical, 146
  false, 276
  important, 249
  media, 204
  medical, 257
  preparatory, 170
  religious, 82, 96, 192n19, 311
  scientific, 95
practice sessions, 129
practices of ngoma, 115
practitioners, 10, 112–13, 169, 256
  tantric, 259
pradāyas, 202
Pradhan, 210, 219
Pragmatics, 43
Prakash, 139, 143
Pramahamsa, 101
Pramukh Swami Maharaj, 245–46, 256, 258–59, 266n1, 267n8
Prasad, 164n5, 166, 286–87, 304
prasadam, xii, 171, 180, 185
prasang, 250, 255–56, 266n1
pravachan, 257
pray, 89, 233, 240, 256
Prayagraj, xii, 197–99, 209–11, 214, 216n2
prayer meetings, 85, 87, 89, 99n23
  monthly, 86
prayers, xi, 40, 82, 87–90, 97, 99n21, 99n22, 99n23, 107–8, 238, 257
  answer, 236
  daily communal, 87
  dutiful, 226
  mission-related, 87
  offering, 192n20
  persevering, 88
  vow, 240
praying, 89, 122, 259
precarity, 7, 14, 86, 149, 198
Predrag, 16
Prem Baba, 206, 217n10, 219
Prem Prakash, 218
Presbyterians, 80
presences, 107, 110, 281
Price, editor Robert M., 65

priests, 21, 31–34, 71, 73–74, 150, 153, 166–67, 170, 179, 181–82, 189n3, 190n9, 251
  chief, 1
privileging, 135
PR Newswire, 299n12, 300n21, 300n22
problem, 14, 51, 75, 93, 101, 113, 147, 195, 229, 256
  ethical, 16
  moral, 1
proceedings, 16, 57, 99n25, 99n29, 99n30, 274
process
  associative labor, 291
  conversionary, 82
  dynamic, 22
  exaggeration, 294
  generative, 229
  symbolic, 117
processions, 168, 170, 179, 183, 203, 215, 217n12
  raucous, 179
production, 86, 197, 199, 210, 212, 216, 272, 277, 282, 291–94, 298
  circulatory, 14
  conscious, 286
  cultural, 134
  literal, 210
  manufactured, 215
  textual, 46
programming, 206
prohibitions, 164n10
projects, 52, 82, 166, 210, 250, 263, 297, 311
  colonial, 48
  comparative, 93
  racial, 83
proliferation, 9, 156–57, 163, 283
Propagation, 102
prophecies, 65, 67, 299n13
  biblical, 55

Prophet, 114, 224, 233–34, 242n15
propitiate, 67, 189n6
prosperous, 151, 228
protagonist, 48, 69, 74, 299n16
protection, 21, 43, 114, 172, 278–79
  spiritual, 113
Protestant Christianity, 94, 97
Protestant communities, 90
Protestant missionaries, 80–81, 97
Protestants, 80, 87–88, 90, 93, 96–98
Prothero, Stephen, 102
provocation, 5, 96, 200, 307–8
  initial, 11
provokes, 5–8, 245, 252, 266n2, 275
prowess
  ascetic, 201
Proxemic Desire, 304
proximity, 149
  ambivalent, 96
PTI, 210–11, 219
Puar, 131–32, 142n9, 143
  paraphrase, 133
Public Culture, 101, 313
Public Health, 217n19
Public Works Department, 51
Puerto Rico, 80
puja, xii, 49, 86, 94, 170, 175, 180–81, 183–84, 256
  big, 256
pukka, 49
Punjabi, 281, 283
punkah-rope, 50
Puranas, 91
Puranic Hinduism, 53
Puri, 24
purity, 168, 184, 188, 232
  cultural, 232
  inherited scholarly, 184
pursuit, 6–7, 10, 96, 241, 254, 267n14, 294, 308, 310
Pushkal, 195
puvadai, 189n6

puvadaikkari, 189n4
Puvali ka Devji, 28–29, 42n7
pūvāṭaikkāri, 311
Pym, 56

qabar, 241n2
qawwal, 223, 237–38, 240
qawwali, 38, 107, 120n21, 223, 225, 237, 243
Queens, 67, 284
quotations, 119n9, 119n10, 119n13, 300n28, 300n29, 301n30, 301n45
Quranic acceptability, 224
qutb, 235

race
　instantiated, 80
races, lesser, 61
racism, 56, 60, 80–81, 131
radical social hope, 310
Ragini Amma, 147, 158–59, 161–62, 165n16
　narrative, 162
Rajasthan, 11, 21, 23, 26, 35, 42–43, 208, 254, 266, 307, 312
　provincial, 23
　rural, xi, 26
Rajasthani-Hindi Shabad-Kosh, 43
Rajasthanis, 22–23, 283
　local, 253
　provincial, 25, 34
Rajneesh, 287
Rajput, 31
Ram, 289, 299n14
Ramadan, 38
Ramakrishna Math, 302
Ramakrishna Mission, 293
Ramakrishnan, 155, 166
Ramana Maharshi, 293–94, 302
Ramanandacharya, 203
Ramanathan, 190n10, 194
Ramanujan, 138, 144

Ramayanam, 142n14
Ramberg, Lucinda, 156, 161
Ramcharitmanas, 199
Ramdev, 28, 273
Ramlila, 283
Ram Mandir, 212
Ram Rahim, 287, 292
Ram temple, 212–13
Rangachari, 189n3, 190n8, 190n9, 191n13, 191n14, 195
rape, 273, 278–79, 300n18
rasa, 134, 138–40
rationality, 56
　economic, 157
　instrumental, 154
Ravi Shankar, 126–30, 132–33
reactionary, 61
reader, 46, 48–50, 53–54, 57, 60, 68, 70, 144, 310
readerships
　intended white Victorian, 54
　youthful, 75
reading, 11–13, 75, 126, 131, 133, 139–41, 142n11, 150, 152, 268
Reaktion, 304
real estate mafias, 235, 239
realities
　economic, 311
　new, 4
reality, constructed, 291
realms, parallel, 236
reciprocity, modal, 275
recitation, 108, 115, 276
Reclamation, 121
Reclassification, 302
recognition, 6, 74, 88, 93, 148–49, 155, 159, 206, 265
recollections, 25, 27, 57, 246–47, 263
Record Holder, 299n14
Reddy, 152, 156, 164n9, 166, 268, 302
reenchant, 14, 86, 198
reexamination, 266n2

Reform, 144
refuge, 65, 72, 160, 240
refusal, 159, 309
regeneration, 170, 175
regimes, 150, 153, 156, 294
   global, 68
   worldly, 237
region, 11, 22, 58, 164n3, 253, 286
   drought-prone, 36
   guru's, 279
   linguistic, 22
Regional Communities, 193
registers
   affective, 148
   authoritative, 60
   scopic, 293
   sensory, 296
regularities, 85
rehabilitates, 262
reify, 15, 263
reiki, 112–13, 120
   channeling, 119n15
reimagining, 309
reincorporation, 251
relation
   reshapes, 168
   social, 228
relationality, 157, 314
   ethical, 162
relationships, 112, 116, 148, 152–54, 156–57, 159, 162–63, 168, 187–88, 246–49, 251, 258–59, 262
   devotional, 186, 298
   enduring, 152, 154
   ethical, 146, 148, 154, 163
relief, 47, 146, 181, 251, 261
religion, 9, 76, 78, 99n17, 101, 165–66, 192n14, 193–95, 233, 241, 243, 284, 286, 302–4, 312–14
   holy, 102
   local, 312

religiosity, 10, 82, 87, 95–96
   congregational, 283
   inauthentic, 227
religious change, 311
religious economy, 207, 229–30, 234–36, 240, 243
religious fanaticism, 199
Religious Pluralism, 305
religious publics, 10
Religious Studies, 311–13
remembrance, 114, 118, 121
Reneau, Don, 303
renouncer, 154–55
renunciation, 146, 155–57, 225, 263
repetition, 93, 124, 131–32
repositories, 92
representations, 164n3, 203, 286, 303–4, 312
   nonfictional, 46
reprieve, 240
   peaceful, 205
Republic Day, 256
reputation, 48, 147–48, 224, 226
   idealized, 14
   moral, 146
research, 41, 75, 163, 250, 266, 277, 298, 311, 313–15
   ethnographic, 15, 106
reservation, 205
resonating, 296
resources
   archival, 298
   financial, 13, 146, 149, 151
revelation, 6, 61, 69, 224, 234
reverie, 34, 73
Revolutionary Era, 285, 287, 294–95
Reynolds, Susan, 43
rhythms, 106, 108, 115–18
   particular, 117
Riamsara Kuyakanon Knapp, 43
Richard, 16, 77, 101, 121, 217
Rifai Sufi, 107
Rishikesh, 206

risk, 139, 142n9, 161, 167, 183, 291
rites, 171, 183, 189n6
ritual context, 107, 118, 150, 162, 189n4, 228, 239–40
ritual creativity, 1, 14, 173, 190n10, 228
ritual drummers, 182, 190n9, 190n10, 191n13
ritual economy, 149
Ritual Innovation, 7, 193, 311
ritual musicians, 169, 171–72, 182, 188
ritual performances, 169, 184, 249, 251
rituals, 81–82, 94, 96–97, 145–47, 149–51, 162–63, 164n3, 168–69, 195, 205–6, 228, 237, 251, 264, 276–77
  graveyard, 307
  hierarchical, 202
  lifecycle, 155
  modern, 145
  public, 149
  religious, 157
  superstitious, 277
ritual spaces, 86–87, 227, 251
ritual symbolism, 239
ritual technique, 149
ritual therapies, 311
ritual transvestism, 189n5
ritual vessel, 170
river
  clear, 214
river Ganga, 125
Rivkin, Julie, 302
R'lyeh, 58–59
Robbins, 119n1, 121
Robbinsville, 250, 267n7
rock
  live, 272
  mainstream, 283
rock concerts, 283
  massive, 283

Rock-star Saint, 283
roles, 117–18, 125, 128, 130, 132, 156, 225, 229, 252, 254, 259, 272, 275
  active, 49
  authoritative, 186
  causal, 151
  central, 108, 182
  cosmogonic, 54
  important, 49, 138
  mediumship, 112
  nonnormative gender, 154
Rollier, Paul, 304
Roman Catholics, 96
Roscoe, 154, 166
Rotman, Andy, 312
Royapuram, 158
Roychowdhury, 41n1, 43
RSS, 213
Rubenstein, 5, 17, 274, 294–95, 297, 304–5
  followed, 295
rudimentary, 200
Rudisill, 138, 144
rudrākṣa, 202
Rudyard Kipling, 11, 46–48
ruhani mehfils, 286
ruhani satah, 233
rules, 138, 154, 212, 230, 264, 290, 293
Rumya Putcha, 135
rupture, 62, 199, 241, 264, 309
  ontological, 8
Ruud, 304
Ryan, Michael, 302

Sabarimala, 213
Sabbath schools, 87
sabha, 138–40, 257
Sabha, Lok, 278
Sacha Kahoon, 281
Sachi Shiksha, 301n32

sacred ash, 31, 34, 202
sacred destination, 242n16
sacrifice, xi, xiv, 67, 70, 90, 150,
    160–62, 172–73
  animal, xii, 178
  blood/animal, 183
  human, 58
sacrificial victims, 191n13
Sadhguru, 273
Sadhna, 281
Sadhu Ishwarcharandas, 266
Sadhu Paramtattvadas, 267n6
sadhus, 76n5, 200, 203, 248, 254,
    267n8, 281
sādhus, xii, 197, 199, 201–2, 207–9,
    211–13, 217n9
sadhvi, 279
sages, 137, 224, 268, 302
saheli, 118
sahib's-eye, 53
Sailaja Krishnamurti, 141
Saint Gurmeet Ram Rahim Singh
    Ji Insan, 271, 282, 300n19,
    301n37, 301n43, 301n44,
    301n46
saints, 12, 14, 38–39, 105–15, 117–
    19, 119n1, 225, 233, 235–36,
    241n1, 276–77
  living, 223
Saints, Sidi, 106, 114, 116, 122
Saiva ritual practices, 93
Saivite, 92
Sajjid, 230–34, 242n11
  left, 231
Sakaria, 42n2, 43
Salamink, Oscar, 17
Salammbô, 62, 78
salvation, 88, 90, 224, 257
samādhi, 205, 217n11
Samooga Varaiviyal, 166
samyutahastamudra, 136–37
sanctification, 84

sanctum, 170
  inner, 192n15
sandai saccharavu, 158
Sangam, 197, 202, 205, 209–11,
    214–15, 216n2, 217n19
Sangh Parivar, 212–13
Sanskar, 281
Sanskrit, 92, 130, 134–35, 137, 139
  complete, 141n1
Sanskritization, 135, 144
  overt, 137
Sanskritized, 138–39
Sanskrit terms, 136
sant, 276–77
Sant Gurmeet Ram Rahim Singh,
    298n2
Santosh, 305
Saraka, 267n14, 268n15, 268
Saraswati, 160
Sargent, Carolyn F., 43
saris, 171, 173
sarkar, 214, 219, 236
Sarv-Dharam Sangam, 281
Sasikala Penumarthi, 127
Sathya Sai Baba, 290
Sathya Sai Movement, 305, 314
satsang, 271, 281, 283
satsangis, 248–52, 254–57, 259–60, 265
  dedicated, 257
satya vaakku, 160
Saudi Arabia, 233–34
savarna, 138–39
sawari, 106, 119n5
sāyuchchiyam, 94
Sayyid, 224
Sayyid Sufis, 226
SBNR, 314
scale, 51, 199, 203, 205, 209, 287
  breaking, 275
  spectacular, 215
scandals, 237–38, 273, 280, 314
  high-profile, 239

schema, 278
  provisional, 291
Schinkel, 3–4, 17
schismatic core, 297
scholars, xiv, 7, 48, 57, 62, 80, 120–21, 184, 191n13, 297, 312
scholarship, 107, 143, 191n14, 225, 228, 280
Schultz, David E., 77
science fiction, 47
scope, 76, 83, 95, 140, 296
  ordinary, 106
scope of art, 76
Scott, Michael W., 148, 159
screens, 279
  cinema, 293
Scripture, 101
scripture readings, 89
Scudder, David, 91, 99n28
sea, 45, 51, 59, 64, 66, 283
  open, 274
  southern, 55
secular, 163n1, 287
  multiple, 162
secular carnivalesque, 208
secular materialism, 14, 198
secular modernity, 294
seduction, 275
seedlings, tender, 189n4
Seeger, Anthony, 120
Seigworth, Gregory J., 144
self, 11, 69, 75, 162, 165, 246–47, 249–52, 258–59, 261, 263–66, 266n2
  agentive, 261, 263
  autonomous, 247
  corporeal, 249, 258, 265
  ethical, 247
  sentient, 255
self-assertion, 163n1
self-cultivation, 266
self-disciplining, 249

self-examination, 88, 250, 252, 259
self-expression, 159
selfhood, 145, 154
  authentic, 132
  transfeminine, 152
self-identification, 159
self intensification/extensification, 294
self-narrativization, 291
self-promotion, 204
self-reliance, 74
self-sacrifice, 89, 98n1, 189n5
self-transformations, 76, 250, 260
Sembadavars, 170, 189n3
seminaries, theological, 92
semiotic ideology, 241, 242n9
  on, 243
Semitic languages, 57
Semmalar, 159, 165n15, 166
Sen, 212, 219
sensations
  memorable, 263
  remembered, 252
sensibilities, aesthetic, 200
sensory responses, 251
sentient beings, 85
sequences
  climax, 281
  liturgical, 97
  mythic, 190n8
Sequestered, 56
Serampore, 83
service, 49, 88–89, 91, 205, 234, 260, 277
  church, 88
  compassionate, 106
  medical, 260
  taxing, 109
set, 50–53, 56, 71, 74, 148, 150–51, 170–71, 252–53, 276–77, 294, 298, 308, 310
  magicians, 208
  procession, 173

seva, 249, 252, 254–57, 259–61, 265, 281
  doing, 255
  offering, 249
sevaks, 249, 259
sex, 16, 49, 143, 166
  procreative, 155
sexuality, 143, 146, 166, 201, 313–14
Shahmina Shah, 230
Shailaja Paik, 132
Shaitan, 225
Shaiva, 192n19
Shakar, Alex, 297
Shakthi, 166
Shambala, 210
Shambhu, 32–35, 41
Shaviro, Steven, 297
Shea, Vernon, 55
Shenk, Petra, 141
Sher-e-Hind, 300n16
Sherma, Rita, 194
Shi'i Imam, 234
shikharbaddha, 253
Shiva, 52, 124–26, 128–30, 132–33, 170, 181, 205
  cursed, 181
  miniature, 205
Shivaratri, Maha, 170
shrines, 28, 30, 33–38, 52, 105, 108–9, 111–13, 115, 117–18, 119n2, 223–26, 228, 230–33, 236–39, 241n2
  abandoned, 53
  central, 248
shrine-tombs, 225
Shriya Sridharan, 194
Shroff, 106–7, 109, 112, 115, 119n1, 119n2, 119n7, 120n20, 121
Shubha Chaudhuri, 120
shudh hava, 33
Shulman, David, 195

Sidi, 12, 105–6, 111, 113–16, 118, 119n3, 119n6, 120n20, 120–21, 312
Sidi devotional tradition, 12, 110, 113, 116, 118–19, 119n1, 120n25
Sidi medium, 110
signals, 3, 12, 150, 170, 187, 189n3, 248, 250
  young male person, 155
significations, 229, 247
signifiers, 100n34, 229, 233
Sikhism, 289
Sikhs, 131, 276, 284
  nonUdāsin, 216n7
  turbaned, 131
Sikh tradition, 288
silhouettes, 77n9
  cyclopean, 67
Silva Jayasuriya, 121
sindhikka vaikkudhu, 158
sinhasana, 248
sins, 88, 197, 234
siratthaiya, 151, 158
Sir Harold Wilberforce-Bell, 200
Sitala, 52–53
Siva-Gnâna-Potham, 93–94, 101
Siva-Pirakâsam, 94, 101
skulls, 173, 177, 181, 183
  decapitated, 190n8
Sloterdijk, 294, 300n24, 305
Sluis, Katrina, 304
Smarta Vaidiki Brahmin, 12
Smith, Jonathan Z., 46
Smriti, 219
snakes, 27, 124, 193
snān karne, 207
Sneath, David, 43
Socialism, 305
sociality, 208, 228, 245, 249, 260–61, 263, 266
  ethics of, 15, 246–48, 250, 252, 258–62, 264–65

social sciences, 34, 157
social strictures, 226
society, 161, 163, 217n12, 218, 229, 239, 243, 262, 265, 303, 309, 313
   civil, 229
   neoliberal, 241
   non-Western, 8
Socratic, 3
Sohi, 80, 102
son, 29, 31, 33, 36, 125, 129, 156, 172, 182, 240, 256
Soneji, 135, 137–38, 142n12, 144
songs, 116, 124–25, 191n13, 281, 283, 312
   popular devotional, 211
Sood, 280, 305
Sophia, 17
soteriological, 76
sound, 56, 67, 127, 179, 197, 267n11, 302, 304
soundscapes, 80
South Asia, 8–10, 12–13, 80, 82–83, 115–16, 120, 122, 238, 242n7, 303–5, 307, 309–10, 312–14
South Asian, 5, 7, 91
South Asian Religions, 193, 304, 311
South Asian Studies, 303
Southern India, 83, 86, 145, 195
sovereignty, 54, 61
spaces, 5, 7–8, 84, 86, 90, 94–97, 108, 110–11, 138, 192n19, 195, 262, 264, 303, 305

   brahminical, 139
   liminal, 97
   ontological, 97
   popular, 95
   racialized, 96
   utopian, 14
   wondrous, 188
spatial, 7, 168, 188, 261

spawn, 70
spectacle, 13, 15, 39, 48, 167–69, 197, 199, 201, 207, 271, 276
   creative, 215
   visual, 228
spectators, 13–14, 167, 171, 275, 296, 303
Spider Web Anthropologies, 302
spirit mediums, 115, 118
spiritual egalitarianism, 81, 87
spirituality, 120, 233, 310
spiritual organization, 276
Srinivasa Kalyanam, 128
Sri Sathya Sai Seva Organization, 206
Sri Sri Anandamayi Sangha, 206
Sri Sri Ravi Shankar, 203, 206
Srivastava, 254, 269, 281, 305
Sri Venkateswara Temple, 126, 129, 143
state, 3, 13–14, 73, 77n9, 106, 109, 111, 115, 118, 145, 147, 228–29, 243
   climactic, 115
   ecstatic, 12, 106, 114
   emotional, 109
   subjective, 54, 290
   trancelike, 57
Steiner Verlag Wiesbaden, 194
Steinmetz, George, 243
sthala puraanam, 165n16
stone, 25–26, 28, 31, 36, 41, 50–51, 73, 84, 250, 254, 257
stories, 1–2, 11, 26–27, 38, 47–48, 51, 53–54, 56, 62, 65, 68–70, 161, 181–82, 260–61, 280
storytelling, 41
stotra, 123, 141n1
strength, 23, 140, 210, 212, 256
   physical, 111
Strickland, 49–51
stri-vesham, 12–13, 133, 137

structure, 139, 164n10, 166, 194, 227–28, 233, 263, 292, 309
  authoritarian, 278
  casteist, 139
  institutional, 263
study, xiv, 21, 59, 65, 106–8, 169, 192n14, 242n10, 242n12, 312
Study of Hinduism, 165, 193, 195
styles, 53, 232, 286–87, 292
  architectural, 36
  didactic, 69
subalternity, 312
subject, 15, 22, 51, 87, 95, 131, 136, 241, 246, 284–85, 308
  agentive, 263
  autonomous, 47
  excessive, 274
  perceiving, 74
  potential, 293
  scientific, 91
subjecthood, 291
  excessive, 296
subjectivities, religious, 246, 265–66, 313
subject positions, 75, 274–75, 290, 295
  hegemonic, 55
  normative, 60
subjugation, 6, 265
Sufi, Sidi, 105–6, 115
Sufi markets, 230, 234, 237, 240
Sufis, 12, 106, 223–26, 235, 241n1, 243
Sufi shrines, 14, 225–26, 229, 231
  mystical, 9
Sufism, 225–27, 232, 239, 242n7, 242n12, 243
  authentic, 227
  modern, 226
Sukhdev Gujar, 42n4
Sunni Muslim, 105, 109
superstition, 81, 84–85, 89, 95, 304
supplication, 12, 109

Surat, 107, 122
surprise
  complete, 272
  initial, 260
  sensorial, 252
suspension, 183, 251, 266, 275
Swacch Bharat, 214, 217n18
Swaminarayan, 248–49, 260–61, 265, 267n3
Swaminarayan Akshardham, 250
Swaminarayan bhakti, 260, 267n6
Swaminarayan community, 248, 264, 266n3
Swaminarayan Hinduism, 268–69
Swami Nithyananda, 203–4, 206
Swayed, 301n31
Sydney Bulletin, 58
symbols, 54–55, 140, 244, 284
symptoms, 8, 50, 60, 109–10, 114
syncretic claims, 289

tahzib, 231
taiyar, 25
Taj Mahal, xi, 25–26, 41
Tamanna, 305
tamasha, 277, 297
Tamil, 92, 186, 189n1, 192n14
Tamil brahmins, 138
Tamil Catholic, 192n20
Tamil Lexicon, 188n1, 190n8, 195
Tamil month, 170, 176, 189n2
Tamil Nadu, 13, 126, 151, 164n3, 165, 168, 181, 183, 190n6, 193–94, 218
Tamil region, 159, 163n1
Tamil Rituals, 165, 193–94
Tamil transgender women, 145
Tamizhini Publications, 166
tantri, 256, 259
Tanzania, 116
Tapas, 195
Taraknath, 315

Tarzan, 76n2
tasawwuf, 242n12
Tattuva-Kaṭṭaḷei, 92, 101
tattuvam, 92–93, 101
tauviz, 239
TDR, 142
teacher
    reiki master, 113
teachings, 45, 82, 128, 257, 273, 276, 312
    moral, 258, 260
technologies, 12, 106, 195, 199, 249, 266, 292
    modern, 293
Tehri dam, 214
Telugu, 136–37, 140, 313
Telugu brahmins, 138
Telugu Culture, 313
temple community, 174, 189n5
temples, 23–24, 36, 49–50, 86–87, 148–51, 153, 155–56, 160–61, 168–71, 173, 176–82, 185–87, 189n2, 248, 252–53
    mega, 250
temporalities, 294–95
temporary inhabitations, 288, 294
tensions, 86, 212, 224–25, 266, 276, 287
    distinct, 265
terror, 5, 67
    supreme, 59
terukkūttu, 191n13
Texas, 75, 144, 166, 195, 315
Thakore, 137, 140, 144
Thappattai, 170
thaumatazein, 3
Thazhanoor, 160
theatricality, 281
theme, 14, 47, 225, 241n5
    central, 232
    consistent, 225
    primary, 24

theology, 54, 96, 231
theory, aesthetic, 126, 130, 134–35
therapeutic cults, 115, 117
therukoothu, 191n13
Thiagarajan, Deborah, 195
Thirumanappu, 194
thirunangai-maruladis, 13, 145–47, 150–51, 153–54, 157, 162, 165n16
thirunangais, 13, 145–63, 163n1, 163n2, 164n7, 164n8, 164n9, 166, 191n14
    company, 154
Thirunankai, 307
Thomas De Bruijn, 121
threshold, 72, 97, 235, 241n2
    ever-expanding, 198
Thrift, Nigel, 274
throne, 65, 70–71, 203, 208
thuggees, 79
thunai, 182
thunderbolt, 75
Thurston, 189n3, 190n8, 190n9, 191n13, 191n14, 195
Thurston, Edgar, 191n14
ṭikās, 202
tilak, 49
time, xiv, 7–8, 24–25, 27–29, 57–59, 77n9, 97, 110, 126–31, 220, 223–24, 251, 253, 255–57, 280–82, 293–94, 302
    chronological, 264
    election, 300n17
    frozen, 283
    intimate, 177
    particular, 258
Tinakaran, 193
Tirchhi Nazar, 303
tirth, 25
tirthasthan, 25
tirthayatra, 25

title
  honorary, 216n8
  official, 289
Todd, William, 85, 94, 98n4, 98n9
tomb, 26, 108, 112, 223, 226, 230, 233, 238, 241n2
  hilltop, 38
tomb-shrines, 105
touchstone, 191n13
tours, transnational, 138
traces, 50, 60, 106, 126, 247, 263
tracks, 58, 72, 77n9, 83, 283
Tracy, William, 91, 99n27
Traditional Music, 144
traditions, 55, 74–75, 105–6, 114–16, 118–19, 143, 189n5, 233, 268, 276, 286–87
  cultural, 286
  encyclopaedic, 46, 76n1
  historical, 70
  musical, 115
  reformist, 277
  religious, 92, 203
Tragic Allahabad Stampede, 219
trance, 13, 59, 102, 107, 120n21, 145, 147
  ecstatic, 110, 118
transactions, 149, 151–53, 240
  fraught, 85
  substantive, 86
  unanticipated, 84
transcendence, 86, 96, 276, 297
Transcendentalist, 79
transformation
  authentic, 75
  emotional, 186
  great, 228
  iconographic, 190n10
  mutual, 159
  next, 132
  personal, 252, 259
transgressing, 226

transitory, 249, 290
translations, 58, 79, 82, 91–97, 141
  contributed, 91
  linguistic, 9
  scriptural, 92
Trans Movements, 166
transnationalism, 314
transvestism, 192n18
traps, 274–75, 296, 303
Traversing, 207
Treza, Raphael, 220
Tribes of Southern India, 195
trio, indefatigable, 266
trisul, 31
triumphs, 89, 195
Triveni, 199–200
tropes, 9, 46, 96–97, 273
truth, 2–3, 33, 93, 121, 131, 294
Tsalal, 55
Tully, 209, 212, 220
Tulsidas, 199
Turner, 154, 164n10, 166, 228, 239–40, 244

Uddi Gujar, 24, 27, 40–41
Udo Simon, 195
udukkai pattu, 191n13
Uganda, 245
ugra, 160
Ujjain, 216n2
UK, 268, 303–5
Ulman, Clark, 65
Ülo, 195
ummah, 234
uncertainties, 7–8, 43, 251, 309
uncontain, 274
undeniability, 53
United States, 45, 62, 68, 75, 101–2, 125–27, 129, 138, 200, 250, 297
Unnao, 214
unpredictability, 198
  dangerous, 198

Untouchable Community, 194
Untouchables, 132
upasana, 248
Urdu, 121, 231, 235, 241n2, 242n11, 242n13, 242n16, 312
urs, 108, 114–16
uruvam, 173
Ute Hüsken, 195
'Uthmān Sullābı, 243
Uttara Asha Coorlawala, 135
Uttarakand, 214
uttaravu, 171
Uttar Pradesh, 211

Vaibhav, 166
Vaishnavi Ramanathan, 188
vajra, 75
Valk, 191n13, 192n17, 195
valorization, 157, 162
valuation, 85, 107
  binary, 107
Vanniyar, 152
vāpsı, 212
Varanasi, 205, 220
Vasant Panchami Snān, 217n12
Vasudevan, 14, 151, 166, 191n14, 195
Vasudha Narayanan, xiii, 121
Vedantam Rattayya Sarma, 142n14
Vedas, 91
Veer, 107, 122
vegetarian, 169
veil, 124–26, 132–33, 224
Velcheru Narayana Rao, 313
Vempati Ravi Shankar, 125, 127, 141n2, 141n4, 141n5, 141n6, 141n7, 141n8, 143
vendors, 151–52, 179
veneration, 12, 105, 234
Venkatachalapathy, 192n17, 195
verisimilitude, 61
Verlag, 194

vermillion, red, 205
Vernacular Islam, 121
vernacular practice, 184, 193
Vernon, 77
Verso, 101
Vertika, 219
vesham, xi, 129, 134, 139, 171–72, 189n5
VHP (Vishwa Hindu Parishad), 207, 212–13
vibhava, 134
vibhūtı, 202
Viceroy, 216n5
vichitra bat, 42n2
Victorian architects, 48
vigyanik log, 33
Vijaya, 154
Vijaya Dashami, 128
Vijayawada, 127
Vikaṭan, 193
vilakku, 170–71
village, 25–28, 32, 136–37, 160
  elected, 35
villagers, 254
  tribal, 208
vil pattu, 191n13
Vimalassery, Manu, 100
vimarisaiya, 148, 151
Vinayaka Chaturthi Festival, 218
violence
  glorify, 301n33
  intimate, 96
  structural, 96
virtuous, 82, 273
Vishakapatnam, 137
Vishnu, 1, 54
Vishwajit, 220
Vishwarupa, 2–3, 5–6, 9
vision, 55, 102, 186, 236, 285, 313
  inner, 41
  picture-postcard, 24
visionary elements, 47

visit
  first, 27
  hospital, 33
  unscheduled, 213
visitation, 53, 241n2
visual culture, 285, 312
visual exchange, 178
Visuality, 303
Visweswara Rao, 313
Vivekananda, 286–87, 293
Viviana, 166
viyappu, 186
vocabulary, 93, 106, 118, 164n9
volunteers, 174, 227, 238–39, 248, 250–52, 259–60
Voodoo orgies, 61
votaries, female, 172
vow-keepers, 172, 182
vows, 31, 170, 172, 175, 241n1
voyeuristic, 215

Wadsworth Publishing Company, 165
Wahhabis, 241n5
wajd, 12, 106–7, 109–10, 115, 118
Wales, 56
wali, 225, 230, 235, 238
Walker, Caroline, 16, 100
Walsh, Catherine E., 16
wander, 181, 207
Wanderlust, 314
waqf, 226, 241n5
Waqf Boards, 224, 239
war
  fratricidal, 1
  late, 61
Warrier, Maya, 268, 302
Waste, 219
water, 25, 28–29, 36, 58, 171, 176, 201, 206, 214, 267n11
  clean, 214
  fresh, 210

glittering, 284
holy, 201
wealth
  financial, 235
  staggering, 239
  unending, 235
wealth inequality, 231
wealthy, 162, 234
weapon, effective, 68
wear, 160–61, 171, 182
Webb Keane, 164n4
website, 299n14
  official, 276
  personal, 277
weirdness, 73–74
Weird Tales, 11, 45–75, 77n8, 78, 307
Welshman Arthur Machen, 55
Wesley, 102
West Africa, 80
Western civilization, 11
Westernization, 144
Western philosophies, 3, 308
West Godavari, 137
West Warwick, 77
whimsical, 206, 277
wife, 38, 107, 174, 188n1, 191n14, 253–54
Wilberforce-Bell Collection, 216n5
Wilcox, 76n7
Wilden, Eva, 195
Wilkerson, 81, 102
William Channing Webb, 60
Williams, Raymond B., 268
window, bedroom, 49
wish-fulfillment figure, 75
witnesses, 52, 60, 146, 153
Wodtke, Petra, 304
women, 13, 83, 87, 106, 108–9, 154, 167, 171, 177, 180, 183–85, 189n5, 245–46
  possessed, 167

women (continued)
  pregnant, 155
  transgender, 163n1
wonder, 13–17, 19–35, 38–41, 74–76, 79–85, 87–98, 100–103, 105–63, 166–69, 171–87, 193–215, 227–28, 239–41, 245–48, 250–52, 258–66, 274–75, 280–82, 295, 307–10
wonder effects, 246, 273, 278, 283, 285, 288, 291, 294, 296, 298
wonder encounters, 252, 263
wonderment, 3, 6, 12, 22, 285
wonderstruck, 2–3, 162
wonder-trash, 14
wondrous, 22, 133, 263
work, xiii–xiv, 9–10, 53, 55, 90, 92, 94, 131–33, 149–51, 156–58, 162, 184–85, 237, 257, 274–75
  literary, 134
  medical, 259
  spiritual, 113
workers, 252–53
  migrant, 232
work ethic, 254
world, 6, 11, 60–61, 68–69, 71–72, 74–75, 89, 102, 139–40, 153–54, 157–58, 183–84, 186–88, 195, 227–28, 249, 284, 299n14, 302, 307–10
  heathen, 85, 90
  modern, 75, 237
  natural, 4, 41, 84, 228
  transformative, 7
  wondrous, 140
World Records Union, 299n14

World Records University, 299n14
World War II, 45
worship, 82, 84, 86, 94, 154, 158, 164n3, 179, 183–84, 192n20, 194
worshippers, 74, 188
wristlets, 181
wry smile, 233
Wulf, 275
Wunderkammern, 4

Yale University, 92
Yama Lokam, 173
Yamuna River, xi, 26, 215
yantras, 207
Yara, 71–74
Yashoda Thakore, 140
Yellamma devadasis, 156
Yoga Institute, 206
Yoga Studies, 218
Yogimata Keiko Aikawa, 206
yogis, 79, 101, 200, 216n5
Yogi Trivedi, 268
Yorke, 208, 220
youth, 71

zamindar, 161
Zamora, 71
Zamora's myriad, 71
Zavos, John, 268, 302
Zelizer, 164n12, 166
Zen, 288
zikr, 114
ziyarat, 242n16
Zotter, 183, 192n19, 195
Zupanov, Ines, 102